BRINGING OUT THE TREASURE

BRINGING OUT THE TREASURE

Inner Biblical Allusion in Zechariah 9–14

edited by

MARK J. BODA AND MICHAEL H. FLOYD
WITH A MAJOR CONTRIBUTION BY REX MASON

T & T CLARK INTERNATIONAL
A Continuum imprint
LONDON • NEW YORK

Published by T&T Clark International
A Continuum imprint
The Tower Building, 11 York Road, London SE1 7NX
15 East 26th Street, Suite 1703, New York, NY 10010

www.tandtclark.com

Copyright © 2003 Sheffield Academic Press
First published as JSOTS 370 by Sheffield Academic Press
This edition published 2004

British Library Cataloguing-in-Publication Data
A catalogue record for this book is available from the British Library

ISBN 056704310X (paperback)

Typeset by Sheffield Academic Press
Printed on acid-free paper in Great Britain by Cromwell Press Ltd, Trowbridge,
Wilts

To Rex Mason
for his many contributions to the guild
for his encouragement of the next generation

CONTENTS

Contents

For those of us researching and writing on the book of Zechariah in a new millennium, Rex Mason continues to exert considerable influence through his many scholarly contributions on this prophetic book. One disappointment, however, is the fact that his superb dissertation from the University of London in 1973 under Peter Ackroyd was never published. This work provides an excellent review of inner-biblical exegesis in Deutero-Zechariah but has been difficult to consult, especially for those writing in North America and on the Continent. The enduring quality of the work, evidenced in its constant appearance in footnotes in research on the book of Zechariah, has led to the present volume which reproduces this dissertation 30 years after it was defended. The dissertation has been reproduced here as close to its original state as possible with a few exceptions, most notably corrections of the few inconsistencies in spelling and the employment of the author-date system of the Press. Because of this the style of the dissertation will be slightly different than that of the essays to follow (for instance, in gender specific language), a feature that ironically highlights the intertextual character of this volume. The original page numbers of the dissertation are retained in the text and indicated in bow brackets (e.g. {100} = p. 100 in the original dissertation). This will enable researchers to find references from secondary literature which cite the dissertation as well as cross references within both the dissertation itself and the responses in the latter half of the volume.

Of course, since Rex Mason's work was completed much has happened in the field of biblical studies and, in particular, in the scholarly study of the book of Zechariah. Because of this, the present volume not only reproduces Mason's seminal work but adds a series of papers from those who have contributed to the guild in the three decades since that time. These responses are arranged in three groups. The first two articles (Petersen, Floyd) are more general in nature, discussing the approach of the guild to the phenomenon of intertextuality and inner-biblical allusion/exegesis. The following four (Nurmela, Tigchelaar, Person, Boda) trace inner-biblical connections between Zech. 9–14 and major prophetic traditions (Isaiah, Jeremiah, Deuteronomic literature, Ezekiel) while the final three contributions (Nogalski, Redditt, Schart) explore inner-biblical connections between Zech. 9–14 and the Book of the Twelve as well as the role of Zech. 9–14 in this larger corpus. These scholars, however, are not given the last word. That is reserved for none other than Rex himself, who has responded to our invitation to reflect on his original work as well as on the various articles in this volume.

There are many who we want to thank for their assistance in bringing this volume to press. First of all, we are grateful to Rex Mason for his willingness to allow us to showcase his seminal work and to participate with us in the project. Second, we are thankful for the positive response of so many within the guild to the venture: to Philip Davies for his initial excitement and acceptance of the proposal and to the participants for their rigorous scholarship for and participation in the colloquia. Third, we are indebted to those who have assisted us in the editing process as we transformed a 1973 dissertation into a manuscript ready for publication: to Gail Jones who digitized the original text, to Timothy Harvie who transformed a considerable portion of the dissertation into Sheffield house style and assisted in the Denver colloquium and to Audrey Mann of Sheffield Academic Press whose attention to detail mixed with grace resulted in a superb finished product. Fourth, we are grateful for academic institutions (Canadian Theological Seminary and Episcopal Theological Seminary of the Southwest) who have supported us in this venture by offering administrative assistance and funds to help attend the conferences and complete the manuscript.

Most of these articles were presented and discussed at two colloquia held during 2001, the first for European participants at the meeting of the European Association of Biblical Studies (Rome, July 2001) and the second for North American participants at the meeting of the Society of Biblical Literature (Denver, November 2001). We are grateful to these two scholarly organizations for showcasing this project and fostering critical dialogue which has enhanced the quality of the present volume.

Rex Mason concluded his work in 1973 with these words:

> What is not in doubt is that these chapters, for all their difficulties and obscurity, testify to the fact that the Word of God which once spoke in living tones through the great prophets of Israel's history, did not fall silent and inactive when the era of the written word began to replace the living voice of prophecy. As men collected the words of these prophets, and pondered the Word which had spoken through them, it proved to have

continuing vitality and relevance to address them as they were challenged, judged and stirred by it to hope and faithfulness in successive generations and widely differing circumstances.

Not the least noble expression of such an encounter and commitment is that expressed in Zechariah ix–xiv. These chapters show us that during this 'dark' period such a living process of re-interpretation continued and that the vital pulse of Israel's faith continued to throb.

There could be few more fitting tributes to 'Deutero–Zechariah' than the words attributed to Jesus in Mt. 13.52:

Therefore every scribe who has been trained for the kingdom of heaven is like a householder who brings out of his treasure what is new and what is old.

For this reason we have entitled this volume *Bringing out the Treasure*, not only because it alludes to the intertextual dynamic in Zech. 9–14, but also because there is a sense that this project is a replication of the social process which gave rise to Zech. 9–14, as a new generation of scribes (scholars) bring out of this treasure (Rex Mason's dissertation) that which is new and that which is old.

Mark J. Boda, Regina, Saskatchewan, Canada
Michael H. Floyd, Austin, Texas, USA

ABBREVIATIONS

AB	Anchor Bible
ABD	David Noel Freedman (ed.), *The Anchor Bible Dictionary* (New York: Doubleday, 1992)
AcOr	*Acta orientalia*
AJSL	*American Journal of Semitic Languages and Literatures*
ANET	James B. Pritchard (ed.), *Ancient Near Eastern Texts Relating to the Old Testament* (Princeton: Princeton University Press, 1950)
AnOr	Analecta orientalia
ASTI	*Annual of the Swedish Theological Institute*
ATANT	Abhandlungen zur Theologie des Alten und Neuen Testaments
ATD	Das Alte Testament Deutsch
Aug	*Augustinianum*
AUSS	*Andrews University Seminary Studies*
AzTh	Arbeiten zur Theologie
BBB	Bonner biblische Beiträge
BDB	Francis Brown, S.R. Driver and Charles A. Briggs, *A Hebrew and English Lexicon of the Old Testament* (Oxford: Clarendon Press, 1907)
BHK	R. Kittel (ed.), *Biblia hebraica* (Stuttgart: Württembergische Bibelanstalt, 1937)
BHS	*Biblia hebraica stuttgartensia*
BibInt	*Biblical Interpretation: A Journal of Contemporary Approaches*
BJRL	*Bulletin of the John Rylands University Library of Manchester*
BKAT	Biblischer Kommentar: Altes Testament
BN	*Biblische Notizen*
BZAW	Beihefte zur *ZAW*
CBC	Cambridge Bible Commentary
CBET	Contributions to Biblical Exegesis and Theology
CBQ	*Catholic Biblical Quarterly*
CBRS	*Currents in Biblical Research*
CR	*Critical Review of Books in Religion*
EBib	Etudes bibliques
ErIsr	*Eretz-Israel*

ETL	*Ephemerides theologicae lovanienses*
FOTL	The Forms of the Old Testament Literature
FRLANT	Forschungen zur Religion und Literatur des Alten und Neuen Testaments
GKC	*Gesenius' Hebrew Grammar* (ed. E. Kautzsch, revised and trans. A.E. Cowley; Oxford: Clarendon Press, 1910)
HAR	*Hebrew Annual Review*
HAT	Handbuch zum Alten Testament
HUCA	*Hebrew Union College Annual*
IB	*Interpreter's Bible*
IBS	*Irish Biblical Studies*
ICC	International Critical Commentary
IEJ	*Israel Exploration Journal*
JBL	*Journal of Biblical Literature*
JETS	*Journal of the Evangelical Theological Society*
JNES	*Journal of Near Eastern Studies*
JSNT	*Journal for the Study of the New Testament*
JSNTSup	*Journal for the Study of the New Testament*, Supplement Series
JSOTSup	*Journal for the Study of the Old Testament*, Supplement Series
JSS	*Journal of Semitic Studies*
KAT	Kommentar zum Alten Testament
KB	Ludwig Koehler and Walter Baumgartner (eds.), *Lexicon in Veteris Testamenti libros* (Leiden: E.J. Brill, 1953)
LD	Lectio divina
LUÅ	Lunds universitets årsskrift
LXX	Septuagint
MT	Massoretic Text
NCB	New Century Bible
NEB	*New English Bible*
NEchtB	Neue Echter Bibel
Neot	*Neotestamentica*
NIB	*The New Interpreter's Bible* (12 vols.; ed. Leander E. Keck *et al.*; Nashville: Abingdon Press, 1994–)
OBO	Orbis biblicus et orientalis
OTL	Old Testament Library
OTS	*Oudtestamentische Studiën*
PEQ	*Palestine Exploration Quarterly*
PTMS	Pittsburgh Theological Monograph Series
RB	*Revue biblique*
RevExp	*Review and Expositor*
RSR	*Recherches de science religieuse*
SBLDS	SBL Dissertation Series
SBLMS	SBL Monograph Series
SBT	Studies in Biblical Theology

SE	*Studia Evangelica I, II, III* (= TU 73 [1959], 87 [1964], 88 [1964], etc.)
SJT	*Scottish Journal of Theology*
TBC	Torch Biblical Commentaries
Transeu	*Transeuphratène*
TU	Texte und Untersuchungen
TynBul	*Tyndale Bulletin*
VTSup	*Vetus Testamentum*, Supplements
WBC	Word Biblical Commentary
WMANT	Wissenschaftliche Monographien zum Alten und Neuen Testament
ZAW	*Zeitschrift für die alttestamentliche Wissenschaft*

LIST OF CONTRIBUTORS

Mark J. Boda, Professor of Old Testament Literature, Canadian Theological Seminary, Regina, Saskatchewan, Canada

Michael H. Floyd, St Michael and All Angels Professor of Old Testament, Episcopal Theological Seminary of the Southwest, Austin, Texas, USA

Rex Mason, Emeritus Fellow, Regent's Park College, Oxford, England; Lecturer in Old Testament and Hebrew (retired), Oxford University, England

James D. Nogalski, Associate Professor of Old Testament Interpretation, M. Christopher White School of Divinity at Gardner-Webb University, Boiling Springs, North Carolina, USA

Risto Nurmela, Docent of Old Testament Exegetics, Åbo Akademi University, Åbo (Turku), Finland

Raymond F. Person, Jr, Associate Professor of Religion, Ohio Northern University, Ada, Ohio, USA

David L. Petersen, Professor of Old Testament, Candler School of Theology, Emory University, Atlanta, Georgia, USA

Paul L. Redditt, Professor of Old Testament, Georgetown College, Georgetown, Kentucky, USA

Aaron Schart, Professor of Old and New Testament, University of Essen, Essen, Germany

Eibert Tigchelaar, Nederlandse organisatie voor Wetenschappelijk Onderzoek fellow, Qumran Instituut, University of Groningen, the Netherlands

Part I

Rex Mason
THE USE OF EARLIER BIBLICAL MATERIAL IN ZECHARIAH 9–14:
A STUDY IN INNER BIBLICAL EXEGESIS

ABSTRACT

Since the time of Stade it has been repeatedly observed that Zech. 9–14 abounds in allusions and references to other biblical material.

The aim of this thesis is to examine the use which is made of this material and to ask whether any general principles of exegesis can be detected. A further aim is to see if the treatment of the material shows the outlook of any particular tradition and whether this throws any light on the circles from which these chapters came.

The general conclusions are that a very varied use is made of earlier biblical material including allusion by the use of particular words or phrases, occasionally (but seldom) direct quotation, and reinterpretation of earlier eschatological pronouncements which are now seen as about to be fulfilled, or sometimes reversed, in the events of the writer's own time.

Further conclusions are that there is cumulative evidence to suggest origin for these chapters among a circle which had been influenced by the tradition of Proto-Zechariah and also which became increasingly sectarian in outlook in opposition to the official Judaism of its day. {i}

INTRODUCTION

It was Stade (1881, 1882) who attempted the first comprehensive analysis of the reference to earlier biblical material in Zech. 9–14. He was not the first to observe traces of such dependence in these chapters, however. Earlier, apologists who wanted to defend their integrity by assigning them, with 1–8, to the authorship of Zechariah, had appealed to such dependence upon the earlier prophets against the critical view which separated them from 1–8, but which, at that time, dated them in the pre-exilic period (cf. Stade 1881: 2ff.; Otzen 1964).

Since the time of Stade, not only has the post-exilic dating of 9–14 been generally accepted and the assigning of them to an author other than Zechariah, but the dependence on earlier biblical material has also been very widely acknowledged, and almost every commentary on these chapters traces the 'sources' of each pericope, many of Stade's original suggestions recurring time and again. Stade's main interest, however, was that of dating the oracles, although it is to his credit that he realised the importance of traces 'sowohl aus der innerjüdischen als der aüsseren Geschichte für die nachexilische Abfassung…' (Stade 1881: 13, 96; 1882a: 152ff.), and in the second part of his work he examined Deutero-Zechariah's estimate of the Houses of David and Levi, his attitude to the ruling circles, the significance attached to Jerusalem {ii} and his conceptions of the kingship of God and the conversion of the heathen.

Since Stade, and increasingly recently, the principle of biblical exegesis within scripture itself has been widely recognized.[1] It is the aim of this

---

1. As examples the following might be cited: Weingreen (1957) pleading for a positive attitude to so-called 'glosses' as examples of a beginning within the biblical period of the later, Mishnaic methods of commentary. 'One may even hazard the conjecture that these notes, preserved as glosses, may well represent the beginning of what became in later times standard and approved commentary' (Weingreen 1957: 155). He developed this last point further in Weingreen (1963). Similarly, Vermes (1961), while concentrating mainly on post-biblical Mishnaic tradition, allows that the process had already begun in the post-exilic scriptural writings (e.g. Vermes 1961:

thesis to examine the use of earlier biblical material in Deutero-Zechariah in the attempt to see what principles of exegesis, if any, can be detected in such use, and, above all, to see if this affords any clue to the place of this author, or authors, in the developing traditio-history of the community of post-exilic Judaism.

It is not intended as a commentary and, therefore, many of the issues raised by commentators are here either ignored, relegated to a secondary role or discussed only when they have an immediate bearing on the investigation in hand. No systematic review of the history of such critical opinion is offered although many references to the work of commentators are made as the discussion proceeds. Such a summary may be conveniently found in the work of Otzen (1964: 11-34).

All that need be said at this point is that a post-exilic date for the present form of the whole of Zech. 9–14 (without precluding the possibility that some oracles or parts of oracles may have been pre-exilic in origin) is

4, 6, 37, etc.). See also Childs (1972: 58): 'Although the early biblical parallels to full-blown rabbinic midrash are often only remotely connected, there is enough similarity to speak of proto-midrashic form within the Old Testament'. Cf. also Ackroyd (1962b: 18): 'The Old Testament awareness of history as the sphere of divine activity is to be found not only in the way in which a prophetic word belongs in a historic setting, but in the way also in which a prophecy or a law or a psalm may be seen to illuminate some new moment of history'; as well as Ackroyd (1968b: 10): 'At no point can there be absolute separation between a message which was spoken on a specific occasion... and the way in which that message has been incorporated into the larger presentation to which it now belongs, and the subsequent understanding of that message in new contexts of which later Christian history and later Jewish history offer two related but distinct types'; also Ackroyd (1970). See also Jones (1955: 237): 'Isaiah's insight into the mind of Yahweh...was deeply learned and understood by the disciples of Isaiah, both by those who used again and again in new situations the oracles of Isaiah of Jerusalem and by that more creative, unknown poet of the exile who outstripped his master'. See also Willi-Plein (1971: 123), a work whose subtitle may be rendered, 'Investigations into the Literary Development which has its Origin in the Books of Amos, Hosea and Micah'. The attempt of Louis Finkelstein (1969) to take the methods of rabbinic exegesis back to an oral stage in pre-exilic times and to find its origin in the pre-exilic prophets themselves, is somewhat extreme and involves a certain amount of special pleading. But that even here there has been conscious re-interpretation of the words of earlier prophets seems arguable. The influence of the preaching of Hosea on the earlier oracles of Jeremiah is widely acknowledged; see, e.g. Skinner (1936: 21-22); Bright (1965: xci); Weiser (1969: xv); Eissfeldt (1965: 358), etc. The influence of Jeremiah on Ezekiel has been vigorously argued by Miller (1955). See 10.3–11.3 {108} n. 10, now p. 76.

assumed. Sufficient grounds for such an assumption will, it is hoped, become clear throughout the course of the argument. {iii}

The fact is, however, that there is no consensus of opinion on such matters as date, unity, or authorship of these chapters, nor about the relation of its parts to each other, either by origin or in their meaning and significance. So much about them has remained obscure and such a wide variety of results have been obtained by different commentators that it is often hard to feel great confidence in the conclusions of any one. It may be justifiable for this reason alone to suggest that the traditional questions are not the ones to ask of these chapters, at least in the first place. Another line of approach seems to be called for.

Two comparatively recent commentaries may indicate what such a line should be. Saebø (1969: 309) has said that what is required (he is speaking of ch. 14 particularly but not exclusively) is not only literary and form critical investigation but also 'milieugeschtlichen Fragestellung' and Otzen (1964: 199) has come close to this in his appeal for an 'ideengeschichtliche Ansetzung des Textes...' It may be that special attention to the use of earlier biblical material will yield some clues as to the place of this author or circle in the line of traditio-history, and that this will then, even if indirectly, not be without its significance for the more traditional questions of authorship and date.

Each method of biblical investigation has its own difficulties or pit-falls, however, and it is as well to mention some of those which obstruct this particular line of approach. There is, first, the danger of subjectivity in {iv} the investigator. Because he finds an analogy between a particular verse or passage with some other part of scripture it is all too easy to imagine that the writer himself intended such an analogy and so a subjective assessment too readily has objective status and honour conferred upon it. Further, once having found some important clue in one place, it is easy to find it in many. Again, it is all too easy, even when confronted by 'objective' criteria such as identity of vocabulary or phraseology, to assume that one passage is dependent upon another, forgetting that both may have had a common origin, for example, in the language of worship in the cult, or in common everyday usage, and so be only indirectly, if at all, related to each other. Again, to solve an equation with two unknown quantities, one on each side, is a notoriously difficult mathematical process. We cannot be sure of the date of Zech. 9–14 as a whole, or any particular section within it. So when we find parallels to it in some passage in the books of Isaiah, Jeremiah, Ezekiel, or Joel, how can the question of dependence be determined? Often there are reasons for believing that such passages may be later additions to the prophetic books. How can we know, then, what written material our author had before him? How far had the process of compiling these collections progressed towards its final stages? In what form were they known to Deutero-Zechariah? Even if the dating of this last were certain, the answers would be {v} difficult ones in each case. When these dates also are uncertain, they become doubly difficult and great caution is called for.

To say that a task is hazardous, however, is not to say it should never be attempted. It will be seen in the following pages that 'identification' of individual sources has often to be tentative. We are on surest ground when we stand, not on isolated instances of dependence of this text on that, but in so far as we are able to trace continuity within broad lines of tradition within the Old Testament literary corpus, and, more particularly in these chapters, within lines of prophetic tradition. For the question of closer and more detailed correspondence and dependence, nevertheless, there can emerge a certain cumulative picture. A great number of probabilities—let us say arbitrarily, for example, that Zech. 12.1–13.6 is based on a knowledge of Ezek. 36.18-32 in its present form—adds up, not to certainty, but to the strong probability that this pericope was already part of the written corpus of the Book of Ezekiel by the time of the author of that section of Deutero-Zechariah, and was known to him as such.

If, in the end, many important issues remain disappointingly unclarified, one may hope that some light will have been shed on the methods and purpose of biblical exegesis of this author or circle, and so reveal something of their theological outlook and, indirectly, of their place {vi} in the context of post-exilic Judaism. Such a study might serve in some ways as prolegomenon to further investigation of these difficult chapters concerning which such a welter of conflicting opinion and interpretations abound.

The English of the RSV has been followed in translation of the Hebrew text wherever the Hebrew appeared to demand no modification. Chapter and verse references are given in Arabic numerals (e.g. Zech. 1.8), except in quotations, where the numeration of the original is retained. Old Testament references are to the Masoretic Text (MT), and the reference to the English Versions, where this differs, is added in brackets, e.g. Zech. 2.1 (1.18). {1}

Chapter 1

ZECHARIAH 9.1-8

The opening oracle, or series of oracles, of 9.1-8 presents the reader with a number of enigmas which might wryly be felt to be characteristic of the chapters they introduce. Critical opinion and interpretation of these verses have been almost as numerous as for any oracle in Deutero-Zechariah.

In form we have, following a superscription whose extent is disputed, a prophetic oracle in which Yahweh is spoken of in the third person in the style of proclamation by a messenger in vv. 1-6a. With v. 6b the form changes to that of a first person divine word (with a lapse back into third person speech in v. 7aγ), while it is not clear whether the last line (v. 8bβ), though still cast in the first person, is the word of the deity or the prophet.

At first glance the content appears to change markedly with the change in form. The first oracle appears to be one of threat against foreign nations in much the same manner, although on a smaller scale, in which oracles against foreign nations appear in most of the collected words of the classical prophets. Yet, even here, some ambiguity attaches to the force of vv.1f. In the second (vv. 6b-8) the tone changes to one of promise for the Philistines and for the Judeans themselves.

There is a wide divergence as to the date and the historical allusions which are to be found in these verses. {2} A number of commentators have found it to be pre-exilic in origin. Some have seen allusions to the advance of one of the Assyrian kings, Tiglath Pileser III, Shalmaneser or Sargon, even if, in its final form, it has been applied to a later situation.[1] Otzen (1964: 45ff., 62ff.) finds the oracle to have originated towards the end of the seventh century BC.

The majority, however, have attributed the oracle to the time of Alexander the Great, seeing a particular reference to his campaign in Syria and against Phoenicia.[2] Some have felt that it belongs to a later point in the

---

1. Horst (1964: 247); Grützmacher (1892: 46); Kraeling (1924); Kuhl (1961: 225).
2. This has been argued particularly vigorously by Delcor (1951a); Elliger (1964:

Greek period and that the references to 'Assyria' and 'Egypt' in ch. 10 are
veiled allusions to the Seleucids and Ptolemies (cf. Weiser 1961: 273).
Others have argued that it is related to no specific historical situation as
such, but is to be seen as a general eschatological promise of the overthrow of the enemies of the people of God when the Messianic kingdom is
established.[3]

Finally, we should note the view of those who believe that there are
insufficiently precise details to be found in the text for us to assign them to
a particular point in history. So P.R. Ackroyd (1962a: 651) has said,

> The variety of datings to which sections of these chapters have been
> assigned does not inspire great confidence in any of those proposed.

Similarly M. Bič (1962: 108n) says,

> Will man historische kriterien machen, fuhrt der Text selbst zu keiner
> eindeutigen Auffassung. {3}

While all these critical opinions, and the grounds which gave rise to them,
must be assigned due weight, our concern here is primarily with the text as
it stands and not only a supposed 'original' core, if we could ever claim
with confidence to have bared it of all additions. For the very elaborations
themselves are important evidence for the way in which this original was
understood and interpreted. They may afford some testimony to the theological outlook and interpretative methods of the traditio-circle which
preserved them.

The oracles which follow the superscription relate to Syria (vv. 1-2a),
Phoenicia (vv. 2b-4) and the Philistines (vv. 5–7), with a concluding word
of Yahweh in v. 8.

It is the oracle concerning Syria which presents us with our first difficulty. In what sense is it to be taken, and why is the region of Syria singled
out for mention? Is it, in the first place, an oracle of threat? The Hebrew
reads literally,

147; 1950: 63ff.); Eissfeldt (1965: 437); Gaide (1968: 65), who puts the references to
such places as Hadrach down to conscious archaisms on the part of the author, a point
also made by Weiser (1961: 273); Dentan (1956: 1092); Pfeiffer (1952: 610-11);
Fohrer (1970: 466-67). Mitchell (1912: 260) believed the oracle originally referred to
Alexander the Great, but was later issued by someone who saw in his advent and the
struggles involved, a pre-figuring of a still further, greater and more lasting deliverance
of his people in the future.

3.   So Robinson (1896); cited by Otzen (1964: 65 n. 9) (the writer has not had
access to this work); van Hoonacker (1908: 650).

The word of Yahweh (is) in the land of Hadrach, and Damascus (is) its/his
resting place. For unto Yahweh (is) the gaze of mankind, and all the tribes
of Israel.

The 'word of Yahweh' is a phrase especially connected with prophetic
utterance. 'The word of Yahweh came to (or "by")...' is a formula found
at, or near, the beginning of the books of Jeremiah, Hosea, Joel, Jonah,
Zephaniah, Haggai, and Zechariah, and is often repeated throughout them,
most frequently in Jeremiah. Phrases such as 'hear the word of {4} Yahweh' also often recur. By it he acts, so that it not only announces the will
and purpose of Yahweh, but is itself a means by which he acts to effect his
purpose. So Isaiah can say,

> The Lord has sent a word against (בְּ) Jacob, and it will be a light on Israel,
> and all the people will know... So the Lord raises adversaries against
> them...' (9.7 [8], 8 [9])

The familiar words of Second Isaiah in 55.10-11 posit the same truth.[4]
So the phrase here suggests that Yahweh is present and active in Syria and
perhaps carries the overtone that once more an authentic voice of prophecy
is being heard as the old formula is used to announce his message and
intentions.

The near parallel construction of Isa. 9.7 with the preposition בְּ also
used, may argue for a hostile sense, although of course בְּ need not carry
any such a connotation.[5] Strangely, a similar ambiguity exists when we
turn to the parallel line

> and Damascus is its/his resting place (מְנֻחָתוֹ)

What force has מְנֻחָתוֹ here? Very often it has a favourable sense. It can
refer to the eschatological 'rest' of God's people when the Spirit is poured
out (Isa. 32.18). Canaan itself is described as just such a resting place
(Deut. 12.9; cf. Gen. 49.15). It can denote God's resting place (Isa. 66.1-2)
whether the Temple, or, even more, the man whom he regards with favour.
The מְנֻחָתה of the root of Jesse (Isa. 11.10) which the {5} nations shall
seek, shall be glorious. In Solomon's words of thanksgiving at the

---

4. Cf. also Ps. 107.20. See Johnson (1961: 17); Grether (1934: 59ff., esp. 103-107:
'Die Dynamis prophetischen Gotteswortes').
5. E.g. Ps. 11.4. The lack of any verbs of motion in Zech. 9.1 reduces the parallel
to Isa. 9.7, although it could, of course, be argued that one is implied. It is taken to
mean 'in' rather than 'against' by Ackroyd (1962a: 652); Jones (1962a: 124); Delcor
(1951a: 110). LXX renders בְּ by ἐν.

dedication of the Temple (1 Kgs 8.56) there occurs again the thought that God's promise of the land and, by implication, the Temple, is his promise of 'rest' for them.

It is this kind of context which leads D.R. Jones (1962a: 124) to state categorically that the term 'does not suggest the idea of a hostile incursion of the Word of God against Damascus'.[6] On the other hand Mitchell (1912: 262) can say, 'No Jew of the time of the author would have entertained the idea that Yahweh would find a resting place at Damascus'. This should at least caution us not to forget that the root נוח is ambivalent, and can certainly be employed in a pejorative sense. Elliger's suggested parallel in Isa. 9.7 (8) and his phrase 'as lightening strikes' is scarcely just, for it is the root נפל which is used there, parallel to שלח ב. Yet the root נוח can mean, in the qal, 'to settle down on' in the sense of 'press down on' or 'overbear', as in Isa. 7.2, where the MT has probably just the right word to describe the historical circumstances in which Syria, as senior partner, was forcing Israel into alliance with and compliance to her own anti-Assyrian policy. It is used also of locusts 'settling' upon Egypt (Exod. 10.14). In one form of the hiphil (הִנִּיחַ) it can speak of God's judgment in the form of his 'abandoning' the people in the wilderness if they disobey him, or, in another (הֵנִיחַ), to declare that the name of the rebellious will be 'left' {6} for a curse by his chosen ones (Isa. 65.15).

There is a striking parallel to the use of the root in this verse in Proto-Zechariah. In the vision of the chariots and the horses we read, 'Behold, those who go towards the north country *have set my Spirit at rest* in the north country' (6.8), where the form of the verb is הֵנִיחוּ. It is not clear exactly which chariots and horses do go to the north, whether the black alone (v. 2), or whether the white ones accompany them (so MT). But, commenting on this latter possibility, Ackroyd (1968a: 182-83) says, '…it is possible that the ambiguity of the verbal form in v. 8 is deliberate, i.e. judgment on Babylon which thus gives rest to God's anger, and yet promise in the spiritual renewal of the exiles in preparation for their return (the theme of vv. 9-15) by virtue of the fact that God's spirit would "rest" upon them'.[7]

6.　See also Jones (1962b: 244): 'מְנֻחָתוֹ bears no suggestion of hostility'. But while he is right to say, 'In all instances of the word מְנֻחָה there is no hint of hostility: emphatically the reverse' (p. 244), we need to remember the other uses of the verbal root mentioned in the text.

7.　Cf. Bič (1962: 77). The suggestion that the white ones went to the west rests on the emendation of אֶל־אַחֲרֵיהֶם to אֶל־אַחֲרֵי הַיָּם (lit. 'to the sea').

Of course in this oracle it is the 'word of Yahweh' rather than his spirit which finds rest in the north country, but it may be that a similar theme of the two-fold process of judgment and deliverance occasioned by the presence and activity of Yahweh is intended. At least it is one possibility amongst the many others which must be considered in any attempt rightly to interpret this oracle.

The obscure v. 1b continues the difficulty and ambiguity. As it stands the MT can be rendered, 'For unto Yahweh is (shall be) the gaze of man, and all the tribes of Israel'. {7} However, the עֵין אָדָם may be understood objectively and rendered, 'For to Yahweh belongs the gaze of man...' Both contractions seem awkward; the first because, when it is man's eye which is spoken of as being upon Yahweh, it is normally the preposition אֶל which is used (e.g. Pss. 25.15; 123.1; 141.8) and the second because the much more natural way of expressing the truth that Yahweh watches over men is that of Pss. 33.18 and 34.16 (15) where אֶל is also used. It is just possible that עַיִן is used here to stand, by a kind of metonymy, for man's faculties and powers, perhaps his apparent control over his own destiny, and so to mean 'the powers of man belong to Yahweh'. But such a use is without parallel in the Old Testament. Elsewhere, if it stands for man's pride or arrogance, it is accompanied by a qualifying noun.[8]

Another possibility is that the phrase should be taken literally to mean 'the eye of man belongs to Yahweh', i.e. he opens their eyes to give them insight into his purpose, or alternatively blinds them, on analogy with 12.4, 10. The versions vary. LXX has, 'for the Lord looks upon men', while the Vulgate takes it the other way and renders, 'to the Lord is the eye of man', a similar sense to Rashi who has, 'the eye of man is turned toward Yahweh'. The Targum apparently interprets, 'Before Yahweh the works of men are manifest'. Some commentators have emended the difficult עֵין to עָרֵי[9] and have read then either 'the {8} cities of men belong to Yahweh', or 'the cities of the earth belong to Yahweh',[10] or, more often, by emending אָדָם to אֲרָם, read 'the cities of Aram (Syria) belong to Yahweh'. This certainly fits the context but one wonders how so obvious a reading could have become corrupted to the more difficult one of the extant text. R.C. Dentan (1956: 1093) reads, 'eye of Syria', taking this to be a reference to Damascus. Gaide (1968: 59-60) suggests that we should take the word עַיִן as 'spring' or 'well', and that it is a metaphor such as that

---

8. So in Isa. 2.11; 5.15; 10.12; Pss. 17.28; 131.1; etc.
9. So, e.g., Mitchell (1912: 263); Driver (1906: 237).
10. By emending אָדָם to אֲדָמָה Gaide (1968: 59) cites Matthes.

found in Deut. 33.28 to suggest the 'prosperity' of a people, or even, as in
Ps. 68.27 (26) to suggest 'off-spring' of Israel. This would mean that the
inhabitants of Aram are to be as much in the hand of Yahweh and to
experience their prosperity from him as the tribes of Israel. The thought is
then somewhat akin to that of v. 7 where the Philistines are to share a
similar fortune. M. Bič (1962: 111) retains the reading of the MT but finds
something of a similar meaning, and says that the reference to the 'tribes
of Israel' should not be excised since it shows that Israel's role was to be
the priestly one of mediating the knowledge of Yahweh to all nations.

One can only conclude, therefore, by saying that this note of ambiguity
is extended throughout vv. 1, 2aβ. The verse can be taken as threat against
the region of Syria to the north as Yahweh's 'word' alights upon its people
and its proclamation of judgment is effected, a fate which can {9} certainly come to pass since Yahweh's writ runs as certainly in that region
as among the tribes of Israel. (This general sense of v. 1bα remains clear
whatever emendations are adopted or rejected.) If it is threat, it is not clear
whether this is being identified with some present, or imminent historical
event (there is certainly nothing in this oracle alone to enable us to identify
that event with any confidence), or whether it is future, a proclamation of a
coming eschatological judgment. If that is the case, is Syria meant literally,
or is it, as Bič (1962: 110) takes it, a general reference to a 'typical' enemy
in the spirit of the night vision of Proto-Zechariah in 2.11 (7), where
Babylon is a type of an original enemy ('Urfeinde', cf. Rev. 16.19; 17.5)?

Or, is the whole to be taken as promise of weal and, if so, to whom is it
directed? Is this an example of an adventurous, universalistic thinking such
as may be found in 9.7 and 14.16ff., and indeed, in Proto-Zechariah (Zech.
8.20ff.)? Has an original threat against a foreign nation been interpreted in
this sense? In which case, if the phrase 'and all the tribes of Israel' is taken
on metrical and stylistic grounds to be a gloss, it becomes a highly significant one, since it may reflect the distinctive viewpoint of the traditio-circle
which gathered such oracles, preserved them, perhaps modified them and
used them to express their faith and future expectations? {10}

Again, we may ask whether the remarkably sustained note of ambiguity
is so persistent as to be intentional. Is there here anything of the kind of
ambiguity that Ackroyd found in the vision of the horses and chariots?[11] It
is interesting to observe that both here and in Zech. 6 the root נוח is used in
reference to the presence and activity of Yahweh in the north country, and
that vv. 2b-7 go on to speak of Phoenicia in the north west and Philistia in

11. See Ackroyd (1968a: 182-83) and p. {4} n. 4 above.

the south west. Does this indicate in any way that this oracle has been coloured by the earlier night vision of Proto-Zechariah to suggest in the same way that all territories are subject to Yahweh and that he will act in mercy to all who respond to his word there, but in judgment to all who refuse it? But this would be a remarkable extension of the idea of Yahweh's activity among his own people. Foreigners are to have an equal chance of hearing and responding to the word of Yahweh. In Proto-Zechariah there is the same two-fold emphasis. The people of Yahweh know both the judgment and the cleansing of God (3.1-5; 5.1-4, 5-11) and hear the call to respond (3.7-14; 7.8ff., 14ff.), and yet are promised the blessings of his salvation (1.1; 2.5 [1]ff., 11 [6]ff., etc.) Yet other nations also hear the word of threat and judgment in so far as they oppose the will of Yahweh by oppressing his people (1.15; 2.1 [1.18]ff.), and yet to them also are addressed words of promise and salvation (8.20ff.). One further {11} parallel between 6.1-8 and 9.1-8 can be mentioned. The first is followed immediately by a promise of the completion of the Temple and the institution of a divinely ordained leadership.[12] 9.1-8 also culminates in a promise that Yahweh will again encamp at his house and offer the protection of the divine presence and leadership of his people. Both thus have been editorially arranged so that they lead towards a Zion-centred tradition. It is possible, then, that in this opening oracle themes of Proto-Zechariah's teaching are being taken up and made the basis for the expression of eschatological hope. That which Zechariah saw as being fulfilled in his day in the completion of the Temple is now about to be realised in a new, final climax to the saving history. This is a possibility which must be considered with others in the light of all that follows.

Yet still questions remain. Why should Syria be chosen to represent the typical 'Urfeinde' of the north, allowing Bič's suggestion to stand for the moment? Why not Babylon, for example, to whom the references to the 'north country' in Zech. 6 must almost certainly have applied? Such a question raises another possible way of understanding and interpreting the reference to this region. If, of course, the original allusion was to a specific historical event, no difficulties arise, since Syria must be mentioned in correspondence to some event or movement which had taken place, or had yet to take place there, whatever the actual {12} event and its date are seen to be. But it has to be considered that the reference may not be historical at all, but that this, and possibly the other places mentioned, have a theo-

---

12. On the relation between Zech. 6.1-8 and 6.9-15, see Ackroyd (1968a: 183).

logical rather than a geographical or historical significance.[13] As we shall
see, certain references and allusions in 9.1-8 suggest that earlier prophetic
material is being recalled, both from the book of Amos and that of Ezekiel.
Has this opening verse been similarly influenced, and, if so, what source in
the prophetic material that is alluded to could reasonably be suggested?

It has in fact been noted before (Jones 1962b: 244-45) that Amos predicted an exile of the northern kingdom of Israel, *'beyond Damascus'*
(Amos 5.27), as a punishment for her improper sacrifices (vv. 21-27) and
her idolatry (v. 26). All the places mentioned in Zech. 9.1, 2a are in fact
'beyond', that is, north of Damascus. Is allusion to this older prophetic
threat being made here, and, if it were, for what purpose? Is it to suggest
that the old threat is now to be reversed? Is Yahweh himself to go amongst
his dispersed people and, by implication, bring them back? This is yet
another possibility to be considered, especially since the reunion of the
two former kingdoms in God's final act of salvation is sounded elsewhere
in these chapters.[14]

D.R. Jones (1962b: 242) is confident that we should not look here, in the
manner of many commentators, for specific historical allusions. {13}

> May it not be that the prophet is wont to quote or use older prophetic
> passages because he sees their relevance to his own day? Then he will not
> be adapting earlier oracles to the precise historical situation of his day. He
> will merely be recognising that his situation is generally envisaged in
> earlier prophecy.

Nevertheless, Jones (1962b: 244, 250, 258-59) himself provides a kind
of historical occasion by saying that this is the work of a prophet who
lived and ministered among these exiles of the former northern kingdom
of Israel in the fifth century BC. This is not impossible but has the weakness of building far-reaching conclusions on slender evidence. One would
expect further indications pointing unmistakably to this *locale* of the

---

13. Mention could well be made here of the lecture given by P.R. Ackroyd as the
Presidential Address to the Winter Meetings of the Society for Old Testament Study,
1972, 'Theological Geography', for the general consideration of the theological
significance of geographical locations mentioned in the Old Testament, although the
particular passage under discussion was not mentioned, nor was the influence of earlier
prophetic influence on later writers being considered.

14. E.g. 9.10, 13; 10.6-7. The relationship between the two kingdoms envisaged by
11.4-14 is a more complex issue and will be discussed in its own place. The northern
kingdom receives no mention in chs. 12ff.

prophet's activity, but in fact there is little compelling to suggest this to the impartial reader.

However, one could accept Jones's method of interpretation without identifying oneself with its results in this particular instance. It need not be the work of a prophet who actually lived among this community. It might be a general allusion to the northern community in exile in the light of Amos 5.27, and constitute a general promise of their ultimate return and reunion with Judah in the final act of salvation. In which case we should have here a general eschatological prophecy in which salvation is seen in terms of reversal of the former judgment of earlier prophecy against those whose sin and idolatry had rendered them unfit to continue as the covenant people. Such a concept of continuing exile appears elsewhere. For {14} example, Dan. 9.24 must be seen as more than a device for explaining away the failure of earlier prophecy to be realised. It is rather an understanding of contemporary suffering as a continuing exile in judgment for sins. The Chronicler also saw not only the past disobedience of the fathers as responsible for the exile (2 Chron. 36.15-16), but also the sins of his contemporaries, Ezra 9.13; Neh. 9.33ff. and esp. vv. 36-37, which speaks of the present in terms of a continuation of their time of subjection.

One further possibility may be mentioned although at this stage left as such, to be examined in the light of further evidence from chs. 9–14. For one feels that a prophet might well have identified himself more closely with a people to whom he was making such a promise, if promise it be. Prophets did tend also to relate their oracles to specific events in history.[15] In this sense Jones may have shown a sure instinct in wanting to identify this prophet geographically and historically with the people of whom, and to whom he was speaking. Yet, as we have suggested, evidence to link him with the districts to which the exiles of the old northern kingdom were taken is slight. Is it possible that the name Damascus here carries a significance other than a purely and strictly geographical one? We know how later the Qumran Covenanters could speak of themselves as 'dwelling in Damascus'.[16] {15} The significance of this is disputed, but it does seem as though the wilderness to them was more than a geographical entity. It

---

15. See Otzen's (1964: 35ff.) strong insistence on this.

16. See *The Damascus Rule* 6.5; 6.19; 7.14-20 which is a kind of apocalyptic re-interpretation of Amos 5.16-27. These passages include the phrases, 'the repentant of Israel who went out from the land of Judah and sojourned in the land of Damascus' (6.5) and '…those who entered the New Covenant in the land of Damascus' (6.19) and 8.21–19.33.

symbolised their isolation and exclusion from the Judaism of their day as represented by Temple and priesthood from which they had separated themselves. Cross, interestingly enough, in his discussion of this, comes to the conclusion that the idea was based on the very prophecy of Amos which we have been considering. They saw this fulfilled in their own being 'sent out' into the wilderness, but believed this was also to be reversed at the end.[17] Certainly the wilderness had once stood for just such a reality to Elijah who, rejected by the royal line then ruling in Israel, had escaped to the wilderness. Yahweh told him to go 'into the wilderness of Damascus' and there anoint as king over Israel one who would be the true leader of Yahweh's appointing in succession to the line which, by its apostate and sinful ways, had forfeited the right to control the affairs of Yahweh's people (1 Kgs 10.9, 15-16).

So at least the possibility can be put forward that such a kind of interpretation of the Amos prophecy as we have reason to believe was held by the men of Qumran, had already been given to it by others. It would mean that this is a promise by the prophet to a circle who are in 'spiritual exile', in isolation from the people and land of Yahweh as typified by its present representatives. He sees {16} Yahweh's word as active among them, perhaps through his own ministry, and Yahweh himself as active among them, and that they are his care as much as the official 'tribes of Israel'. This could be, but of course need not be, the interpretation of the significance of the allusion to the region of Syria beyond Damascus here, and could only be further entertained if sufficient evidence of such a viewpoint were to be found elsewhere in these chapters.

However, one point may be made in passing. If the ambiguity throughout this verse *is* intentional, then it may be that this comes with the force of a pastoral exhortation. To some group the prophet is saying, 'The word of Yahweh has come among you once more. Upon your response depends whether the consequences of this are to be for weal or woe'. If that is so, then we should have the paradoxical situation that it is the point of greatest ambiguity in vv. 1, 2a which is its only source of light. Its aim would be one both of encouragement and promise, and yet also of pastoral exhortation and warning to faithful response, and this would not be without its implications for our understanding of its meaning, its purpose, and its origin in the circle in which it was preserved.

In summary, however, we must reiterate that vv. 1, 2a face us with a

---

17. See Cross (1958: 59-60n) for the various views of the significance of the phrase as it related to the Qumran community.

bewildering array of possible alternative interpretations. It may be threat against a foreign people as the context may most naturally suggest, and be {17} related to some particular historical event which we cannot now identify with certainty. Or it may be threat of a general eschatological nature, in which case Syria may not be meant to be an actual, but a typical enemy power. It is possible that the vision of Zech. 6 has had some general influence. On the other hand, it may be promise, either of a universalist kind which proclaims that even Syria shall belong to Yahweh and know his word, or it may be allusive to the earlier prophecies of Amos and intended to refer, either to the exiled Israelites, or to a group who saw themselves as 'spiritually' or 'theologically' rather than geographically isolated. Or it may be deliberately ambiguous, being neither a simple prediction of woe or weal, but instead a proclamation of the word of Yahweh which may be either, according to the response of those to whom it is addressed. Such an embarrassing wealth of options should counsel caution before any one interpretation is too quickly and too confidently said to be the one which alone fits vv. 1, 2aα.

Clearly, the answer to the question as to whether it is interpretative of earlier prophetic themes rather than a statement of specific historical allusions cannot be discovered apart from examination of what follows. In what sense are the oracles concerning Phoenicia and Philistia to be understood, and how do they relate to what has preceded? If the references are literal we have to decide {18} why these places in particular are singled out for mention. Jones, as we have seen, believes that the places in Syria represent the actual location of the prophet's ministry. Delcor (1951a), and others, find here an itinerary of the march of Alexander the Great. Otzen (1964: 120ff.) has found here a recalling of the ideal boundaries of the Davidic kingdom, as Josiah sought to reconstruct it. If, however, these places are mentioned because of the occurrence in earlier prophetic material to which allusion is being made, their significance becomes somewhat different. We have seen that the references to Hadrach, Damascus, and Hamath may be due to, and intended to recall, Amos 5.27, by way of announcing its reversal. We have to ask how this could apply to the mention of the cities of Phoenicia and Philistia.

Phoenicia is represented by Tyre.[18] Here the inspiration of earlier

18. The mention of Sidon may well be secondary since: (a) the חָכְמָה which follows is in the singular; (b) no further reference to Sidon is made at all; and (c) it could well have been added because of the close association of the two names in earlier biblical references, e.g. Isa. 23; Jer. 25.22; 27.3; 47.4; Ezek. 28, where the possible source of

prophetic material seems to be clearer and the resemblances between the references to Tyre here and those in Ezekiel especially have often been noted. Ezek. 28.2ff. ironically lampoons the self-styled wisdom and divine status which claims, in the person of their king,

> You are indeed wiser than Daniel; no secret is hidden from you:
> you have gotten wealth for yourselves
> and have gathered gold and silver into your treasure.
> By your great wisdom in trade
> you have increased your wealth
> and your heart has become proud in your wealth.

Ezek. 26.12 foretells that: {19}

> they will make a spoil of your riches and a prey of your merchandise; your pleasant houses; your stones and timber and dust they will cast into the midst of the waters.

Tyre, who is so proud of the rampart defense of her island which she has built (וַתִּבֶן), is the same one who received in Ezek. 26.14 the threat, 'you shall never be rebuilt' (לֹא תִבָּנֶה עוֹד). Her gold which is like the 'mire of the streets' (כְּטִיט חוּצוֹת, Zech. 9.3), a term of contempt in Mic. 7.10 as, later, in Zech. 10.5, ironically recalls the threat of Ezek. 26 that the streets of Tyre will be trampled by the invader following the breaching of the walls, while her silver, which is 'like dust' (כֶּעָפָר, Zech. 9.3) recalls the threat of Ezek. 26.12 'your dust (עֲפָרֵךְ) they will cast into the midst of the waters'. These allusions are strikingly echoed in Zech. 9.3-4:

> Tyre has built herself a rampart,
> and heaped up silver like dust, and gold like the dirt of the streets.
> But lo, the Lord will strip her of her possessions
> and hurl her wealth into the sea...

This echoing and evoking of the oracles of Ezekiel against Tyre raises the question as to how our prophet is here using the material, whether he is 'expounding' it, as we should say, and if he is, in what way he is relating it to his own day. It is, of course, possible, as we have seen with a number of scholars, to identify it with some specific historical event in which Tyre is threatened by an invader in whose activity our prophet sees a fulfilment of these earlier oracles. But here it is pertinent {20} to enquire a little more closely into the nature of the Ezekiel oracles.

the words about Tyre in Zech. 9.2b-4 may have inspired the reference to Sidon, and Joel 3.4.

The oracles against Tyre occupy a prominent place in Ezekiel, extending through chs. 26–28. Next to the oracles concerning Egypt they are the longest of those relating to a foreign nation, confirming no doubt the prominence and power of both these powers in Ezekiel's time. She is attacked basically on three counts; her gloating over the fate of Jerusalem in its fall (26.2) so that she can enjoy unrivalled power; the confidence which she places in her wealth and resources (27.3ff.); but, above all, for her *hubris*, personified in the person of her 'prince' (נָגִיד) who claims in the pride of his heart, 'I am a god, I sit in the seat of the gods' (28.2, possibly a reference to the concept of divine kingship testified to in the Ugaritic literature).[19] It is generally accepted that the reference here is not specifically and exclusively to King Itobaal II, of whom no individual characteristics are specified, but to the king as personifying the whole spirit, outlook and temper of Tyre.[20] Zimmerli (1969: 666) says, 'Der könig von Tyrus wird auf seinen überheblichen Hochmut hin angeredet'.

He points out that גְבַהּ לֵב is an abomination to Yahweh in the wisdom literature (Prov. 16.5). But the idea of Yahweh bringing down the proud and lofty and raising the lowly is a prominent theme in Ezekiel (17.22-24 {21}; 21.31; 19.11; 31). Thus it may be said that the whole tenor of Ezekiel's attack against Tyre was its spirit of proud independence, of confidence in the powers of her own wisdom and wealth, her strength and alliances, all of which were the very antipathy to the spirit of humble faith in Yahweh which is a dominant feature of all Old Testament theology.

This raises the question whether it is a specific allusion to some historical event in which Tyre was threatened, or whether it is rather this whole spirit which our author is echoing in taking over the traditional material against Tyre, the very epitome of that attitude so opposed to Yahweh's will. The contrast with the lowly and obedient king of vv. 9-10 could not be more marked. Is he, in fact, referring to Ezekiel's words against Tyre to make the same kind of theological point which Ezekiel himself makes the material serve? This would mean that older prophetic material is being used and expounded to suggest that, just as in vv. 1, 2a, the word of Yahweh is coming with its life and death ambivalence equally to men, all of whom are subject to him, so vv. 2b-4 are predicting that this final act will be the occasion for the bringing down of all that pride of man by which he sets himself in opposition to, and independence of, Yahweh. It was of this spirit that Tyre was the typical historical example as earlier

19. For a discussion of this, see de Langhe (1958: 122-48).
20. So Zimmerli (1969: 666); Eichrodt (1970: 390); Stalker (1968: 216).

prophecy showed, but the prediction of her downfall will be fulfilled against all who exemplify the {22} same spirit now.

But, if the reference to Tyre is 'typical' rather than historical, the question can again be asked, whether this is limited only to non-Israelites, or whether foreigners and Israelites are alike open to the word of Yahweh by responding to which they will know salvation, but by rejecting which they will suffer the same fate as the lofty, the wise and the proud. And is it further possible that any reference is intended to a particular group within Israel? Ezek. 28 was addressed to the 'prince' of Tyre. Could there be any veiled reference to the leadership within Israel itself which might be thought to be arrogating to itself claims to power which are too lofty, attitudes of scorn to the faithful within the community, and reliance on resources by which they have become rich? Again, at this point, the question can only be posed, but ought to be kept in mind, in case such a viewpoint appears elsewhere to characterize these chapters.

With the threat of judgment against the Philistines it is found that there are also echoes of earlier prophetic material, this time from Amos. A possible link between the two may be found in the phrase וְהִיא בָּאֵשׁ תֵּאָכֵל which, while it refers here to Tyre, recalls the opening lines of Amos's oracles against the Nations, וְשִׁלַּחְתִּי אֵשׁ בְּחוֹמַת צֹר וְאָכְלָה אַרְמְנֹתֶיהָ (Amos 1.6-9f.). This Amos passage does seem to be in mind here, for in {23} Amos 1.6-9 Tyre, Gaza, Ashkelon, Ashdod, and Ekron are all brought together following reference to Damascus, in each case Gath being omitted.[21] Similar judgments are related to different subjects. In Amos, the threat is 'to cut off the inhabitant from Ashdod', which is parallel to cutting off 'him who holds the sceptre in Ashkelon'. In Zech. 9 it is Ashkelon which 'shall be uninhabited', while Ashdod is threatened with a bastard population.[22] The threat to Ashkelon is parallel to the warning that 'the king shall perish from Gaza'.

If in fact, then, this is another example of the use of earlier prophetic material we have again to ask in what way it is being used, how it is being expounded, and for what purpose it is being recalled.

The oracles in the opening two chapters of Amos against foreign nations have a very clear purpose in their own context. They suggest that God has

---

21. It should, however, be pointed out that Gath is also missing elsewhere, e.g., in Zeph. 2.4; Jer. 25.20.

22. The term מַמְזֵר occurs elsewhere in the Old Testament only in Deut. 23.3 (2), where it refers to the descendants of mixed marriages, one of the groups to be excluded from the cultic community of the Temple.

one standard of justice for all men and will judge all alike, except in so far as Israel's special privileges of covenant status involve the greater responsibility (3.1-2). In his eyes now Israel is no different from them. This coincides with the theme that Israel, by her actions, has forfeited her covenant status which should have entitled Yahweh to a special response from her, but in fact, in God's eyes, Israel and the nations are all alike (6.1-3). The most remarkable expression of this thought occurs in 9.7 where {24} the special theology of privilege is turned aside.

Does this throw any light on the use of this material in Zech. 9? This is an unusual structure in that the announcement of judgment comes first (vv. 5, 6a) while vv. 6b, 7 continue the announcement of judgment but alone include the nature of the charges against the various Philistine towns. This, as has been said, coincides with the change to first person divine speech and includes the very remarkable modification of the traditional announcement of judgment to show that the ultimate purpose for the Philistines is redemptive.

The charges are now specified. Just as the sin of Tyre had been the false estimate of her own wisdom by which she believed she had amassed her wealth by herself, forgetful of the truth that it is Yahweh's wisdom alone which is 'better than silver and gold' (Prov. 8.19), so it is the גָּאוֹן of Philistia which is now to be ended by God. This is what needs to be cleansed. Throughout the Old Testament this is the term used often to denote the magnificence of nations, their military and political power, wealth, fame and pomp, all of which tend to make them self-sufficient in their own eyes, and thus independent of Yahweh. True גָּאוֹן, however, is Yahweh's alone to bestow. Trito-Isaiah sees how Zion will have its גָּאוֹן renewed by Yahweh (Isa. 60.15). Just as the oracles against Tyre, therefore, spoke of that human wisdom which must {25} topple before Yahweh, so those directed against Philistia may well be directed against all false self-reliance. In addition sinful practices and cultic defilement must be removed, the reference in v. 7 being to the eating of blood, forbidden in Deut. 12.16, 23f., and animals forbidden by the Mosaic law (Deut. 14.3ff.). Perhaps also the 'mamzer' of v. 6a suggests cultic impurity (cf. Deut. 23.3). Then they too may become part of the Covenant People.

In the Amos passage it was the remnant of the Philistines which was to perish (1.8), presumably meaning that the destruction was to be total. Here, however, the idea is of the destruction of that within her which is contrary to God's will, so that she may be fitted to take her place among God's people. After purification she will become a 'remnant' (וְנִשְׁאַר) for

God, a very different use of the remnant idea from that found in Amos, indeed, what might be termed at least a partial reversal of it. She shall become 'like a clan in Judah' which, however, we point אלף, either as אַלֻּף meaning 'clan', or אַלָּף meaning 'tamed', 'intimate', the force would seem to be the same. These people will become the intimates of God's people. To this is paralleled the thought that Ekron shall become like the Jebusites, presumably a reference to the apparently gentle treatment of the Jebusites after David's capture of Jerusalem, so that they became absorbed into the people of God and, as {26} we now know, exerted a great influence on Israelite worship and theology.[23] Why Ekron should have received special mention is not clear. Perhaps when the oracle was crystallizing some incident involving them brought them into a position of leadership or special prominence, or it was because they were those whose own hopes had been disappointed (v. 5, cf. Isa. 20.5-6) and so who had had their own גָּאוֹן cut off in a particular way.

Then Philistia will know the same protection of God which the faithful of his own people will know. People of God and foreigner are to be treated exactly alike. Judgment is not seen in the form which these oracles have finally assumed, simply as the overthrow of a national enemy. It appears to take the form, in foreigner and home-born alike, of all that prevents the purpose of God in them. Again, one is reminded of Proto-Zechariah with his emphasis on the spiritual renewal of the returned community which must precede her experience of Yahweh's salvation. This found expression in the symbolic cleansing of Joshua as representative of the whole community (ch. 3) and the two visions of the removal of sin under the figures of the flying scroll and the woman removed to Babylon (ch. 5). What seems to be suggested is that the purifying work of judgment is not for one people alone.

It is a lofty and noble outlook suggesting a circle whose zeal for moral and cultic obedience to Yahweh is {27} matched by a breadth of vision and universalist thought somewhat akin to the circles in which the final form of the oracles of Zech. 1–8 took shape. That Philistines should become like the Jebusites is truly amazing, but it reminds us again of Jerusalem, the place which God had chosen for his own special habitation and which, for all its foreignness of origin, became the site of the Temple,

---

23. One may instance David's purchase of the threshing floor from Araunah, the Jebusite (2 Sam. 10.14, esp. vv. 16ff.). For a treatment of the possible Jebusite influence on Israelite worship and theology, see Rowley (1939); Johnson (1967: 31-53).

with its worship acceptable to God, the focal point of the nation's covenant relationship with Yahweh.

Such a thought, indeed, provides a bridge for the passage to the concluding verse, but before we turn to that we have to ask how this oracle relating to the Philistines is to be understood in its present context. Again, it is possible that it has an historical reference as those concerning Aram and Phoenicia may have had. But also, the use of earlier prophetic material leads us to ask whether Philistia is to be seen in a 'typical' sense, by whose mention the original prophecy is being evoked, reinterpreted and reapplied to a new situation. We have seen that in its original context it suggested that the Israelites could not hide behind the special privileges of a covenant, election theology. If she sinned like other nations she would be judged like other nations. If Tyre typified all that was lifted up in *hubris* against Yahweh, does Philistia typify all which can likewise be spoken of as גָּאוֹן and whose worship and idolatry are in opposition to his {28} requirements? Is what is being said that, in the final act of salvation, Yahweh will judge this, wherever it is found? But, if so, it must be a two-edged word. It is a remarkable instance of Universalism that Yahweh will judge foreigner and Israelite alike. But it brings home to the people of God the uncomfortable challenge that they can hide behind no special privilege. In so far as they exhibit גָּאוֹן, and their worship is corrupt and unworthy of Yahweh, they are liable to judgment. Yet, if the threat of divine judgment applies to all alike, so, the oracle triumphantly concludes, does the purpose of divine cleansing and salvation. The Philistines, after all, were always 'the uncircumcised' *par excellence*. If such can be cleansed by God for his own, then so can any.

So understood, this application of older prophetic material would become a vital and urgent message for the prophet's hearers in the light of the coming final act of salvation of Yahweh. It would mark the evocation of earlier prophetic teaching in order to bring its lesson home to his contemporaries in the light of this imminent and final fulfillment.

Again, the question would arise whether this warning implies that, in the prophet's view, such attitudes of *hubris*, גָּאוֹן and cultic apostasy which once typified these nations are to be found within the Israel of his own day as well as outside it. {29}

We have suggested that a link between the end of the oracles concerning foreign nations and v. 8 is to be found in the reference in v. 7 to the Jebusites with their association with Jerusalem and the site of the Temple. Verse 8 proceeds to mention the 'house' of Yahweh. In view of what has

gone before, and the promise that follows that no 'oppressor' will again
pass over them, some commentators believe that the reference here is to
the 'land' rather than specifically to the Temple. Elliger (1964: 146) takes
the reference to be to the Temple but says that the plural 'them' shows that
it stands for the land and people of Judah and Jerusalem. Gaide (1968: 63)
says, 'D'après la plupart des commentateurs modernes, le mot désigne ici
non pas le Temple de Jérusalem, mais la Palestine'.[24]

Clearly it can signify the whole land, but since the Temple was seen as
very much the cultic centre of the land and nation's life, the place where
Yahweh's presence was made known, it is perhaps of added significance
that this term is used, rather than 'the land'.[25]

In fact, the text is obscure here. The Targum renders freely, but has the
same rendering for 'I will encamp' (וְחָנִיתִי) as in Zech. 2.14 (10), which
calls on men to rejoice for Yahweh will dwell in the midst of them, but
adds, 'in my holy house'; it also adds 'like a wall of fire', based on Zech.
2.9 (5). The LXX has, 'I will set up a defense' (ἀνάστημα = 'height', or
'prominence'), {30} a reading of MT מִצָּבָה which seems to have influenced the Vulgate's 'Et ponam in domo mea elevationem', which may
have followed a reading מַצֵּבָה. The vocalization is often emended to
read מַצָּבָה from the root נצב, 'I will encamp at my home *as a guard*'.
Jansma's (1949: 69ff.) conclusions concerning the MT is that, taken with
the 'apparently redundant' מעבר ומשב, three texts may have been combined: (i) 'I shall set a watch for my house'; (ii) 'and I shall encamp at my
house against the army'; (iii) 'and I shall encamp about my house against
him that passeth through and returneth'.

It is interesting that at least one interpretation, that represented by the
Targum, linked this with Proto-Zechariah. Saebø (1969: 159-60) says that
both textual tradition variants (he sees מצבה and מעבר ומשב as parallel
variants) relate to Proto-Zechariah. The first relates to Zech. 2.8b-9 (4b-5)

---

24. He cites as parallels, Hos. 8.1; 9.15; Jer. 12.7; cf. also Mitchell (1912: 269ff.).

25. For this connection between the land and the Temple, see Clements (1965:
73ff.). In commenting on Hos. 8.1, Mays (1969b: 115-16) says, 'The "house of Yahweh" is Hosea's phrase for the land as God's gift to Israel of a place to live in'. He
goes on to say that the use of 'house' with a proper name to designate places was a
formulation current in the general speech of the ancient Near East, and refers to Tiglath
Pileser's name for Israel as 'House of Omri', and place names with the 'Beth-'
compound. This is true, but, it might be added, that the fact that Israel was called
'Omri's House' was because at the heart of it Omri ruled in its palace. If a place was
called 'Beth-el', it was because there was a sanctuary of 'El' there. One can easily
follow the progression of thought—holy place, holy city, holy land.

which looks back to 1.16-17. Those also were in the first person of the divine speech which sometimes occurs in the night visions. Both concern Jerusalem, now without walled protection, but to which Yahweh himself will be a wall of fire. In 1.16-17 the 'house' is central as in 9.8, and in both the word עוֹד occurs. The second relates to Zech. 7.14 (cf. Ezek. 35.7).[26] Certainly there is reflected a kinship of theme. Verse 8 has the effect of rounding off vv. 1-7 with the promise {31} that God will protect his people, cleansed and forgiven, stripped of all false self-reliance and cultic apostasy, Israelite and foreign, from the Temple, whither all come to seek him. This echoes the themes of the divine return to Jerusalem and protection of it, the cleansing and renewing of his people, and the making of the Temple a centre for all, Israelite and foreign alike, to come and worship, themes, all of which, are prominent in Proto-Zechariah.

We should note that protection is to be provided from 'the oppressor' (נֹגֵשׂ). This may refer to foreign invaders and overlords. It is certainly used in the Old Testament of the Egyptian taskmasters who oppressed them (Exod. 3.7; 5.6, 10, 13, 14). Sometimes, it refers unmistakably to foreign domination (e.g. Isa. 9.3 [4]; 14.2, 4). But it can also refer to unworthy native leaders who oppress their own people by the burdens they place upon them. So, for example, Jehoiakim 'exacted' from his people the silver and gold needed to pay tribute to Egypt (2 Kgs 23.35).[27] A very similar thought in Joel 4.17 (3.17) is expressed less ambiguously:

> So you shall know that I am the Lord your God, who dwells in Zion, my holy mountain. And Jerusalem shall be holy, and strangers (זָרִים) shall never again pass through it (לֹא־יַעַבְרוּ־בָהּ עוֹד).

Here the idea of Yahweh's presence in his sanctuary is strongly emphasized. But the use of נֹגֵשׂ in Zech. 9.8 may be used in place of a word like זָרִים {32} intentionally to convey a *double entendre*. All injustice and oppression of the people of God will cease from whatever source, foreign invaders or unworthy national leaders.

The concluding phrase 'Now I see with my eyes' is enigmatic. It may be word of Yahweh in which case בְעֵינִי could be emended to בְעָנְיוֹ, 'I have looked on his (their) affliction'.[28] Or the same sense could be achieved

---

26. Compare also, the remarks of Elliger (1964: 146-47).

27. See also Deut. 15.2f. The use of the word in Zech. 10.4 seems to suggest that, what her conquerors had been to Israel, she will be to her former captors, as in Isa. 14.2.

28. Cf. *BHS*—one can compare Exod. 3.7.

without emendation. Yahweh has turned his eyes upon his people in their
need, this possibly affording a counterpart to the phrase in v. 1b. Saebø
(1969: 161) has pointed out how much emphasis on the 'eye' of Yahweh
there is in Proto-Zechariah.[29] It could even carry the overtone that Yahweh
will watch over his own directly and immediately, rather than through the
mediation of leaders who have proved unworthy of their pastoral charge.
On the other hand, this could be the word of the prophet who claims
he can see all this coming to pass in the events of his own time, and perhaps be an evocation of the 'vision' style of oracle familiar from Proto-
Zechariah.

If now we attempt to summarize our investigation of 9.1-8 as a whole it
can only be with the recognition that the more closely we examine it the
more questions it tends to raise, and that, strictly from the data within this
section alone, certainty is hard to come by.

We have seen that it may be related to an historical {33} context, to
events in which the prophet sees foreign nations coming under judgment
as the people of God experience deliverance and salvation. As these
oracles now stand, they have been modified, at least as far as the Philistines are concerned, by a remarkable universalism, certainly reminiscent of
Proto-Zechariah.

Again, the references to these nations may not be literal, but the whole
be an eschatological prophecy of that which has yet to happen, not as yet
related to any specific event.

But we have also seen that the oracles concerning Tyre and the Philistian
cities, and even possibly those relating to Aram, appear to have been influenced by earlier prophetic oracles and this has raised the question as to
why this should have been so. It may be that the prophet, or prophetic
circle responsible for the final form of these oracles, believed that, in the
events of their own time, those older prophecies were finding a literal fulfilment. But it may have been also that the teaching of the earlier prophets
was being expounded and reapplied with a pastoral concern by the
preacher to announce their fulfilment in a more general way and prepare
his hearers for the crisis which is at hand. Thus the reference to the region
beyond Damascus may be a reference, in the light of Amos's prediction of
exile and judgment there, to God's judgment on his people, with the
promise that that judgment is about to be reversed. To such, the word of
God comes with {34} ambivalent force. The announcement will be judg-

---

29. He cites Zech. 2.12 (8); 3.9; 4.10; 8.6.

ment for those who reject it but salvation for those who respond. Again, Tyre and the Philistian cities may typify all that is opposed to, and independent of Yahweh by way of human pride, false trust in human resources and cultic apostasy, and these oracles declare that judgment is to fall on all who exemplify such attitudes. But such judgment is aimed at redemption and, just as Yahweh's writ runs among all men (v. 1) so, from even the Philistines, he can raise up for himself a people cleansed and restored (v. 7).

There thus seems to be a universalist note sounded which was heard also in Proto-Zechariah. Yet the teaching of Proto-Zechariah is also to be heard in the prominence given to the activity of Yahweh in destroying all that is contrary to his will and which checks his purpose of redemption for his people, in returning to guard his 'house' and protect his people, but also to cleanse them from all that defiles them.

Implicit in this, however, is the note of exclusivism. If these foreign nations really do typify attitudes of mind and spirit and, in the case of the echoes from Amos, remind that his oracles served to introduce a pointed warning to those who claim to be the covenant people of God, then there would seem likely to be implicit here also a word of warning and pastoral entreaty to the prophet's own people to be ready. And always we have seen the {35} possibility to exist that this prophet, or circle, identifies with some groups, and perhaps especially with influential circles of leadership within the community, the very attitudes, spirit and sins which Yahweh must punish.

This would suggest, then, a prophet or circle who: (i) venerated the teaching of the earlier prophets and not only recalled them, but expounded them for their own preaching, announcing their imminent fulfilment in their own time and echoing the teaching of those prophets; (ii) a prophet or circle which seems to have been particularly influenced by the teaching of Proto-Zechariah and bearers of that tradition; and (iii) possibly a prophet or circle who had such a critical evaluation of some elements in the Jewish community, and who were perhaps particularly critical of the leadership of that community and saw the need for renewal within the Temple itself.

Such conclusions can only be tentative from an examination of 9.1-8 which have managed to support so many and such varied conclusions within the history of criticism. They must be held as possibilities to be tested as examination of Deutero-Zechariah proceeds further. {36}

Chapter 2

ZECHARIAH 9.9-10

This oracle is in the form of a messenger proclamation in which Zion/ Jerusalem is addressed in the second person feminine singular and called to rejoice because of the approach of her king. Verse 10 consists of first person divine speech referring to the king in the third person. By metre, and the common themes of the king and his victory, the two verses appear closely related, and are usually taken as a unity.

The relation of this oracle to its context has been much discussed. However, the new form, the style of the proclamation, if not the metre, would seem to lend weight to the view that we have here to do with an oracle that was, at least in origin, a detached one; yet for all that, its editorial placing here can hardly have been accidental, and in this connection, a general resemblance to the pattern and emphases of Proto-Zechariah may be recalled. We have already seen that the earlier section culminated in 9.8 with the thought of the Temple. Indeed, the fact of God's protective presence in his house was treated as the climax of this picture of the new age. We see also that the Temple played a central role in the oracles of Proto-Zechariah in that its completion was an essential preparation for the ushering in of God's decisive act of salvation. This is seen in 4.6-10; 8.20-23 and 2.13-17 (9-13), where the phrase, 'I will dwell in the {37} midst of you' suggests the Temple. Twice the prophet suggests that the authenticity of his calling and ministry will find its vindication in this (2.15 [11]; 4.9). Yet inextricably bound up with this task of the completion of the Temple is the person of Zerubbabel, the agent God has chosen for the task (3.8; 6.12ff.). He is spoken of as God's 'servant' (3.8), the 'Branch' (3.8; 6.12), a Messianic term (see Jer. 23.5; 33.15; Isa. 11.1; cf. Ps. 132.17). He is endowed by God's spirit (4.6) and is to bear royal honour and sit and rule upon his throne (6.13).

Here, in ch. 9, mention of the Temple leads immediately to the introduction of the royal agent of God's rule in Jerusalem. We are not, of course, suggesting any necessary or facile equation between Zerubbabel and the Messianic figure denoted in these verses. Indeed, as we shall see, there appears to be here important modification of traditional Messianic hopes. Yet the general parallel is of interest. In both the promise of the new age, with the role of the Temple central in its fulfilment, leads on to thought of the agent of the rule of God, and in both, certain features of royalty are emphasized. Have these emphases of Proto-Zechariah influenced the arrangement of oracles here, and, if so, does it mean that the promises of Zechariah concerning the Temple and the leadership are being reinterpreted in a new situation and their fulfilment announced as being at hand? {38}

It is interesting to speculate whether our writer or the editor who arranged this oracle did not see in the role and ministry of Zerubbabel an open-ended promise that, later than the time of Zerubbabel, another, of whom the earlier was but the pre-shadowing, would come, and that this coming would mark the establishment of the new of which Zerubbabel and the work of his day were but the herald.[1]

The person of the king spoken about in 9.9-10, and the date of the oracle have also been much discussed. Some have seen in him a Judean king of pre-exilic times, Uzziah (König 1893: 358), Hezekiah (Kraeling 1924: 29ff.) or that this cry reflects the welcome given to Tabe'el in 733 BC (Masing 1938)[2] or Ahaz (Otzen 1964: 134n). Horst (1964: 247) thinks it is a pre-exilic or exilic figure since no such messianic figure as this emerges in post-exilic times, least of all in the time of Haggai and Zechariah. Some have seen a link here with the figure of the 'Suffering Servant' of Second Isaiah (Mitchell 1912: 273). Others have found a cultic background to the description of the figure and related it to the concept of sacral kingship and the New Year Festival (Otzen 1964: 134ff.; von Rad 1962: 319n, 322; Jones 1962a: 129). Some speak, more guardedly, of the influence of the Psalms of the Zion tradition (Ackroyd 1968a: 652).[3] D.R. Jones (1962a:

---

1. For such a use of earlier material one can compare Beuken's (1967: 10-20, 281, 331ff.) suggestion that the activity of the prophets Haggai and Zechariah (shown as standing together in the Chronicler's tradition in Ezra 5f.) was viewed as indicative of events still to come. Its fulfilment was to be realized, at least in part, in the Chronicler's own time, even if not fully so, as Neh. 9 shows.

2. The writer has not had access to this work, which is cited by Otzen (1964: 134n).

3. Saebø (1969: 183), who thinks, however, that the figure is intended to be more political than sacral—one by whom the rule of foreign overlords is ended.

130) believes it has been based on the tradition of David's return to Jerusalem after his flight at the rebellion of Absalom, while Gaide (1968: 69-70) suggests that Solomon affords the model. {39}

Wellhausen (1892: 186) put it in the Maccabaean period, believing that it showed a deliberate contrast with the martial kings of the pre-exilic period. It shows, he thought, that the king of peace will not come 'from the godless ruling parties in Jerusalem, but from the oppressed pious'. Much more recently Weiser (1961: 275) has spoken of the Messianic picture of this oracle as being 'drawn from the circles of the "meek" and the pious'.[4] Eisenbeis (1969: 215-21) also dates it as late as c. 150 BC and believes it represents the viewpoint of the priestly circle of the Sadducees within the ruling Maccabaean house, or the Hasidim, from whom the Pharisees came and ultimately, the Qumran community. It represents the rejection by such circles of the warlike methods of the Maccabaeans.

The form of a messenger proclamation addressing the inhabitants of the city collectively in the second person feminine singular as the 'daughter of Zion' or of 'Jerusalem' and calling upon them to rejoice is strikingly reminiscent of two other passages. The first, interestingly in the light of other similarities which have begun to emerge in our investigation, occurs in Proto–Zechariah at 2.14 (10). This reads:

רָנִּי וְשִׂמְחִי בַּת־צִיּוֹן כִּי הִנְנִי־בָא וְשָׁכַנְתִּי בְתוֹכֵךְ

With which may be compared Zech. 9.9:

גִּילִי מְאֹד בַּת־צִיּוֹן הָרִיעִי בַּת יְרוּשָׁלַם הִנֵּה מַלְכֵּךְ יָבוֹא לָךְ {40}

When we consider the context of the call in Zech. 2.14 (10), some interesting points in common arise. The context is that of judgment against the 'nations' (2.12 [8]f.; cf. 9.1-8), which have plundered and oppressed his people. In contrast to their former servitude the call to the inhabitants of Zion is to rejoice because of the fulfilment of the promise of Yahweh to come himself into the midst of his people in the city and dwell there, a promise which, as we have noted already, implied the centrality of the Temple and its significance for the coming of the new age (cf. 9.8). But even this is not all. For one sign of that new age will be that 'many nations shall join themselves to the Lord in that day and shall be my people', with which we may compare 9.7-8, which we have already considered and

---

4.   Similarly, T. Chary (1955: 229), speaking of the quality of עָנִי in the king, says, 'Cette qualité lui vient certainement des milieux piétistes et pauvres'.

where we have seen that exactly the same group of ideas seems to be interwoven.

Another passage, also strikingly similar in terms to Zech. 9.9, is Zeph. 3.14ff., with its similar call to rejoicing: רָנִּי בַּת־צִיּוֹן הָרִיעוּ יִשְׂרָאֵל שִׂמְחִי וְעָלְזִי בְּכָל־לֵב בַּת יְרוּשָׁלָם. It is difficult to date too confidently the Zephaniah passage. Almost unanimously commentators have assigned it to a time later than that of Zephaniah himself, indeed, to some point after the exile. Reasons adduced are that {41} the exile is presupposed, the spirit is as different from the first chapters as Isa. 40–55 are from those of Isaiah of Jerusalem, and that they suggest that the time of judgment and trial is now in the past.[5]

The general run of ideas appears to be remarkably akin between the two passages. In Zephaniah, Zion and Israel are called upon to rejoice (note the linking of Ephraim and Jerusalem in Zech. 9.10) because God has intervened decisively. He has removed the sentence which was against them, and, because of this and in demonstration of it, he has turned away their enemies. In language reminiscent of the cultic announcement of the theophany it is proclaimed that Yahweh is now in their midst as king (מֶלֶךְ יִשְׂרָאֵל יְהוָה בְּקִרְבֵּךְ) as divine warrior, appearing to remove their reproach. It is most unfortunate that the text is tantalizingly corrupt in vv. 17f. If, as seems most likely, the strangely out of place יַחֲרִישׁ (contrast the parallel יָשִׂישׂ עָלַיִךְ) is to be read as יְחַדֵּשׁ, following the LXX (καινιεῖ), we have the thought of the renewal of the welfare of the community, which seems to have been so integral a thought of the Enthronement Psalms. Whether or not there is specific cultic allusion to be found in v. 18a (reading כִּי מֵי מוֹעֵר after the LXX, Syriac and Targum), the whole atmosphere of this passage is that of a hymnic celebration of the kingship of Yahweh and its beneficial {42} victory over the enemies of the people, which is entirely in the spirit of such Psalms as 47, 76, etc. Finally, we should note that there follows in vv. 19ff., in a clearly eschatological context (witness the phrase בָּעֵת הַהִיא) a promise to deal gently with the halt and outcast of the scattered dispersion. God himself will gather them and lead them home, so reversing their fortunes that he will make them a 'name and a praise'. The two sides of Yahweh's deliverance are explicit judgment on

---

5. So Taylor (1956: 1011, 1028ff.); J.M. Powis Smith (1911: 172ff.), who gives a summary of critical opinion until that time; Eissfeldt (1965: 425). Weiser (1961: 266) sounds a note of qualified caution here, suggesting that 'it could be explained by the prophet's dependence on the ideas of the festal cult'.

his people's foes, restoration and renewal for them. It is the first which makes the second possible.

Such judgment is to be directed against the 'oppressors' of the people (מְעַנֶּיךְ, cf. עָנִי of Zech. 9.9) and Yahweh will 'deliver/save' (וְהוֹשַׁעְתִּי) his people (cf. וְנוֹשָׁע of Zech. 9.9). But not only is what follows of interest here in the oracle of salvation of vv. 14-20 which is so often thought to be later, but what has preceded also. Verses 1-4 form an oracle of judgment, introduced by 'woe', against the corruptions of the city at all levels of its life, the officials (judges, prophets and priests) in particular being singled out for censure. But vv. 9-13 say that the judgment which is to fall is redemptive in aim. This will affect all nations:

> Yea, at that time I will change the speech of the peoples, to a pure speech, that all of them may call on the name of the Lord, and serve him with one accord. {43}

Of course, the unity of Zeph. 3 cannot be assumed. Almost certainly its various parts come from different bands at different times.[6] Yet, even so, the additions are significant, since they would show how the eschatological hopes which burned brightly in some circles (and terminology and theme show them to be not too far distant from the thought world of Zech. 9) were seen as God's answer to the needs of his people as revealed by the earlier prophets: in this case the corruptness of the city of Jerusalem as expressed particularly in the lives and deeds of her officials, is to be met by the redemptive act of Yahweh who will not only judge the 'oppressing nations' (vv. 6-8), but will also aim at refining and reducing both foreigners (vv. 9-10) and the home community, from whom will emerge a faithful, proven remnant.

> for then I will remove from your midst, your proudly exultant ones (עַלִּיזֵי גַּאֲוָתֵךְ)
> and you shall no longer be haughty in my holy mountain (לְגָבְהָה)
> For I will leave in the midst of you
> a people humble and lowly (עָנִי וָדָל).
> They shall seek refuge in the name of the Lord,

---

6.   J.M. Powis Smith (1911: 172ff.) assigns vv. 1-5 to Zephaniah and finds vv. 6f. to be 'isolated fragments'. Verses 8-13 and 14-20 are two distinct post-exilic additions; C.L. Taylor (1956: 1028) questions if even vv. 1-5 are Zephaniah's, while vv. 8-20 'originated after the time of Zephaniah'. Eissfeldt (1965: 425), on the other hand, while allowing that vv. 14-17 and 18-20 are more likely to be post-exilic additions, says of vv. 1-13, 'This poem is certainly genuine, and has merely been elaborated in vv. 8-10'.

those who are left in Israel:
they shall do no wrong
and utter no lies,
nor shall there be found in their mouth,
a deceitful tongue.
For they shall pasture and lie down,
and none shall make them afraid.

This is such a clear counterpart to the 'officials' formerly within her (vv. 3-5) that it is difficult to {44} believe it was not seen as the divine answer to her former condition, and thus appended to this chapter intentionally, whether by Zephaniah or a later, post-exilic circle.

Zechariah 2.14 (10) and Zeph. 3.14 appear, then, in contexts which announce joy to the 'Daughter of Zion' because of this reversal of judgment for former sins proclaimed by the earlier prophets. For Zechariah it is the reversal of the exile and punishment of the community at the hands of the 'nations', which has already been declared to be judgment for the sins of the fathers (1.4ff.). In the Zephaniah context there is also to be judgment on 'nations' (3.8), but a judgment aimed at their redemption (3.9-10), but its climax is in the replacing of an earlier evil community, typified by the corruption of its officials, with a faithful, humble community. For both, this is the work to be accomplished when Yahweh comes in person amongst his people. We cannot of course claim that Zeph. 3.14 has influenced Zech. 9.9-10, since we cannot be sure of its date. Yet it seems to suggest a source with a very similar range of ideas, with one important modification, to Zech. 9.9-10.

The note of conscious reversal seems to be strengthened when we trace the background of the address to the inhabitants of Zion in the second person singular. For in Isaiah particularly, this was most often used in {45} the context of threat of judgment.[7] But in later usage it appears in a context of the coming salvation of Yahweh.[8] Now, in these two contexts,

---

7. E.g. Isa. 1.5ff., 10ff., 22ff.; 29.1-6; cf. Mic. 4.8-13. Isa. 10.24 is an exception, a passage which is usually assigned to Isaiah, but which Kaiser (1972: 149) interestingly assigns to the Greek period, for 'it breathes the atmosphere of a zealous study of Scripture'. Another exception is Isa. 12.6, which Kaiser (1972: 167) also assigns to the post-exilic period.

8. E.g. Isa. 62.11, based perhaps on cultic usage as shown in Ps. 48.12 (11). Indeed, the Zion cult tradition seems the most likely background for such a call to joy, but, if that were so, then Isaiah must have challenged the current false and optimistic interpretation of the Zion tradition as interpreted from the cult. For a discussion of the

the address is being used to call the people to rejoice for Yahweh's presence in their midst, bringing salvation.

If we have then in the similar form of Zech. 9.9 a like proclamation of the reversal of earlier judgment, we have to note next a most significant variation in the tradition as it appears here from the manner in which it finds expression in Zech. 2.14 (10) and Zeph. 3.14. They speak of the direct and immediate presence of Yahweh in the midst of his city and its people, even although the broad context of Proto-Zechariah speaks much of the provision of civil and priestly leadership in the persons of Joshua and Zerubbabel. In Zeph. 3 the thought is of a faithful and restored community to replace former corrupt officialdom. Yet in Zech. 9.9-10, it is a 'king' whose coming is spoken of, and we have to ask why this should be so.

But, in doing so, another question needs to be borne in mind which seems seldom to be raised. How is it that so much emphasis is given to a Messianic figure here, but scarcely elsewhere in Deutero-Zechariah? The only possible Messianic references are to be found in 10.4, which, however, as will be argued, seems to be more the promise of a general provision of adequate leadership to {46} replace the unworthy ones than to a Messianic figure specifically of the Davidic line; 11.4, which there is no reason to believe is Messianic; 12.7ff., which we shall suggest, if it envisages a Davidic leadership, sees it as only of a very limited kind;[9] and 12.10, which cannot be taken as Messianic in any recognized sense. Chapters 13–14 have no possible reference to a Messianic figure. Why then is this special variant of the coming of Yahweh to his people tradition, apparently so strongly stressed here? Of course, if these chapters consist of nothing but a loose collection of entirely unrelated oracles, no problem arises.[10] But if there is any continuity of tradition represented in them, this appears as a difficulty which needs explanation. So, from considerations of form and type of material and its possible antecedents, we must turn to examine the person of the 'King' and the characteristics of his mission, whose coming is announced.

He is described, in the first place, as being צַדִּיק. צֶדֶק can bear the meaning 'victory', and is so used, particularly by Second Isaiah. In Isa.

---

form of address to Zion personified as a woman in Lamentations, Isaiah and elsewhere, see N. Porteous (1961: 238ff.).

9.   See below, pp. {225ff.}.

10.   E.g. Flügge (1784: 82-85), who saw in Zech. 9–14 not a 'Deutero-Zechariah', but nine independent pericopes, cited by Stade (1881: 2) (the present writer has not had access to this work).

41.2 it clearly has this sense of 'victory' applied to Cyrus, while in 45.8 and 11.5 it is also paralleled, as here, with the root יָשַׁע. The NEB translates Zech. 9.9 clearly in this sense: 'his cause won, his victory gained'. Perhaps it comes to have this sense from the idea of 'righteousness vindicated', that is, the victory of Yahweh experienced {47} by the one who is in a 'right' relationship to him.

In this latter sense, it is a characteristic of the king in the Psalms, as Johnson (1958: 221-22) has said.[11] One has only to think of Ps. 72.1ff., and the so-called 'Last Words of David' (2 Sam. 23.2-7, esp. v. 3b). By virtue of the king's right relationship with Yahweh, the whole collective life of the community is thereby brought into the same right relationship and so is able to experience both God's יֶשַׁע and שָׁלֹם. We have noticed how clearly in Second Isaiah צְדָקָה and יֶשַׁע are paralleled, and Porteous (1961: 239ff.) has shown how יֶשַׁע and שָׁלֹם were connected especially with the city of Jerusalem. All of this may well have afforded a general background of thought which could colour the use of the term in connection with the king here. The one who comes, by his right relationship with Yahweh, is able to be the bearer of יֶשַׁע and effect שָׁלֹם for the nations. But it should not be forgotten that this idea had earlier received a special adaptation to the Servant of Second Isaiah. In the third 'Servant Song' of Isa. 50.4-9, where he describes the persecution he has suffered for his faithfulness to the call of Yahweh, he turns in v. 8 to the imagery of the law-court. Let those who will wrongfully accuse him come into the divine assize together with him for קָרוֹב מַצְדִּיקִי, i.e. 'he who declares me to be "in the right", i.e. God, is near'.

The next characteristic of the Servant is that he {48} is נוֹשָׁע.[12] What

---

11. See also Johnson (1967: 4ff., 7ff., 35ff., 116f., 120, 126, 135).

12. The root יָשַׁע has often traditionally been associated with the basic idea of 'liberty', 'spaciousness'. See, e.g., Driver (1913: 118-19). Sawyer (1965: 475ff.), however, has challenged this etymology. He believes it had a forensic origin: 'The most probable etymology suggests a forensic origin for the root *yš* " (486). He believes the noun came to indicate an advocate, playing the role for the defense that the Satan played for the prosecution. Finally, it came to be a title of God in a general sense because it was thought that such was his role. In a later article (Sawyer 1967–68), he allows that it is sometimes contrasted with צָרוֹת in the Old Testament and to the root יָצָא, but so, he argues, are other roots, for there are a number of other Hebrew words which bring to the vocabulary of salvation the idea of 'room', and 'there is no need to resort to faulty linguistics to find it there' (20). See, more recently, Sawyer (1972: 94ff.). In the light of this, our understanding of the term must at least be enlarged to include the forensic concept.

significance is to be given to the niphal form here? It is possible that it may bear a reflexive sense, in which case we should render by some such phrase as 'bearing salvation', or, 'the one in whom victory is revealed'. Yet the only other two instances of the use of the niphal participle in the Old Testament occur in contexts which suggest more a passive sense, where the emphasis is laid on the fact that the deliverance is God's achievement and his gift to his people. It occurs in Deut. 33.29:

> Happy are you, O Israel! Who is like you,
> a people *saved* (נוֹשָׁע) by the Lord,
> the shield of your help,
> and the sword of your triumph.

And even more significant for our passage, Ps. 33.16:

> A king is not *saved* (נוֹשָׁע) by his great army;
> a warrior is not delivered by his great strength.
> The war horse (הַסּוּס) is a vain hope for victory,
> and by its great might it cannot save.

One almost wonders if this was in the writer's mind when he goes on to say, 'I will cut off...the war horse from Jerusalem', although, of course, the idea is a familiar enough one in the Old Testament. The context of these two passages suggests, however, that the salvation that is true is that which is won for men by God; it is not man's achievement, even if that man be the king. Even if we render Deut. 33.29 as 'a people victorious in Yahweh' it remains that Yahweh is their shield and sword in battle. Only these three instances of the niphal participle occur {49} in the Old Testament, but wherever the niphal in some form occurs, the context seems to be of that victory which is experienced only by reference to Yahweh. One thinks of the well-known example of Isa. 30.15, 'In returning and rest [i.e. to Yahweh], you shall experience יֵשׁע', or in the Song of David (2 Sam. 22.4), 'I call unto Yahweh...and I shall experience victory (אִוָּשֵׁעַ)', cf. Ps. 18.4 (3). Or we may also recall Ps. 80.4 (3), 'let thy face shine that we may experience deliverance (וְנִוָּשֵׁעָה)'. Also significant for our purpose here is the thought expressed in Zech. 4.6b-10a where, though the root יֵשׁע is not used, it is stressed that Zerubbabel's victory will not be 'by might not by power', i.e. not by human strength.

What seems to be indicated here, therefore, is that the king who comes brings victory and deliverance with him for the people. But it is God's victory which he has experienced, and which he mediates to the community by virtue of his right relationship to God. But again we should notice, that this is a characteristic of the Servant of Second Isaiah. In the second 'Servant Song', it is said again, after the Servant has proved faithful through suffering, that his call is not only to 'raise up the tribes of Jacob and to restore the preserved of Israel', but also

> I will give you as a light to the nations
> (גּוֹיִם) that my salvation (יְשׁוּעָתִי)
> may reach to the ends of the earth! (Isa. 49.6) {50}

The Servant also, then, is to be the bearer of salvation.

The third attribute of the King is that he is עָנִי. The word can mean 'poor', 'afflicted' or 'humble'. It is a strange epithet to find employed of a royal figure.

In considering its significance, attention must be paid to an important treatment of the theme of the 'poor' in the Psalms and the book of Amos by A.S. Kapelrud (1966: 193-206). He follows Birkeland in saying that דַּל עָנִי עָנָו and אֶבְיוֹן alike designated those who were suffering and needed help (Kapelrud 1966: 200-201). But he goes beyond Birkeland in saying that they were regarded as those who had a claim on the prosperous, the צַדִּיקִים. The poor were in fact persons on the outskirts of society. Sometimes they are referred to as those who had sinned in the past, but who were now entitled to be treated as צַדִּיק again (e.g. Ps. 25). But again, such a man might see himself as one who was deeply afflicted without being able to see any reason for it (Pss. 10, 22). In fact, he was really a צַדִּיק, yet not permitted by God to live as a צַדִּיק. The Psalms of Lament are petitions that the poor may be readmitted to the world of the צַדִּיקִים, while the Psalms of Thanksgiving proclaim that the worshipper had been so readmitted. The distinction between the צַדִּיק and the עָנִי was in their fortune and circumstances. Amos shattered this scale of values by his shocking attacks on those who were apparently the צַדִּיקִים, the wealthy {51} and powerful, for their shameful treatment of the poor. The apparent צַדִּיקִים were in fact רְשָׁעִים, the oppressors and enemies of their fellow-countrymen. By contrast, the implication is clear, the afflicted and oppressed were the real צַדִּיקִים, which is made clear from the parallelism of 2.6-7a. Thus, as in the Psalms, Amos identifies the poor and needy with those who were despised and downtrodden and who were suffering ill fortune. He went beyond the Psalms in showing that these men were in fact the צַדִּיקִים, 'Their condition and their position in society were an integrated part of their צְדָקָה'.

This is an important distinction for our purpose, for in the final 'Servant Song' of Second Isaiah exactly the same can be said of the Servant:

We esteemed him stricken,
smitten by God, and afflicted (מְעֻנֶּה, Isa. 53.4).

In fact, however, it was he alone who was צַדִּיק, but, in his case, his suffering was to have a redemptive effect for those who were not צַדִּיק, for
because 'he was oppressed and afflicted' (וְנַעֲנֶה, v. 7) and submitted himself
in trust and obedience to Yahweh, the only proper response for the
'poor',[13] he will make 'many to be accounted righteous' (יַצְדִּיק צַדִּיק).[14]

We have to ask whether the adjective עָנִי here is a simple description of
his general attitude of pious trust, or whether it indicates one who, like the
Servant of Second {52} Isaiah, and perhaps the עָנִי of some of the Psalms,
has suffered wrongfully, and been deemed to be 'afflicted'; but, who, in
fact, is צַדִּיק, and even more, the bearer of salvation to others. It hardly
needs to be said that the characteristics so far enumerated could not be
in starker contrast to the attitude of pride and cultic apostasy depicted in
vv. 1-8, upon which the judgment of Yahweh is to fall.

The picture of the Messiah riding upon an ass has been variously understood. Some have taken it as an implied contrast with the proud pomp and
warlike spirit of pagan kings, as Dentan (1956: 1095-96) does. Others
however, like Horst (1964: 247), have suggested that this was a traditional
royal mount, and that there is a parallel with Gen. 49.10-11, where the ass
seems to be linked in some way with the rule of the tribe of Judah. Elliger
(1964: 149) says there may be some echo here of a primitive Messianic
tradition: perhaps this was the mount of the king in some early form of
'Konigsrituals'. But even so, we would follow him when he goes on to say
that in this place the meaning has been inverted, and it serves to demonstrate a repudiation of all forms of warfare.[15] The context would seem, to
suggest again that his is the way of humble trust on the arm of Yahweh.

13. So, e.g., Ps. 18.28 (27), of which Johnson (1967: 120) says, 'For it is only a
humble people (עַם־עָנִי) proved to be such in the person of their king, whom Yahweh
consents to save'. The spirit of such trust in the Psalms is well caught by Mowinckel
(1962, I: 195): 'For he is great, and we are small; he can do everything, we can do
nothing; nobody else can help, and if he does not save, it will be the end of us, but we
confide in him'.

14. Omitting the צַדִּיק as dittography from the preceding יַצְדִּיק. C.R. North (1964:
65, 232-33) favours retaining it as in the construct case, as a kind of superlative, and he
translates, 'My Servant, himself righteous, shall bring righteousness to many'.

15. Also in connection with the whole discussion at this point, the article of M.A.
Beek (1972), on the meaning of the expression, 'The Chariots and the Horseman of
Israel'. See the discussion at 10.3f. below.

How far the 'cutting off' of the chariot and the warhorse are merely the aftermath of victory, or the establishment of an eschatological peace is not clear. {53} For it is possible it should be seen rather against the background of the often repeated protests of the earlier prophets against the 'horse' and 'chariot'. They stood for human statesmanship, for human self-reliance upon the force of arms. They were the product of shameful alliance with Egypt. But they will form no part of the programme of the king at the time of Yahweh's intervention for the judgment of his enemies and the deliverance of his people. The king will lead his people in that attitude of faith and dependence upon God which is the condition of experiencing the salvation which he alone can win and which is his alone to bestow (cf. Isa. 31.1-3). Perhaps it is this last sense which answers most fittingly to the idea of his being עָנִי. Finally it is said of the king,

> and he shall command peace to the nations:
> and his rule shall extend from sea to sea,
> and from the river to the ends of the earth.

This is very reminiscent of Ps. 72.7 (8)f.

> In his days may righteousness (צֶדֶק) flourish[16] and peace abound,
> till the moon be no more.
> May he have dominion from sea to sea,
> and from the river to the ends of the earth.

The coincidence of the last lines (with the interesting exception of the וְדִבֶּר שָׁלוֹם in Zech. 9.10 for the וְיֵרְדְּ of Ps. 72.8, and even for the וְרֹב שָׁלוֹם of the preceding verse) suggests that an originally cultic phrase is being echoed to indicate a universal, or literally 'world-wide' rule. How far it retains its original {54} significance and how far it has become simply a *terminus technicus* by this time is not clear.[17]

An equally interesting link between the language of the Psalm and Zech. 9.9f. is that bringing together the ideas of צְדָקָה and שָׁלוֹם to which Porteous (1961: 239ff.) refers. He notes how the two ideas were often

---

16. Reading צֶדֶק for צַדִּיק with three MSS, LXX, Syriac and Jerome.
17. It has often been said that the reference in the Psalm is to the River Euphrates, and that therefore it reflects Babylonian influence; e.g. Mowinckel (1962, I: 55), and for the same view of Zech. 9.10, see Horst (1964: 247). Others, however, have seen the reference to be to the cosmic waters that encircle the earth; see Johnson (1967: 10ff.), the reference there being taken to be to 'the circuit of the great cosmic sea which nourishes the holy city', and so stresses the centrality of Jerusalem, a point also made by M. Bič (1962: 118); cf. Otzen (1964: 141).

connected with the city of Jerusalem, possibly because of very ancient mythological ideas, and possibly because Sedek and Salem were names of tutelary deities of the city at a very early stage.[18] Isaiah's play on the idea of 'righteousness' and the name of the city in 1.21, 26 is familiar. שָׁלוֹם also appears in the names of Solomon and Absalom, and both aspects characterize the future ruler of Jerusalem (Isa. 9.5ff.; 11.1ff.). Micah 3 stresses that the two characteristics belong inseparably together, and the 'rulers' and 'prophets' are castigated for failing both to exhibit and establish them in the life of the community. Jeremiah sees that Yahweh has plans for שָׁלוֹם even in exile (ch. 29) but that it would finally characterize Jerusalem again after its judgment (33.14-16; cf. Ezek. 37.24-26). In one sense, therefore, the coming king of Zech. 9.9-10 will restore the city of Jerusalem, traditionally the city of צֶדֶק and שָׁלוֹם, to its original character and function. For, it is clear from such references, that שָׁלוֹם is much more than a negative quality, 'peace' only in the {55} sense of an absence of strife, but rather signifies that wholeness of life which characterizes the man and the community in a 'right' relationship to Yahweh.

A very thorough analysis of the use of the root שׁלם in the Old Testament has been made by Eisenbeis (1969: 215-21), which reveals something of the breadth of meaning which can be attributed to it, both secular and religious. In his examination of Zech. 9.9-10, he comes to the conclusion that it has to be dated as late as 150 BC, a conclusion which he bases on the description of the bearer of salvation. It reveals, he believes, a concept of שָׁלוֹם not met with in the Old Testament before, an idealization of the conditions of spiritual salvation which is unique. It sees it as being not only for Israel, but for all nations, for the גּוֹיִם, for whom thoughts of vengeance are entirely absent. Further, it will be brought about by the preaching (דִּבֶּר) of the message of salvation. He does not need to engage in war with the nations since God will help him (נוֹשָׁע) and will make his word alone effective, a significant understanding of the powerful and creative word of God. Further, the concept of שָׁלוֹם here carries with it strongly the idea of inner peace, with its description of the attributes of the spirit, צַדִּיק, עָנִי and נוֹשָׁע. Such ideas are all relatively late. Nor does mention of Ephraim necessarily imply an early date, for the term may well be an archaism such as is found in the Qumran {56} literature. A date in the Maccabaean period, argues Eisenbeis, fits the concept of שָׁלוֹם found here, which is of both inner and outer peace.

18. See Porteous (1961: 239) and references cited there.

Eisenbeis asks the important question, 'In which Jewish circles could such ideas have existed?' He believes it can only have been within the priestly circles of Sadducees within the Maccabaean movement, or among the Hasidim, from whom came the Pharisees and even the Qumran community itself. The peace-loving spirit of this oracle is in marked opposition to the apocalyptic and nationalistic feeling which characterized so many periods in Israel's history, and in particular the military spirit of the Maccabaeans.

These conclusions of Eisenbeis can be accepted in general as helpful and significant, although his criteria for dating such a passage as this need to be questioned. Were the groups he mentioned the only ones in Jewish history to evince this spirit? Was there not a concept of the power of the divine word much earlier than he allows in the prophetic movement?

As was noted above, the fact that the king will 'speak', or 'command', peace is an interesting variant from Ps. 72, which it otherwise so closely resembles as is (and so Eisenbeis rightly points out), the extension of the promise of peace to all nations. For, although it is said in Ps. 72 that the king's rule will be a universal one, the foes are there only to be conquered, {57} to bow down and to lick the dust, to render tribute and to serve him (vv. 9-10). This is very different from the picture of Zech. 9.9-10. What can be the source, and the significance, of the distinctive tradition concerning the king here?

Again, as with the other qualities and attributes, both ideas can be paralleled in the person and ministry of the Servant of Second Isaiah. He, too, was to be 'a light to the nations' (גּוֹיִם, 49.6). But Yahweh made his 'mouth as a sharp sword' (49.2), and again, he is able to say,

> The Lord God has given me
> the tongue of those who are taught,
> that I may know how to sustain with a word
> him that is weary (50.4).

But, in addition, by virtue of his sufferings it can be said of this one, מוּסַר שְׁלוֹמֵנוּ עָלָיו.

Each of the descriptions of the king can therefore be seen to be that which was characteristic also of the Servant. The same features can, of course, be used to justify seeing here a reference to the supposed role of the king in the Autumnal Festival of pre-exilic Jerusalem.[19] It seems,

---

19. See Johnson (1967: *passim*); and for its application to this passage, Jones (1962a: 129-30).

however, that there is no need to make such an assumption which, even if it could be established beyond doubt as characteristic of such a pre-exilic cultus, is hardly likely to have been a living and powerful influence for long after the exile. Rather, it would seem that {58} we may have here a re-interpretation of the Messianic role in the light of the mission of the Suffering Servant of Second Isaiah. The use of the word מֶלֶךְ and the apparent allusion to such a Psalm as 72 suggest that it *is* intended to be the role of the king which is referred to. But equally, the allusion to the characteristics of the Servant would seem to suggest that a conscious modification of that role is being made here.

Why should that be? We began this discussion of the 'king' in order to see if we could better explain why, having addressed Zion in terms similar to those of Zeph. 3.14-15, and Zech. 2.14 (10), the prophet, unlike them, speaks not of the direct and immediate advent of Yahweh to his city, but the advent of his 'Messianic' representative.

But one more general observation needs first to be made. This is not the only re-interpretation of the role of the Davidic Messiah offered in post-exilic literature of the Old Testament. Second Isaiah himself, as has been often noticed, extends the hopes concerning the Davidic Messiah of First Isaiah to the whole restored community. In 55.3-5 the promise is made that what David was to the people of Israel, the whole community is to be to the 'nations' (גּוֹי). They are to inherit both the blessings of the Davidic Covenant and the task of being a 'witness to the peoples'.[20]

Nor is that the only 'collectivisation' of the {59} Messianic hope. The Chronicler also seems to offer such a re-interpretation. Commenting on the stress the Chronicler places upon the reign and achievement of David, P.R. Ackroyd (1967: 501-15) says,

> ...it is not in terms of the future Davidic monarchy and hence a hope for the future... It is rather the embodiment of the David/Jerusalem theme no longer in political but in theological terms, in relation to the life and worship of the little Judean community of his own time.

20. See, e.g., the discussion of this passage in Westermann (1969: 283-84): '...he (i.e. the author) does not take as the way of comforting his people telling them of some supernatural king who is to come at some time in the future and effect their salvation. Instead, he is daring enough to proclaim that...the tokens of grace vouchsafed to David are transferred to Israel'. One could also compare the comment of J. Mauchline (1970: 303): 'There is no evidence that Second Isaiah put any emphasis at all upon a renewal of the Davidic kingdom or even upon a ruler in Judah of David's line. But...he did maintain emphasis on Jerusalem, not, indeed, as an exclusive sanctuary for Jews alone, but as a spiritual centre from which the rule of Yahweh would go forth to the ends of the earth.'

Therefore a still further question arises concerning this passage. Is it possible that some such collectivisation of the role of the king has taken place here, especially remembering that, according to Second Isaiah, it was the Servant's role to enable the community of God's people to realize its divine vocation (Isa. 49.5), and so properly fulfil its call to inherit the terms of the Davidic covenant? And would this explain the use of so 'Messianic' an oracle in a collection in which the concept of the 'Messiah' plays so insignificant a role?

We have, then, to marshal such evidence as can be found for forming a judgment concerning this oracle, as to its meaning and the kind of traditio-circle from which it could have come.

It seems to be in line with the glad expectation that, at the last time, God himself will come to his community in Zion to reverse the judgment of former times, and so calls that community to the joy of eschatological hope and expectation, in the same manner as that found {60} in Zech. 2.14 (10) and Zeph. 3.14. Therefore, as elsewhere, the old prophetic address to the community as a collective, feminine person has also been reversed from announcement of judgment to one of joy and hope. In Zechariah it was the old judgment of exile and dispersion which was to be reversed. There too, the provision of proper leadership in Zerubbabel, who is spoken of in Messianic terms, and Joshua, as High Priest, is seen as playing a part in effecting God's purpose and, in a real sense, this is a manifestation of Yahweh's own return and activity. Zerubbabel will rebuild the Temple. Joshua is cleansed as representative, perhaps even 'on behalf of' the community. Already there is possibly some limitation of the role of the Davidic line in the reminder to Zerubbabel that his mission will be accomplished not by *human* power or might, but by the Spirit of Yahweh entirely.[21] In a sense, therefore, the role of leadership is more a manifestation of the divine presence and activity than it is an urgent and vital prerequisite for the community to experience the coming salvation. Or, if it is a prerequisite, it is so only because Yahweh has chosen to effect his programme through this leadership, in this way rather than by any other.

Again, in Zephaniah, it is the direct and immediate presence of Yahweh which is emphasized. But here, since this later part of the chapter seems

---

21. One may compare the conclusions of Beyse (1971: 102-103) who says that in both Haggai and Zechariah there is a deuteronomistic-type and prophetic criticism of kingship in which the realms of world politics and military power are left far behind. It is Yahweh himself who guarantees the new kingdom. The great 'royal' task has become the rebuilding of the Temple.

consciously to look {61} back to the earlier part which attacked the corrupt leadership, it looks as though the judgment seen within the circles from which this came was not just the exile and the oppression of foreigners, but the rottenness of Israel's own 'body politic' and its religious life as typified and personified by its leaders. It is tempting to believe, therefore, that Zeph. 3.9ff., 11ff., and 14ff., represents the outlook of a circle in post-exilic Judaism which had grown disillusioned by its official leadership and found an answering echo to that which Zephaniah had attacked long before, and looked for God's coming especially in terms of its overthrow and replacement and consequent renewal of the life of the whole community. Both Zechariah and the author of this later part of Zeph. 3, it may be said finally, look for this future restoration to be extended to all nations.

Is it possible that in Zech. 9.9-10 we have yet another interpretation of what the coming of God will mean? This too will consist in the reversal of judgment upon all that is contrary to his will in the community, only now, it is seen that those ills go so deep that this must be effected, not just by a restored Messiah of the old Davidic line, even in the limited sense in which that hope had attached to Zerubbabel in Proto-Zechariah, but rather one whose Messianic role was already being interpreted in the light of the Mission of the Suffering Servant of Second Isaiah. And is the need for such a {62} suffering role seen because there is a more deeply pessimistic evaluation of the state and condition of the Jewish community of its time than would certainly have been the case at the time of the bright hopes of Zechariah, and that we have here also a further development later than that represented by Zeph. 3.14? It may be that this oracle has been placed after 9.1-8 because it is seen that the prevalence of those attitudes of pride and cultic apostasy is so widespread that, if the community is to fulfil its role of 'bearer of salvation' to the nations, it will only be at the cost of its faithful and humble acceptance of suffering. Is this how collectively it is to inherit the 'democratized' Davidic covenant as Second Isaiah saw it?

But may we have to go even further? What is the significance of the fact that this 'king' will bring about 'peace' by the word of proclamation alone? Is it possible that this suggests an identification of this figure with the *prophetic* office?[22] In which case, is the prophet addressing the faithful within the community (his own circle of faithful devotees?), and calling them to the role of righteous, humble trust and faithful acceptance of suffering, rejection and, perhaps, persecution, in order that, like the Ser-

---

22. Here it is important to remember von Rad's (1965, II: 259) insistence that the role of the Suffering Servant of Second Isaiah is a *prophetic* rather than a royal one.

vant, they may fulfil a mission *to* the people of God as well as equipping
them effectively to engage in their mission to {63} 'the nations'? In which
case, is the contrast here not so much with Alexander the Great, or the
heathen cities of Tyre and Ashkelon and the rest, but between the faithful
pious ones and the corrupt leadership which exhibits all the qualities
which are the opposite of those for which God looks in his people? The
judgment of Wellhausen on the person of this 'king', to some extent
echoed by Weiser (1962: 275) may well prove to have been one of the
more significant which have been offered.

Again, it has to be said that it is easier to raise questions than confidently and dogmatically to answer them. But, if they have to be set on
one side and left open while investigations go further, there are enough
indications within the text to suggest that it is just such questions which
need to be asked. At this stage, therefore, it is sufficient to summarize by
saying that the hopes expressed here for the coming of the king appear to
have arisen among those who had been deeply influenced by the figure of
the Suffering Servant, and who seem to regard the weapons, aims and
methods of militant nationalists as to be repudiated, and who see themselves rather as among the 'god-fearing pious'. {64}

Chapter 3

ZECHARIAH 9.11-17

This section also begins with an address in the second person feminine singular, linked by *gam* (גַּם־אַתְּ), a stylistic feature which has already appeared in v. 2 (cf. v. 7). This seems to be an editorial device (either by the prophet himself or another) to relate to the oracle of 9.9f. There are certain similarities between the two. This is also an announcement of deliverance and final victory; Zion is spoken of, and Ephraim is given a place, although here it is Judah with which Ephraim is paralleled rather than Jerusalem. The indications are, however, that it was an independent oracle. The 'king' receives no mention, the attitude to foreign nations typified by 'Jawan' (but see the discussion below) appears more uniformly hostile (vv. 13, 15), with no place apparently given for their inclusion in the final act of Yahweh's deliverance. In form, vv. 11-13 are in the first person divine speech addressing, first, an unspecified second person singular (v. 11), then, those who are addressed as 'prisoners of hope' (v. 12) and, finally, 'Sons of Zion' (v. 13). Verses 14f. switch to prophetic announcement speaking of Yahweh in the third person, and recounting the theophany when God will defend victoriously an unspecified third person plural 'them'. Verses 16f., introduced by a new oracular formula 'on that day' and marked by a sudden switch in mood to a description of the beneficent effects for land and {65} people in the new age, appears to be a separate oracle placed, not inappropriately however, after the account of the theophany and victory of the preceding verses.

The opening oracle announces the restoration of the captives, the theme of Second Isaiah. It is significant therefore that certain echoes of the later chapters of Isaiah appear to be sounded. There, 'Israel' was sent 'to pro-claim liberty to the captives', לִקְרֹא לִשְׁבוּיִם דְּרוֹר וְלַאֲסוּרִים פְּקַח־קוֹחַ (61.1)[1]

---

1. The rendering of פְּקַח־קוֹחַ is not certain, so that it is impossible to be sure of the exact nature of the promise to those who are 'bound'. Is it that their prisons are to be opened, and, if so, is Westermann's (1969: 366) opinion that this refers, not to the

whereas our prophet exclaims, שׁוּבוּ לְבִצָּרוֹן אֲסִירֵי הַתִּקְוָה. But the passage in Trito-Isaiah itself recalls Isa. 42.7 where part of the ministry of
the servant is, לְהוֹצִיא מִמַּסְגֵּר אַסִּיר מִבֵּית כֶּלֶא יֹשְׁבֵי חֹשֶׁךְ while in Isa. 51.11
there had been the promise, וּפְדוּיֵי יְהוָה יְשׁוּבוּן וּבָאוּ צִיּוֹן בְּרִנָּה. The promise
of Yahweh to restore double to his people recalls again the promise of
Isa. 61.7, תַּחַת בָּשְׁתְּכֶם מִשְׁנֶה which itself echoes the statement of 40.2,
כִּי לָקְחָה מִיַּד יְהוָה כִּפְלַיִם בְּכָל־חַטֹּאתֶיהָ. When we compare a similar use of
the phrase in Jer. 16.18 it may be that Isa. 61.7 is speaking of a deliberate
reversal of an earlier 'double' judgment by a promise of double restoration, and that this has influenced the interpretation of Zech. 9.12. A similar
idea is to be found in Job 42.10.

If, then, we have here echoes of an Isaianic {66} tradition, this should
not be without significance for our understanding of who it is who is being
addressed here. Opinions have differed on this. Otzen (1964: 126-29)
believes the reference is, not to the exile of Judah in Babylon in 586 BC,
but to the exiles of the northern kingdom of 734 and 722 BC. The address
to Zion is akin to that in Mic. 4f., where it is the return of the northern
exiles to Zion which is being announced. A similar point is being made
here in that Ephraim is spoken of as one of the 'sons' of Zion. He argues
that the word תִּקְוָה is elsewhere used more of the exiles of the northern
kingdom (e.g. Hos. 2.17; Jer. 31.17; Ezek. 19.5). Others have seen here a
reference to the Babylonian and Persian exiles in which some are still
bound, even in the later Greek period (e.g. Mitchell 1912: 277-78). Horst
(1964: 248) believes it is a reference to the Diaspora in general, but Elliger
(1964: 153) believes it relates more specifically to the prisoners taken by
the Greek forces. The general theme of return from captivity does seem to
recall the promises of Second Isaiah and therefore to have had the Babylonian exile particularly in mind. Yet, as we have seen, there is some indication that in Trito-Isaiah this idea has already received some measure of
re-interpretation to represent the idea of the captivity of the oppressed,
particularly in 58.6, which perhaps also lies behind the idea of captivity in
61.1. Has it received some re-interpretation here, whether in the light of
the Diaspora, the persecution under the Greeks {67} or in some other
direction? Saebø's taking up the idea of R. Bach that v. 12 belongs to a

exile, but to those who are in prison for debt, to be accepted? Cf. Isa. 58.6. Or is the
LXX to be followed in reading, 'recovery of sight to the blind', and the MT accordingly
to be emended? If this were a reference to the oppression of the innocent, as Isa. 58.6
suggests, it would be of the greatest interest to know whether this has influenced the
interpretation of Zech. 9.11b, 12a. We cannot, however, be sure.

literary type of an 'Invitation to Flight' similar to that found in Zech. 2.10-13 (6-9), and earlier in Jeremiah, is of interest here, and would again suggest that the return from Babylonian exile is being taken as a type of that which Yahweh is now about to do (Saebø 1969: 191 and references cited there). It still leaves open, however, the question of exactly what it is that answers to the original type, and who is now being invited to flight.

They are addressed as those who (a) because of the blood of your covenant (בְּדַם־בְּרִיתֵךְ) will (b) be set free from a 'waterless pit', and are called on (c) to return to the 'stronghold' (לְבִצָּרוֹן) and finally, apostrophized as 'prisoners of hope' (אֲסִירֵי הַתִּקְוָה).

תִּקְוָה is several times used in connection with return from captivity. In Hos. 2.17 (15) it is said that, after a period in the wilderness, where Yahweh will accompany Israel to allure her back to himself, he will 'make the valley of Achor a door of hope'. Similarly, in the letter to the exiles, Jeremiah announces that it is Yahweh's plan to bring her back and so to 'give you., a future and a hope' (29.10). Again, it is said in Jer. 31.17,

> There is hope for you, says the Lord,
> and your children shall come back to their own country. {68}

Perhaps such prophetic promises are themselves echoes of the hope expressed in worship, as reflected in Pss. 9.19 (18); 62.6 (5); 71.5, where God himself is the ground of hope for the 'poor'. The phrase 'prisoners of hope' would therefore seem to suggest that those who are at present suffering may rejoice for they are about to experience the final act of Yahweh's deliverance.

The place and nature of their captivity is described as a 'waterless pit' (אֵין מַיִם בּוֹ בּוֹר). The term בּוֹר can be used in a metaphorical sense of a place of despair, constriction and suffering, as in Pss. 40.3 (2); 58.7 (6), but it is probably closely allied in such instances to the idea of Sheol, towards which a man sinks through the waters of chaos in any condition which marks a diminution of his full powers of life and vitality (cf. Johnson 1964: 91ff.). As a designation of Sheol it occurs in Isa. 14.15-19; 38.18; Ezek. 36.20; Pss. 28.1; 30.4 (3), etc. The dreadful thing about the 'Pit' or 'Sheol', to the Israelites was that it cut a man off from the presence of Yahweh. Perhaps, insistence here that it is a 'waterless pit' is not only, as Gaide sees it, a counterpart to the promised eschatological gift of rain (14.8, 16ff.; cf. 10.1ff. and the discussion of that passage below), but owes something to the imagery of passages such as Jer. 2.13. It is the very reverse of this which is {69} promised in Isa. 41.17f., for when

הָעֲנִיִּים וְהָאֶבְיוֹנִים מְבַקְשִׁים מַיִם וָאַיִן לְשׁוֹנָם בַּצָּמָא נָשָׁתָּה אֲנִי יְהוָה אֶעֱנֵם

and he will do so by making the wilderness a pool of water and the dry land springs of water. Again, in Isa. 49, Yahweh will say to the prisoner, 'Come forth and by springs of water he will guide them' (vv. 9f.).

Such general prophetic concepts and promises may lie behind the use of the picture here. Like the phrase 'prisoners of hope' it may indicate that those who seem to be cast away from the presence and help of Yahweh in their distress, are about to experience a reversal of this as Yahweh comes among them to deliver them. But, in fact, there are two instances in the Old Testament where this concept of the 'pit' appears to receive a more specific interpretation.

In Gen. 37.24 we read how Joseph was the victim of his brothers' plot when they decided to rid themselves of him for good, so that they took him 'and cast him into a pit'. A further detail is added, the pit was empty, 'there was no water in it' (אֵין בּוֹ מָיִם). Is this a purely fortuitous detail, provided to explain why he did not drown, or could it be that the 'pit' in this wisdom story is related to larger soteriological themes? Was Joseph whom God delivered from the plot of those who sought his life and caused to prosper in Egypt {70} and to gather all its wealth, in some way seen as a symbol of Israel itself, delivered by God from captivity in Egypt having gathered the wealth of Egypt, preserved from the plot of those who would have destroyed her and finally led into the land of plenty? If so, the picture of God's deliverance as from a 'waterless pit' must be an early one, known already in the form of the tale used by the Yahwist. Certainly it would express his strong emphasis on the land of Canaan as God's gift, the goal of his redeeming purpose for his people from the time of Abraham onwards. But again, a similar motif occurs in the Jeremiah narrative. In Jer. 38.6 it is related how the prophet was cast into a pit, and again the apparently fortuitous information is added, וּבַבּוֹר אֵין־מַיִם. Here, however, it is added also that there was 'mire' (טִיט) into which Jeremiah 'sank' (וַיִּטְבַּע).[2] This is also a feature of the cry of the Psalms. Ps. 40.3 (2) reads,

> He drew me up from the desolate pit (מִבּוֹר)
> out of the miry bog (מִטִּיט הַיָּוֵן).

Again, it may be coincidence, but the hiphil imperfect of the root עלה occurs here as in the account of the Midianites drawing up Joseph from the

---

2. For the significance of this incident in the Jeremiah tradition see Ackroyd (1971: 7-8).

pit (Gen. 37.28) and of Ebedmelech and his friends drawing up Jeremiah (Jer. 38.13).

A similar paralleling of טִיט and בּוֹר is found in Ps. 69.15 (14),

> Rescue me from sinking in the mire...
> Let not the flood sweep over me...
> or the pit close its mouth over me. {71}

Whether, therefore, in the Joseph and Jeremiah narratives there is a conscious adoption of the motifs and familiar imagery of the divine protection and deliverance, or whether the features in the narrative are fortuitous, it is difficult to say, But certainly both do treat the theme of Yahweh's deliverance of those who were faithful to him in spite of the persecution and rejection of their fellow-Israelites who wanted to be rid of them. E.W. Nicholson's (1970: 108) comments on the general theological purport of Jer. 37–40 are of interest here:

> The faithful prophet who is the spokesman of the Word is himself subjected to violent treatment by those who reject the Word (xxxvii–xxxviii). But both he and the Word of Yahweh which he proclaimed are now vindicated; the word of judgment upon Judah's disobedience now finds fulfillment and is actualized in the destruction of Jerusalem and the exile of 586 BC (xxxix. 1-10), whilst Jeremiah himself is released by the Babylonian victors from the imprisonment imposed on him by his fellow-countrymen (xxxix. 11-14, xl 1-6).[3]

Is the reference in Zech. 9.11 to the captives in the 'pit where there is no water' in any sense intended as an allusion to such specific instances of the theme of Yahweh's deliverance as these? If so, does it suggest that those who are addressed are not merely the people of God in general, suffering either imprisonment or the banishment of the Diaspora, but those who regarded themselves as in the tradition of Joseph and Jeremiah, cast out by

---

3.   For the general line of argument here, that a use of a word or a phrase can indicate comment on and interpretation of some earlier incident or biblical theme, see Weingreen (1968: 209-15). Just as the use of the יצא at the beginning of the Decalogue in Exod. 20.2 and Deut. 5.6 leads it to have the meaning, 'deliverance from some great peril', so its use in Gen. 15.7 with regards to Abraham suggests some allusion to the tradition later found in *Genesis Rabbah*, 38, of Abraham's ordeal in the fiery furnace of King Nimrod. It suggests 'that in special circumstances, a word or phrase in an Old Testament passage may have been deliberately selected by the writer to hint implicitly at some well-known item of information not immediately apparent from the sense, as determined by impeccable scholarly methods' (Weingreen 1968: 209-10).

their fellow-countrymen and rejected because of this word, but who will now be vindicated by the action {72} Yahweh is about to perform? Again, the question needs to be asked although, taking this reference alone, it can remain only a possibility.

Is any further clue afforded by the strange phrase 'by the blood of your covenant'? Horst (1964: 249) sees it as a reference to the sacrificial offerings which they have brought, on whose account God is about to intervene for their deliverance, and so feels that the verse reflects the viewpoint of later Judaism. Of course, if reference to their 'imprisonment' were to the exile or to the Diaspora, it might be argued that such would not have been offering sacrifice, nor would a prophet representing the viewpoint of later Judaism have approved if they had. But Horst might then argue that it was the continuous offerings in Jerusalem which were effective for the Jews of the Dispersion. Mitchell (1912: 278) finds here a reference to the Priestly account of the covenant with Abraham, associated as it is with the gift of the land. Certainly in Jewish writings the phrase 'blood of the covenant' is used to designate circumcision (*Yeb.* 71a), but, within the Old Testament, blood is not referred to in that tradition (while in the enigmatic 'J' passage, Exod. 4.24-26, there is no mention of covenant).

Usually the phrase is taken to be a reference to the Sinaitic covenant with its ceremony of the sprinkling of blood by Moses upon both altar and people (Exod. 24.8).[4]{73} This means taking the sense of this phrase, with the RSV, as 'the blood of my covenant with you'. This may be right, but it should be noticed that the use of בְּרִיתֶךְ in this sense is not attested elsewhere in the Old Testament, apart from Ezek. 16.61 where, again, the meaning is ambiguous. There it occurs in a later addition to the chapter in which Jerusalem is threatened with the same judgment as her sisters, Sodom and Samaria. In the addition, the promise, set within the context of the covenant, is that all three will be renewed, with Jerusalem in the place of chief prominence, but 'not on account of your covenant'. This could mean 'not because of the covenant relationship you formerly acknowledged with them but because of my covenant with all of you', as Cooke (1936: 181) takes it. Or it could mean 'not on account of my former covenant with you [linking with v. 8] but because of a new covenant of my grace'.[5] It is of interest to note that the phrase occurs here also in a promise of

---

4.   So Gaide (1968: 76); Elliger (1964: 153); Driver (1906: 242).
5.   So, Davidson (1916: 127). Eichrodt (1970: 201) sees the phrase as a 'corrupt addition'. Zimmerli (1969: 370) wonders whether it means that the two sisters will be accepted, but not on the same basis as the covenant with Jerusalem.

restoration to Jerusalem and is linked to the reunion of Judah and Ephraim (v. 61; cf. Zech. 9.13).

Saebø (1969: 189-90) thinks that the similarity between the phrase in Zech. 9.11 and Ezek. 16.61 suggests that it is a Zion tradition which is also finding expression here. Then the 'blood of your covenant' refers to some aspect of the Zion tradition, perhaps to the Temple with its offerings and cult, to which those now exiled will be re-admitted. Perhaps the strange noun בְּצָרוֹן, {74} a ἅπαξ λεγόμενον, strengthens this suggestion, for in Isa. 22.10 the same root in the piel infinitive occurs in connection with the wall of Jerusalem which was to be fortified, and, in connection with the same attempt, a reservoir was to be made between the walls to collect water. This is of interest when we again connect it with the concept of the 'waterless pit' from which the captives are to return. Again, the imagery of Jerusalem as a place 'watered' by Yahweh's presence is familiar from the old Jerusalem cult (e.g. Ps. 46.5 [4]f.).

If, in the Isaiah passage, this occurs in a context of judgment upon the futility of their effort because they did not look to Yahweh, here, it seems to be said by contrast, this 'fortification' of Jerusalem will now make the city all that it was meant to be, since it will again be the place of Yahweh's presence.[6]

There is another possibility in the understanding of the phrase, 'the blood of your covenant', which can only be offered tentatively. By a very familiar Hebrew idiom it would be quite correct to render this phrase, 'your blood of the covenant'.[7] This would bring the emphasis more fully on the blood of the captives and prisoners who are about to be rescued and restored. In Second Isaiah (42.6) occur the words, וְאֶצָּרְךָ וְאֶתֶּנְךָ לִבְרִית[8]

6. The בְּצָרוֹן is often emended. *BHS* suggests וְשָׁבוּלֵךְ בַּת־צִיּוֹן. Mitchell (1912: 279, 283) rejects it as a gloss based possibly on a marginal note for בַּצָּרָה ('trouble') cf. Pss. 9.10 (9); 10.1, which would have been comment on the מִשְׁנֶה לָךְ. But the Versions support the MT. LXX ἐν ὀχυρώματι; Syriac *bḥsn'*; Vulgate, 'ad munitionem'.

7. Cf., e.g., הַר קָדְשִׁי, literally, 'the hill of my holiness', or 'my holy hill' (GKC §135n).

8. This is a well know *crux interpretum*. The phrase בְּרִית עָם is strange, especially as paralleled with 'light to the nations'. Lowth suggested the emendation to בְּרִית עוֹלָם (cited by Muilenburg 1956: 468). Torczyner (1936) suggested that this is a form of the Akkadian root, *brr*, 'to shine out', and so translates, 'brilliance of the people', which affords an excellent parallel to 'light of the nations', and this suggestion has been adopted by NEB, 'to be a light to all peoples, a beacon for the nations'. Muilenburg (1956: 468) objects that 'the Hebrew Bible offers no linguistic analogy for this meaning', while North (1964: 112) finds as an objection that since בְּרִית ('cove-

עַם לְאוֹר גּוֹיִם and this in the context of the release and return of the prisoners who will be led on their way home by Yahweh {75} 'by pools of water', a passage we have already suggested may have been in the prophet's mind at this point. But the role of Israel is one which is not accomplished without affliction and suffering, even to death, as the Servant Songs show. Yet, as Second Isaiah also makes plain, it is because they have now completed their suffering, because they have received of the hand of Yahweh 'double' (a phrase we suggested might be hinted at in v. 12) that they are now to be brought back through the wilderness to Zion, and will become the 'sign' of Yahweh's saving power to all nations. Is it possible that v. 11 is speaking of what they have suffered by virtue of their destiny to be a 'covenant' to the nations and which will be the very means of implementing that purpose?

The possibility that our prophet is reminding his hearers of the general theme of Second Isaiah's words of restoration in an earlier context of captivity and suffering is strengthened by v. 13. The picture of God's judgment in terms of the loosing of an arrow from a bent bow is familiar in the Old Testament. In Ps. 7.13 (12)f., such judgment is directed against the unrepentant, while in Lamentations it furnishes the image for Yahweh's treatment of Jerusalem for her sins (2.4), and again in 3.12f., against the one who speaks either for himself alone, or who personifies the apostate community. This judgment is now to be reversed, and the renewed and reunited community is to become the {76} instrument of judgment in the hands of Yahweh against his enemies. Perhaps it is an example of allusive word choice that this particular terminology is employed here to evoke memory of the earlier oracles and to re-apply them by way of reversal of the judgment they announced.

nant') 'occurs some 300 times…it would hardly be obvious even to a contemporary that in this one instance it meant vision'. If it does mean 'covenant of the people' it would seem most obvious that the 'people' should be the same as those in v. 5 where it is normally understood as referring to 'all mankind' (so Westermann 1969: 100). In that case the reference must be to Israel, or to the 'Servant', as being an instrument in the purpose of God's covenant with all mankind. This might look back to the terms of the Abrahamic covenant (Gen. 12.3) or, as North (1964: 112) suggests, to the rainbow covenant of Gen. 9.8-17. If North is right in saying that a *double entendre* may have lain behind the use of the word בְּרִית, it would show how the term and concept of 'covenant' had come to be understood in some circles, and such an understanding is clearly at home in the thought of Second Isaiah. But neither is it foreign to the thought of Deutero-Zechariah.

But at this point we are reminded again of the Servant in Second Isaiah of whom it is said,

> He made my mouth like a sharp *sword*...
> he made me a polished *arrow*
> in his quiver he hid me away (Isa. 49.2).

The Servant is the instrument of God's word and his ministry is not to be a domestic one only. He is given also to be 'a light to the nations'. If it was the role of Cyrus to make the kings of the earth 'like dust with his sword and like stubble with his bow', it is the role of the Servant to subdue the nations by the word of Yahweh (cf. 9.10). It is not impossible that, just as Second Isaiah's widening of the Davidic hope to the whole community may have influenced the preceding oracle, so this promise of restoration has been influenced by the same prophet's conception of the servant-people. They, having suffered as the covenant people of God, will, by their return and restoration, witness to the grace and power of Yahweh.[9] This idea occurs not only in the Servant Songs but very remarkably also in a passage of Trito-Isaiah in Isa. 61.7. Here it is said that the nations will minister to Israel's material needs in {77} order that they may be able to function as 'priests of Yahweh' and 'the ministers of our God'. Finally, we should notice in this connection, that this is a theme given some prominence in Proto-Zechariah where, in 2.14-16 (10-12), after the daughter of Zion has been summoned to rejoice because of the advent of Yahweh into her midst, it is said that 'many nations shall join themselves to the Lord in that day, and shall be my people'. Even more strongly, in 8.20ff., it is said that 'many peoples and strong nations shall come to seek the Lord of hosts in Jerusalem', and his people will play a mediatorial role in this, for 'ten men from the nations of every tongue shall take hold of the robe of a Jew, saying, "Let us go with you, for we have heard that God is with you"'. We seem to have here, then, something of a similar re-interpretation of Second Isaiah to that found in Trito-Isaiah, an interpretation and application of his teaching which is fully in line with the thought of Proto-Zechariah.

The 'enemies' against whom Yahweh will direct the 'sons of Zion' are

---

9. Saebø (1969: 189-90) approaches a similar conclusion along different lines. If this is based on an 'invitation to flight' type oracle such as was found in Zech. 2.10 (see above), it is not now conceived in a military situation. The בָּם seems to link it with other sections in ch. 9, e.g. vv. 1f., 7aγb, which have a pacifist tendency, where the emphasis is on the 'Word' of God, where Zion is central, and where the offer of salvation is open to all.

termed 'the Sons of Jawan'. If this refers to the Greeks, then it is the most explicit reference to the period of these oracles provided in these chapters.[10] Often, however, these words are regarded as a gloss.[11] Even if that were so, an interpretative gloss can be highly significant for appreciating the way in which the text was understood {78} and applied in the circles which preserved it. It does seem to disturb the parallelism of the couplet of v. 13b, so that it might be held to be additional. Such a reference to the 'Greeks' would fit well a description of the oppression under Ptolemies or Seleucids as a captivity from which the people of God are about to be delivered.

Again, criteria for certainty are not found within the passage itself. Is it possible, however, that there is intended a play on words? יָוָן may be 'Greece', but pointed יָוֵן it means 'mire'. We have already commented on the close connection between the imagery of the 'pit' and the 'mire' into which the sufferer sinks and from which he needs to be rescued by Yahweh. But need this mean literally 'Egyptians' as Bič suggested?[12] Remembering the two close analogies to the 'pit with no water' in the Joseph and Jeremiah narratives, in which faithful Israelites were delivered from the schemes of false fellow-Israelites who opposed God by opposing them, could 'Sons of Greece' refer to the succession of priests who secured their position under the Diadochoi by bribery and compromise? Could the title 'sons of Greece' be an ironic one suggesting that they owe their status to Greek overlords rather than to Yahweh, and in that sense, are no true 'sons of Zion' or even 'sons of Yahweh'? They would then be

10. Gaide (1968: 74) is emphatic that this should be allowed to stand and be taken as regulative for the date of origin of this passage.

11. Mitchell (1912: 279, 284), since it destroys the symmetry of the couplet. Nevertheless, 'it doubtless embodies the authorized Jewish interpretation of an early date'. Ackroyd (1962a: 652) also finds that it overloads the line and is therefore probably to be regarded as a gloss. 'It is, however, an indication of an early application of the prophecy...' R.C. Dentan (1956: 1097), who sees vv. 13ff. as an appendix added to the preceding section when its promises appeared not to have been fulfilled and when Greece had become the world power, thinks it unlikely that, within such an appendix, this phrase was a gloss. D.R. Jones (1962a: 136-37) says it is either a gloss, or, on the basis of Gen. 10.4 and other passages, symbolic of distant nations in general. M. Bič (1962: 121-22) believes that here, and in Joel 4 (3).6ff., the word should be יָוֵן ('sons of mire') and refer to Egypt, such reference fitting both the idea of the 'waterless pit' and Joseph in Egypt (see discussion below). Otzen (1964) finds the reference to be to the Egyptian use of Greek mercenaries in the seventh century BC.

12. See previous note.

those who have excluded the faithful and perhaps persecuted them. But Yahweh is about to {79} intervene, to bring his faithful back to Zion which will be restored to its first cultic purity and covenant relationship with Yahweh because of the suffering and fidelity of his own. The usurpers will then be ejected, as the whole community is once more united about the cultic centre of Zion.

Such an interpretation needs to be tentative, yet it would be consistent with the very sharp attacks on the leadership of Yahweh's people met with elsewhere in these chapters.

Briefly surveying, however, the few conclusions that can be held to emerge unambiguously from this section, it would appear that we have here a strongly Zion-centred tradition. Possibly the whole community, or a faithful remnant oppressed by their fellow-Israelites, are about to be restored to Temple and city by the fulfillment of the eschatological 'hope' of Yahweh's self-manifestation and act of deliverance. In his hands they will be instruments of divine judgment on those who, either externally or internally, can be described as the oppressors and captors of his people. This return is seen in the light of the promise of Second Isaiah concerning the return from the Babylonian exile, possibly as those promises were re-interpreted and applied by Trito-Isaiah to a later situation of hardship within the land among the returned community. Perhaps in both the form of this oracle as an 'invitation to flight', and in its {80} understanding of the restored community serving to enlighten others beyond its own ranks, some influence of Proto-Zechariah is again to be observed.

Verse 14 continues appropriately in this line of thought. That which made Israel a mediator of the knowledge of God for Second Isaiah was supremely their return and restoration. For Zechariah, for whom this was an accomplished fact, it was more the manifest signs of God's own presence in the midst of his people, now returned to Jerusalem, such signs being the cleansing of the community, the worship in the rebuilt Temple, and the divine safeguarding of Jerusalem. It is the presence of Yahweh among his people which is now stressed here, cast in the traditional language of the theophany. Although it is most probably in origin an independent oracle, as it stands it is now smoothly jointed in to the preceding oracle, for all its change of form, by the linking word of the 'arrow' of God which goes forth 'like lightening', and saying that the return of the people will be both the sign of, and the occasion of, the manifestation of God's presence in all his might and glory.

Traditional elements from the old cultic language are certainly here, as seen in Pss. 18.8-16 (7-15); 72.17-21 (16-20), and in Exod. 19.13-22 where the account surely had its home in the cultic celebration of the covenant (witness, *inter alia*, the trumpet blast in v. 16). Even the tradition that God comes to his people {81} from the south was familiar from Judg. 5.4f., and Hab. 3.3.

The note of this verse is not missing from Second Isaiah. One thinks of 43.13:

> The Lord goes forth like a mighty man,
> like a man of war he stirs up his fury;
> he cries out, he shouts aloud,
> he shows himself mighty against his foes.

Similar passages occur in 43.16f.; 49.24f., and often in Trito-Isaiah: 59.15bff.; 62.1f.; 63.1-6; 64.1-3; 66.15f. It occurs also in Proto-Zechariah, as in the vision of the Four Horns (2.1-3 [1.18-21]) which also occurs in the context of the deliverance of Jerusalem. The promise of 2.10-13 (6-9) also shows that Yahweh's judgment on the foes of his people played an essential part in the defense and deliverance of Jerusalem, yet it is not seen in any way to be inconsistent with the 'universalism' of the verses immediately following, or of 8.20-23. By the judgment of his foes Yahweh will so restore the fortunes of his people that they will become the witnesses to his redeeming might, and so the instruments of his word. This integration of judgment and salvation is as old as the 'Enthronement Psalms', whose language v. 14 so closely resembles (cf. Pss. 47, 97, 99, etc.). It is after such a pattern that the place of v. 15 must be seen, and we should note that there is something of a connection between vv. 14f. and the accounts of the divine theophany for the deliverance of {82} Jerusalem which appear in a muted form in 12.1ff., and more clearly in 14.3f.

So many interpretations of v. 15 have been offered that it is difficult to be confident of any of them. The confusion in the Versions over this verse argues probably that there has been some textual corruption, so that conclusions drawn from it must remain conjectural (see Jansma 1949: 76ff.).

But the interpretive difficulties need not concern us here, for the general sense is plain. It conveys the obverse of God's salvation for his people, namely, the judgment of all who oppose his will. There is in vv. 14f., however, nothing which would relate it by origin to the same traditio-circle of the other oracles of this chapter. There is no hint of universalism, of judgment aimed at redemption, or of any demarcation within the community of God's people themselves. It would appear to be a general eschatological promise appropriated by such a group but neither their

original work nor modified by them in such a way as the earlier oracles
appear to have been. In some ways it is akin to the oracles of 12.1ff. and
14.1ff., but, as will be shown later, these have preserved some of the
features which appear elsewhere as characteristic of this traditio-circle.

What of vv. 16f.? With this oracle, again presumably a detached one
because of its introductory formula 'On that day', we return to the positive
side of the {83} deliverance. Yahweh will deliver them 'like the flock of
his people', a strange phrase, from which some have assumed that the verb
of the root רעה has dropped out (Mitchell 1912: 281). Yet it might well, as
it stands, be evocative of Ps. 95.7: 'אֲנַחְנוּ עַם מַרְעִיתוֹ וְצֹאן יָדוֹ'. Again, it
might echo Ps. 79, which calls on Yahweh to deliver his people so that.
We thy people, the flock of thy pasture (וַאֲנַחְנוּ עַמְּךָ וְצֹאן מַרְעִיתֶךָ) will give
thanks to thee forever (v. 13). Yet the earlier part of the Psalm had
complained that the heathen had defiled the Temple (v. 1), they 'have
given the bodies of thy servants to the birds of the air for food...', and
they 'have poured out their blood like water'. Possibly again, therefore,
general imagery drawn from the covenant worship of Zion lies behind the
imagery of this oracle in its sequence to vv. 11ff. When Yahweh acts in
final salvation to cleanse his Temple and avenge the blood of his servants,
he will be acting in the manner of the 'shepherd' to whom his people had
appealed over the centuries in their need.

Again, the picture of Yahweh's powerful, yet careful, deliverance of his
people as being like that of a shepherd's care for his flock is a familiar one
from Second Isaiah (40.10f.) and Ezekiel (34.11-16), where the faithfulness of Yahweh as shepherd is contrasted with the infidelity of those
who should have been 'shepherds' to his people, a point which is to be
emphasized repeatedly {84} in the succeeding chapters.

A rapid transition of picture leads on to the thought of the Israelites as
precious stones in a crown. Most commentators feel that the unusual
מִתְנוֹסְסוֹת should be emended to some form of the root נצץ, to 'sparkle', or
'glitter'. This may be so, although it would be a strange corruption from a
simple reading like that suggested, to the more difficult. In Isa. 62.3 there
is the promise:

> You shall be a crown[13] of beauty in the hand of the Lord.

This also occurs in the context of restoration. Later in the same chapter
(v. 10), where the people are exhorted to prepare the way for the triumphant
return to Zion, they are instructed, הָרִימוּ נֵס עַל־הָעַמִּים. This strophe in

---

13. עֲטֶרֶת; while in Zech. 9.16, נֵזֶר is the word used.

Trito-Isaiah is taken by most commentators to be itself a series of echoes from Second Isaiah, particularly here, 49.22, where the promise is made that God will raise his standard as a rallying point for the returning exiles.[14] It is just possible that the two points are recalled in the MT of Zech. 9.16. The people whom God restores will be like precious stones in his crown, that is, tributes and witnesses to his sovereignty over all other gods and nations, and, as such, will serve as Yahweh's standard by which people of all nations shall be guided to Jerusalem to seek him in his land, a thought taken up {85} again in 10.8.

A rather more tentative suggestion may be in place. For, in Proto-Zechariah we cannot overlook the fact that both stones and crowns are given some prominence.[15] There is the stone which is set before Joshua whose inscription Yahweh cuts himself, with its seven facets. This is linked with the cleansing of the land (Zech. 3.9f.), and appears to be the stone in the high priest's turban. Further, there is the reference in 6.9-14 to the crowns which are to be made, set upon Joshua's head, and then placed in the temple as a 'memorial' (לְזִכָּרוֹן). The passage raises many difficulties and it has usually been suggested that the text has been tampered with. Ackroyd (1968a: 194ff.), who argues for the general sense of the MT, here suggests that Joshua was symbolically crowned when Zerubbabel's return from Babylon was heralded but not yet accomplished, in token of the coming of the Branch whose function was to be to rebuild the Temple. The two crowns then do have a place and speak of the joint rule of high priest and 'civil' governor in the restored community.[16]

In v. 14 a new use for the crowns is suggested, however. If the verse suggests that it was spoken at a time when the Temple now stood again (which is a reasonable although not an essential interpretation of it), it may also testify to the fact that the promised event had taken place and yet some disappointment remained. The {86} crowns remained then as a

---

14. So Muilenburg (1956: 722): 'The strophe is almost a catena of quotations from Second Isaiah'; Westermann (1969: 378).

15. This is also observed by Saebø (1969: 269ff.) in relation to 12.3; also see the discussion of 12.3 below.

16. See also here, Rignell (1950) who maintains that it was Joshua who was crowned. 'Er sollte aber nicht selbst als ein Messiaskönig gekrönt werden, sondern der Akt solite symbolisch sein und vorausweisende Bedeutung haben'. Rignell (1950: 223f.) links this with the clothing of Joshua in ch. 3 which was also intended to be symbolic of the coming 'Branch' (v. 8). He thinks, however, that in spite of the plural form, only one crown was intended.

'memorial' to men (and perhaps to God?) of the full blessings which were to come, and of which the joint rule of Joshua and Zerubbabel were the pledge and the foreshadowing. These crowns, then, represent the cleansing of the whole community by the intercession of the high priests, and the political prosperity which the rebuilding of the Temple presaged.

Independently of this Gaide (1968: 75) points out that the MT probably suggests a gleaming like the stones of a tiara. Taken in conjunction with the promise of the rich fertility of the land (corn, flocks, etc.), it perhaps evokes the idea of the restoration of the monarchy. He points to Ps. 132.17f. (וְעָלָיו יָצִיץ נִזְרוֹ) and to Isa. 62.3ff. But, of course, this is a promise extended to the community of Zion (v. 1).[17]

Is it possible that in this verse there is the thought that the promise of the stone and the crowns, particularly in Proto-Zechariah, is to be fulfilled in the life of the community? If so, it would be a most interesting re-interpretation of the specific promise of Proto-Zechariah at the time of the joint ministry of Joshua and Zerubbabel. For this would mean that it is the community of which the prophet speaks who are to become what Joshua and Zerubbabel had been. It would be a further example of the 'democratization' of the future hope of earlier times, from the specific figure to a larger circle, in line with the tendencies which we {87} have suggested may be found elsewhere in this chapter. At some point in the dark period of the Jewish history between the rebuilding of the Temple and the arrival of Nehemiah, the figure of the governor of Jerusalem disappeared and with it, presumably, any of the old Davidic hope that some may still have cherished. Does this oracle reveal the new note of hope that some of the faithful may have seen, namely, that the faithful people of God were to become the inheritors of the old promises, and the mediator of them to the nations? A quotation from Westermann (1969: 378-79) is not inappropriate here. Commenting on the passage in Trito-Isaiah (62.10-12) to which we have already referred, he quotes Muilenburg's judgment, 'The strophe is almost a catena of quotations from Second Isaiah', and continues,

> These final verses give us our clearest picture of Trito-Isaiah as his master's disciple. They also show us that it was impossible, even when the thing initiated was a message of salvation, to return to the words used in the original. The situation as between God, the prophet and the nation was a

17. Muilenburg (1956: 718) believes this reference is derived from the ancient custom of representing the tutelary deity of a city as being crowned within the city walls. 'The crown is a visual representation of Israel's glory. It expresses the close relationship between Yahweh and Zion'.

different one from Deutero-Isaiah's, and for that reason the same words no longer said the same thing. But…the quotations here were not made at random. Both, in subject matter and style they entirely correspond.

Can we begin to discern the same kind of relationship between Zechariah and the author of the chapter we are here considering, whereby the general themes of Zechariah's hopes have been taken, but re-applied and re-interpreted in the light of a quite different situation in which {88} earlier hopes of the leadership of Zerubbabel and Joshua had been disappointed?

The passage ends with an exclamation concerning the prosperity of the land in the new age, a traditional feature of the future hope, as in Ps. 62.16; Joel 2.23ff., and again in Zechariah (3.10) where prosperity follows the cleansing and restoration of Joshua, the high priest. 'Grain' and 'new wine' are the traditional terminology for the bounty of the land of Canaan (see e.g. Gen. 27.28, 37; Deut. 11.14; 2 Kgs 18.32, etc.). This connection between salvation and the fertility of the land is, however, no mere formal convention for our author, but a constant theme of his picture of the future (see 10.1; 14.6-9, 16-19).

If we attempt a brief interim summary of findings in our study of ch. 9, we have to admit that few hard and fast conclusions can be claimed as having been established on the elusive evidence provided by these oracles. They have raised a number of questions which can only be asked and left open pending vindication or refutation in the light of study of future passages. And even such results will depend in large measure on the way the relation of these chapters and oracles to each other are viewed.

It would seem, however, that we have here a number of eschatological pieces, either composed by the prophet or prophetic circle which transmitted them, or taken over {89} and modified from a particular traditionist standpoint. Perhaps they serve as a collection of eschatological hymns for such a group.

Common to most of them is a strong dependence on earlier biblical material. Allusions abound to prophetic collections, such as the books of Amos, Ezekiel, to the Isaianic corpus and in particular, the oracles of Second and Trito-Isaiah. Allusion is also made, however, to the general imagery and themes of the language of the cult and worship as shown in some Psalms. It is as though earlier prophetic hopes and biblical 'types' are being seen as receiving their imminent fulfillment in the prophet's own time, and, in some cases, modification and re-interpretation of such promises can be traced in the light of later circumstances.

There seems to be a strongly Zionist emphasis apparent, for example in

vv. 7b, 9f., 11ff., and even perhaps in 16f., if the allusions to Zechariah and Trito-Isaiah traditions suggested here can stand.

Again, something of a universalist note is found, possibly in. v. 1, in vv. 7b-8, 9f., and possibly even in vv. 11ff., if there is in fact there some echo of the Servant figure of Second Isaiah also. Of course, there are variations of theme and interest between such an outlook and that suggested in vv. 14f., between the emphasis now upon Judah, now upon Jerusalem, now upon the pairing of Ephraim with Jerusalem or with Judah. {90}

Such variations may well be explained by the suggestion that some of these oracles were originally independent, or were formed from originally independent nuclei, and have been taken over by this prophet or prophetic circle, and modified.

Further, the question of leadership receives some emphasis, obviously in vv. 9f., and possibly in v. 16, but there are also indications that traditional 'messianic' hopes have been modified in a 'democratizing' direction. It may be, although at no point has this been capable of clear proof, that there is a note of hostility to the existing leadership of the community centred on Jerusalem, and that our prophet or circle saw themselves as Yahweh's true and faithful remnant, inheritors of the role of the servant, excluded and persecuted now, but about to be restored and vindicated in the final act of Yahweh's salvation which is even now at hand.

These three main emphases, the centrality of Zion, the divine provision of leadership as a sign of the new age, and universalism, are all found in Proto-Zechariah, and there are indications to suggest that the circle from which these oracles came, or among which they were preserved and handed on, represented the continuance of a 'Zechariah tradition', or, at least, of the tradition in which the oracles and narratives of Zechariah received their final form. {91}

Chapter 4

ZECHARIAH 10.1-2

With an apparently abrupt transition from promises of final salvation with its accompanying manifestation of fertility, we are confronted with an oracle depicted by Horst (1964: 249) as 'Mahnspruch'.[1]

The references in it to the teraphim and diviners have been variously estimated. Some, believing that general access to them after the time of the exile is unlikely, take them to be indications of a pre-exilic origin for this oracle.[2] Some have seen them as indicative of a 'deliberately archaic' style,[3] while others insist that our lack of knowledge of such features of post-exilic Judaism precludes any certainty of judgment here.[4] Elliger (1964: 155) suggests that, just as in the Hellenistic period, 'soothsayers' came to be equated with 'false prophets' (see 13.2-6), so, in the same period, 'teraphim' stand for false gods and indicate no more than this. They represent, as it were, any object of worship or source of prayer other than Yahweh himself.

The fact is, however, that they can be shown to have acquired some such pejorative significance earlier than that in the teaching of the canonical prophets themselves. Ezekiel portrays the king of Babylon consulting both before the gates of Jerusalem (21.21ff.) and, while the obscure v. 24 appears to indicate that, contrary to the expectations of the city's inhabitants, they offer {92} a true divination, it is worthy of note that it is in the hands of a pagan king that they are to be found, one for whom, presumably, there was no more direct medium of communication of the word of Yahweh. Elsewhere, such references as 1 Sam. 15.23 (where the condemnation of tera-

---

1.　Elliger (1964: 154) sees it as part invective, part admonition.

2.　So Horst (1964: 249); Otzen (1964: 216-17) also dates this passage, with all chs. 9–11 in the latter part of the seventh century BC, and believes the historical retrospect of 10.2b refers to the exile of the northern kingdom in 722–21 BC.

3.　So Dentan (1956: 1099).

4.　So Ackroyd (1962a: 653); cf. Jones (1962a: 141).

phim as equivalent to 'iniquity' couched in such strongly prophetic terms,
v. 22, is attributed to the prophet Samuel) and the account of Josiah's reforms in 2 Kgs 23.24, support the view of Lods (1932: 431) that teraphim
came to be 'one of those terms of reproach, like "shame", "abomination",
"filth", which the Jews of later times substituted in the text for the names,
abhorrent to them, of idols and false gods' (so also Ackroyd 1950–51:
379). Nor should it be forgotten that the prophets often attack the diviners
and visionaries, whose activity is parallel in this Zechariah passage with
the use of teraphim (see e.g. Mic. 3.6f.; Isa. 3.2f.; Jer. 27.9; 29.8; Ezek.
13.9).

The inference is not without warrant, therefore, that rather than seeking
a particular date for such a reference, or detecting in it a piece of 'conscious archaism', we should see here a conscious re-application of
traditional prophetic teaching. Let the people recall the prophets' stern
denunciation of the practice of seeking sources of guidance alternative to
Yahweh and remember that he alone can be their true source of supply.

Similarly, we should recall the place that the gift of rain holds in
traditional prophetic teaching concerning {93} the activity of Yahweh on
behalf of his people. As the rain is itself his gift (Job 5.10; 28.26; Ps.
147.8, etc.), so it becomes symbolic of that life-giving activity and presence of his by which his people live (Isa. 30.23ff.; 6.2f.; Mal. 3.10f.; Pss.
62.6; 68.8f.; Hag. 1.5-11; Zech. 8.9-13, etc.). When we recall the importance given to rain in 14.17 as a sign of Yahweh's kingship (cf. v. 9)
and the connection of both motifs there with the Feast of Tabernacles, it
hardly seems rash to find with Elliger in the oracle before us an allusion to
'Heilsregen', a reference again quite in line with traditional prophetic
preaching.

This impression is much strengthened when we see how all the elements
of this oracle had earlier appeared together in Jer. 14, a collection of oracles
headed 'Concerning the Drought'. The chapter as a whole, with which
15.1-4 appears closely connected by virtue of the theme of prophetic
intercession already introduced in 14.11f., has the appearance of a prophetic liturgy, somewhat similar to that found in Hos. 6.1-3, and even
more strongly, in Hos. 14.1-8. Its various component sections may well
have had independent origins as Bright, among others,[5] has urged, for

---

5. Bright (1965: 100ff.); E.W. Nicholson (1970: 100f.) finds chs. 14–15 to be
'composed of four separate and originally unconnected blocks of material in both
poetry and prose', i.e., a lament in 14.1-10, a prose discourse in vv. 11-16, another
lament in vv. 17-22, followed by a further (predominantly) prose discourse in 15.1-4.

while some sections indicate drought (e.g. 14.2-6), others seem to relate more appropriately to times of invasion and war (e.g. 14.17f.).[6]

Of special interest here is the nature of Yahweh's {94} condemnation of the prophets,

שֶׁקֶר הַנִּבְאִים נִבְּאִים בִּשְׁמִי לֹא שְׁלַחְתִּים וְלֹא צִוִּיתִים וְלֹא דִבַּרְתִּי אֲלֵיהֶם חֲזוֹן שֶׁקֶר וְקֶסֶם וֶאֱלִיל וְתַרְמִית לִבָּם הֵמָּה מִתְנַבְּאִים לָכֶם

with which may be compared Zech. 10.2,

כִּי הַתְּרָפִים דִּבְּרוּ־אָוֶן וְהַקּוֹסְמִים חָזוּ שֶׁקֶר וַחֲלֹמוֹת הַשָּׁוְא יְדַבֵּרוּ הֶבֶל יְנַחֵמוּן.

Verses 17-19 are a poem rather than an oracle, showing that identification of the prophet in his grief with the suffering of his people which is so markedly characteristic of Jeremiah. It culminates again in the attribution to the misdirection of the erroneous priests and prophets of the calamities which have overtaken them. Verses 19-22 constitute a renewed cry of communal lament by the people, again acknowledging their sin. Here however, the connection with drought is explicit, and, most interestingly, leads to an affirmation, by way of question, of the very faith which is the central theme of Zech. 10.1:

> Are there any among the false gods of the
> nations that can bring rain? (Jer. 14.22)

> Ask rain…from the Lord who makes the storm clouds,
> who gives men showers of rain… (Zech. 10.1)

The tragic finality of Jeremiah's message of rejection becomes plain in 15.1-4 in which the divine repudiation of the prophet's intercession of 14.11f. is renewed and re-emphasized. Not even the intercession of Moses and {95} Samuel (*the* prophets *par excellence*) would turn the heart of Yahweh back to his people. The final oracle of doom is pronounced.

One of the main interests of the whole passage, therefore, seems to be the problem of the nature of false prophecy. Its relation to the role of the prophet, and the responsibility of such false prophets for the state of the whole community is an issue which was of particular concern to the Deuteronomists. This is noticed by Nicholson (1970: 102), who says,

> …it seems clear that xiv–xv 4 must be regarded as having assumed its
> present form at the hands of the Deuteronomists. If this is accepted we may

---

For an examination of the relation of the concept of the root שֶׁקֶר to the theology of Jeremiah as a whole, see Overholt (1970: 86ff.).

6.   So also Weiser (1969: 121f.).

conclude that the prose passage xiv 11-16 is to be taken together with xxvii-xxix as giving expression to the concern of the Deuteronomists with the problem of false prophecy.

The likelihood of this is greatly strengthened when such a passage as Deut. 11.10-17 is recalled, where the beauty and fertility of the land, and its dependence on rain, which is Yahweh's gift, are stressed, but these are still dependent on their obedience to the law and refusal to have anything to do with idols.

If we are right, then, in believing that this passage of Jeremiah is being alluded to in Zech. 10.1f. with its combined emphasis on the misdirection of false prophets and Yahweh as the sole giver of rain, it becomes possible to discern a more positive connection with the preceding oracles than some have found.

The prophet has been proclaiming what is to be {96} the great final act of Yahweh's salvation. Now he turns in pastoral concern towards the community, summoning them to a proper response to Yahweh who alone is the giver of the blessings of the new age, a response which is, therefore, the essential condition of experiencing it. To underline the point he echoes (by allusion) the passage in Jer. 14.1–15.4 which, by its unrelenting note of judgment on an earlier generation which had failed to make that response in time, is a solemn witness to the urgency of the pastoral call. They too face the choice of judgment or salvation. Let them not fail as their fathers did by turning to false sources of reliance and so missing the 'Heilsregen' which it is Yahweh's alone to give.

But here it is important to note that the Jeremiah/Deuteronomist tradition which appears to be re-interpreted and re-applied is one in which polemic against the wrong leadership and direction of false prophets is strongly to the fore. Has this element also been taken up in Zech. 10.1f.? How this is answered will depend to a great extent on how v. 2 is rendered, whether the verbal tenses are taken to refer to conditions contemporary with the writing of the oracle, or are to be taken as referring back to conditions which obtained in the past. The Hebrew tenses do not provide decisive evidence. In v. 2aαβ, דִּבְּרוּ and חָזוּ are simple perfects, but in v. 2aγδ we have two simple imperfects, יְדַבֵּרוּ and {97} יְנַחֵמוּן. In v. 2bα the tense is perfect נָסְעוּ, and in v. 2bβ, imperfect יֵעֵנוּ. This by itself is not determinative since the perfect tense can be used specifically of past events which are still of constant recurrence and 'hence are matters of common experience',[7] while the imperfect may be used to express actions 'which *continued* in the past through a longer or shorter period'.[8]

Saebø, speaking of the form-structure of v. 2, sees the first strophe as bearing the marks of the type of prophetic reproach. Where we should expect in the second strophe, however, the announcement of judgment introduced by the עַל־כֵּן, we have instead an historical retrospect ('einen geschichtlichen Rückblick') over judgment which fell in the past. This break in formal structure and sudden switch is indeed remarkable. Mitchell (1912: 286ff.) also believes that we have here historical retrospect as does Otzen (1964: 217-218). Saebø cites Eissfeldt (1965: 16) who says that historical retrospect and exhortation are common features of the sermons in the historical books.

It is, therefore, possible that this prophet, in calling on his contemporaries to worship Yahweh alone, points to the moral to be drawn from history when the people turned from the true prophets to seek divination by other means, and so suffered judgment. This is much then in the spirit of Zech. 1.4. But it is also possible that he is setting his own prophetic word deliberately in {98} the spirit of the Jeremiah/Deuteronomist tradition from which he draws, in order to apply the same spirit of polemic against the false spiritual direction in terms of the situation of the community of his own day, as he sees it. Is his own assessment of the contemporary situation such as can justly be described by v. 2b? This would mean that his picture of the people wandering and suffering for lack of true leadership is a comment on the contemporary situation. Why should he mention teraphim, diviners and the visions of dreamers? Were they really a major cause of religious apostasy in his time, perhaps under Persian or Greek influence? Or are they objects of attack mentioned in the tradition on which he is drawing, and so seen as symbolic of the poor spiritual direction and false teaching of those who were meant to be Yahweh's spokesmen?[9] Is this 'mahnspruch' urgent and real because it reveals this prophet's diagnosis of the condition of community and leadership in his own time? Within the passage itself conclusive evidence is again lacking, but the nature of the attack on the 'shepherds' in 10.3; 11.4ff., 15ff.; and

7. GKC §106k. Mitchell (1912: 287) takes the variation in tenses to indicate additions to the original text.

8. GKC §107h.

9. The exact role of 'shepherds' in these chapters is discussed below, but here conclusions may be anticipated by saying that the equation 'shepherd' = 'king' seems too narrow and rigid a concept to fit what is said of them.

13.7 may suggest that, of two equally possible interpretations, the more probable is that which sees in 10.1f. a diagnosis of, and an address to, a contemporary situation of the prophet's own time.

Finally, we may note that this passage, in its position in context and in its pastoral purpose, affords {99} another strong link between these oracles and those of Proto-Zechariah. Such a link may be found in both substance and pattern. The oracles of Proto-Zechariah, as we now have them, open with a call to return to Yahweh and so avoid the sins of their fathers, those very sins which called down upon them the judgment of the former prophets (1.2-6). They go on to give central place to the Temple and its rebuilding whose significance is that it will be the place where Yahweh dwells again in the midst of his people (1.16; 2.9 [5], 14 [10]ff.). But this means that they will again be able to call on Yahweh and recognize the authentic accents of his voice in genuine prophecy (2.15 [11]). There will be no false dealings with any other for they will then live in a renewed relationship to Yahweh. They will seek (בקש) him and him alone for guidance (8.21) in the house in which Joshua is faithfully keeping his charge (3.7). Indeed, the promise overflows from the members of the restored community for 'many people and strong nations' (8.22) shall also come to 'seek' Yahweh, forsaking their false gods and other sources of oracular direction to do so. There is thus a remarkable similarity of substance between the themes of the two at this point.

But also to be noted is the pattern of such pastoral concern which occurs in the same key in both Proto-Zechariah and in our later section of the book. For in both there is found to be that same admixture of proclamation of {100} coming deliverance, the *eschaton* of God, and pastoral entreaty to be ready to enter it and appropriate its blessings. It occurs in Proto-Zechariah in the call, to which allusion has already been made, to avoid the sins of their fathers. The cleansing of Joshua in ch. 3 may be seen in some way as expressing the cleansing of the whole community of which he is representative, a cleansing which is graphically portrayed in the vision of ch. 5. Chapter 6 ends with the words addressed by the prophet to his contemporaries in v. 15b, 'And this shall come to pass if you will diligently obey the voice of the Lord your God'. There are the reiterated calls to just living in chs. 7–8, in which post- and pre-exilic prophecy join hands (7.8-13; 8.16f.).

Thus in both substance and pattern 10.1f. show the same lines of dependence and similarity running from these chapters to Proto-Zechariah which we observed in the oracles of ch. 9. Further, they see the same allusive evocation of earlier prophetic teaching serving not only the proclamation of those oracles, but the urgent pastoral entreaty of 'the good shepherd', and appear to reflect the same kind of hostility towards the established leadership of the Jewish community and negative evaluation of the consequences of that leadership in the life of the community as a whole which were suggested at several points in ch. 9. {101}

Chapter 5

ZECHARIAH 10.3-12; 11.1-3

This section, which, for all its awkwardness of construction and problems of textual corruption, is sufficiently linked by theme and terminology to be taken as a unit, is often associated with 9.11-17[1] and shares with it the general note of deliverance of his people by the power of Yahweh.

As it stands now it contains three distinct words of Yahweh (in vv. 3a, 6, 8-10) each followed by oracular material (vv. 3b-5, 7, 11f.). Verse 3a contains a general threat against the leaders of the people (whether foreign or false leaders of their own remains to be discussed) and is followed by a promise of deliverance when Yahweh shepherds the House of Judah. Verses 6 announces the divine deliverance of both the Houses of Judah and of Joseph, and v. 7 contains a promise addressed specifically to Ephraim. Verses 8-10 predict the return of the exiles, led home by Yahweh himself from Assyria and Egypt, a promise echoed in v. 11, while v. 12 contains a concluding oracle of general well-being, the whole ending with the oracular formula, יְהוָה נְאֻם. There then follows (11.1-3) a call for lamentation over the destroyed glory of Lebanon and Bashan, which, for reasons to be discussed, appears to have some relationship to 10.3-12.

In an article entitled 'The Shepherd-Ruler Concept in the Old Testament and its Application in the New Testament', J.G.S.S. Thomson (1955) points out that the {102} shepherd concept came naturally to a pastoral community such as the Israelites, and that it was, in any event, current amongst other ancient Semitic peoples. This is certainly attested quite early[2] and several examples can be cited throughout the Old Testament as Thomson shows, in reference to Yahweh, to certain national leaders in Israel, to Israelite nobility, to Gentile military commanders and to the

---

1. See, e.g., Elliger (1964: 156ff.).
2. E.g. *The Code of Hammurabi* 1.50: 'Hammurabi, the shepherd called by Enlil, am I' (*ANET*: 164). For fuller references to the Mesopotamian and Egyptian parallels, see Saebø (1969: 215n) and also the list given by Zimmerli (1969: 835).

Messiah. Such uses are found in the eighth century prophets, in the historical books of Samuel and Kings, and elsewhere. But there is no doubt that the greatest use of the picture is found in Jeremiah, Ezekiel and Zechariah, as C. Brouwer (1949: 11) has shown and which he attributes to the influx of Mesopotamian influence at this period.

The question therefore arises whether its presence in Zechariah may be due to the influence of Jeremiah and Ezekiel's usage of the picture, and, with the themes and ideas of this passage before us, it is interesting to study its appearances in these earlier prophetic writings, where it is the falsity of these 'shepherds' and their betrayal of their pastoral trust, which is the constant theme of attack.

Jer. 2.8 is important:

> The priests did not say, 'Where is the Lord?'
> Those who handle the law did not know me;
> וְהָרֹעִים פָּשְׁעוּ בִי
> The prophets prophesied by Baal,
> and went after things that do not profit. {103}

Thomson argues that the term 'shepherd' is applied only to political rulers.[3] To some extent it depends on whether we take these lines as referring to four distinct groups of people, as J.P. Hyatt (1956: 814) maintains, or whether by the parallelism 'those who handle the law' is a synonym for the priests. If it were, it would become more likely that the 'shepherds' would then be a synonym for prophets with which they would stand related by the parallelism of the lines. To take it, however, that four distinct groups are meant implies, as Hyatt (1941) explicitly states elsewhere, that there already was in existence a class of expert interpreter of the law, forerunners of the later scribes and referred to here as וְתֹפְשֵׂי הַתּוֹרָה.[4] It is true that Jeremiah does, on several occasions, refer to 'scribes' (סֹפְרִים) of whom, of course, Baruch was one, and that the existence of such a class is attested from an early period in the monarchy. Whether the term had yet

---

3.   Thomson (1955: 410): 'Perhaps Ezek. 34 does emphasize the spiritual rather than the political aspect of their work, but in v. 23 the false shepherds are contrasted with the true shepherd of the House of David, *which suggests the prophet had in mind the political not the priestly office*' (italics mine).

4.   This is an unusual use of the root חפש, which does not occur elsewhere in the Old Testament in reference to exponents of the law. The LXX renders with ἀντέχειν, the only occasion in which the root חפש is so rendered. Bright (1965: 15) takes it as a parallel reference to the priests ('the handlers of the law', i.e., priests and Levites whose duty it was to interpret the law); Cunliffe-Jones (1966: 54) to 'law-givers'.

acquired its later meaning, or still had its older sense of 'secretary', is not quite as clear as perhaps Hyatt assumes. For our present purpose it is sufficient, but important, to note that Jeremiah can use the term in parallel to the 'spiritual' leaders, i.e. the priests and the prophets who were so often the joint target of his attacks.[5] The question may at least be permitted as to whether, during the period of the exile and after, the distinction can have remained so clear and relevant that the term {104} הָרֹעִים might not imply collectively all men of authority whom Yahweh had set over his people, responsible to him as 'under-shepherds' as it were.[6]

Jer. 3.15 is also significant:

> And I will give you shepherds after my own heart,
> who will feed you with knowledge and understanding.

This is usually regarded as part of an exilic expansion[7] in a passage (vv. 6-18) which is itself seen as intrusive, separating as it does 3.1-8 and 3.19–4.4.[8] Nevertheless, such interpretation of God's redemptive action in the time of the exile is interesting and important. It may explain why the function of the 'shepherds' is seen now in terms of דֵּעָה וְהַשְׂכֵּיל, terms more often associated with the 'wisdom' teachers than political rulers, and suggests again that by the time of the exile and beyond, a broader under-standing of the role of the leader was current, matching the changed political circumstances which gave rise to the joint role of Zerubbabel and Joshua in Proto-Zechariah, and the priest-rulers of later periods. It is interesting to note that the promise that Yahweh will himself give true and faithful leaders to replace the false, is matched by Zech. 10.4, and that Jer. 3.6-18 includes, like Zech. 10.3-12, references to the faithlessness of both

---

5. See, e.g., Jer. 6.13; 8.10; 14.18. Brouwer (1949: 25) believes that in Jeremiah, the 'shepherds' represent priests, princes and prophets and, in 11.1ff., believes that the close relationship with Jeremiah suggests that it is Israel's leaders which are indicated (Brouwer 1949: 130ff.).

6. Note should also be taken of several instances in Jeremiah where the three types of officials are mentioned together, namely, king, prophet and priest, see 4.9; 8.1; 13.13, but where the term is not used. This might suggest that where it is used it may be construed as a general term for all types of leadership in the nation, both 'spiritual' and 'political' if such a distinction had meaning for the Israelites. See also Zimmerli (1969: 835), who argues that, especially in Jeremiah, 'shepherds' applies to leaders other than kings.

7. So Bright (1965: 25ff.); Hyatt (1956: 827); Paterson (1962: 542).

8. In addition to those cited above, see Cunliffe-Jones (1966: 61). Weiser (1969: 29-30), however, is much more cautious.

kingdoms, North and South, with a promise of their joint restoration (Jer. 3.18). {105}

Another attack on the shepherds is found in Jer. 10.21:

> For the shepherds are stupid,
> and do not inquire of the Lord;
> therefore they have not prospered
> and all their flock is scattered.

The context of Jer. 10.17-22 is of the imminent approach of the foe before the gates of the city, which is portrayed as uttering a lament:

> My tent is destroyed,
> and all my cords are broken...
> there is no one to spread my tent again (10.20).

The רֹעִים have not 'inquired of the Lord' as Zech. 10.1 counsels them to do, and therefore Yahweh is to 'sling' (הִנְנִי קוֹלֵעַ; cf. Zech. 9.15, אַבְנֵי־קֶלַע) them out of Jerusalem at the hands of besieging invaders. The tent is collapsing. It is this which is to be exactly reversed in Zech. 10.3-12. The people are to be given true leadership by Yahweh (v. 3) for from out of them will come the 'tent peg'(יָתֵד) so that the tent of the city may again be fastened; under this God-given leadership it will be they who trample their enemies like the dirt in the street and they who will be restored to their land. The hope of Isa. 33.20 is to be fulfilled when Jerusalem would be

> a quiet habitation, an immovable tent,
> whose stakes (יְתֵדֹתָיו) will never be plucked up,
> nor will any of its cords be broken,
> because Yahweh will be our judge, ruler and king, to save us (v. 22). {106}

In Jer. 12.10 it is complained, 'Many shepherds have destroyed my vineyards', an instance where רֹעִים could well apply to foreign powers. Yet in Zech. 10.7, the restoration will, it is said, cause the hearts of the people to 'be glad as with wine'. Vineyards will be restored in the reversal of fortunes which is coming.

Another attack on the 'shepherds' in Jeremiah occurs in Jer. 22.22, where the context also includes motifs found in Deutero-Zechariah. Various members of the royal line are compared and contrasted with the standards of righteousness called for by the terms of the Davidic Covenant. In vv. 20ff. the doom of Jerusalem is announced and the city called to lamentation on the mountains of Lebanon, Bashan and Abarim. These last may be mentioned as the seat of the worship of other gods in whose cults the leaders and people had so often indulged, or as symbols of power on which reliance had so often been placed:

> The wind shall shepherd all your shepherds,
> and your lovers shall go into captivity (v. 22);

and later,

> O inhabitant of Lebanon,
> nested among the cedars (v. 23)

presumably a reference back to 22.15 where Jehoiakim is scathingly asked,

> Do you think you are a king
> because you compete in cedar? {107}

It is interesting to note, therefore, that our passage which begins with an attack on the shepherds, is preceded by an appeal to worship Yahweh alone, and is followed (11.1-3) by a summons to Lebanon and Bashan to bewail the fate that is about to overtake them. Not only does this recall Jer. 22.23, but it is also strikingly reminiscent of Jer. 25.36, 38:

> Hark! the cry of the shepherds,
> and the wail of the lords of the flock...
> Like a lion he (Yahweh) has left his covert,
> for their land has become a waste.

Again, of importance for our section is the prose oracle of Jer. 23.1-6 where a further attack on the 'shepherds who destroy and scatter the sheep of my pasture' is followed by a promise that Yahweh himself will gather them and bring them back. He will set over them 'shepherds who will care for them' (or 'really shepherd them' as we might render it). This is followed by a promise of a descendant of David described as צֶמַח (one is reminded of the description of Zerubbabel as the 'branch' in Zech. 3.8; 6.12) in whose days 'Judah will be saved and Israel will dwell securely'.

In the 'Booklet of Consolation' a further use of the 'shepherd' simile occurs in Jeremiah, where it is said,

> He who scattered (מְזָרֵה) Israel,
> will gather him (יְקַבְּצֶנּוּ),
> and will keep him as a shepherd keeps his flock.
> For the Lord has ransomed (פָּדָה) Jacob
> and has redeemed him from hands too strong for him (Jer. 31.10f.) {108}

while in Zech. 10.9ff. it is said of the people Yahweh[9] 'scattered' (אֶזְרָעֵם),
that

> I will bring them home from the land of Egypt
> and gather them (אֲקַבְּצֵם) from Assyria

which follows the assurance כִּי פְדִיתִים.

Of course, the terms and pictures used are general and nowhere can direct quotation be proved. Yet it is difficult to avoid the total impression that Zech. 10.3–11.3 has been influenced by Jeremiah, not only by virtue of the terminology but of the connection of ideas, and that the verses announce the reversal of the state of affairs denounced by the earlier prophet and reaffirm the promises made there for the future.

The ideas are also closely akin to those found in Ezek. 34. Indeed, so closely does that chapter follow the ideas found in Jeremiah that it would be easy to believe there has been some interaction of thought between the two.[10] One cannot simply assert the dependence of Ezekiel on Jeremiah since later elements are probably involved in both books in the relevant sections. But clearly a sense of betrayal on the part of the pre-exilic leaders, and the hope of the provision of truer leadership in the future would be natural to the time of the exile and it is not surprising that the teaching of both prophets on the subject received further expansion. Nor is it surprising that the theme received further re-interpretation at a later time of crisis represented by the Zechariah passage. {109}

Ezekiel 34 says that the scattering of the sheep and their impoverishment is due to the falsity of the shepherds who have fed and clothed themselves at the expense of the flock. God will therefore reject the shepherds and take their charge away from them, and will himself become shepherd to them. He will gather them from all the places where they have been scattered. He will judge between sheep and sheep, rams and he-goats (עַתּוּדִים). Further, as the text now stands, part of his provision for them

---

9. See discussion below.
10. A point noted by Muilenburg (1962: 585). So also Zimmerli (1969: 835), '…ist aber vor allem Jer 23 1ff zu nennen, eine Stelle, *die unverkennbar Vorbild für Ez 34 geworden ist*' (italics mine). A strong relationship between the preaching of Ezekiel and Jeremiah is argued for by J.W. Miller (1955), particularly in their pictures of national (pp. 173-81) and individual (pp. 181-83) renewal. On the relationship of their use of the 'shepherd/flock' imagery (pp. 105f.) he says emphatically, 'Der Eindruck, den all diese Berührungen zwischen den beiden Stellen machen, kann schwerlich anders interpretiert werden, als das die Stelle Jer. 23.1-2 dem Hesekiel bekannt war' (p. 106).

will be a shepherd who is spoken of as 'my servant David', presumably, therefore, a prince of the Davidic line. The 'wild beasts', i.e. those who ravaged and harassed his flock, will be banished and peace and fertility will again be known. This will be because of a covenant whose terms, for all the reference to David, are strongly reminiscent of the Sinaitic covenant:

> And they shall know that I, the Lord their God, am with them, and that they, the house of Israel, are my people... (Ezek. 34.30, cf. Exod. 6.7).

Now it is often held that Ezek. 34, as it now stands, is composite, although it has also been pointed out that Ezekiel's characteristic vocabulary and style are to be found throughout.[11] Once more, however, this need not delay the present enquiry, for, as has been suggested above, whether they are all the words of Ezekiel himself or a development and re-interpretation of his teaching in the light of later conditions when hopes of restoration began to become more specific, the present {110} state of the text shows how promises of Yahweh's leadership of his own people following his judgment on their false leaders, and his provision of true leadership, in this

---

11. The composite nature of this chapter is upheld by Muilenburg (1962: 585), who, in allowing for the possibility of composite authorship, follows, *inter alia*, Cooke (1936) who believes vv. 17-31 to be secondary; Hölscher (1924), who allows nothing of the chapter to Ezekiel; and Irwin (1943), who, with his rather more drastic approach to the book along the line of differentiation between the source of the poetic and prose oracles, limited Ezekiel's part in this chapter to a tristich in v. 2. H.G. May (1956: 251), believes that the 'homogeneity of the thought and diction within the chapter' show unity of authorship, but that 'The diction and ideology, with the picture of the Davidic Messiah and the doctrine of the new covenant, point to the editor as most probably author'. The reasons usually advanced for the composite nature of the chapter are that in v. 17 a judgment *within* Israel separating good and bad is inconsistent with the theme of chs. 34–37; that the shepherds are no longer kings but leaders within Israel generally; the replacement of the direct shepherding of Yahweh himself with the promise of 'David' as shepherd; and a 'falling off in style' (Cooke 1936). Zimmerli (1969: 847), however, retains the verse concerning David for Ezekiel: 'Das Davidswort 23f. meinten wir Ezechiel nicht absprechen zu müssen...' since it forms a fitting conclusion to vv. 17-22. He acknowledges that the chapter is the result of a gradual process of editing in which words of disciples have been added to those of Ezekiel, but believes it possible that vv. 1-15 and 17-22 belong to Ezekiel. The treatment of the same theme from two different angles is characteristic of Ezekiel (cf. ch. 16). Zimmerli argues that if it was Ezekiel who brought them both together then all vv. 1-23 may be assigned to him, for the promise concerning David is a fitting climax which binds both sections together, for, in the first section, v. 12 reflects the catastophe of the exile, for which the historical line of the Davidic kings in Jerusalem is the only final remedy.

instance from the house of David, could be brought together. The same sequence of ideas occurs in our passage, where v. 4 goes on immediately to speak of the leadership Yahweh will provide for them.

The sudden transformation of image from the people as the flock which needs gentle shepherding, to the horse which bears Yahweh's majesty in battle, is astonishing. That we are dealing here with general imagery rather than specific and literal detail is suggested by the fact that in v. 6 they are apparently on foot again confounding 'the riders on horses'. Unless we are to make a heavily pedantic approach to this passage and find a different hand behind each conflicting element we may assume that general picture language is being used. Yet they are pictures with very clear associations.

This transformation of his people from the oppressed flock to Yahweh's majestic battle-horse (כְּסוּס הוֹדוֹ בַּמִּלְחָמָה) is emphatically the work of Yahweh. He will 'set them up' (שׂוּם) in this role.

Normally the horse, as we have seen, is regarded by the prophets as a sign of human reliance and strength, so often opposed to the will of Yahweh and its use contrary to the spirit of faith. It is in such a sense {111} that v. 5 must be understood. No human might will be able to withstand the people of God in the holy war when they become the instruments of Yahweh's vengeance on his foes. The thought of this verse is wholly in line with the spirit of Isa. 31.1-3. But there are not wanting in the Old Testament references to the idea that Yahweh employs his own horses in beating down his opponents. Their much-vaunted strength and resources are nothing compared with his.

There is the vision granted to Elisha's servant at Dothan, recorded in 2 Kgs 6.17, where the prophet prays that his eyes might be opened when he fears the size of the Syrian army: 'and behold, the mountain was full of horses and chariots round about Elisha'.

Before such heavenly cavalry the horses of the Syrians are useless, and when the sound of them is heard they flee, *forsaking* their horses. There is not even a battle (2 Kgs 7.7).

There is further the imagery which pictures the victory of Yahweh in the deliverance from Egypt in terms of the mythological victory over the waters of chaos:

> When thou didst ride upon thy horses (עַל־סוּסֶיךָ)
> upon thy chariots of victory?...
> Thou didst trample the sea with thy horses (סוּסֶיךָ)
> the surging of mighty waters (Hab. 3.8, 15).

That he can use human horsemen for his purpose of vengeance is to be seen from Jeremiah's vivid poem of doom for Egypt at the hand of the Babylonians: {112}

> Advance, O horses,
> and rage, O chariots!...
> That day is the day of the Lord God of hosts,
> a day of vengeance (Jer. 46.9f.).[12]

Thus the picture used here in Zech. 10, while startling, is in line with a certain strand of Old Testament tradition. What is striking is that there (alone), he makes his own oppressed people his instrument for judgment.

Perhaps, however, even this idea has an interesting history in the light of an article by M.A. Beek (1972). This apparently strange designation could be given to a prophet because the 'words of the prophet and consequently the man who bears these words of God, the prophet himself, is guarantee of Israel's salvation. Therefore every prophet has a right to the title רֶכֶב יִשְׂרָאֵל וּפָרָשָׁיו.' He believes that the phrase stems from the liturgy of the Passover Legend because of the frequent occurrence of the words in the Exodus narratives. It leads, in the prophetic material, to an understanding of them in a symbolic way, as expressive of all human might which is opposed to trust in God alone. The title expresses 'what the function has been of every prophet in the light of Israel's faith. He is not only a representative of the power of the Almighty, he is a power himself...' (Beek 1972: 10). If now this is extended to the whole 'flock, the House of Judah' it may be a kind of {113} democratization of such a concept of the prophetic office, and would give slightly more support for the view that the leadership spoken of in v. 4 is seen as emerging collectively from the restored community.

There are two critical points at issue in vv. 3f. The first is whether the phrase 'the House of Judah' in v. 3 is a gloss,[13] and the second is the exact

---

12. Verse 10 is often denied to Jeremiah, e.g., Skinner (1936: 239n), who finds in the whole chapter 'the work of an anonymous, perhaps contemporary, poet, with a genius akin to that of Nahum'; also Hyatt (1956: 1107) and Cunliffe-Jones (1966: 252). Its apocalyptic language and concepts suggest it is a later intrusion, but there can be no doubt that Jeremiah sees in the defeat of the Egyptians a just judgment of God. He is (*contra* Cunliffe-Jones) quite capable of such sentiments; e.g. 10.25; 11.20; 18.21ff.; 20.12.

13. So BH and Mitchell (1912: 288). Magne Saebø, however, argues that it is original here in view of v. 4 and Judah's traditional role in the provision of messianic leadership.

force of the מִמֶּנּוּ at the beginning of v. 4. Are we to take it as a reference to Yahweh himself? In which case it emphasizes that from him these leaders shall come. Or is the reference to the people, that this leadership will come from among *them*, whether the 'flock' or the 'House of Judah'? The answer to both depends, to some extent, on how we are to understand that which is being promised.

פִּנָּה, the 'corner stone', which occurs first, already has connotations of leadership in the Old Testament. In Judg. 20.2 it is used of the 'chiefs of all the people' who assembled before Yahweh at Mizpah. It is used in the same sense in 1 Sam. 14.38 where Saul, the king, addressed all the 'leaders of the people'. It can be used of foreign leaders as for example in Isa. 19.13, where the deluded princes of Zoan and Memphis who have led Egypt astray are ironically addressed. The RSV legitimately brings out the irony by rendering it as 'those who are the corner stones of her tribes' for the word is clearly suggestive of strength and dependability, and these were exactly the qualities the Egyptian leaders {114} failed to show.

So far it is seen to have no necessary Messianic connotation. Indeed, when Saul uses it to address the leaders it clearly has none. But the well-known instance in Ps. 118.22 stands by itself:

> The stone which the builders rejected has become the head of the corner (פִּנָּה).
> This is the Lord's doing—it is marvellous in our eyes.

The psalm is one of thanksgiving for deliverance. The worshipper called on Yahweh in his distress, for he knows it is better to trust in him than 'put confidence in princes'. Yahweh delivers him and the 'glad songs of victory' are heard in the tents of the righteous. In triumphant cultic procession he calls for admittance to the Temple (vv. 19f.). The similarity of vocabulary and thought to Zech. 9.9f. is striking. Nowhere in this psalm is the speaker identified explicitly with the king. But of whom else would the words of v. 22 have any significance? Indeed, not only does v. 22 seem to imply the king, but vv. 10ff. can hardly refer to anyone else. That it is the king speaking in the individual passages in this liturgical celebration has been widely acknowledged,[14] although v. 22, of course, would be part of

---

14. E.g. Weiser (1962: 724): '...the thanksgiving of an individual according to vv. 10ff., 22, presumably that of the king...' See also, Johnson (1967: 123): 'It is true that the king is not specifically mentioned, but the language and thought of the psalm as a whole are obviously in harmony with other psalms in this series which centre in the person of the Messiah.'

the congregational response which extends from v. 22 to v. 27.

It is of interest that an identification of the 'stone' in Ps. 118.22 with the Messiah is attested in the writings of later Judaism. Strack and Billerbeck (1922–28, I: 875ff.) quote Rashi on Mic. 5.1 (2) in which he sees the Messiah {115} as the one who comes forth from Bethlehem, and continues: 'Just as Ps. 118.22 says, "The stone which the builders rejected".' The Targum on Zech. 10.4 also interprets it of the Messiah, and of course, Christian interpretation of it in this sense is well attested in the New Testament.[15]

The idea of a leader of the community as a 'tent peg' (יָתֵד) is obviously closely related. There is the well-known passage in Isa. 62.23 where it is said of Eliakim,

> And I will fasten him like a peg (יָתֵד) in a sure place,
> and he will become a throne of honour to his father's house.

Of course the idea here is of a peg driven into a wall. Another interesting use of the same Hebrew word metaphorically as a 'tent peg' occurs in Isa. 33.20:

> Look upon Zion, the city of our appointed feasts!
> Your eyes will see Jerusalem,
> a quiet habitation, an immovable tent,
> whose stakes (יְתֵדֹתָיו) will never be plucked up,
> nor will any of its cords be broken.

Here the picture is not so much of leadership of the city, as the secure centre of relationship to Yahweh through its ordered and unhindered cultus in which Yahweh himself (v. 22) acts as judge, ruler and king.

It is possible, then, that Deutero-Zechariah is here using the term יָתֵד in its significance within the Isaianic corpus, and expounding it as indicative of the provision of true leadership in his own time. When one remembers the close connection of Eliakim with the House {116} of David (Isa. 62.22) and that he is seen as 'a father to the inhabitants of Jerusalem and the house of Judah' (v. 20) and 'a throne of honour to his father's house' (v. 23) and, further, that he is one 'called' by Yahweh to replace a worthless leader (Shebna) the appropriateness of the reference here becomes the more apparent. Naturally, to an eastern people of nomadic origins, imagery inspired by tents is bound to figure prominently anyway, and we must be careful not to press suggestions of inter-dependence. But that it

15. For a citation of the principal passages in which the imagery of Ps. 118.22 is used in the New Testament, see Taylor (1953: 476).

did lend itself in a general way to pictures of restoration may be illustrated from Isa. 54.1f.:

> 'For the children of the desolate will be more than the children of her that is married', says the Lord. 'Enlarge the place of your tent, and let the curtains of your habitations be stretched out; hold not back, lengthen your cords and strengthen your stakes'.

And even in Ezra 9.8 it is said that by the return from exile God has given the remnant 'a secure hold' (יָתֵד) *'within his holy place'*.[16] As with פִּנָּה, so by the use of יָתֵד the prophet is speaking primarily of the provision of leadership, but, in so doing, can awaken echoes of prophetic promises that speak of the restoration of Jerusalem which such leadership will bring about. Since also both terms can be indicative of building, there may be some *double entendre* here of the thought of the rebuilding of Jerusalem and its community as, for {117} example, in Zech. 2.6 (2). True leadership will result in the rebuilding of a true community.

The 'battle-bow' (קֶשֶׁת מִלְחָמָה) is reminiscent of 9.13, where it is said of Judah that she is bent by Yahweh as his bow, and so affords another thread in the strand that links these two sections. Reference has already been made to the use in the Old Testament of the picture of God's 'bow' directed against evil-doers (see above pp. {75-76}). It is clearly an echo of the earlier 'Holy War' concept[17] as is implied by Josh. 24.12 where the deeds of Yahweh are recalled at the covenant ceremony:

> I sent the hornet before you which drove them out before you, the two kings of the Amorites; it was not by your sword or your bow.

It can be a picture of the people in the Old Testament, for in Ps. 78.57 and Hos. 7.16 they are likened to a 'twisted' or a 'treacherous' bow which does not shoot straight. It passes naturally over into a picture of strength, as in 'the Blessing of Jacob' in Gen. 49.24, where it is said of Joseph that even when under attack

> his bow remained unmoved,
> his arms were made agile
> by the hand of the Mighty One of Jacob,
> by the name of the Shepherd, the Rock of Israel.

---

16. So MT Esdras has ῥίζαν and LXX στήριγμα. BH suggests emendation to יָתֵד. This may afford an instance of a parallel, if independent, method of exegesis by both the Chronicler and Deutero-Zechariah.

17. See von Rad (1958) for a full discussion of this whole concept. For Cross's criticism of von Rad, see {259} n. 3, now p. 176 n. 3.

Some suspicion attaches to this last line, since it is too long metrically, the two nouns in apposition as given by the MT seem strange, and the Versions offer renderings based on apparently variant readings. However, even if the term 'Shepherd' is a later interpretation {118} one wonders if it is the basis of the application made in Zech. 10.4 that as Yahweh once shepherded Joseph and so made them strong, so he will care for his flock now with the same result. The rather abrupt and sudden transition from imagery of battle to that of the pastoral care of Yahweh in Gen. 49.24 might even be behind the abrupt transition of imagery (which occurs the other way round in Zech. 10) which has so puzzled commentators.

The question arises whether this is a general promise that the people as a whole shall be made strong, or whether the phrase קֶשֶׁת מִלְחָמָה is used as the title of a leader, in a way that both פִּנָּה and יָתֵד could be elsewhere in the Old Testament. G. Gaide (1968: 87) follows Marti in believing that the prophet is drawing here on a symbolic representation of the king, common amongst ancient Semitic peoples. It is not a picture which occurs in the Old Testament, although the king is described as a 'shield' to his people (Ps. 84.9), unless it be, as Gaide suggests, in Jer. 49.35-38. There it is said that Yahweh will break 'the bow of Elam, "the mainstay" of their might', a prediction which ends with the threat of the destruction of their kings and princes. The phrase רֵאשִׁית גְּבוּרָתָם certainly could fit the king well, although, on the other hand, since the Elamites were famed as archers (Isa. 22.6) the 'bow' in a literal sense could also be intended here.[18] {119}

The Egyptian kings sometimes bore the title of 'He who repels the Nine Bows'[19] where the 'Nine Bows' represent traditional foes of Egypt. It seems, then, that this may be another title of royal dignity and power, however it is applied. However, that military leadership of some sort is implied is suggested by the parallelism, by which קֶשֶׁת מִלְחָמָה is parallel to כָּל־נוֹגֵשׂ.

The use of this latter term is interesting, since it nearly always occurs in

18. It is possible, however, that the identification of the Elamites with archery had become almost a conventional phrase. It is interesting to observe as early as the Sumerian King List a reference to one, En-men-barage-si, who 'carried away as spoil the "weapon" of Elam' (*ANET*: 265).

19. See, e.g., *The Legend of the Possessed Princes* (*ANET*: 1969: 29ff.), where it is apparently used of Ramses II, but in reality of Thut-mose IV. Later he is addressed by the messenger of the Prince of Bekhten as 'O Re of the Nine Bows'. With this may be compared line 50 of the Merneptah Stele, 'Not one lifts his head among the Nine Bows'.

a pejorative sense. Particularly does it figure in Exodus in describing the treatment of the Israelites by their Egyptian taskmasters (e.g. Exod. 3.7; 5.6, 10, 13, 14, etc.). The word has already occurred in 9.8 in the promise that the people shall never again be oppressed by a conqueror. The suggestion would seem to be that, not only will the deliverance from captivity in Egypt be repeated in the renewed deliverance of the people, but that the people of God will know a reversal of roles. That which their traditional persecutors have been to them throughout their history, they will in turn become to them. An almost exactly similar development of thought is seen in Isa. 14.1f. God will take vengeance on his enemies by empowering his people to subdue them, and thus the recurring theme of the old Enthronement Psalms will be realized (e.g. Pss. 46.6f.; 47.2, 8f.; 97.3, 7ff.; 98.1f., etc.).

In this connection it is tempting to see significance even in the יַחְדָּו. For, more than once, the enemies of Yahweh are spoken of as concerting their attacks *together* (e.g. Pss. 2.2; 74.8; 133.5, etc.). It would be a nice twist of ironic fate {120} if now, it is being said, the people of God should attack them *together*. But there is a more specific instance where this word has already been used in a promise of restoration. In Jer. 3.18, in a promise of restoration of the people of God to Jerusalem following the promise of v. 15, 'I will give you shepherds after my own heart', and that of v. 17, that 'all nations shall gather' to Jerusalem when it has become his throne, we read, 'In those days the House of Judah shall join the House of Israel and together (יַחְדָּו) they shall come from the land of the North to the land that I gave your fathers for a heritage'. Of course this is probably later than Jeremiah himself, but it is remarkably akin to the outlook of Zech. 10.3-12 which goes on to speak (v. 6) of the return of the Houses of Judah and Israel together.

It would seem, then, that what is being promised in v. 4 is leadership of Yahweh's own provision, by which the people will not only be nurtured like a flock but empowered to become the agents in the holy war against God's adversaries, as v. 5 makes plain. The promises of Second Isaiah (cf. Isa. 41.8-16; 51.21-23), themselves reflecting the terminology and ideology of the Enthronement Psalms, will be realized by a like gathering of the people from exile (vv. 6, 8ff.) in what is also described as a second Exodus.[20]

---

20. Reading in v. 11 the much-favoured בְּיָם מִצְרַיִם for בַּיָּם צָרָה, an emendation rendered plausible by: (a) the reference to Egypt in the context; (b) the parallel phrase כֹּל מְצוּלֹות יְאֹר; and (c) the likelihood of haplography where a final and initial מ stood next to each other.

We must now return to the two critical problems whose consideration was deferred earlier. Seeing that what is promised is leadership, how is the מִמֶּנּוּ to be {121} understood? It has been suggested that Jer. 30.21 is in view here:[21]

> Their prince shall be one of themselves,
> their ruler shall come forth from their midst,

or even Isa. 11.1[22] There shall come forth a shoot from the stump of Jesse, in which case either the 'flock' or 'Judah' is in mind.

But this in turn raises the question whether the reference to Judah is secondary. This would appear to be the more likely. For the emphasis in the text is on the transformation of the people as a whole (vv. 6f.) and particularly upon their unity, in a manner which suggests that Israel and Judah will again be joining forces. It is possible, then, we should see the whole community inheriting a kind of democratized charismatic leadership, as the NEB renders this. Perhaps the וְיָחַד of v. 4 supports this, as does the reference in v. 3 to the whole community of Judah becoming his 'warhorse' in the way the earlier prophets had been seen to be. But whatever it is, it is provided by Yahweh. Indeed, this is the point of the contrast with the previous reference to inadequate leadership. So it is not so much on the leadership as such that the emphasis falls. It is rather on the activity of Yahweh and the effect on the people. It is much more understandable that a later hand, seeing the Messianic connotation possible in these descriptions of {122} leadership, should, in the light of Gen. 49.10, and the general Davidic and Messianic hopes attached to Judah (cf. Mic. 5.2; Isa. 11.1, etc.) introduce the name of Judah as the only possible source of such leadership. Yet a feature of these chapters is the close unity of North and South (cf. Zech. 9.10; 10.6). If this is so, then the gloss represents an early re-interpretation of this original verse along Davidic lines as we have in Micah.

Our conclusion would be, therefore, that the מִמֶּנּוּ is ambiguous, and possibly, deliberately so. The promise of Jer. 30.21 is to be fulfilled, but there is no doubt from whom all true leadership really comes, and of whose act of final salvation its appearance is a sign. It comes from him and so מִמֶּנּוּ is primarily to be understood.[23]

---

21. By Elliger (1964: 156); Jones (1962a: 143).

22. By Jones (1962a: 143).

23. The LXX translators appear to have found difficulty with this verse, but appear to have started with something near the MT. The reference to Judah is there in v. 3. פֶּנָּה

The remainder of the section continues to connect with earlier themes of prophecy but there is space only to discuss one or two of the more significant.

The 'I will answer them' (which *BHS* deletes) recalls the promise of Jer. 33.3, 'Call to me, and I will answer you', again from a later expansion of the prophet's work, which goes on to speak of a restoration of Jerusalem, and the provision by Yahweh of a representative both of the Davidic line and of the Levitical order of priesthood.

Of course, the idea of the saving work of God as an 'answer' to the lament of the people is neither new nor {123} unique. It is found in Deutero-Isaiah. For example, in Isa. 41.17 occurs the promise:

> When the poor and needy seek water and there is none, and their tongue is parched with thirst, I the Lord will answer them (אֲנִי יְהוָה אֶעֱנֵם),

which can be compared with Zech. 10.6 כִּי אֲנִי יְהוָה אֱלֹהֵיהֶם וְאֶעֱנֵם. The Isaiah passage is preceded by the promise to make his people a 'threshing-sledge' which introduces a promise of the restoration of the wilderness to fertility and plenty. In Zech. 10 the same two concepts are brought together. Ephraim will become like a mighty warrior and their hearts will be 'glad as with wine', always the sign of fertility in Canaan. In Isa. 58.9 there is the promise:

> Then you shall call, and the Lord will answer:
> You shall cry, and he will say, 'Here I am',

which comes within the context of a call to the true fasting of ethical behaviour. Finally, in Trito-Isaiah there occurs the (late) near apocalyptic picture of salvation in ch. 65 of the re-creation of Jerusalem as 'A rejoicing', of the place of vineyards and the eating of their fruits, culminating in the promise,

---

appears to have been linked (erroneously) with the root פנה, 'to turn', and therefore 'to turn and look', giving καὶ ἐξ αὐτοῦ ἐπέβλεψεν. The τόξον ἐν θυμῷ clearly represents קֶשֶׁת מִלְחָמָה and πᾶς ὁ ἐξελαύνων ἐν τῷ αὐτῷ the כָּל־נוֹגֵשׂ. But καὶ ἐξ αὐτοῦ ἔταξεν is more difficult. Did they fail to recognize יָתֵד as a metaphorical reference? In the Eliashib passage, LXX has ἄρχοντα for יָתֵד (Isa. 42.23) although where the word stands literally for a tent peg it is uniformly rendered by πάσσαλος (e.g. Judg. 4.21), as also is a peg for hanging things on (ef. Ezek. 15.3). Or did they read the root עָר, which is translated by τάσσειν in Exod. 29.43 and 2 Sam. 25, either from a failure to grasp the metaphorical usage, or because they had a text which read root הַיֵּעֵר? This would be an unusual occurrence and would indicate a process of interpretation towards a more specifically 'messianic' type figure.

> Before they call I will answer,
> while they are yet speaking I will hear (v. 24).

In this connection, the reference in Zech. 10.7 to Ephraim by name, may be an allusion to the play on the word found in 'the Blessing of Jacob' in Gen. 49. Joseph will indeed become fruitful as his name suggests. Not only, however, does v. 6 echo promises of salvation from Second {124} and Third Isaiah, but it affords a remarkable reversal of the judgment of Zech. 7.13.

Verse 7, as has been said, is closely akin to 9.15, and answers to the promise of 10.5. There is hardly need to follow the literalism of Gaide (1968: 92-93) who takes the reference to children as implying that not the present, but a future generation will return. Surely it may equally well be taken as a renewal of the terms of God's blessing which was never to the individual recipients alone, but to 'children's children' as a Psalm like 128 makes clear. This aspect of the promise had already been taken up in Ezek. 37.25, where it is said,

> They shall dwell in the land...that I gave to Jacob: they and their children's children shall dwell there for ever...

and this itself was set in the context of the promise of the 'one shepherd' they all should have over them, namely, the Davidic king.

But once more there is a striking echo of Proto-Zechariah here. In Zech. 8.5, in the idyllic picture of the restored Jerusalem, it is said, 'And the streets of the city shall be full of boys and girls playing in its streets'. The picture is completed there also with a restoration of the people from the 'east country' and the 'west country' and the vine yielding its fruit. Again it seems there is a line of continuity between the kind of re-echoing {125} of earlier prophetic material to be found in Proto- and Deutero-Zechariah.

The יְזְכְּרוּנִי in v. 9 is significant. Gaide is surely right when he says,

> Se souvenir de YHWH est une expression qui a dans la Bible un sense très fort. Ce n'est pas un vain souvenir. C'est toute une conversion profonde, avec tout ce que cela implique de foi en YHWH, d'obéissance à ses commandements, d'action de grâces pour ses bienfaits.[24]

---

24. Gaide (1968: 92), and see references cited in footnote. Also M. Saebø (1969: 217n). A detailed analysis of the root זכר in the Old Testament, and an examination of its theological development is carried out by B.S. Childs (1962). In Deuteronomy it means, 'Present Israel has not been cut off from redemption history, but she encounters the same covenant God through a living tradition' (Childs 1962: 55). For Second Isaiah, '...Israel's memory is an active response in faith which links her to the

It corresponds to Yahweh's 'answering' them. Whether or not the passage cited above in Isa. 58.9 was in the prophet's mind, with its context of true fasting marking a true penitence before Yahweh, the whole concept of a 'call' to Yahweh which he 'answers' within prophetic liturgy suggests that such a response alone is appropriate to those who are suffering his judgments. In which case we have here some idea of Ezekiel's view of a 'regeneration' of the people (see esp. Ezek. 36.24f.) as the inward reality of Yahweh's work of which the outward expression and result is the return to their own land. And the context of this passage suggests, as does Ezekiel, that this is something which is likely to happen when the worthless leaders who led them astray from making a true response to Yahweh are replaced by leadership of Yahweh's own appointing.

The פְּדִיתִים of v. 8 (although excised by *BHK*, presumably on metrical grounds) serves to introduce another concept of the restorative work of God already {126} found in Second Isaiah, namely, the idea of a new, or second Exodus. It is a word frequently associated with the Exodus (e.g. Deut. 7.8; 13.6, Mic. 6.4; Ps. 78.42, etc.) and occurs in Second Isaiah in a similar way, notably in Isa. 51.11, where following a reference to the Exodus in terms of Yahweh's victory over Rahab in the drying up of the waters, it continues,

> And the ransomed of the Lord (וּפְדוּיֵי יְהוָה)
> shall return and come to Zion with singing.

That this idea is present to the writer of the passage is suggested by v. 11, which says, 'and the waves of the sea shall be smitten and all the depths of the Nile dried up'.[25] The mention of Assyria and Egypt in particular has been much discussed. Elliger's suggestion that the reference here is to the Ptolemies and Seleucids is precarious, showing his constant tendency to pin-point these oracles in historical events, a hazardous undertaking in view of our lack of knowledge of the details of the period. It could be, of course, that they are mentioned as 'traditional' and therefore 'typical' historical oppressors of the people of God. Mitchell (1912: 293) cites

redemptive action of God's entrance into history' (p. 59). With Ezekiel it means, 'A recognition or discernment which turns one towards God' (p. 60). In the Complaint Psalms, 'Israel encounters again through the medium of her memory the God of the past' (pp. 64f.). Childs has been criticized by Sawyer (1972: 32n) for drawing the semantic field for this study too narrowly.

25. Assuming that the generally accepted emendation of v. 11a to read וְעָבְרוּ יָם־מִצְרַיִם is plausible; cf. {120} now p. 83 n. 20 above. So LXX.

instances, gathered both by himself and by Stade where Assyria and Baby-
lonia may be used, not literally, but to designate the ruling world power of
the time. Certainly Assyria was the enemy of the old Northern kingdom
and perhaps the location of these nations in North and South {127} is
significant for the idea of the eventual re-unification of both the kingdoms.
Ackroyd's suggestion that their use is influenced by Isa. 52.4 would be
wholly in keeping with the kind of allusive echoes of earlier prophetic
material which characterizes this passage. It is, in any event, one further
confident assertion that all who oppress the people of God, and so oppose
Yahweh himself, will be finally defeated.

Some interest attaches to the uncertain word in v. 9, וְאֶזְרָעֵם. The waw
has to be read in an adversative sense, although one would normally
expect it then to be pointed וְ. More significant, however, is that the root
זרע does not appear to be used of 'scattering' people, but only of sowing.
For this meaning, זרה is regularly employed. Many therefore emend to
וְאֶזְרֵם. The LXX does not help much here. It has σπερῶ αὐτοὺς ἐν λαοῖς.
Σπείρω, at least in Classical Greek, carries the double sense of 'sow' as
well as 'scatter'. It can be used in this latter sense of people.[26] It is difficult
to believe that the prophet would speak of Yahweh 'sowing' his people
'among the nations'. We must either therefore assume that this is an
isolated use of זרע or accept the emendation. There is a possible echo from
Proto-Zechariah to strengthen this last impression. In 2.4 (1.21), in the
vision of the four horns, Zechariah is told that they represent 'the horns
which scattered Judah (אֲשֶׁר־זֵרוּ אֶת־יְהוּדָה)... {128} and they have come to
terrify them, to cast down the horns of the nations who lifted up their
horns against the land of Judah to scatter it (לְזָרוֹתָהּ)'. It is possible that
this promise of deliverance by the defeat of the nations who have held
them captive is being recalled here. Again, in 7.9-14, reference is being
made to the disobedience of their fathers to the voice of God which came
to them through the prophets. For this reason, it is said, 'I scattered them
with a whirlwind (סער) among all the nations which they had not known.
Thus the land they left was desolate, so that no one went to and fro, and
the pleasant land was made desolate.' Again, it is possible that this is
being recalled by way of contrast. 'Though I scattered them [because they
"forgot" me] now in far countries they shall remember me'—and so the
way for their return shall be opened.

---

26. E.g. Thucydides II.27, where it is said of the Aeginaetae who were expelled
from their island by the Athenians, οἱ δ' ἐσπάρησαν κάτα τὴν ἄλλην Ἑλλάδα.

This return is to be 'to the land of Gilead and to Lebanon'. The mention of these two areas has also proved puzzling. It has been suggested by Gaide and Horst that it is because they will be so numerous that there will not be room for them all in their former territories. Saebø suggests they represented the extent of David's boundaries which will be re-occupied in a new 'golden' age. It has also been pointed out that Gilead was the first area to know the ravages of the Assyrians (2 Kgs 15.29) although this would not explain the {129} mention of Lebanon.

Such suggestions may be too literal. Both were famed for their wealth and beauty of natural resources: Lebanon, of course, for its cedars, but Gilead also.[27] Jeremiah records an instance where these two very place names could be used metaphorically. Yahweh addresses the king of Judah:

> You are as Gilead to me, as the summit of Lebanon, yet surely I will make you a desert, an uninhabited city (Jer. 22.6).

Now this judgment is to be reversed. The land and the returned community are to be rescued from desolation and made as Gilead and Lebanon in Yahweh's sight again. The beauty and fertility of the land will be such, and perhaps even the character of the whole community so different from that of the old Judean kings, that it can be described as Gilead and Lebanon again. As in Zech. 7–8 the restoration of the people will be accompanied by the blessing of the land.

We have included 11.1-3 with 10.3-12 since it is closely related to it. The use of a taunt-song or dirge by the earlier prophets to enforce their warning of judgment on the enemies of Yahweh is often encountered.[28] This lament for the spoiled glory of Lebanon may have been placed after 10.3-12 on the 'catchword' principle, following the mention of Lebanon in 10.10, but its position is wholly fitting. The idea of the giant trees of {130} Lebanon, or elsewhere, as symbols of human might and pride, so often opposed to the spirit of humble dependence on Yahweh, occurs elsewhere in the Old Testament.[29] This then falls naturally after the promise of salvation for Israel and Judah. It is the negative counterpart to Yahweh's act of deliverance for his people. His judgment will fall on their foes since they oppose his purpose in opposing his people. But if our earlier suggestion is correct that this too echoes thoughts and images from the same parts of

---

27. See Num. 32.1ff.; Song 4.1; Jer. 8.22; 50.19.
28. E.g. Amos 5.2; Isa. 14.4-20; Jer. 6.1-5.
29. Judg. 9.15; Ps. 29.5; Isa. 2.13; Jer. 22.7; Ezek. 17.3.

Jeremiah which inspired the words against the false shepherds,[30] its position here is the more appropriate.

In summary, then, we can say that 10.3–11.3, whether it is itself a collection of originally independent oracles or not, now forms a whole, related in general theme as an oracle of salvation and deliverance for the people of God. It is closely akin to 9.11-15, which it echoes at several points. It is related to 10.1f. in that it builds on the pastoral call to the people who were being led astray by false leaders, and promises, as part of the act of Yahweh's deliverance, the provision of leaders of his choice. It is possible that by 'shepherds' are meant, not only military leaders in the narrower sense, but all who exercised responsibility, including prophets, priests and others. This promise to substitute the false leadership by that of divine appointment owes much in its terminology and ideas {131} to the books of Jeremiah and Ezekiel and, like them, sees such appointment as an eschatological sign of the final act of salvation. This may suggest that it is their own leaders, and not foreign rulers, which are being spoken of. Details of this final act of salvation, the strengthening of the people for victory over their former persecutors, the reunion of the old Northern and Southern kingdoms, the homecoming of the dispersed, the fertility of the land, the inward reformation of the people, echo in both language and concept, earlier prophetic material, especially that from Jeremiah, Second Isaiah and Ezekiel. Some striking similarity of thought in particular to that of the circles amongst whom the words and traditions of Jeremiah received expansion, can be detected. A continued link with the thought of Proto-Zechariah is apparent in the promise of divinely-appointed leadership, the destruction by the power of Yahweh of those who opposed his people, perhaps the avenging horsemen who execute Yahweh's will, the joy of the returning exiles extending even to their children, the fertility of the land with its vineyards, the reversal of the 'scattering' and the picture of the restored community 'walking' in the name of Yahweh (v. 12; cf. Zech. 8.21).

What is missing from 10.3–11.3 as from 9.11-15 is any thought of the universalism of Proto-Zechariah or of 9.7, 9f. The 'enemies' are there merely to be worsted. This may be coincidence or may be due to the fact that a nucleus of an originally independent oracle has been {132} 'taken over' as it were. There is a possible hint in 9.11 that the suffering undergone by the people, or the group from which the oracle finally came, may

---

30. See pp. {106-107}, above.

have had something of the vicarious value for others that the Servant's suffering had. But such an idea is not pursued or given prominence here at all.

This raises the question of the relation of this section to the rest of chs. 9–10. Taken together, these seem to have been a collection of eschatological prophecies which inner differences and disparities may indicate are of diverse origin. Some are more militarist, others more 'pacifist' in tendency; some are 'universalist', some more nationalistic in outlook; some stress the immediate presence of Yahweh himself in the future, others suggest that his rule will be exercised through some human leadership.

Yet there are certain signs to suggest that this material has been shaped and given its final form in one broad circle of tradition. Much of it is evocative of earlier biblical material and leans heavily upon material in the earlier major prophetic collections. This argues for a post-exilic milieu for this final shaping. In particular, emphases and themes of the Proto-Zechariah tradition appear persistently throughout, suggesting that even though that material has been subject to some degree of modification and re-interpretation, a circle has been influenced by that tradition and stands within {133} its viewpoint and line of development. Especially do the hopes attaching to Zerubbabel and Joshua appear to have been modified. It continues to suggest a Zechariah 'school' in the same way that 'Second Isaiah' is felt to be representative of an Isaiah 'school'.

If anything distinctive of such a circle could be known, does it lie along the line of the critical attitude towards the official leadership which, we have suggested, is another feature which may be found throughout this material? Several indications are there to suggest that they viewed this leadership as corrupt and that it had a corrupting influence on the life of the whole community, necessitating the emergence of a new type of leadership as expressed in 9.9f. Such new leadership is spoken of in rather more traditional terms in 10.4, but here the emphasis appears to fall on the fact that it will be of Yahweh's provision and appointing. Possibly, the concept of such leadership has been to some extent 'democratized', although it has been less modified than in 9.9f. where a much more advanced view of leadership is expressed. There is no strongly Davidic Messianic hope of the earlier type apparent in these oracles anywhere. This negative attitude to existing leadership could also be responsible for the pastoral entreaty of 10.1f., which perhaps characterized some (early?) stage of the ministry of the prophet was behind this traditio-circle. He still appears to have some hope of being able to summon his fellow Judeans to

{134} the true worship of Yahweh by abandoning worship which he sees as little better than idolatry. Does all this suggest a traditio-circle of the covenant, dissenter type within the Judaism of their day, who saw themselves as upholders and guardians of the true prophetic tradition of the past, which they now faithfully expound in the light of the circumstances of the day and the belief that the final act of salvation to which those traditions pointed is now about to be fulfilled? This would explain the heavy dependence on earlier prophetic material in these chapters. Chapters 9–10 might well have formed a collection of the eschatological hymns of such a group. A great deal depends on their relation with chs. 11ff., to the examination of which we now turn. {135}

Chapter 6

ZECHARIAH 11.4-17

There are indications of an elaborate history of growth and re-working of this text to which must be, in part at least, attributed the difficulties of interpretation which commentators have found. But, beyond these, it has proved difficult to know how this narrative is to be understood. It has often been interpreted historically. It is well known that Kremer (1930: 83) could cite in 1930 no fewer than 30 different interpretations of the three shepherds in v. 8a. It is sometimes overlooked that he also added, 'Ich bemerke jedoch, dass diese Übersicht noch nicht erschöpfend ist und dass nicht die Namen aller Vertreter der jeweiligen Deutung in Klammern beigegefügt wurden'. A recent example of such interpretation is that of D.R. Jones (1962a: 150) who finds here an allusion to an episode between 516 and 445 BC in the ministry of a prophet who worked amongst Israelites of the northern Dispersion at that time in and around Damascus.[1] Most commentators who have found historical allusions here assign them to the time of the Maccabees, or more generally to the rivalry between the Ptolemies and the Seleucids although, as we shall see, some have found reference to the Samaritan schism. In addition, as Kremer has shown, both Jewish and Christian exegetes have treated it Messianically and eschatologically.

More recently, there has been a turning away from a purely historical explanation. Some have suggested that {136} it should be taken in an allegorical sense. So R.C. Dentan (1956: 1103) speaks of it as 'an allegory of God's attempt to rule an oppressed but still refractory people'. While

---

1.   See his introductory remarks (Jones 1962a: 116-19). More recently, Otzen (1964: 146ff.) has suggested that the reference is to Saul, David and Solomon. He finds this passage (which he dates in the period of the exile) to show a strongly anti-monarchic outlook. The contrast between this and the more favourable view of monarchy in chs. 9–10 is due to the fact that they stemmed from the time of Josiah, but this after the time of Zedekiah, to whom reference is made in vv. 15ff.

the section is modeled on the old narratives of prophetic acts of symbolism, this has by this time become only a 'literary device'. Horst (1964: 251) also denies that these actions were ever undertaken. We have to do here not with prophetic symbolism but with written allegory. Ackroyd (1962a: 653) agrees that 'the nature of the symbolic act he is instructed to carry out is such that it is impossible to be sure how far it could actually be carried out'. It is, perhaps, rather to be regarded as literary device. Elliger (1964: 160) finds that the passage represents an example of the 'Gattung' of prophetic symbolism which, however, has by this time become only a literary form, a matter of words rather than of actions. The style has become mixed with allegory. This, however, is not due to the original writer but to a 'later hand'. The aim of the earlier symbolism was to give a theological 'apologia' for the schism between the Samaritans and Jews. As we shall see, other commentators have found such an allusion here.[2]

On the other hand, Saebø believes that this is not purely imitative, literary device, but a narrative which, at least in its core, rested on an actual deed of prophetic symbolism.

Many commentators beside Saebø, point to the influence of earlier prophetic material on the form of the account of {137} this action, and its interpretation, have taken. Passages such as Ezek. 37.15ff. and 34, as well as more general examples of acts of prophetic symbolism are cited, and to these we shall be giving more detailed attention in our own examination of the passage.

Not only the complicated process of growth of the text, to which text-, form-, and traditio-critical methods have alike pointed, but also the obscure nature of the original passage which has been subjected to such interpretative comments, combine alike to justify Gaide's (1968: 107) comment on this section: 'L'interprétation de Za. 11.4-17 est l'une des difficultés les plus célèbres de la Bible'.

Our own examination of the section may start from the observation that any reader must immediately be impressed by the difference between this

---

2. Elliger (1964: 164). Ackroyd (1962a: 654) allows that the Samaritan schism may have been an appropriate occasion for this breach between north and south, but adds cautiously, that the allusions are too obscure to justify a dogmatic statement. Horst follows Elliger here (1964: 253). Gaide (1968: 111) also supports this view; Saebø (1969: 250ff.) takes the reference as possibly a later interpretation of the original action. Others, however, have attributed it either to the Maccabaean risings (so most older commentators) or to the time of the Ptolemies and Seleucid rivalries (so Mitchell 1912: 310f.; Dentan 1956: 1102f.).

section and the oracles which have preceded it in chs. 9–10. There the atmosphere has been strongly optimistic; they confidently assert the imminence of Yahweh's final act of salvation; the people of Zion are called upon to rejoice; the dispersed of both the former kingdoms of Judah and Israel are to be brought back and re-united; the scattered remnants of the nation will 'remember' Yahweh; the wonders of the Exodus are to be repeated. It is true that a cautionary note has been sounded in 10.1f. which we have suggested is to be understood as a pastoral call to the people as a whole, indicating, perhaps, at least the tendency to lapse back into the old ways of idolatry. Further, there has {138} been the anger expressed against the so-called 'false shepherds' of the people in 10.3, leading to the promise of the provision of other leadership, and other indications of a negative attitude to the leadership of the community in general. Yet, even so, the emphasis falls there upon the renewing work of Yahweh. In this section, however, at least as it stands now, the tone appears to be almost wholly pessimistic. It appears to contain, not only another attack upon the shepherds, but to speak also of the abandonment of the people to their fate of judgment, symbolized by the breaking of the two staves, the one signifying God's favour to the people and the other the unity of Judah and Israel.

It has been this abrupt appearance of contradiction which has been the despair of so many commentators, and has led so many to assign these chapters to a multiplicity of authors, and a variety of sources.[3]

3.   So Eissfeldt (1965: 440), having seen two booklets in 9–11 and 12–14, goes on to say that whether this division 'is sufficient may indeed be doubted. There is in fact little relationship between the prophecies of 9.1–11.3 and the parable of 11.4-17...' Fohrer (1970: 468) also, dividing chs. 9–11 and 12–14 as between Deutero- and Trito-Zechariah, describes the former as 'a collection of sayings of several unknown prophets', agreeing substantially with the view of Oesterley and Robinson (1958). G.W. Anderson (1959: 167) says, 'It may well be that the authorship of these chapters is still more diverse'. Horst (1964: 213) follows Kuenen, Baudisson, Steurnagel and Kraeling in believing that in these chapters a collection of earlier, pre-exilic oracles has received later additions in the Hellenistic period. Of this section in particular he says, 'Der Abschnitt 11.4-17, 13.7-9, bestehend aus einem Kern, einer Erweiterung und Spruchbeifügungen stellt sich somit als ein von anderer Hand stammender Anhang zu 9.1-11.3 dar'. Kuhl (1961: 225) also finds the mixture of prophetic words and oracles indicates 'that we are here dealing with pre-exilic portions which have subsequently been transferred by Deutero-Zechariah to his own contemporary conditions and to suit his purpose'. He goes on to remark that this was the kind of stealing of the דְּבָרִים of other prophets denounced by Jeremiah. In a more general way, Gelin (1951: 23) speaks of a 'lien assez lâche' in these chapters, Robert (1935: 515) spoke of a succession of pieces with no progression, and Touzard (1917: 128) of a collection of oracles of very

In addition to difference of tone and atmosphere, there is the marked difference of the style and character of this section. For the first time, apparently, the 'I' of the prophet's own person intrudes. The type of material here is less that of the preceding oracles and has more in kin with the narratives of acts of prophetic symbolism in earlier prophetic material, especially that found in Ezek. 37.15-28, although of course the differences between the two should not be minimized. There appears to be also some general similarity, at least, to the {139} 'Night Visions' of Proto-Zechariah, also recorded in the first person. The similarity is most marked perhaps with the last of these in 6.9-14, in which Zechariah is also directed to take symbolic action in having the silver and gold brought by three returned exiles smelted down to make crowns for Joshua (and Zerubbabel?) which are to be placed in the Temple. Such general similarity may be recognized without necessarily accepting Saebø's (1969: 252) suggestion that Zechariah was the prophet who originally carried out the action recorded in 11.4-17.

We must note first that the section is introduced by a formula otherwise seldom met in other Old Testament prophetic literature: כֹּה אָמַר יְהוָה אֱלֹהָי.

In the LXX this reads, τάδε λέγει κύριος παντοκράτωρ, the familiar rendering of יְהוָה צְבָאוֹת. However, this need mean no more than that the term אֱלֹהָי struck the translators as strange in this context.[4]

The word does occur often in the Old Testament of course, but generally in certain well-defined categories. It is used often in the language of prayer and devotion where the special relationship of the worshipper to God is naturally being emphasized. Hence its frequent usage in the Psalms (e.g. Pss. 3.8 [7]; 7.2 [1]; 13.4 [3], etc.), and in such passages as the Song of David (2 Sam. 22.7, 22, 30), the prayers of Solomon (e.g. 1 Kgs 3.7; 5.17; 8.27, etc.), of Ezra (e.g. Ezra 7.28; 9.5), Nehemiah (e.g. Neh. 5.19; 6.14; 13.29, etc.), and many others (e.g. 1 Kgs 17.21; Isa. 25.1; Jer. 31.18; Dan.

diverse types. These last were cited by P. Lamarche (1961) who, on the contrary, finds a tightly knit structure throughout these chapters which he finds convincing demonstration of their unity of design and authorship. Otzen (1964: *passim*) also finds a closely knit (but different) structure in chs. 9–10, which he attributes to the time of Josiah. Chapter 11 (the Shepherd Allegory) he assigns to the Judean exile and finds it to reflect a Deuteronomic anti-royalist point of view. 12.1–13.6 comes also from the time of the exile, while ch. 14 reflects a later apocalyptic outlook (see especially the Danish conclusion, Otzen 1964: 273ff.).

4. P.R. Ackroyd (1962a: 653), suggests that in line with vv. 13a and 15 the original reading might have been 'The Lord said unto me...' But note its reappearance in 14.5.

9.9, etc.). But there is another important group of occasions when the term is used, {140} as, for example, when the speaker is setting his own relationship with Yahweh *over against* that of his hearers. Thus Balaam to Balak says that, however much the king might pay him, 'I could not go beyond the command of the Lord *my* God' (Num. 22.18). Joshua condemns the foreign Gibeonites to be servants 'for the house of *my* God' (Josh. 9.23). David uses the term in speaking to the Jebusite, Araunah (2 Sam. 24.24), Solomon to Hiram of Tyre (1 Kgs 5.17), and perhaps Isaiah's use of the term to the faithless Ahaz should be seen in this light also (Isa. 7.13). A similarly ironic use of the term may be found in Joel 1.13 where the prophet seems to draw a distinction between his relationship to God and that of the priests whom he is apparently charging with neglect of duty, or at least, with lack of penitential zeal.

> Gird on sackcloth and lament, O priests,
> Wail, O ministers of the altar,
> Go in, pass the night in sackcloth,
> O ministers of *my* God!

The contrast is drawn more sharply in the following couplet:

> Because cereal offering and drink offering
> are withheld from the house of *your* God.[5]

Of this, J.A. Thompson (1956: 740), says, 'The priests, *from whom the prophet seems to distinguish himself*, are summoned to lament' (emphasis mine).

So we are entitled to ask whether its use in Zech. 11.4 in the introduction to this section suggests that the prophet is setting himself over against his hearers. Since the passage appears to be charged with tension and conflict it would hardly be surprising. If that is so, we have {141} further to ask, against whom is he setting himself and his own relationship with God?

There remain two important uses of the term not so far considered, with both of which Moses is concerned. The first occurs in Deut. 4.5 where Moses, addressing the Israelites, says, 'Behold, I have taught you statutes and ordinances, as the Lord my God commanded me'. This may be taken as a typical instance of the kind of usage we have discussed already, where the speaker's relationship to God is being set over against that of his hearers. There can be little doubt that Moses was regarded as standing in a special relationship to God (e.g. Exod. 19.9; 20.19; 24.2; 33.9, 17-23,

---

5.   It should be noted that J.A. Bewer (1911: 85) finds this couplet to be secondary.

etc.), an impression which gains strength from the other passages which need to be considered here. In Deut. 18.16 the phrase occurs on the lips of the people, but by way of repudiation as it were, or rather, by way of transferring the responsibility of this special relationship to Moses, a reference back to their words in Exod. 20.19:

> The Lord your God will raise up for you a prophet like me from among you, from your brethren—him you shall heed—just as you desired of the Lord your God at Horeb on the day of the assembly, when you said, 'Let me not hear again the voice of the Lord my God, or see this great fire any more, lest I die'.

And such a sentiment here receives divine approval and sanction, for it is followed by the statement,

> They have rightly said all that they have spoken. I will raise up for them a prophet like you...and I will put my words in his mouth, and he shall speak to them all that I command him. {142}

There follows the threat that whoever fails to obey the word of God which he speaks through such a prophet will be answerable to God, and so is provided also a test by which the people may examine whether what he speaks is an authentic word of Yahweh or not. The (somewhat unsatis-factory) test of the word's fulfillment is what is given.

It has been the subject of much discussion as to exactly what was being promised here; whether this is an eschatological promise of one specific figure to come, as understood, for example, in the later Jewish hope of the coming of Elijah,[6] or whether it is seen as legitimizing the succession of prophets as such.[7] But its use is such as to set the bearer of the prophetic office over against the false prophets and, indeed, to establish him as one who stands in a special relationship to Yahweh compared with the people as a whole, a relationship which at once authorizes his message and clothes it with divine sanction and power.[8]

The question arises, then, whether the use of this strange opening

---

6. See Mal. 4.5; Mt. 11.14; 17.10-13; Jn 1.21. For a treatment of this theme in Jewish literature, see Strack and Billerbeck (1922–28: 779-98).

7. For a discussion, see von Rad (1966: 124); also Kraus (1966: 106ff.). Kraus sees it as referring to the specific role of a mediator of the covenant whose task was to proclaim and expound the law. He has been followed, *inter alia*, by E.W. Nicholson (1967: 76-77).

8. Cf. Jer. 23.18, 21f., where the relationship of the prophet to Yahweh is made the test of his authenticity.

formula to the prophetic oracle, related as it is to a most unusual act, or series of acts, is deliberate: that, in effect, the prophet is setting himself over and against others, whose words and deeds in his view had no such divine sanction or authority. But if this is so, we have further to ask, Who are these from whom he distinguishes himself so sharply?

Since v. 6 is usually held to be intrusive with its {143} reference to judgment on 'the inhabitants of the land', and his ire tends to be directed against the shepherds who have no pity for their flock, and for the 'traders'[9] who oppress them (the two groups are very closely related as comparison between vv. 5, 7, 11 shows, indeed, if the waw of v. 5 were taken as *explicative* they could be regarded as related groups), it has often been supposed that it is against the leaders of the community that he inveighs, while feeling pity and concern for the community as a whole.[10] But here, consideration of the strange description of the flock as צֹאן הַהֲרֵגָה needs to be considered. The phrase does not occur exactly in this way elsewhere. Indeed, the noun הַהֲרֵגָה occurs only five times in the Old Testament, three times in Jeremiah and twice in this chapter. This only makes its near parallel in Jer. 12.3 the more striking. Jeremiah 12.1-6 is one of the

---

9. Following the customary redistribution of the consonantal text in v. 7 of the לִכְנַעֲנֵיּ to לָכֵן עֲנִיֵּי.

10. P.R. Ackroyd points to the possibility that the last phrase of v. 5 suggests, by contrast, that their new shepherd is to be a good one, and 'so the gloomy note of v. 6 is intrusive'. But he also allows that the singular verb of v. 5 לֹא יַחְמֹל (usually emended to a plural) could suggest that the shepherd they employ, now represented by the prophet, will not spare them. The reference to 'traders' has been variously estimated. H.G. Mitchell (1912: 303) believes it denotes those who collected taxes under the Ptolemies, that is, fellow-Jews who oppress their own people for a foreign ruler. D.R. Jones (1962a: 151) takes it as a reference to the foreign rulers who buy and sell them with impunity while their own leaders (i.e. 'the shepherds') exercise no real pastoral care. R.C. Dentan (1956: 1103) also feels that the traders are foreign rulers, while the shepherds are their own native leaders, both groups being condemned by the prophet for being harsh and selfish. Horst (1964: 251) understands the 'sheep-dealers' as the people's upper classes and the 'shepherds' as the political and religious leaders. Gaide (1968: 107) sees the shepherds as kings and the 'merchants' as false prophets (cf. 10.1f. and 13.1-6) but also priests. Elliger (1964: 161) says it is not always clear which circle is responsible for the oppression of the sheep: a distinction is always made between 'sheep-dealers' and 'shepherds', but they are certainly not heathen since they give thanks for their profit to *Yahweh* (v. 5). Saebø (1969: 243ff.) believes that behind the oldest stratum in this pericope stands the influence of Jer. 23.1ff. and Ezek. 34.1-31 where the false shepherds are not only kings, but also royal ministers and officials.

passages which have been called the 'Confessions' of Jeremiah.[11] The prophet has been complaining to God that the wicked prosper:

> Thou plantest them, and they take root;
> they grow and bring forth fruit;
> thou art near in their mouth and far from their heart.

Yet he is convinced of the righteousness of Yahweh (v. 1) and continues,

> But thou, O LORD, knowest me;
> thou seest me, and triest my mind toward thee.
> Pull them out *like sheep for the slaughter* (כְּצֹאן לְטִבְחָה),
> and set them apart *for the day of slaughter* (לְיוֹם הֲרֵגָה). {144}

In this instance, therefore, the sheep for slaughter who are to be set aside for the day of slaughter are the wicked within the community. Several commentators have suggested that 11.18-20 is related to this passage and that 12.6 should be read between 11.18 and 19.[12] If this is so, it is not only the wicked in general within the community who are being referred to, but more specifically those who have rejected the prophet and his message, the men of Anathoth, who may well have represented the interest of the priestly circles.[13]

The use of this phrase,[14] therefore, may suggest a prophet who saw, not

---

11.   The point drawn from this passage is not affected by the recent discussion as to the exact nature of the so-called 'Confessions' in the book of Jeremiah. The traditional understanding of them as affording insights into the inner spiritual 'autobiography' of the prophet (e.g. Skinner 1936: 201-30) has more recently been challenged by von Reventlow (1963) who sees the passages as liturgical in character, akin to the Psalms of Individual Lament, in which the 'I' is that of the community as a whole and not that of Jeremiah's own personal experiences. This view has been challenged by Bright (1970). My own view would be that it is neither necessary nor legitimate to set these views too sharply in contrast to one another.

12.   So H. Cunliffe-Jones (1966: 107); Bright (1970: 189-90) follows Peake and Cornill in placing all 12.1-6 before 11.18-23. See also J.P. Hyatt (1941: 912) and Rowley (1925–26: 217-27).

13.   J.P. Hyatt (1941: 912f.), rejects the view that Jer. 11 refers to the reaction of Jeremiah's own priestly family against his support for the reform of Josiah. He follows Volz in believing that it was the Jerusalem priesthood, working through their colleagues at Anathoth, who were behind this, incited by the attacks of Jeremiah against the Temple, the prophets and the priests at a later stage of his ministry. Such a view has much to commend it, although this interpretation of 11.18-20 turns on the literal sense of 12.6. If the latter is seen as metaphorical, the relevance to it of 11.18-20 is less obvious.

14.   The echo of the terms of the Jeremiah passage in Zech. 11, but in different

only the leadership, but much of the community as well, no doubt under the influence of their leadership, as under judgment, as shown by their rejection of the prophet and his message (v. 8b).

It is difficult to say, of course, whether v. 4 would have represented an actual call to 'pasture' (רְעֵה) the flock, and so have represented an early stage when this prophet felt a responsibility to the community at large whom he felt to be oppressed and misled by their leaders, a responsibility fulfilled in such a pastoral call as in 10.1f. If that were the case, the phrase describing the flock as 'for slaughter' must be a proleptic one, given in the light of later events. Such, for example, have some seen to be the case with the call which came to Hosea, 'Go, take to yourself a wife of harlotry'.[15] On the other hand, Isaiah could be called {145} to a ministry whose terms from the beginning were without any real glimmer of hope,[16] and it is equally possible that this prophet embarked on his ministry with scanty hopes of the community at large. Indeed, the other possibility is that the whole course of this ministry may have been simply an act of symbolism, as perhaps the parallel with the call in v. 15 might suggest, designed at once to show how the people were rejecting Yahweh in turning from the one he had commissioned to speak and act in his name.[17]

order, might be an instance of the break-up of stereotype phrases as an artistic device in biblical poetry of which E.Z. Melamed (1961: 115-44) has given many examples. Similarly, R.C. Culley (1967) where he argues that in spite of great variety introduced into their compositions by good composers of cultic songs, repeated formulae show that they do belong to the Temple personnel, as Gunkel argued, and are not to be seen as occasional poems. The recurrence of similar formulaic structures is to be explained in this way rather than by assuming 'borrowing' from one psalm to another.

15. For a full documentation of those who have taken this view, see Rowley (1956–57), later republished in Rowley (1963, see esp. 75n).

16. So Isa. 6, regarding the final line of v. 13, 'the holy seed is its stump', as interpretative comment which does not find its justification in the image of the burned-out stump left over after the felling of the tree. The phrase is generally regarded as indicative of the view-point of post-exilic Judaism, as the analogy of Ezra 9.2; Mal. 2.15 and its absence in the LXX of Isa. 6.13 suggests. See e.g. Scott (1956: 213); Mauchline (1962: 93); Whitehouse (1905: 126); Gray (1970: 111). However, the interpretative comment, if, as seems possible, it reflects a view-point from the time of post-exilic Judaism, is of interest and relevance to the present inquiry, It suggests that the emergence of a new 'remnant' from the other side of what appears to be total judgment could be, and was, envisaged. Such thoughts are not absent from these chapters, see e.g. Zech. 12.10–13.1; 13.8-9.

17. This very close relation between Yahweh and his prophet, and between the symbolism of word and deed and the act of Yahweh in bringing about that which word

We have already suggested that in these chapters the term 'shepherd' may carry with it connotations wider than purely political ones, as it appears to have done in Jeremiah and Ezekiel, and that, in any event, if, as seems possible, we are in the days of priest-rulers, any hard and fast distinction between what we should call 'secular' and 'religious' leadership would tend to be still further weakened. We need not look necessarily, therefore, for some literal act of the assumption of political power here, which in any case is hard to envisage being undertaken at whim, nor even the symbolic representation of the rule of some historical king.[18] Whether an actual ministry, or an act symbolic of one, as mentioned above, is meant, can hardly be settled at this stage of our knowledge. But that it is seen in terms which are mainly *prophetic* would seem to be suggested by the symbolic acts so characteristic of the actions of the earlier prophets. {146}

However, there is no need to set 'prophetic' in this context over against 'priestly'. Such an understanding of what is involved in the call רְעֵה need not preclude the idea that this was someone who originally had some official position within the Temple and its hierarchy as one interpretation of vv. 12f. might possibly suggest. Since the term 'shepherd' is used loosely in these chapters, it is best not to try to define the role here too closely.

If it is difficult to be precise about the nature of the 'shepherds', what of those who are described as 'traders', who 'buy and sell' the flock and 'slay' them? Again, it is difficult to know how literally this is to be taken, but the phrase is often used in prophetic literature, usually in a derogatory sense.

---

and deed designate, should cause us to be careful before dividing this passage on the grounds of that which is 'word of the prophet' and that which is 'word of Yahweh'. For a treatment of prophetic symbolism, see H. Wheeler Robinson (1927: 1ff.), and, more recently, J. Lindblom (1962: 165ff.) and G. Fohrer (1970). It is possible that in 1 Sam. 8–9, we have an exposition of this truth in narrative form.

18. As, e.g., with H.G. Mitchell (1912: 303): 'It is clear from v. 6 where the term *shepherd* is a synonym for *king*, that the command given requires the prophet to personate a king and illustrate the character of his government'. He suggests Ptolemy III as the king in question. Unless the conjunction is taken to be a use of waw explicative, v. 6 seems rather to suggest a distinction between shepherds and kings. P.R. Ackroyd (1962a: 653) says that the nature of the action is such 'that it is impossible to be sure how far it could actually be performed; it is perhaps rather to be regarded as a literary device...', a view also shared by Elliger. Gaide (1968: 111) allows for a wider kind of interpretation of the terms of the commission in suggesting that the prophet here represented Ezra who, as a kind of prophet, offered in the law a salvation from God which the people rejected. It should be noted that the kind of representation called for in 11.15 appears to be purely symbolic.

On occasions they are mentioned in a general way as being amongst those who will share in the general judgment of Yahweh, as in Isa. 24.2, where a number of groups within the community are mentioned to indicate the totality of such judgment on all alike, or again in Ezek. 7.12. But there are more specific references to the practice of buying and selling fellow Israelites as slaves, a practice referred to in Jer. 34.8-22, where the people let their slaves go free, an action understood in this passage to be in obedience to the law of Deut. 15.1, 12-15 relating to the setting free of fellow Hebrew slaves at the end of six years service. This action, apparently intended to placate Yahweh in the critical period of the Babylonian siege, was revoked when {147} the danger appeared to have been averted.[19]

Earlier still the prophet Amos had attacked those who 'sell the righteous for silver, and the needy for a pair of shoes' (2.6), a reference perhaps more to the merciless foreclosure by the wealthy on the freeholds of those who had mortgaged them to borrow money, in defiance of the covenant law (Exod. 22.25ff.) than to actual selling into slavery. Yet slavery was often the all too inevitable result of such harshness.[20]

Even as late as the time of Nehemiah there seems to have been some recrudesence of such practices, for, in a slightly enigmatic reference in Neh. 5.1-13, we hear of those who were being forced to sell their children into slavery by virtue of having had to mortgage their houses and their lands. When Nehemiah accuses the nobles and officials he says,

> We, as far as we are able, have bought back our Jewish brethren who have been sold to the nations; but you even sell your brethren that they may be sold to us! (v. 8)

The emphasis here is on the un-covenant-like treatment of fellow Jews by wealthy and unscrupulous oppressors.[21]

This boast of the 'traders' that they have become rich echoes Hos. 12.7ff.:

> A trader, in whose hands are false balances, he loves to oppress, Ephraim has said, 'Ah, but I am rich, I have gained wealth for myself'; but all his riches can never offset the guilt he has incurred.

---

19. E.W. Nicholson (1970: 63ff.) contends that this passage, as it now stands, represents the preaching of a Deuteronomic traditionalist circle to the exiles, based on an authentic word of Jeremiah. This has much to commend it and his general treatment of the prose material in the book of Jeremiah along this line deserves close attention.

20. Cf. 2 Kgs 4.1-7, and the note on this passage by Mays (1969a: 45).

21. For a discussion of the nature of these transactions, see Myers (1965: 129ff.) and also Ackroyd (1973: 28ff.).

Here is a reference presumably to the wealthy whose oppression {148} has so corrupted and affected the life of the community that the whole nation can be addressed as a false, oppressive trader, gloating in its material wealth, but in fact guilty before Yahweh. The reference to Egypt recalls the basis of the covenant which will be broken in judgment. So the buyers and sellers of Zech. 11.5 even praise Yahweh that they have become rich[22] but are clearly guilty before him, and there will follow, in the act of prophetic symbolism, the threat of the breaking of the covenant.

If this verse is an echo then of the general spirit of older prophecy, its reference to the buyers and sellers could be to the wealthy among the people of God who oppress the poor of their fellow-Israelites, and this with no obstruction from the priests and leaders (their own shepherds) who were supposed to be the guardians of this covenant religion. So corrupt is the society that such men are even invited to bless the name of Yahweh and so receive the approval of the official cultus (no doubt in return for generous support for the upkeep of the Temple and its personnel). This would be another sign of this prophet's view of the corruption of both the national life and official religious institutions of his time.

But it is most interesting to note that, in making such an attack, he would again be continuing and re-applying the teaching of Proto-Zechariah. For in Zech. 7.8-10 {149} occurs a passage on which Zech 11.4f. might almost be comment:

> Thus says the Lord of hosts, 'Render true judgments,
> show kindness and mercy each to his brother,
> do not oppress the widow, the fatherless,
> the sojourner, or the poor; and let none of
> you devise evil against his brother in your heart'.

There follows, as the text now stands, a warning of judgment if, like their pre-exilic fathers, they fail to heed just such commands. God 'scattered them with a whirlwind among all the nations which they had not known', (7.14) so that the 'pleasant land' (אֶרֶץ־חֶמְדָּה) was made desolate. Uncovenant behaviour led to the breaking of the covenant relationship with Yahweh.

In Zech. 11, the description of the state of affairs which merits judgment is also followed by the threat of judgment, in v. 6. Many consider this verse as secondary in its present position. Yet the fact remains that it reveals how some at least saw it possible to interpret the prophet's ministry with

---

22. So they can hardly be heathen, or foreigners, as Elliger (1964: 161) has noted.

its rejection by leaders and people alike. With its prediction of a judgment to fall on all the inhabitants by their being betrayed into the power of their political and religious leaders so that the whole land is crushed by them, we have only a spelling out of what appeared to be implicit in the terms of the call in v. 4, and anticipatory of the wholesale rejection which was to follow. Verse 6 may well be interpretative, but it appears to interpret in line with the original terms of the call and to represent a view which saw the whole body {150} of the nation as corrupt and under sentence of judgment.

Clearly, however, in Zech. 11.4-17 the main emphasis is meant to fall on the act(s) of prophetic symbolism. How far, if at all, are the implications of the attitude and message of the prophet suggested by the terms and basis of his call, to be found to underlie also these actions? We must turn first to the action involving the use of two staves which inevitably recalls the similar action of Ezekiel, recorded in 37.15-28.[23] Ezekiel was also directed to take two sticks (the terminology being different, עֵץ in Ezekiel, מַקְלוֹת in the Zechariah passage). One of them is to be inscribed, 'Belonging to Judah' and the other 'Belonging to Joseph'. These he is to join, foretelling that aspect of the redemptive work of God by which the scattered of both former kingdoms will be brought back and re-united in the land. They shall be under one king, identified with David in v. 24a, who is referred to as נָשִׂיא in v. 25; they will be cleansed from all idolatry and will again know a true covenant relationship with Yahweh, alluded to by the words in v. 23b, 'and they shall be my people, and I will be their God', the old covenant formula. This covenant renewal idea is made even more explicit in vv. 24-28 and the centrality of the sanctuary will be the sign to 'the nations' that God is again in their midst, in covenant relationship with his people once more. Even a superficial reading of Zech. 11.7-14 suggests {151} some link with the Ezekiel passage, and we shall suggest that in fact a very close link exists which, in some measure, helps us to elucidate some aspects of the obscurity of the shepherd-allegory. Nevertheless it remains to be emphasized again that some of this obscurity is almost undoubtedly due to the fact that the passage has received a good

---

23. The unity of this section is often questioned. Zimmerli (1969: 906ff.) believes it contains an original unit in vv. 15-19, a further elaboration in vv. 20-23 (24a) linking the prophetic action with the themes of the preceding chapters with their idea of 'covenant', an elaboration which derives from Ezekiel himself, however, and a third extension in vv. 24b-28 which has nothing to do with the original action and is not the work of Ezekiel.

deal of modification in the course of transmission as interpretative comments have sought to apply its details to later situations. We can never be absolutely sure where the original has been overlaid or distorted.[24]

Nevertheless, one basic fact emerges. In Zechariah the significance of the original act of Ezekiel appears to have been completely reversed. From being a proclamation of the final act of salvation it has become the prediction of judgment.

The theme of the final re-unification of the two kingdoms has been present in these chapters (e.g. 9.13; 10.6). But here it is present by way of repudiation. This prophet also takes two sticks which are not, however, to be joined, but each is to be broken. Not only is the action thus different, but the names given to them (no specific reference to writing on them is found in Zech. 11) are different. One is called 'favour', 'pleasantness', 'beauty' or 'grace'. A number of renderings are possible for the Hebrew נֹעַם. The other is called 'union', Hebrew חֹבְלִים, literally 'those which bind', the only instance of such a use of the participle of the root חבל in the {152} Old Testament. As the narrative now reads, the breaking of the first staff was the sign of the annulling of the covenant 'I' (the divine or the prophetic 'I'?) had made. The breaking of the second signifies the breach of the 'brotherhood' between Judah and Israel.

Where so much is uncertain and obscure, caution is necessary. Yet a comparison of the two sections can suggest a close relation between the action of Ezekiel and the action of the breaking of the two staves, with the significance attached to them in Zech. 11. For, in the Ezekiel passage, the idea of the renewal of the covenant is present together with the idea of the reuniting of the two former kingdoms. Ezek. 37.23b reads, '...and they shall be my people, and I will be their God', the old covenant formula. This occurs in the section which Zimmerli believes to be a first expansion of vv. 15-19, but to be dependent upon Ezekiel himself. It is made quite explicit in the latest section of that pericope, vv. 26f., where we read, 'I will make a covenant of peace with them', while the concluding words of v. 23 are repeated in inverted order in v. 27.[25] It should be noted that v. 28

---

24. This certainly seems to be the case with v. 8a. Speculations on the significance and identity of the three shepherds have been legion (cf. Kremer, 1930). The allusion can hardly be expected to become clear to us now and no attempt is undertaken here to add to the list of speculations as to whom they are supposed to represent.

25. See {150} now p. 105 n. 23. Most commentators on Ezekiel stress the close connection of the idea of the re-union of Israel and Judah behind the act of prophetic symbolism and the concept of the renewal of the covenant. See, e.g., Zimmerli (1969:

speaks of 'all nations' (הַגּוֹיִם) who 'will know that I the Lord sanctify Israel, when my sanctuary is in the midst of them for evermore'. Thus the two ideas, of renewal of covenant and re-unification, are present in the Ezekiel passage, the two apparently being closely connected in his mind, the one the mark of the other. {153}

These two ideas are also present in the Zechariah passage, of the covenant, represented by the first staff, and the unity between the two former kingdoms, represented by the second. Only, of course, here the meaning of the sign in Ezekiel is exactly reversed. The original message is being inverted and the meaning of the action is to announce judgment. If the breaking of the first staff announces the revoking of the covenant, the breaking of the second announces the breach of the relationship between the two kingdoms. In exactly the same way, the second could be said to be the mark of the first, its accompanying phenomenon.

But why the double action of breaking two staves? Again, this can be seen to be wholly consonant with the main purpose of the action, namely, the complete reversal of what had been promised by Ezekiel's action. For, if Ezekiel took two sticks in order to join them in symbolic action, the later prophet takes two that they may be further broken. It is a dramatic portrayal of the radical and complete reversal of the earlier prophecy. Far from indicating an elaboration by a later hand of an original action, now misunderstood, the two parts belong to an original act and are thus integrally related.

It remains to examine the names given to the staves which, of course, are quite different from those inscribed by Ezekiel on his.

נֹעַם the name given to the first can be rendered {154} by a number of English words, but basically it seems often to stand for the presence and favour of Yahweh. So it does, for example, in Ps. 90.17, a Psalm of Communal Lament in which a cry of distress is uttered to Yahweh:

> Let the *favour* of Yahweh our God be upon us.

Again, in Ps. 27.4 we read,

> One thing have I desired of the Lord,
> that will I seek after;
> that I may dwell in the house of the Lord

913ff.). Eichrodt insists that it is a *new* covenant, a covenant of salvation which is spoken of, but, with Zimmerli, points out that for its terminology it is dependant on the P description of the old covenant, Gen. 17.7, 13, 19; Exod. 31.16; Lev. 24.8; Num. 18.19. Zimmerli (1969: 514).

all the days of my life,
to behold the *beauty* of the Lord,
(לַחֲזוֹת בְּנֹעַם־יְהוָה)
and to inquire in his temple.

It is interesting that this speaks of the presence and favour of Yahweh revealed through the cultic life of the Temple. It reminds us that in the Ezekiel passage referred to above special reference was made to the restoration of the sanctuary in the midst of them as at once the sign and means of the renewal of the covenant relationship between Yahweh and his people. The breaking of the staff named נֹעַם, therefore, suggests the reversal of this covenant experience, that knowledge of God's נֹעַם which is made known to the people through the presence of true Temple cultus in their midst. The grace and favour known through the worship of the Temple is to be withdrawn.

If this is so, two things follow. The first is that it offers explanation of why, concerning this part of the action alone, the prophet speaks in the solemn announcement of the 'I' of Yahweh himself. As only the sovereign grace of God could make the covenant, so only he could repudiate it. {155} As Horst (1964: 251-52) has said, rightly in our opinion, 'Aus 10b ist aber zu erkennen, dass dieser Hirt in göttlicher Legitimation und Vollmacht handelt'.[26] The second is that what looks like the elaboration of the Ezekiel passage and the ideas of Proto-Zechariah by reversal affords another indication that this action of breaking the staff named נֹעַם involves repudiation of the Temple and its worship. It suggests again that we ought to look for the origin of this act of prophetic symbolism in one who saw himself over against the official Judaism of his day, and saw the old promises of Ezekiel and Proto-Zechariah as no longer capable of being fulfilled through the Temple and its hierarchy as it had become.

This raises the question as to why the covenant is described as being 'with all the peoples' (אֶת־כָּל־הָעַמִּים). Elliger takes this as a sign of a later hand which interpreted the original act of prophetic symbolism in an almost apocalyptic sense as pointing forward to God's action in judging all the peoples of the world, the same hand responsible for the two references to the 'earth' in vv. 6 and 16. He believes that the original here was singular and spoke of Yahweh's covenant with 'all the people'. This is,

---

26. Others have suggested emendation of the text, taking the ׳ which appears as the pronominal suffix of the noun בְּרִית to be the misplaced ׳ of the Tetragrammaton. This gives the rendering, 'thus annulling the covenant of Yahweh with all peoples'.

however, without textual support and, plausible as it may seem, needs critical examination.

As a general rule, when Israelites are being spoken of as 'the people of God', עַם appears in the singular. In the plural, this word is often parallel to הַגּוֹיִם. {156} This appears, for example, in Gen. 17.16 (P) in which the divine promise is made to Abraham concerning Sarah, 'I will bless her, and moreover she shall be a mother of nations (לְגוֹיִם), kings of peoples (עַמִּים) shall come from her'. Somewhat similar is the blessing of Isaac, meant for Esau but mistakenly addressed to Jacob:

> Let peoples (עַמִּים) serve you,
> and nations (לְאֻמִּים) bow down to you (Gen. 27.29 [JE, E?]),

a thought echoed in that part of the so-called Blessing of Jacob addressed to Judah, '…and to him shall be the obedience of the peoples (עַמִּים)'. (Gen. 49.10 [J?]). These two latter references speak of the covenant with the people of God in terms more political and nationalistic than the majority of the forms in which promises made to the patriarchs appear, so that von Rad (1963: 273) says of the former, 'The blessing is strangely independent of the otherwise rather uniformly formulated patriarchal promises', and of Gen. 49 he says, 'there are no clear signs which lead one to connect J with this collection'.[27]

Perhaps, therefore, one should see J's statement of the promise to Abraham as a refining and transforming of this hope when it is said, 'and by you all the families of the earth (מִשְׁפְּחֹת הָאֲדָמָה) shall bless themselves'.[28] Yet there was something there to be lifted on to a higher plane, namely that from the beginning the thought existed that Yahweh's purposes did not concern Israel alone in isolation. This was also found in Ezek. {157} 37.28 where it is said that 'the nations (הַגּוֹיִם) shall know that I the Lord sanctify Israel'.

The question arises whether such ideas offer any clue for our understanding of Zech. 11.10 which speaks of the annulment of the covenant 'with all the peoples'. Does it refer in some way to those purposes of God in the calling of Israel which, on one plane or another, were to affect other nations? Such an impression is strengthened when we recall the prominent place given to such an idea in Proto-Zechariah, in 8.22f.

---

27. Von Rad (1963: 417). Similarly, Simpson (1952: 818) attributes it to 'a number of originally independent tribal oracles…later added to the J narrative'.

28. Gen. 12.3 (J); 22.17f., כֹּל גּוֹיֵי הָאָרֶץ (E); 28.3f. (P, 'that you may become לִקְהַל עַמִּים') v. 14.

It is possible, therefore, that here too the prophet is saying that the promises made by Zechariah to the returned community are forfeited by them, so unworthy have they shown themselves to be. No longer able to know the covenant relationship by which the נֹעַם־יְהוָה is mediated to them, their place in the divine purpose for all nations is lost also. Their rejection of Yahweh, shown in their rejection of his representative (v. 8b) shows that the whole community, leaders and people alike, have proved themselves unfitted for their destined role.

We turn next to examine the significance of the breaking of the other staff, חֹבְלִים. The root חבל has the basic meaning of 'pledge', and hence that which is joined or united by pledge.[29] It may be, then, that it indicates that union which once belonged to the people of God by virtue of their mutual pledge of obedience to the terms of the covenant with Yahweh. We have already shown {158} that in the Ezekiel passage, the idea of renewal of covenant and renewal of union between the two kingdoms are related, the one being the mark of the other. Just so, the breaking of the second staff חֹבְלִים may be taken as showing that break-up in the unity of the people of God which is the inevitable concomitant of their breaking of the covenant pledge with Yahweh. The two actions are closely related.

But what could this mean for the prophet and his hearers? It may well be that, since the historical break between the two kingdoms was long in the past, this has only a general reference based on the passage in Ezekiel, to indicate the disruptive effects on the community of their rejection by Yahweh in judgment. Many commentators have thought here that there is an allusion to the historical event of the Samaritan schism.[30] Certainly, as that schism opened up, this passage would be seen to have a special relevance and may well have been interpreted as referring to it, though such interpretation has left little obvious trace in the text.

There is just a hint, however, that this is not the only kind of interpretation it received. There is a curious variant reading to be found in some LXX Manuscripts[31] which substitutes Jerusalem for Israel making the tension appear to be between Judah and Jerusalem. It is not implied, of course, that this is weighty textual evidence which should be preferred to the MT, but it {159} does suggest that this breach of relationship, of brotherhood, could be and probably was variously interpreted in different historical circumstances. We can only guess whether this reflects some

---

29. See BDB: 286.
30. E.g. Elliger (1964: 163f.); Saebø (1969: 250f.).
31. In G^{62}, G^{147}

period of tension between the capital city and its surrounding district. All we are trying to show is that it is possible that at various times this verse could have been variously understood and applied. Certainly it could be, and doubtless was, applied to the Samaritan situation, but was any one of these necessarily the *original* significance of the staff called חֹבְלִים?

As we have suggested above, Judah and Israel could be fused here in a 'typical' sense, based on the model of the Ezekiel passage in ch. 37. The thought may have been of the disruption generally which accompanies Yahweh's acts of judgment. But there is another possibility. It could have been understood originally as signifying the break between the prophet himself, and perhaps his community of followers, and the Judaism of their day which they saw as decadent and under sentence of divine judgment, and which had rejected him and his ministry. Elliger (1964: 164) speaks of this passage as being written as a religious confession, a piece of self-justification by the Jewish cult community, showing that, in the continuing rift with the Samaritans, neither God nor the Jewish community bear the guilt. It is possible, however, that while it might have been 'taken over' as such, originally it served this purpose for the prophet himself and his circle as over against the Jewish cult community. The implications of this would be {160} that in him we have a kind of founder of an early dissenting group, rejected by the priests and official cult, but who saw himself and his followers, a rejected remnant of the true Israel, emerging from the purifying fires of judgment as heirs to all the promises of the covenant uttered by the prophets of old. This, of course, can only remain tentative from the little we are given in this particular act of symbolism. Its validity, or otherwise, will depend upon study of other passages in these chapters, not least 13.7-9, but also that piece of action we have not so far considered, which is described in 11.11-13, and to which we now turn.

The first question which must be faced is how far vv. 11-13 relate to the section as a whole. And here it must be noted that it appears to interrupt the related action of the breaking of the two staves. Furthermore, it introduces another, and more distantly related theme, that of the payment the shepherd received for his service and what he did with it, whereas the main thrust of the symbolism is concerned with the nature of that service as such and the actions concerning the staves. Often this is taken as an indication that we are not now dealing with prophetic symbolism in the traditional manner, but are faced with an extended, written, allegorical and later imitation of the earlier prophetic actions. Yet it is important to notice that not only in theme, but in form structure also, vv. 11-13 appear to be secondary in their {161} present position. Verse 11a merely repeats in another form the concluding words of v. 10b. Yet, compared with the parallel conclusion of v. 14, v. 10b appears to be a concluding statement of the first stage of the prophetic symbolism. Thus v. 11a bears all the marks of an editorial link. Again, the form structure of the action described in vv. 11-13 is incomplete. There is no introductory word of command to the prophet from Yahweh, nor is there any explanation of its significance.[32] So it may well be that this short section, with its much, discussed detail of the actual wages paid, is also the result of a considerable process of interpretative comment, and, in the light of some later historical incident, has become misplaced and inserted at this point to which it was then seen to have relevance. The question then remains, Is there evidence of any act of prophetic symbolism behind all the elaboration which can now be discerned?

The MT of v. 13 speaks of his casting the pieces of silver into בֵּית יְהוָה אֶל־הַיּוֹצֵר. Following the Peshitta and the Targum this is usually emended to read הָאוֹצָר, i.e. 'treasury', since the reference to a potter is deemed to be irrelevant. However, 'potter' is not the only possible rendering of יוֹצֵר, for since the root meaning of the verb is to 'form' or 'fashion', it can be applied to those who fashion in metal, not only in pottery.[33] It seems very likely, as Torrey has sought to show, that there was a foundry in the Second Temple.[34] {162} Indeed, Eissfeldt (1937: 164) has also maintained that there was such a foundry in the First Temple.[35] M. Delcor

---

32. Cf. G. Fohrer (1970). Saebø (1969: 234-54) examines 11.4-17 in the light of Fohrer's study, concluding that we have here an original act of prophetic symbolism, and not merely a literary imitation of earlier accounts, but fails to recognize in his study of the form analysis of this section that vv. 11-13 cannot originally have belonged to the account of the action introduced in v. 7.

33. E.g. Isa. 44.9-10: 'Who fashions a god (מִי־יָצַר אֵל) or casts an image (וּפֶסֶל נָסָךְ) all who make idols (יֹצְרֵי־פֶסֶל)'. It is perhaps conceivable that a pottery image might have been in mind, although the parallelism makes this unlikely. There can be, however, no doubt over Hab. 2.18: 'What profit is an idol, when its maker has shaped it' (כִּי פְסָלוֹ יֹצְרוֹ מַסֵּכָה וּמוֹרֶה שָׁקֶר; RSV, 'a metal image'). Finally there is Isa. 54.17: כָּל־כְּלִי יוּצַר עָלַיִךְ לֹא יִצְלָח. It is hardly likely to be a piece of pottery against which immunity is promised! כְּלִי, that portmanteau Hebrew word, clearly has the sense here of 'weapon', given it by the EVV. One wonders, therefore, whether it is necessary to follow Delcor in assuming that the LXX read the word צוֹרֵף or יוֹצֵף in the text available (Delcor 1953: 67-77).

34. Torrey (1936 and 1943).

35. Eissfeldt is followed by T. Chary (1955: 221ff.) who also sees here a reference to the refining process of 13.7-9.

(1962: 353-77, esp. 372-77) has accepted, this and held that יוֹצֵר in Zech. 11.13 should be understood as referring to a 'smelter'.

But why should the prophet have cast his 30 pieces of silver into the Temple for the smelter? Van Hoonacker believed it was to echo the theme of the 'potter' symbolism in Jer. 18, in which Yahweh himself is the potter, and as such rejects the Israel which had failed him. Wellhausen (1892: 186) believed that the Massoretes emended אוֹצָר to יוֹצֵר because, in their view, the sum was so unworthy that it could not have been cast into the Temple treasury. Delcor (1953: 75ff.; 1962: 375) himself believes that by the action the prophet was saying, in effect, that, since they did not want him as their shepherd, they should fashion an idol of their own. It is not quite clear, however, why the natural alternative to response to the prophet should be some form of idolatry. However, it is significant, perhaps, that the root יצר is used in connection with the manufacture of idols (see {161} n. 43, now p. 112). Further, this prophet does elsewhere speak against various forms of idolatry, as, for example, in 10.1f.

At this point a comparison with the LXX becomes interesting, for it introduces into v. 13 an idea not to be found in the MT. The prophet is told to cast the pieces of silver into the χωνευτήριον (i.e. 'smelting furnace'), καὶ σκέψαι εἰ δόκιμόν ἐστιν, ὃν τρόπον ἐδοκιμάσθην ὑπὲρ αὐτῶν. {163} Here the idea of the test by refining is prominent. There is difference between the codices S, A and Q, which read the first person, 'I will see whether it is good', and the others which read the third person, where the prophet is commanded to examine it on behalf of Yahweh. The last phrase is tantalizing. Is the prophet understood as having undergone some refining process on behalf of the people, or is it Yahweh's faithfulness to them which has been found constant in contrast to their fickleness?

In assessing the value of the LXX at this point we have to proceed cautiously. It may itself bear witness to a later way of interpreting this action whose significance was already overlaid and obscure. Yet such a method of interpretation proved persistent, witness the Targum's understanding of the 30 pieces of silver as *30 just men*, for whom the fear of God was something holy and precious.[36]

It raises the question whether, behind vv. 11-13, there may not have lain

36. See Kremer (1930: 9-16). Such an idea is very closely related to the story of Dan. 3, where the three friends of Daniel are proved in the fiery furnace. Has the LXX of Zech. 11.13 been influenced by this? Or does Dan. 3 represent a narrative expression and interpretation of the theme in the prophetic material?

some act meant to symbolize the message that God was about to visit the leaders and people of Judaism in judgment, a judgment from which only that which was 'pure' would emerge. Tentative as such conclusion must remain, three other considerations point in its favour. First, this seems to be the exact meaning of 13.7-9 which is so close to this passage in style, vocabulary and thought. {164}

Further, we should then have had originally another act of prophetic symbolism based upon an original in Ezekiel. For Ezek. 22.17-22 speaks of just such a threat, that God will gather the House of Israel which 'has become dross to me' just as men gather metals 'into a furnace, to blow the fire upon it in order to melt it'.

But again, such a conception would be wholly in line with a theme which is prominent in Proto-Zechariah in a way we have found to characterize these chapters. For, in Zech. 3, Joshua, as High Priest, is spoken of as 'a brand plucked from the fire'. As such, the filthy garments are removed from him, that he may be clothed in rich apparel, with a clean turban on his head. In some way, he is representative of a wider community here, for in v. 8, not only Joshua is addressed by the angel of Yahweh, but also 'your friends who sit before you'. These latter are described as אַנְשֵׁי מוֹפֵת, 'men of portent'. This term is exactly that which was used of the Isaiah and his 'children' (Isa. 8.18). This nucleus of a new community, cleansed by the action of Yahweh on Joshua as their representative, was to portend the new age, the deliverance which was to come. A similar idea of the community being purged of its evil as a prelude to this final act of salvation is found in Zech. 5, with the vision of the woman sitting in the ephah, representing 'their iniquity in all the land', who is cast out of the land, into Babylon. Even in Zech. 6.9-14 there was the literal {165} action of Zechariah in taking silver and gold from three of the exiles who had arrived from Babylon, to smelt it into a crown, or crowns, to be placed on the head of Joshua, and of Zerubbabel also perhaps,[37] whose significance was that the Temple was to be perfected and the joint reign of governor and high priest to characterize the new age.

Thus the idea of a judgment on the official religious life of the time, aimed at refining so that the nucleus of a new community might emerge to inherit the final age of salvation is strongly emphasized in Proto-Zechariah. Added to the agreement with Zech. 13.7-9, with the passage in Ezek. 22.17-22, and the influence the thought of Proto-Zechariah has had

---

37. For a recent discussion of this passage, see Ackroyd (1973: 203ff.).

on these chapters, it does at least make possible the suggestion that behind vv. 11-13 stood an act of prophetic symbolism making just this same point.

What we have suggested, then, is that in 11.4-17 we do not have extended allegory, an example of literary imitation of early acts of prophetic symbolism, but that behind it lay three literal acts of symbolism (the third in vv. 15-17 remains to be considered). The breaking of the two staves was originally one complete and related act. The casting of the silver into the furnace was another, now misplaced and related to the former only in secondary manner. It may be, of course, that the prophet did actually cast wages received from the official representatives of the Temple, to the smelter. He may have once {166} had some standing within the official Judaism of his day and this use of his wages symbolized his repudiation of it. It may be that the use of the term יוֹצֵר instead of the more usual words available to denote smelters in metal, was a deliberate evocation of the Jeremiah passage, as van Hoonacker suggested, or because of what he considered to be the little better than idolatrous worship of the Temple, as Delcor's suggestion could remind us. Or such details may be secondary and related as interpretative comment to some later episode in the life of the Temple. Of such details we cannot now hope to be sure. Yet we have vv. 15-17 to show us what this prophet thought of the official leadership after his repudiation of his office.

The final section of vv. 15-17 introduces what we see as the third act of prophetic symbolism in this passage. It is constructed in the familiar form, with the command of Yahweh, followed by the 'explanation' of the action. In this case there is no narrative of its being executed. It has been argued that this was an impossible action to carry out, yet it could involve the prophet appearing in the dress and with the equipment of a High Priest of his day, or as one of the Temple personnel, whose appearance, and perhaps whose method of carrying out his charge the prophet aped. There follows a 'cry of woe' over the worthless shepherd. The command is to take the implements (כְּלִי) of a worthless shepherd, and its significance is said to be that God is raising up a shepherd in the {167} land who is false in every respect. Indeed, almost all his qualities match those denounced in Ezek. 34 and are the opposite of these which the same chapter says Yahweh will show himself when shepherding the flock.

The 'Wehe-ruf' of v. 17 may of course be a detached piece added on the

editorial catch-word principle.[38] On the other hand, such a cry can appear
in the narrative of earlier acts of prophetic symbolism, as in Ezek. 24.1-14,
where the action of the boiling pot is narrated, a narrative twice interrupted
by a 'Wehe-ruf' in vv. 6 and 9. Perhaps the thought in this verse echoes
Ezekiel's threat against the King of Egypt in Ezek. 30.21f., where the arm
of the Pharaoh is broken in order that it cannot hold a sword. To blind the
right eye in addition would be to render the worthless shepherd utterly
incapable of withstanding the judgment with which he is threatened.

Again, this section need not have a particular historical figure in mind.
Just as 'David' or 'House of David' could be applied to any king in the
Davidic succession (e.g. Isa. 7.13) so this could well be directed against
the official leadership (both 'civil' and 'religious') of Judaism following
the prophet's own withdrawal from them. Such leadership he sees as both
the judgment of God on the people, on the flock 'doomed to slaughter',
and itself the inevitable target of such judgment—the theme of the next
section. {168}

38. So Elliger (1964: 165ff.).

Chapter 7

ZECHARIAH 13.7-9

Few sections, even of these obscure chapters, have so succeeded in polarizing critical opinion as this one. There is division concerning its relation to other sections, and consequently a difference of interpretation as to the identity of the shepherd who becomes the object of Yahweh's 'smiting', and what the significance of his suffering or death is.

It opens with an apostrophe to the sword of Yahweh: חֶרֶב עוּרִי עַל־רֹעִי. The root עוּר is a word closely associated with the activity of Yahweh, either in judgment or salvation. It may call men to arouse themselves fittingly to hymn the work of God;[1] it may form an invitation to Yahweh himself to come in deliverance for his people by taking vengeance against their (and his) foes.[2] Even when it is not used in the imperative it is still often suggestive of the power of Yahweh. He 'raises up' Cyrus[3] as he does other unconscious agents of his purpose.[4] Of course, there may be an internal word-play in 13.7a, between עוּרִי and רֹעִי. Although instances occur in these chapters of word allusion and play apparently evoking other biblical passages, this appears to be an isolated instance of such internal word-play.

The idea of the sword of Yahweh is also one with a long history. It may well stem from the old idea of the {169} Holy War, although the only reference to it is perhaps preserved in the cry of Judg. 7.20, 'a sword for Yahweh and for Gideon', or, as it might be rendered if the preposition לְ is

---

1. E.g. Judg. 5.12, where Deborah is called upon to sing of the deliverance wrought by Yahweh against Sisera, or Pss. 57.9 (8); 108.3 (2), where the Psalmist calls on harp and lyre to awake to enable him adequately to praise Yahweh for his חֶסֶד.

2. E.g. Pss. 7.7 (6); 44.24 (23), or, interestingly, Isa. 51.9, where it is the *arm* of Yahweh which is addressed, for it was he who 'cut Rahab in pieces'.

3. Isa. 41.2, 25; 45.13; 2 Chron. 36.22 = Ezra 1.1.

4. E.g. the Medes, Isa. 13.17.

taken to indicate possession, 'the sword of Yahweh and of Gideon'.[5] There are many references in the Prophets to the sword as the means of Yahweh's vengeance and judgment[6] where the inference seems to be that he will bring the sword of human enemies upon those threatened, and that they will wield their sword at his direction, so that it becomes in truth 'Yahweh's sword'. This can receive vivid and dramatic expression, as in Isa. 34.5f. in an oracle against Edom:

> For my sword has drunk its fill in the heaven;
> behold, it descends for judgment upon Edom
> The LORD has a sword; it is sated with blood...

This sword can be apostrophized, as in Jer. 47.6:

> Ah, sword of the LORD!
> How long till you are quiet?
> How can it be quiet,
> When the LORD has given it a charge?

With such a long and frequent usage behind it, we must be cautious about claiming any one prophetic passage as 'the source' for Zech. 13.7. It is of interest, in view of the connections many have seen between this section and the symbolic action described in Ezek. 5, which will be discussed below, to notice how prominent a part the sword plays there.

Further, in Ezek. 21 a number of originally independent oracles have been arranged around the connecting theme {170} or catch-word, of judgment by the sword. The chapter contains a 'Song of the Sword':

> A sword, a sword is sharpened
> and also polished,
> sharpened for slaughter
> polished to flash like lightening (vv. 14f. [9f.]).

---

5.   Some older commentators have queried the reference to the 'sword' as a gloss. So G.P. Moore (1895: 210) and C.F. Burney (1918: 217). Burney believes the parallel phrase in v. 18 shows that the original cry was 'For Yahweh and for Gideon', the present form of it being due to the redactor who combined the J and E narratives. Even if this is so, the present form of the narrative seeks to emphasize that the victory was Yahweh's alone, and v. 22 probably implied that the sword of the Midianites themselves became Yahweh's sword of vengeance as, in panic, they turned them upon each other. Thus the passage is in line with the many prophetic references to the sword which Yahweh will use in judgment against his foes. There may be an earlier concept of the sword of Yahweh in the Fall narrative in Gen. 3 (v. 24).

6.   See *inter multa alia* Jer. 9.16; 24.10, etc.

The preparation of the sword by polishing and sharpening is that it might 'be given into the hand of the slayer'. The prophet is called to a cry of lamentation, for it is to be directed against Yahweh's own people, and especially against 'all the princes of Israel: they are delivered over to the sword with my people' (21.17 [12]).

Eichrodt (1970: 293ff.) follows Oort[7] in linking such a song with acts of 'weapon-magic' such as that found in 2 Kgs 13.18. He sees in the call of v. 19 (14), 'clap your hands and let the sword come down twice, yea thrice, the sword for those to be slain', a parallel to Elisha's injunction to Joash. Eichrodt continues,

> It (i.e. the sword) is even addressed as if it were a living being, and summoned to strike without mercy on every side so as to carry out completely the destruction on which God has determined.

All this suggests that such sayings furnish, in general, the context for the address to the sword of Yahweh. In our section, and if that section is within the broad circle of Ezekiel tradition, then this makes more probable that what follows is seen in the context of judgment for sin, against the leadership first of all, but also against the people corrupted by its influence. The sword-oracles appear in {171} the earlier prophetic tradition in general, and in Ezekiel in particular, in a context of judgment and punishment.

If then, tradition history suggests that the inspiration for this sword oracle lies in the prophetic concept of the judgment in general, and in the Ezekiel tradition in particular, and that its concept is therefore one of threat and punishment, our attention is directed to those who are the object of this visitation, namely, to the identity of the 'shepherd' and the 'little ones' of the flock. By itself this consideration would not seem to argue conclusively that the 'shepherd' is the bad shepherd of 11.4-17. So it is necessary to turn to examine the way in which he is described.

The one who is to be smitten is described by Yahweh as רֹעִי and גֶּבֶר עֲמִיתִי. The pointing of רֹעִי has been disputed. It can be pointed either רֵעִי, meaning 'my companion', which would certainly appear to harmonize

---

7. The reference is to Oort (1889: 511f.). Attention should, however, be paid to J.H. Eaton (1964). In taking the מַטּוֹת of v. 9 to be a reference to weapons, he comments on the part given to the naming and commissioning of Baal's weapons in the Ugaritic 'Baal and Anath' III, and the fact that 'in the ensuing combat each weapon performs exactly the work to which it had been commissioned'. He also cites Isa. 34.5 and Jer. 47.7 as parallels to this (Eaton 1964: 152).

with גֶּבֶר עֲמִיתִי or as רֹעִי, meaning 'my shepherd'.[8] Nevertheless, the clear reference to the shepherd in v. 7b, and the consequence on the flock of his being smitten tilt the scales in favour of the Massoretic pointing.

Could the term 'my shepherd' be applied to a false and worthless holder of the office? The only clue here is afforded by Isa. 44.28 where this exact term is applied to Cyrus. Even nobler titles are also used to designate {172} him, notably, 'my anointed'. The emphasis, therefore, must be on the purpose which Yahweh has, not so much *for* Cyrus, as through Cyrus for Israel and so for the whole world.[9] By him all men are to come to know that Yahweh alone is God and in control of history (Isa. 45.4-6). It says nothing of Cyrus's own relationship to Yahweh, still less does it hold out any promise of his final salvation. If then, even a pagan king may be the instrument of Yahweh's disclosure of his own nature and purpose, it would not seem inconceivable that an unworthy native Israelite leader, by whose judgment and rejection the same nature and purpose of Yahweh will be revealed, might also be termed 'my shepherd'. Even the unworthy kings of pre-exilic Israel still presumably received the royal appellations.[10]

Elliger has found significance in the use of the term גֶּבֶר for the shepherd. It is a word, he maintains, which belongs to elevated speech, often to emphasize strength and heroic qualities. It is the first component of the name by which the angel Gabriel is represented in the book of Daniel (8.16; 9.21).[11] Elliger's conclusion is that the author has in mind here a Messianic figure. If we are seeking support for such a view, however, one would have thought something more to the point than the Danielic reference to Gabriel lay to hand in the so-called 'Last Words of David'.[12] For there we read: {173}

---

8. BH proposes reading רֹעִי. The only textual variant is Targum which renders by מַלְכָּא ('king') with no pronominal suffix and has שִׁילטוֹנָא הַבְרֵיהּ for גֶּבֶר עֲמִיתִי; but this is presumably interpretive. Lamarche (1961: 91), while accepting the MT pointing wonders whether the author may have had a play on words in mind in view of the further description of the 'shepherd'. Otherwise, most commentators prefer MT pointing (and so *BHS*).

9. See esp. Westermann (1969: 160f.).

10. '…since the Hebrews believed that all rulers were under the control and direction of their God, they could apply it (i.e. the term "my shepherd") to a king, even if he were oppressing them instead of relieving them from oppression' (Mitchell 1912: 317). 'The "foolish shepherd" of 11.15-17 called "Yahweh's shepherd", in so far as, however unworthy, he stands officially at the head of Yahweh's people' (Driver 1906: 271).

11. See Elliger (1964: 175-76).

12. 2 Sam. 23.1ff. The point at issue here is not affected by the authenticity of the

נְאֻם דָּוִד בֶּן־יִשַׁי וּנְאֻם הַגֶּבֶר הֻקַם עָל מְשִׁיחַ אֱלֹהֵי יַעֲקֹב

The word is not used anything like as frequently as the much more common שׁיא. Nevertheless it is hard to determine any thorough-going and consistent significance in its usage in the Old Testament. It can occur in very early writing, as in the Song of Deborah in Judg. 5.30. It can be used in a favourable sense (e.g. Pss. 34.9 [8]; 37.23; 40.5 [4]) but also in an unfavourable (e.g. Ps. 52.9 [7]; Prov. 28.21). It does occur, it is true, in Wisdom literature a great deal,[13] yet it is not a sign necessarily of the late date of a work, since it occurs only three times in the work of the Chronicler, and not at all in Ezekiel. It appears once in Micah, once in Habakkuk and four times in Lamentations. If, therefore, as Elliger says, it bears some specifically Messianic connotations it could only be by echoing some such specific use of the word as in the 'Last Words of David' rather than by the use of the term itself. It is possible that its use in the 'Last Words of David' has found echo in the book of Jeremiah. On the context of a lamentation over Jehoiachin, Jeremiah asks (22.28ff.),

> Why are he and his children hurled
> and cast into a land which they do not know?...
> Write this man (שׁיא) down as childless,
> a man (גֶּבֶר) who shall not succeed in his days;
> for none of his off-spring shall succeed,
> in sitting on the throne of David,
> and ruling again in Judah.

The phrase in which this use of the word (גֶּבֶר) occurs is often regarded as a gloss.[14] If original, the {174} use of the different word for 'man' might

---

words. Most commentators follow Hertzberg (1964: 402) who sees the poem as a prophetic interpretation of what David was and did. However, against H.P. Smith (1899), who finds thought and vocabulary to indicate a late date, and Brockington (1962: 336), who finds 'gnomic' elements in it also suggesting a late date, traditio-historical arguments would suggest an origin among the same circles which forged the Davidic covenant theology, and a time early on in the history of the Davidic dynasty when this still needed apologetic. For the relevant literature, and a rejection of the arguments for the later date on stylistic and linguistic grounds, see A.R. Johnson (1967: 16f.).

13. Fifteen times in Job, eight times in Proverbs, and in some Jeremiah passages which have indications of Wisdom origin, e.g. Jer. 17.5, 7. But it also occurs elsewhere in Jeremiah e.g. 30.6; 31.22. Kosmala (1968) finds it to be used in the Old Testament of: (a) the qualities of virility in a man; and (b) a man who walks with God (especially in the Psalms) and the man who lives rightly with God (especially in Job). Such an emphasis could still point the *irony* of the use of the term in Zech. 13.7.

14. So *BHS*; Bright (1970: 193); Weiser (1962: 193).

be nothing more than poetic device to vary monotony, but it might be a deliberate evocation of the 'Last Words of David' which are by no means inappositely recalled here, since they appear to be reversed in context exactly, the original promise being annulled in judgment. But even if a gloss, it might equally be interpretative comment setting the threat to Jehoiachin against the background which alone sets off its horror in stark relief, namely, the terms of the original promise which proved the bedrock of the theology of the Davidic Covenant concept. Is such a claim mentioned here ironically? Is there intended an allusion to the Jeremianic treatment of this original claim, that it is about to be reversed and overthrown in the rejection of this leadership? The questions would seem still to be open ones.

We must give attention, therefore, to the very unusual term עֲמִיתִי. Surely, by its very rarity, it is meant to carry special emphasis. For, elsewhere in the Old Testament, it appears *exclusively* in the legal sections of Leviticus. Does the author intend any special statement by the choice of a term to describe, the 'shepherd' of so very narrow a range of use and definition?

An examination of its use in Leviticus shows that it occurs in passages regulating the behaviour of an Israelite towards his fellow-Israelites. Nevertheless, the first {175} occurrence of such a passage makes it clear that any wrong treatment of a fellow is a sin against Yahweh himself, a theme which is prominent in the law codes of the Old Testament from the Book of the Covenant onwards, and which receives elaboration and emphasis in the prophets from Amos onwards:

> If anyone sins and commits a breach of faith against the LORD by deceiving his neighbour (בַּעֲמִיתוֹ) in a matter of a deposit or security, or through robbery, or if he has oppressed his neighbour (עָשַׁק אֶת־עֲמִיתוֹ)...[15]

Further instances make reference to lying with the wife of a neighbour (18.20), stealing, dealing falsely and lying to one another (19.11), injustice in judgment against a neighbour (19.15), and hating another in one's heart (19.17); a man is to be treated in similar fashion if he disfigures a neighbour (24.19), he is not to wrong his neighbour in buying and selling (25.14), and there comes finally, as at the beginning, a reminder that this conduct to each other is vitally related to their conduct towards Yahweh:

> You shall not wrong one another, but you shall fear your God; for I am the LORD your God (25.17).

15. Lev. 5.21 (6.2).

At this point it is worth recalling that we have already had reason to point to the stress laid in Proto-Zechariah on neighbourly conduct towards each other as fellow covenanters, and believe that this also has found echo in the chapters of Deutero-Zechariah. {176}

With this legal background to the term עֲמִית and the kind of prophetic comment on it with which the Old Testament familiarizes us, the question again arises as to whether the use of these terms in Zech. 13.7 is not ironic. Does not עֲמִית together with 'my shepherd' and the possible Messianic connotation of גֶּבֶר emphasize what these leaders were supposed to be by virtue of their office and what they themselves claimed to be? Far from shepherding the flock, from ruling according to the terms of the Davidic Covenant or being upholders of the law in the community, they themselves have exploited and oppressed the poor and broken the covenant law whose champions they were supposed to be. If this were legitimate interpretation of this mode of address, and, as we have seen, the tradition history of the terminology strongly suggests a context and milieu of judgment and punishment of what is announced evil, then this section could well be seen as a continuation of the rejection of the official leadership which we have found in 11.4-17, and represent the view of the same circles of tradition. In which case this section does form a very close unity with 11.14-17. It is at least a possibility, and it remains to be seen whether the vocabulary and terminology employed to describe the consequences of the judgment show anything of the same emphasis which has characterized the address to the sword and the terms descriptive of the one who is to be smitten. {177}

The shepherd is to be 'smitten' (נכה). This is a word used uniformly with harmful connotations. It does not always mean to smite fatally as we may see, for example, from Num. 22.23, 25 and 27, not even where God is the subject as in 1 Kgs 14.15, where it involves dispossession of the land following the threat to cut off the royal house of Jeroboam. Of course, very often it does carry with it the associated idea of death, meaning 'to smite fatally'. In such cases the weapon or instrument that deals out death may be mentioned (e.g. 1 Sam. 17.35; 2 Sam. 2.23) but not always (e.g. Gen. 4.15). Often, when used against a ruler it involves the death of that ruler, as, for example, in 2 Kgs 9.7 where Elisha directs Jehu to 'strike down' the house of Ahab. We cannot say, therefore, for certain, that it is the shepherd's death which is threatened, but analogy would certainly suggest an effective end to his rule as being supposed at the very least, and the effect this 'smiting' has on the sheep would re-enforce such a conclusion.

The thought of the succeeding phrase, וּתְפוּצֶין הַצֹּאן, is also one with a pre-history in the prophetic literature of the Old Testament. One recalls the oracular pronouncement of Micaiah ben Imlah against Ahab and his ill-timed venture against the Syrians at Ramoth Gilead:

> I saw all Israel scattered (וְפֹצִים) upon the mountains, as sheep (כַּצֹּאן) that have no shepherd; and the LORD said, 'These have no master; let each return to his home in peace'. {178}

Furthermore, it is significant how the Deuteronomist historian, with his tight-knit *schema* of prophecy and its fulfilment narrates the event. For, after someone had drawn his bow 'at a venture' and 'struck' (וַיַּכֶּה) the king, the cry went up in the evening, 'Every man to his city, and every man to his country'. Thus they were indeed 'scattered' with no leader any longer effectively to shepherd them. Indeed, the whole chapter can be viewed as a conflict between 'true' and 'false' prophecy.[16] Here a shepherd was 'struck' in judgment because of his disobedience to the oracle of Yahweh, and, as a result, the flock was scattered.

This is how so often the prophetic circles diagnosed the disaster which fell upon the nation, and it is an idea often expressed where, the shepherd/ flock metaphor is employed. Ezekiel says of the flock, 'so they were scattered because there was no shepherd' (34.5). In fact they had shepherds, but such worthless ones that Ezekiel can speak as though, in effect, they had none. We encounter the same picture in Jer. 10.21:

> For, the shepherds are stupid,
> and do not inquire of the LORD,
> therefore they have not prospered,
> and all their flock is scattered (וְפֹוצָה).

In Jer. 23.2f. there is a charge against the shepherds that they have 'scattered my flock' (הֲפִצֹתֶם אֶת־צֹאנִי) for which they will be punished. Here there is an interesting drawing together of the idea of judgment against worth-less shepherds who have failed in their charge {179} and a consequent scattering of the flock, leading to a redemption in which the remnant of the flock will be gathered, and given genuine leadership.[17] It does therefore

---

16. In the second edition of his commentary, Gray (1970: 414) says, 'In any case this instance of prophecy and fulfillment in the case of Ahab, whom prophetic tradition in the Elijah-saga presents in such a dark light, was something which the Deuteronomist was sure to emphasize'.

17. E.W. Nicholson (1970: 88f.) finds traces of deuteronomistic style here and believes that the attitude to monarchy also reflects the Deuteronomist view of kingship.

seem that the prophetic traditions referring to the dispossession of the flock do so in a context which sees them as suffering because of the sins of their leaders, so that the calamities which befall the whole nation signify judgment on the sins of their leaders.

That the people too suffer in Zech. 13.7-9 is further supported by the phrase 'I will turn my hand against the little ones'.[18] The phrase וַהֲשִׁבֹתִי יָדִי עַל is used uniformly in a hostile sense in the Old Testament (see Amos 1.8; Ps. 81.15 [14]; Isa. 1.25). Most interesting is its occurrence in Isa. 1.25 where 'I will turn my hand against you' is immediately linked with the idea of refining by fire, 'and will smelt away your dross as with lye, and remove all your alloy' (cf. Zech. 13.8).

This Isaianic oracle is of interest not only because it brings these two ideas together which also occur in our passage in terminology which is similar (Isa. 1.25, וְאָשִׁיבָה יָדִי עָלַיִךְ; cf. Zech. 13.7, וַהֲשִׁבֹתִי יָדִי עַל, and, while the phrasing to describe the process of smelting is different, root צרף is common to both), but because both also have this apparent promise held out in a context of apparent threat. In Isaiah both form and vocabulary are those of pronouncements of woe. לָכֵן nearly always introduces such an announcement, especially in {180} Isaiah, in this case preceding the messenger formula. This is followed by הוֹי which usually introduces the specification of the sins on which judgment is being passed, 'Ah, I will vent my wrath on my enemies, and avenge myself on my foes' (Isa. 1.14). It is indeed a dramatic switch, one of the most striking illustrations in the Old Testament that, for the prophet, the judgment and salvation of Yahweh were obverse and reverse of the same coin, the same divine act.[19] But here a further point of interest occurs. The emphasis in Isaiah's oracle is on the *leadership* of Jerusalem. It is not implied that the leaders have a monopoly of sin, nor that they alone are to be the targets of the divine

This of course in no way vitiates our contention that this is in line with the main stream of prophetic tradition, since the Deuteronomists were clearly influenced by the older prophetic movement of the north, a point E.W. Nicholson (1967: 58-82) himself stresses forcibly in his earlier work.

18. Even the use of הַצֹּעֲרִים for the 'little ones' of the flock echoes this kind of judgment by Yahweh against leader and community alike (e.g. Jer. 49.20), where, in the context of a threat against Edom, and following the question 'What shepherd can stand before me?' (v. 19) it is said, 'Even the little ones of the flock (צְעִירֵי הַצֹּאן) shall be dragged away'. The phrase is repeated in 50.49 against Babylon.

19. One should note that this is also an instance of 'reversal' of a prophetic oracle, in this case within the same oracular unit. Other instances we have examined suggest a reversal of earlier prophetic oracles in the light of a new situation.

judgment. But it is said that they bear special responsibility for the sin of the whole community, and the ultimate aim of making Jerusalem again to be 'the city of righteousness, the faithful city', results from 'restoring your judges as at the first, and your counsellors as at the beginning', for it was they in particular who were addressed in the accusation:

> Your princes are rebels,
> and companions of thieves.
> Every one loves a bribe
> and runs after gifts.
> They do not defend the fatherless,
> and the widow's cause does not come to them (Isa. 1.23).

(Again, it is interesting to note the echo of those very passages from the law codes of Israel which Zech. 13.7 evokes by the use of their technical term עָמִית, speaking as it does of the neighbourly responsibilities of one Israelite for another.) {181}

All this suggests that R.C. Dentan's (1956: 1109-10) conclusions at this point need to be received with caution. He believes that in Zech. 13.7 there is no suggestion that the shepherd is evil; that the smiting, far from being a form of punishment, is but the means of scattering the sheep in order to purify them by suffering; that this is a reference in general terms to the time of 'Messianic woes' as in 12.1ff. Both traditio- and form-critical considerations suggest, however, that we are here dealing with a real threat against a leadership which was seen as evil, but that, as in Isa. 1.25, we have an instance where the judgment of Yahweh, though far-reaching and devastating, is thought not to be finally destructive but ultimately redemptive. Its result is to be the emergence of a purified remnant.

This leads us, then, to a consideration of that which follows in vv. 8f. Of the entire population of the land two thirds will perish and one third will survive. This remaining third will itself be put into the fire, but for the purpose of refining rather than destruction, to go through the same process as that to which silver and gold are subjected. The survivors (and there is no suggestion that this is not the whole of that third) will enter into a new relationship with Yahweh reminiscent of the terms of the original Sinaitic covenant.

Such a division of the population into three thirds for the purpose of judgment calls to mind the symbolic {182} action to which Ezekiel was called and which is recorded in Ezek. 5. This is usually thought itself to be in close relation to the symbolic actions of ch. 4. Zimmerli (1969: 137), for example, speaks of a 'Dreizeichenkomposition' from 4.1–5.17, with an introduction in 3.24b announcing the approaching siege and destruction of Jerusalem. He sees this complex as itself intended to be a conclusion to the narrative of the prophet's call (Zimmerli 1969: 136). The hair which is shaved off is to be weighed exactly into three equal parts (both shaving and weighing in balances symbolizing divine judgment in the Old Testament).[20] The first was to be burned, signifying that some of the population would die during the fighting for the capture of the city; the second was to be struck with the sword round the city, indicating, that some would be slain in the attempt to escape; and the third part was to be scattered to the wind where, with a change of person, Yahweh announces, 'I will unsheathe the sword after them' (Ezek. 3.12). This seems to indicate that even those who are taken away from the city as prisoners, or who might escape, and so, in a sense at least, survive the disaster, will yet be the target of Yahweh's own, immediate punishment. In other words, the picture of the original action is one of *total* judgment.

Yet, of the greatest interest for us, there are not wanting signs in Ezek. 5.3f. which suggest that the original symbolic action was early subjected to a re-interpretation {183} by those who believed that from this third group of exiles in Babylon, the nucleus of a new people of God, a 'remnant' would emerge. For in vv. 3f. there follows a further injunction to an action with this final group which, both by virtue of the impracticability of its actually being carried out, and its profound modification of the totality of the judgment symbolized by the earlier action, proclaims itself as secondary.[21] Further support for this is found in that v. 12 knows nothing of vv. 3f.

Of the third group, a small number is to be collected again and the prophet is to bind them in the skirts of his robe. Of these, yet another 'small number' are to be taken and burned in the fire.[22] This reference to some further catastrophe in exile is significant in that it is not regarded as total. If only 'some' are to be burned then, by implication, some are to be

---

20. Cf., e.g., Judg. 16.17ff.; Isa. 7.20; Job 31.6; Isa. 26.7; Dan. 5.27.

21. The secondary nature of these verses is recognized by Zimmerli (1969: 130, 137), who leaves open the issue of whether they stem from Ezekiel himself later in the period of the exile, or from a circle of his disciples. So also Stalker (1968: 70). For reasons given in the text we question whether they could have come from Ezekiel himself.

22. Verse 4b is notoriously difficult to interpret in this context and must probably be regarded as yet further elaboration of vv. 3, 4a.

preserved.[23] Evidently some group believed themselves to be separated
from others even of their fellow-exiles who would not be allowed a part in
the reconstituted life of the people of God, while they themselves were to
be the nucleus of such a community. This is of interest here since it shows
re-interpretive movement at work from some circles among the exiles,
even although such re-interpretation is taken further and made more explicit
in Zech. 13.8f. What we have there may, however, be only a development
of a mode of interpretation to which the Ezekiel passage had {184}
already been subjected and the application of a concept originally applied
to one group to another.

That as such it is a reversal of Ezekiel's original picture of judgment is
certain, but by this means seen to be more credible. It is certain, since
Ezekiel's own picture of a smelting process in 22.17ff. is so different.
There it means that Israel is nothing but dross and the smelting process
will show this to have been so. Nothing will be left. Perhaps this indicates
that the thought in Ezek. 5.3f. may not have come from Ezekiel himself,
but at the least from a group of disciples. Yet in Zech. 13.8f. something is
to be left. A faithful remnant will emerge from the ordeal of testing who
will 'call on Yahweh's name' and who will be answered by him. They
will be termed 'my people' by Yahweh and will confess that Yahweh is
their God.

For all that, the Ezekiel passage appears to have been in mind here, for
the threat of destruction of the totally false by smelting is followed in
Ezekiel by the word: 'You are a land that is not cleansed, or rained upon in
the day of indignation' (Ezek. 22.24) and the sign of that lack of cleansing
are the charges that are brought upon the princes and the priests. When
one recalls the prominent place given to rain in Zech. 9ff., for example, the
prayer for it in 10.1, the cleansing fountain of 13.1, by which the idols and
the prophets will be {185} cleansed away, the waters of 14.8, and the importance of the Feast of Booths for the provision of rain in 14.17, one sees
a very similar viewpoint represented. The gift of water symbolizes God's
cleansing of the community from a corrupt and tainted leadership. It is yet
another indication that the section before us belongs to that stream of
tradition which sees the re-emergence of a redeemed community following
the cleansing process which strikes down the false leadership of the
old age.

23. It should be noted that, against Zimmerli who finds a 'remnant' concept in this
elaboration of the original text, Eichrodt (1970: 87) says that it is 'more probably
aimed at the destruction of all hope of surviving the judgment with a whole skin'.

The emphasis on the newness of what is to follow is however also strongly rooted in the traditions of earlier prophetic material and adapts to its own expression much of its terminology. The way in which the renewed covenant relationship is expressed is strongly reminiscent of Hos. 2.25: 'and I will say to Not my people, "You are my people"; and he shall say, "Thou art my God"'.

This occurs in Hosea, a prophet who strongly emphasizes the Exodus/ Sinaitic covenant tradition, within the context of promises of its renewal after a judgment which shall take them out of the land with all its idolatrous associations and its corrupting leadership (cf. 'For the children of Israel shall dwell many days without king or prince, without sacrifice or pillar, without ephod or teraphim', 3.4). It is possible that such a concept in Hosea influenced Ezekiel in such a passage as 37.23, 27, especially in v. 23 which reads {186}

> They shall not defile themselves any more with their idols
> and their detestable things or with any of their transgressions;
> but I will save them from all their backslidings in which they have sinned,
> and will cleanse them;
> and they shall be my people, and I will be their God.

Such a line of thought is taken up by Proto-Zechariah in 8.8, for after the return of Yahweh's presence to Zion and Jerusalem which has such a cleansing effect that it can again be called 'the faithful city', there continues the promise to bring back the dispersed from east and west:

> and I will bring them to dwell in the midst of Jerusalem;
> and they shall be my people and I will be their God,
> in faithfulness and righteousness.

It is such a line of tradition which seems to lie behind Zech. 13.8f. It seems to be to such lines of prophetic thought that the concepts there point, and all these lines of traditio-history thus continue to indicate the idea of a nucleus, a remnant emerging purified from the fires of judgment, now ready to enter into new covenant relationship with him, the same process having removed the false leadership and sections of the community whose polluting presence brought about the act of judgment. Does such an outlook not fall naturally to a group who saw in themselves the faithful nucleus of such a new community as over against the false leadership of the Judaism of their day? At hand are the birth-pangs of the new age when God will vindicate his own.

The connections in language, structure, and above all {187} in treatment or theme between 11.4-17 and 13.7ff. are, then, striking. Both use the 'shepherd' imagery; both refer to the place of the sword in striking the shepherd; in both are allusions to smelting; in both allusions to the covenant concepts; the metrical structure of 11.17 is continued in 13.7.

It is our view, therefore, that both internal connections, and the common use made of traditions in earlier prophetic writings indicate a community of outlook and a common origin between these two passages, and that the 'shepherd' is the false one of 11.15-17. We have tried to show by an examination of the traditio-history behind the two passages that both represent the same viewpoint and outlook of the same group. But this does not detract from its connection in general with 12.1–13.6, and indeed may vindicate its positioning where we find it. For not only is a reference to be found here to a general suffering as the prelude to the last time of salvation, but more specifically, a precise reference is found to that convulsion consisting in the cleansing of the land and the community by the removal of its unworthy leadership and those elements in the community which, under the influence of that leadership, have proved corrupting. This is also the outlook of 13.1-6.

Like 11.4-17, however, 13.7-9 goes further in showing that on the other side of this convulsion the nucleus of a new community will emerge. Hidden away in {188} the putrefaction of the whole body is that faithful circle of people who will emerge from the fire, their faith and loyalty for Yahweh proven and vindicated, to be heirs to the promised new covenant relationship. Indeed, is it not likely that the part played by this section in the library of this faithful group would be to serve as encouragement and pastoral exhortation? Let them remain firm. Let them hold on during the trials and conflicts which are ahead. The issue is sure. The domination of the corrupt leadership from which they have severed themselves is only for a time. Seen like this, this section falls into a recognizable category of religious literature, from the oracles of Second Isaiah, through the book of Daniel, to the literature of the Qumran Community, and it is of interest to see that in the Damascus Rule, Zech. 13.7 is interpreted in just this way.[24] {189}

---

24. *Damascus Document* B 19.7 (6QD).

Chapter 8

ZECHARIAH 12.1–13.6

This section is often treated as a related group of oracles clustered around broad, eschatological themes. That they are somewhat different in character from chs. 9ff. is often noted. So R.C. Dentan says that in Zech. 12–14 it is an apocalyptic spirit which dominates. Its concern is not with contemporary events but with those of the 'last days'.[1] Elliger agrees by saying that from ch. 12 onwards all the passages are orientated towards pure apocalyptic eschatology, having lost all traces of history (Elliger 1964: 167). Lamarche says that the doxology in 12.1 fittingly leads the reader towards the cosmic scale of these chapters which deal with a new heaven (14.7), a new earth (14.8-10), as well as the inner renewal of the Israelites (Lamarche 1961: 75).

The related themes in 12.1–13.6 are usually seen as the final, cosmic struggle in which the peoples of the world come to fight against Jerusalem, where, however, there takes place a dramatic and miraculous intervention of Yahweh who rescues his people by confounding the nations. This out-

---

1. Dentan (1956: 1106). The treatment of chs. 9ff. in the present work will have shown that we regard with caution claims that they relate primarily to 'contemporary events' (even though secondary interpretative allusions may have indicated a constant tendency for them to be so used and interpreted). They also, we have sought to show, are eschatological in character. Nevertheless, the change in emphasis and tone in chs. 12ff. is remarkable, in that, somewhat in the spirit of apocalyptic, the coming events are set against a much wider cosmic background. They do not relate to one people and one land alone. For this feature of apocalyptic, see *inter alia*, Rowley (1963: 26f.); Lindblom (1938: 101f.; 1962: 422). But, commenting on Deutero-Zechariah in particular, Lindblom (1962: 275) says, 'Although these chapters contain various ideas which are typical of apocalyptic literature, they are, neither in whole nor in part, an apocalypse, i.e. a book containing a system of secret doctrines concerning the cosmos, history, and the age to come, but a prophetic book, although with a prevailingly eschatological content'. Cf. Russell (1964); von Rad (1965: 301-308); Charles (1914: 24); Koch (1970).

ward act of salvation is matched by an inward act of cleansing and renewal by which the people of Jerusalem are moved to penitence because of the outpouring by Yahweh of a spirit of compassion and supplication, a penitence which appears to be not unconnected with the death of one who is pierced, and which results in cleansing from sin and uncleanness (12.10–13.1); this cleansing has the {190} result that the people turn from the worship of idols and become a community in which the activity of (false?) prophets is no longer tolerated (13.2-6). Such a broad, thematic continuity in this section is acknowledged in many commentaries,[2] although such recognition of broad unity of themes and general apocalyptic characteristics have certainly not meant that the section as it now stands is believed universally to have organic literary unity. It does seem clear that we are faced with a section which, in its present form, is the result of a complicated process of growth. Thus again caution is needed in any treatment. Yet, on the other hand, the broad continuity of theme is acknowledged by a consensus of opinion which is impressive. Further, even additions to the 'original' text are significant in showing how it was understood and interpreted in successive situations. Saebø's suggestion that the whole may represent the on-going and developing views of one circle of tradition and stream of faith is one which needs to be examined carefully (Saebø 1969: 276). Our own concern will again be centred primarily on the influence and treatment of older biblical material in this passage.

After the opening מַשָּׂא, which also appeared at 9.1 and which seems therefore to indicate the introduction of what was regarded as a separate section,[3] we come to the strange superscription דְּבַר־יְהוָה עַל־יִשְׂרָאֵל. It is

---

2. This can be observed from the titles given to this section: 'The Victory of God's People Over The Heathen' (Dentan: 1956: 1106); 'The Deliverance and Purification of Jerusalem and Judah' (Ackroyd 1962a: 654); 'The Jews in their Internal Relations' (Mitchell 1912: 32); 'The Deliverance and Glorious Future of Jerusalem' (Driver 1906: 261; Driver also links ch. 14 with this section under the same heading); Gaide (1968: 114) entitles chs. 12–14, 'Dernières Purifications et Triomphe de Jérusalem', under which he labels 13.1-13.6 as 'Première Série d'Oracles'; 'Jerusalem gerettet und gereinigt' (Elliger 1964: 166); 'Die Rettung Jerusalems vor den Völkern und seine innere Erneuerung' (Horst 1964: 254).

3. It is not possible to say by whom this was so regarded. The appearance of the same heading not only at 9.1 but at Mal. 1.1 might suggest that these two prophetic collections were seen as in some way related, and that the headings are therefore later than the authors of these chapters. On the other hand, if the suggestion put forward in this thesis of an anti-Jerusalem bias in Zech. 9–14 is correct, then those who collected and passed on these oracles may have found in Malachi a congenial and kindred spirit

strange, since what follows appears to deal wholly with Jerusalem and Judah, unlike chs. 9ff., where {191} references to the former northern kingdom do appear (see, e.g., 9.10, 13; 10.6f.). Elliger noted this peculiarity and wondered whether this was because v. 1 was intended as a superscription not to 12.1–13.6 alone, but to the whole of chs. 12–14 (Elliger 1964: 167). This is possible but it does not solve the problem of the reference to Israel since this is nowhere mentioned specifically in 13.7-14 either. Horst also refers to this, contenting himself with the observation that it is 'seltsam' (Horst 1964: 255).

There is, however, a possibility to be borne in mind concerning the use of the term 'Israel' here; it has often been remarked that the Chronicler employs the term 'Israel' when he is clearly referring to the community of Benjamin and Judah (see, e.g., 2 Chron. 11.1; 12.1, 6; 15.17; 21.24; 27.19-27). This is seen as an expression of his faith that it was the southern community, centred on the Jerusalem temple and its cultus, obedient to the Davidic monarchy, which alone constituted the true Israel. It is by no means impossible that some such feeling is behind its use here to introduce a section which deals with the final salvation of Judah and Jerusalem. Those who experience the deliverance of Yahweh's final victory and his work of cleansing and renewal will be the true Israel, heirs to all the promises relating to Israel from patriarchal times onwards, and not least to those especial promises of Ezekiel, whose fulfillment is now to be elaborated and applied to this prophet's own hearers. {192}

This introductory formula is extended by the words of a doxology which, as has often been remarked, is strongly reminiscent of Isa. 42.5. Both use the term נטה for Yahweh's creation of the heavens; both speak of the creation of the earth; both refer to the spirit of Yahweh which he puts within man (Zech. 12.1) or within those who walk on the earth (Isa. 42.5). There is, of course, another source for such terminology and theology, the accounts of creation in Gen. 1ff. A conscious formulation of the doctrine

with its stern words to the priests, its attack on cultic malpractices, and its promise of future cleansing for the cultic personnel. Its final call to heed the Mosaic Law and its naming Elijah, the prophet, as a forerunner of the final act of God, would also parallel emphases we have found in these chapters. It is impossible to be dogmatic about whether Malachi as we have it influenced the writing of Zech. 9–14, and so therefore the use of מַשָּׂא here is influenced by Malachi or whether Malachi was subsequently hailed as a kindred cry from the group who preserved the oracles of Zech. 9–14 and, as it were, integrated it into the corpus of their literature by the parallel form of the headings.

of creation seems to have been made during the time of the exile, which is not by any means the same as saying such a doctrine was not held in Israel much earlier. Indeed, the accounts of the wonders wrought by Yahweh over the forces of nature in the events of the Exodus, as well as many Psalms, some of which at least must be earlier than the exile, suggest that it was. But in the Priestly Code and Second Isaiah it becomes consciously formulated, and, possibly, it even passed into the liturgy of post-exilic Judaism[4] so that a common origin rather than direct borrowing may explain the similarities here. But presumably its introduction at this point suggests that the final act of salvation is to be seen as a new act of creation. The God who made this earth is able to restore it to its original purpose.[5] But this is also the context in which Deutero-Isaiah uses the appeal to creation theology in Isa. 42.5. The God of {193} the 'former things' can be relied upon to perform the 'new things' now declared. Within this concept the role of the servant is stressed. This does raise the question as to whether there is a deliberate evocation of the passage in Deutero-Isaiah here, not only in that in both places the appeal to creation occurs in the same theological context, but because here also the role of one who suffers is to play some part in the spiritual renewal of the wider community. We cannot be sure, but the possibility must not be overlooked.

Verses 2-9 deal with the theme of the coming together of the nations of the earth against Jerusalem, and of God's intervention to confound them and to give victory to his people. The frequent repetition of the phrase

---

4.   This of course is not certain. It is argued, however, by S.H. Hooke (1947: 36). He points out the close resemblances between Gen. 1 and the creation hymn of Ps. 104, which was probably sung at the New Year Festival. He thinks the seven dayś of creation may have been suited to the seven days of the festival. For another view that in origin Gen. 1 was derived from the festal cult, see S. Mowinckel (1962: 169).

5.   It is interesting to see how prominent a part such doxologies play in the Hodayoth, or Psalms of Thanksgiving of the Qumran Community. See, e.g., 1QH 1.7ff.; 13ff.; 19f. Comments of J.L. Price (1972: 12) are apposite here: 'Doxological language serves a variety of purposes: to clarify, to correct misunderstanding, to console, to declare things that are to come, etc'. A passage in the Rule is also important: 'From the God of knowledge comes all that is and shall be. Before everything existed He established their whole design, and, when, as ordained for them, they come into being, it is in accord with their glorious design that they accomplish their task without change' (1QS 3.15ff.). These are quoted here merely in order to illustrate how those who live in the full blaze of eschatological hope find comfort in reflecting how the sun of their hope rose with the creation. That which has been begun in order and wisdom will the more surely continue until its purpose is achieved.

הַהוּא בַּיּוֹם suggests that this is seen as an eschatological event, a final act of deliverance preceded by a time of distress and danger.[6] It has been widely held that this concept is based upon Ezek. 38ff., the chapters which tell of an attack upon the land of Israel by a coalition of nations headed by Gog, of the land of Magog, chief prince of Meshech and Tubal. He comes from 'the uttermost parts of the north' (38.15; 39.2), plotting against the land which seems to him to be a land of 'unwalled villages' (38.11) whose inhabitants are at that time dwelling securely, having been 'gathered from the {194} nations' (38.12). In one place at least it is said that he is brought to the land at the behest of Yahweh (38.2ff., 16), but it is only in order that in his own land Yahweh may destroy him. As the section now stands, this great conflict is accompanied by all kinds of terror: earthquake, pestilence, slaughter, hail, fire and brimstone (38.18ff.). All this is in fulfillment of words spoken 'in former days by my servants

6. Gressmann (1905 and 1929), to whom the preaching of the prophets was through and through eschatological, believed that the phrase 'in that day' of necessity bore always an eschatological meaning. At the other extreme, P.A. Munch took the phrase to be nothing more than a mere adverb of time (Munch 1936). There are places where it seems to be little more than that, as its occurrence in the historical books shows, but Mowinckel appears to be right when he asserts that, especially in later prophetic literature, 'in several passages it is clearly an eschatological formula; and the later prophetic tradition tended more and more to take it in the absolute and specific sense, as referring to the *dies* illa' (Mowinckel 1959: 147 n. 1). His connection of it with the earlier prophetic concept of 'the Day of Yahweh' also appears to be justified, whatever view is taken of his belief that this concept originated in the cult with the annual Enthronement Festival. In a hitherto unpublished work, to the typescript of which I have had access and from which permission to quote has kindly been granted, Simon J. de Vries (1975) undertakes an exhaustive exegesis of all Old Testament passages in which phrases indicating time appear. This confirms the view that the phrase הַהוּא בַּיּוֹם often has no technical sense at all. A passage from the Epilogue in which he discusses its use in apocalyptic, however, is relevant to its use in these chapters: 'Apocalyptic follows in the train of the late prophetic expansions to the prophetic oracles that use (*wehāyâh*) *bayyôm hahû*, in which the day of Yahweh's action often becomes so full and complex that it loses any proximate resemblance to an original situation of crisis. The future has become increasingly abstracted from the present. It is no longer an extension of the present, but an epoch on its own, detached from the present and irrelevant to it. Chronological interests intervene to define a duration of time lying ahead ere Yahweh will come to act. Zech. 14.21 reflects this mentality by itemizing the future day as a state of being rather than as the bearer of a decisive event. Other *bayyôm hahû* passages with forms of הָיָה reflect the influence of this mentality'. (I am grateful to Professor Ackroyd for access to this work.)

the prophets of Israel' (38.17) and has one sole purpose: that Yahweh's name, his power and holiness may be vindicated in the eyes of all peoples by what he does in delivering Israel. The multitude of slain will be so great that, in 39.11ff., it is said that it will take the Israelites seven months to bury them in the region of the Dead Sea, while in 39.17ff., beasts and birds are summoned to gorge themselves at a sacrificial feast on the carcasses and blood of the victims.

This pericope is obviously a complex one and presents many problems of historical, textual and form-critical nature. Even a superficial reading shows that it is not homogeneous, but contains inconsistencies and introduces motifs which are additional to the main theme. Eichrodt, for example, finds it impossible to attribute it at all to the authorship of Ezekiel (Eichrodt 1970: 520ff.) On the other hand, Zimmerli finds this section to be stylistically no different from the rest of the book, and its {195} reliance upon the Isaiah and Jeremiah traditions similar to that found elsewhere. It is characteristic of exilic prophecy (cf. Deutero-Isaiah) to show how earlier prophecy was being, and was to be, actualized. Zimmerli can find no compelling reason for denying Ezekiel's authorship in the realm of Mesopotamia before the appearance of Cyrus to the central core of the passage. In this he supports broadly the views of Herrmann (1924), Eissfeldt (1965: 380) and Fohrer (1955); cf. Zimmerli (1969: 942f.). Of course, he recognizes, with many others, that this central core has received many additions and embellishments.

Nevertheless, the fact that this could attract to itself such various motifs from a wide range of Old Testament traditions, even at the expense at times of what appears to us to be logical consistency, is of interest from the traditio-critical point of view. It shows how different eschatological concepts could be combined together and this is not without significance for our purposes here and our interest in the use made of such traditions in Zech. 12ff. We cannot, of course, be certain about the length of time which Ezek. 38ff. took in arriving at its present form and so say confidently what was, and what was not before our author. What we can do is to examine the motifs that occur there and compare them with the Gog pericope.

Before we do that, however, some attempt must be made to subject the Ezekiel passage itself to traditio-{196}criticism, for we must always be on our guard against assuming too readily that because certain themes occur in Ezek. 28ff. and Zech. 12ff. it is simply a case of Deutero-Zechariah borrowing directly from the earlier prophet. Both may be making creative use of wider traditions that were common heritage to both.

Zimmerli and others emphasize the fact that Ezekiel is here re-applying and re-interpreting the earlier oracles of Jeremiah in which he threatens invasion and disaster at the hands of an unspecified 'foe from the North', particularly in chs. 1 and 4–6. Zimmerli (1969: 939), at least, has no doubt that 'seine Rede vom Feind aus dem Norden auf der ihm vorliegenden jeremianischen Ankündigung fusst'. Yet Jeremiah himself may be kin to still older traditions. Earlier, Isaiah had predicted that the Assyrians should be defeated in the holy land itself:

> I will break the Assyrian in my land,
> and upon my mountains trample him underfoot;
> and his yoke shall depart from them,
> and his burden from their shoulder (14.25).[7]

But mention of Isaiah must recall the Zion tradition which influenced him so markedly and which is reflected in the 'Enthronement Psalms'. Ps. 48, having referred to 'Mount Zion in the far north' continues,

> For lo, the kings assembled,
> they came on together.
> As soon as they saw it, they were astounded,
> they were in panic, they took to flight:
> trembling took hold of them there,
> anguish as of a woman in travail. (vv. 5-7 [4-6] {197})

Similar ideas and language occur in Ps. 46, which hymns the presence of God in Jerusalem so that, when the 'nations rage' and the 'kingdoms totter', the city remains calm, for

> He breaks the bow and shatters the spear
> he burns the chariots with fire (cf. Ezek. 39.3),

and so is

> ...exalted among the nations (cf. Ezek. 38.16, 23; 39.7).

There follows the injunction,

> Be still and know that I am God I am exalted among the nations
> (הַרְפּוּ וּדְעוּ כִּי־אָנֹכִי אֱלֹהִים אָרוּם בַּגּוֹיִם),

7.   While earlier critical opinion divided over the authenticity of this passage, Duhm and Cheyne accepting it, Stade, Marti and Gray questioning it, more recent commentators have been readier to accept it. So Scott (1956: 264f.); Bright (1962: 500). Gray's comment (1912: 263) that the phrase 'my mountains' suspiciously recalls Ezekiel, fails to take account of the critical commonplace that dependence can occur both ways.

which is remarkably close to Ezek. 39.7,

> The nations will know that I am the LORD, the Holy One in Israel
> (וְיָדְעוּ הַגּוֹיִם כִּי־אֲנִי יְהוָה קָדוֹשׁ בְּיִשְׂרָאֵל).

Thus the language of the Jerusalem cultus seems to have exerted an influence here, an influence which is taken up in Isaiah and perhaps in Jeremiah, who in turn exert their own influence by the use they make of it. Yet history must have played its part in determining the shape this tradition assumed in the course of transmission, for the defeat of the exile, and the advantage taken of Judah's plight by neighbouring states, especially Edom, has left its impact of revulsion on almost all exilic and post-exilic Old Testament literature.[8] It is in this connection that Ezek. 36 {198} must be considered for, in the context of an attack against Edom and others for giving Yahweh's land to themselves 'as a possession with wholehearted joy and utter contempt that they might possess it and plunder it', the promise is now made to the mountains of Israel that these nations shall themselves suffer reproach, while they themselves become fertile and prosperous again.

This prediction of a victory against the nations who have taken possession of the land during the time of the exile is significant, because it is taken up again by Proto-Zechariah after the exile. However, in contrast to Ezekiel who speaks of the land as a whole, Zechariah speaks more particularly of Jerusalem and Judah. So, in the first vision, the word of God comes,

> I am exceedingly jealous for Jerusalem and for Zion. And I am very angry with the nations that are at ease; for while I was angry but a little they furthered the disaster (Zech. 1.14-15).

In the second vision of the four horns this theme is taken farther:

> These are the horns which scattered Judah, so that no man raised his head: and these have come to terrify them, to cast down the horns of the nations who lifted their horns against the land of Judah to scatter it (Zech. 2.2 [1.19]).

---

8.   We cannot, however, be certain of Edom's exact role at the time of the fall of Jerusalem. There is no hard evidence of their moving in to Judean territory before the late sixth or early fifth century BC (Cresson 1972: esp. 132). Cresson suggests that evidence of earlier hatred of Edom may be due to Nebuchadnezzar's use of Edomite troops in 587 BC, although we cannot be certain of that. He believes that later the Edomites 'became the exemplification of a nation and a people opposed to the Jews', and so 'became a symbol for "the enemy"' (Cresson 1972: 147f.).

In the following vision comes the invitation to the exiles to return:

> Flee from the land of the north, says the LORD...for thus said the LORD of hosts, after his glory had sent me to the nations which plundered you, for who touches you {199} touches the apple of his eye. Behold I will shake my hand over them, and they shall become plunder for those who served them (Zech. 2.10-12 [2.6-8]).

In the light of the interest shown in Zech. 12 in the part played by the surrounding countryside and the enduring security of Jerusalem, the promise in that same vision of Proto-Zechariah is interesting which says,

> Jerusalem shall be inhabited as villages without walls, because of the multitude of men and cattle in it

and the whole finishes with

> The LORD will inherit Judah as his portion in the holy land, and will again choose Jerusalem.

Thus we may conclude that the concept of a final victory of Yahweh over his foes in the holy land is a multi-stranded one.[9]

This brief survey of the lines of tradition which appear to lie behind Ezek. 38ff., and the various forms in which they appear in the Old Testament is necessary before any direct comparison of Zech. 12.1–13.6 is taken in hand.

We may note by way of similarity that the Ezekiel Gog pericope in its present position follows the act of prophetic symbolism involving the two staves, as the corresponding section in Zech. 12 follows the similar act recorded in the preceding chapter. Even if its position in Ezekiel is secondary it is nevertheless possible that it has influenced the arrangement of Zech. {200} 11ff. Like the Ezekiel tradition it depicts an actual invasion of the land by an assemblage of nations and their defeat by an act of divine intervention in the land itself. Both make frequent use of the connecting phrase 'On that day'. Further, there is some general resemblance between the language descriptive of terror and confusion in the two passages, some of which may be secondary to both (cf. Zech. 12.2ff.; Ezek. 38.19ff.; 39.3ff.).

On closer examination, however, much of this resemblance proves to be

---

9.   Eichrodt suggests that a still further variant of this tradition in the Old Testament is to be found in such passages as Isa. 60 and 66.18ff., for whereas these share the same longings as Isa. 63.1-6; Zech. 9.11ff., and 14.1ff., they see it achieved by peaceful means (Eichrodt 1970: 521).

general only, and more detailed examination suggests that Zech. 12 has been influenced more closely by passages other than Ezek. 38ff. In fact, the difference between the two sections are at least as striking as the parallels. There is a concentration upon Jerusalem and Judah in the Zechariah passage which is not found in Ezek. 38ff., where the whole land is the object both of the attack and the deliverance (cf. Ezek. 38.8ff., 11ff., 16, 19; 39.2ff., where the phrase is 'the mountains of Israel'). It may be that behind a phrase like 'the mountains of Israel' is a suggestion of the mountain of God,[10] or that a Temple theology is behind the phrase 'And my holy name I will make known in the midst of my people, Israel' (39.7), but it has not the explicit attention directed to it of the Zechariah passage. Indeed, whereas in Ezekiel the aim appears to be the vindication of Yahweh's name, the emphasis in Zech. 12 is much more on the deliverance wrought for Judah and Jerusalem. They will certainly come to {201} realize the power of Yahweh, but, except again by implication, there is no thought of the other nations being brought to a like acknowledgement. Nor are the nations that come actualized in any sense, or apostrophized. Nor is their destruction made the subject of such extension of thought and metaphor as that represented by the image of the sacrificial meal. Their role here is all but subsidiary with no details provided of their advance or their destruction. The whole scene is centred on Jerusalem and on Judah, and on the effect this victory has on them. Here it is indissolubly linked to the salvation of the community itself, to whose inward conversion the victory over the nations is but the prelude.

This is in no way to deny that Ezek. 38ff. has played any part in influencing the tradition of Zech. 12ff., but it is difficult to believe it has

---

10. This, however, is unlikely. Nearly all commentators agree that the use of the term 'mountains of Israel' is a term for the whole land. So Stalker (1968: 76ff.); Eichrodt (1970: 93) sees a further suggestion of the interaction between men and nature since nature has been made to subserve human life. Zimmerli (1969: 146ff.) says it has to some extent an archaic flavour about it stemming from the fact that at first Israel settled the mountain territory and Yahweh was seen as a mountain God. The influence of Isaiah may have been felt here by Ezekiel; cf. Isa. 14.25; 28.3. After the Deuteronomic reform, the mountains were seen as the locations of Israel's cultic apostasy, and it is as such that Ezekiel apostrophises them in his oracles of judgment: 6.2ff.; 9.9; 12.9; 33.28; 34.6. But, by the same token, his use of them in the oracles of promise and hope probably carries the idea that these former centres of apostasy will become the scenes of Yahweh's deliverance and blessing. In other words, the use of the term conveys a promise of Yahweh's regeneration as well as military deliverance of his people. So in 34.13ff.; 35.12; 36.1, 4, 8; 37.22 (cf. v. 23); 39.2, 17.

played a sole part. Elements from the other traditions glanced at above are also found. In Ezek. 36 the idea of the 'nations' around 'the mountains of Israel' occurs particularly in relation to Edom and those who took advantage of Israel's weakness during the time of the exile. The thought is of a defeat of such powers in order that the mountains may again be inhabited freely by the Israelites themselves in peace and plenty. It is not explicitly said that the defeat is to take place on Israelite soil, nor is the picture one of invasion {202} against a people already dwelling in the land in security as in Ezek. 38ff., and, presumably, in Zech. 12. Yet it is closely associated with an immediately succeeding section which promises a cleansing of the land subsequently from the stains of defilement by bloodshed and idolatry, and the provision for the people of a sprinkling with clean water and the putting within them of a new spirit. Not only is the same sequence to be observed in the Zechariah passage, but the same image for the defilement of sin as by 'menstruation' is used. Thus, in sequence of thought, in some terminology and in ideas there is a closer connection between our passage and Ezek. 36 than with Ezek. 38ff.[11]

It has already been suggested that a variant of the tradition of Yahweh's final victory over his foes around Jerusalem appears in Proto-Zechariah. Like Ezek. 36, this relates more specifically to the situation occasioned by the exile, but in that Zechariah spoke *after* the first return, slightly more of a futuristic note has crept into it, the fulfillment not now being identifiable exactly with the return but is closely connected with the completion of the re-building of the Temple itself. In Zech. 1.14 Yahweh announces,

---

11. But here also questions of direct relationship are complicated by critical questions of a difficult nature. These refer not only to the relationship of 36.1-15 with 16-38, both of which are probably of complex origin as they now stand, but the relation of these oracles to Ezekiel himself. H.G. May (1956: 47ff.), e.g., follows Irwin and Matthews in locating the substance of the chapter in the fifth century, probably about the time of Nehemiah. Zimmerli (1969: 874), on the other hand, finds that vv. 1-5 belong certainly before the return under Zerubbabel whether they are the work of Ezekiel or a disciple. Verses 16-38 he finds so close in spirit and matter to Second Isaiah, with its concern for the cleansing of sin and the rebuilding of the desolated homeland, that it must stem from the school of Ezekiel in exile at about that time. Zimmerli rightly points out that similar concerns are to be found in Zechariah. Neither view, however, prevents our accepting that it is possible that the author of Zech. 12 knew Ezek. 36 substantially in its present form. Certain terminology, as we shall see, suggests more than a general converging of thought, and a set of ideas of common origin. More recently, Zimmerli has reacted strongly against the assigning of passages of hope to a 'Deutero-Ezekiel', even while recognizing the place of a 'school' of Ezekiel in transmitting and re-interpreting his words (1972: esp. 515ff.).

> I am exceedingly jealous for Jerusalem and for Zion. And I am very angry
> with the nations that are at ease; for while I was angry but a little they
> furthered the disaster.

This is followed by the assurance, {203}

> I have returned to Jerusalem with compassion; my house shall be built in it
> (1.16).

What little has already happened *is* the work of God. He *has* come to Jerusalem and, as a consequence, signs of his activity will follow. The Temple, the sign of his presence and the means by which his relationship with his people is realized through due observance of the cult, will be rebuilt. Further, Jerusalem and the cities of the land will know prosperity and 'well-being' again.

But are not the nations which threatened Judah and Jerusalem still strong? Does not so weak a state and city hang on to its slender thread of life by their tolerance? The second vision assures them that the threat posed by these powers is to be removed by divine action. More re-assurance is to follow. In the third vision of the man with the line, presumably to measure Jerusalem's defenses, he is told by the messenger that Jerusalem shall be inhabited like villages without walls because of the multitude of men and cattle in her, that is, she will be immeasurable in size, while lack of walls will not matter,

> For I will be to her a wall of fire round about, says the LORD, and I will be
> the glory within her (2.9 [5]).

Much of this is the general and familiar language of the old Zion tradition of the Psalms, although the connection of military victory with inward cleansing {204} and renewal (ch. 3), the concern for Yahweh's reputation, his 'glory', and the idea of a divine military encounter with oppressing nations typified by Babylon, show some understanding of these traditions perhaps influenced by Ezekiel. The very forms of the 'night visions' may also show Ezekiel's influence.

A striking number of these features of the tradition in Proto-Zechariah find echo in Zech. 12ff., however. There, as in Proto-Zechariah, Jerusalem is at the centre of concern, explicitly mentioned by name, a feature absent from the Ezekiel versions of the traditions. There, as here, as the passage now stands, the fortunes of Judah and Jerusalem are seen as interrelated. Here, even more than in Proto-Zechariah, all this is seen as an impending action of the future, the divine future salvation. While Proto-Zechariah does not specifically speak of an invasion by these nations (although the traditional Zion language of Zech. 2.17 [13] suggests that at least it is from the Temple that the divine initiative starts) the idea of a cosmic conflict is common to both. Although Deutero-Zechariah emphasizes (at least in part) the active role of the people of Judah and Jerusalem which they are empowered to play, while Proto-Zechariah speaks more of the immediacy of the divine action, both share the similar imagery of the 'fire' which will play its part in the divine protection (Zech. 2.9 [5]; cf. 12.6) and both have the idea of this protection which Deutero-Zechariah describes as Yahweh's being a 'shield' to his people (12.8; cf. 2.9 [5]). Both these last two {205} references come close in their common idea of Yahweh being the 'glory' of his people, and both, above all, emphasize the close connection between the outward victory over the 'nations' and the inward cleansing and renewal of the people of God (Zech. 3; 5; 12.10; 13.6). Both see a restored leadership as playing a vital part in that cleansing, Joshua cleansed in ch. 3, Zerubbabel empowered by the Spirit of Yahweh, 4.6ff., the House of David being 'like God', 12.8, and all sections of the community moved to penitence when the 'spirit of compassion and supplication' is poured out on them by God (12.10ff.).

A general survey of the passage and its antecedents in the Old Testament suggests, then, that no one source for Zech. 12ff. can be claimed as exclusive for its inspiration and re-interpretation. The theme of Yahweh's miraculous deliverance of Jerusalem by the defeat of the peoples ranged against it has a long pre-history, appearing in several different forms.[12] The closest relationship appears to be with Proto-Zechariah, yet with two striking variations: the action is spoken of in slightly more futuristic terms and is waged against those who have actually invaded Judah and are besieging Jerusalem. If, however, as several indications appear to show, we have to do in these chapters with a re-interpretation and re-application of Zechariah's prophecies, such variants would be easily explained. {206}

Although the Temple was rebuilt, Zechariah's promises of what would follow that event were not wholly or lastingly fulfilled. It is possible, then, that the later prophet, or the circle of tradition from which these chapters come, has taken up the twin themes of deliverance for Judah and Jerusalem and a cleansing and renewal of the community and related them to the final act of salvation which is yet to come. Although it is thought of as 'at hand' it does not seem to be tied to any specific or imminent event such

---

12. The closest analysis of these themes is that by H.M. Lutz (1968), a study which compares 12.1-8 and 14.1-5 and seeks to trace their antecedents. It is examined more closely in our treatment of ch. 14.

as the arrival of Zerubbabel in Zechariah's time. Nor, in Zechariah's time, were the foes at the door of Jerusalem. They were identified with those countries into which so many Jews had been taken captive and where they, or their descendants, willingly or by necessity, were still in exile. The victory of Yahweh was seen primarily therefore as achieved against them, on their soil, with the result that such people might be free to return. But in the time of these later chapters, while there would, of course, be an even larger 'Diaspora', they must have known again what it was to hear the march of the invader's boot and to fall again under political domination. This could apply to a wide range of many possible periods in which the passage could be dated. It would be natural, therefore, to think in terms of the Ezekiel tradition which spoke more closely in the terms of the Zion tradition of the defeat of an invading foe {207} bent upon plunder and conquest. The relation of this in Ezekiel to the situation following the exile, as in Ezek. 36 with its reference to Edom's treachery, would make this the more appropriate. Such Ezekiel traditions were therefore used to supplement the Zechariah tradition, to show the relevance of biblical material generally to this contemporary situation.

Turning now to a more detailed examination of the contents of the passage itself, we may note first that the use of the construction of הִנֵּה with the participle is a very common one with the earlier prophets (e.g. Isa. 3.1; 10.33; 17.1, etc., and often with first person singular pronominal suffix, e.g. Jer. 8.17; 9.22) where it signifies *futurum instans*, that is, an event in the immediate future (Driver 1892: §135.3; GKC §116p; BDB: 244). This emphasizes the view, first identified with Stade, that the dependence on earlier prophets in these chapters indicates the viewpoint that God is, at the time of their being written, about to fulfill the unfulfilled prophecies of earlier times.

We are then introduced to two striking metaphors, descriptive of Yahweh's defense of Jerusalem and the overthrow of her foes. He will make the city a 'cup of reeling' (סַף־רַעַל) to all the peoples surrounding her, and a 'stone of burden' (אֶבֶן מַעֲמָסָה) for 'all the peoples'. The idea of judgment or blessing as a cup handed out by Yahweh to be drunk is a familiar one in the Old Testament.[13] Two instances are of particular interest. The first occurs in Isa. 51.17, 22ff. {208} Jerusalem, who is said to have

---

13. E.g. Pss. 11.6; 16.5; 75.9 (8); Jer. 51.7; Ezek. 23.31ff.; Hab. 2.15ff. Whether the original idea for the figure comes from the banquet where the host singles out the guest he wishes to mark for special honour, or from the idea of trial by ordeal is not certain. Cf. Weiser (1962: 157, 175, 523).

drunk at the hand of the LORD
the cup of his wrath

and to have

drunk to the dregs
the bowl of staggering (אֶת־קֻבַּעַת כּוֹס הַתַּרְעֵלָה),

is now called on to rouse herself because God, who pleads the cause of his people, is about to reverse her judgment. This cup is to be taken from her hand

and I will put it into the hand of your tormentors.

Such an idea had already figured in Jer. 25.15ff., in a passage whose authorship is disputed, but which is generally thought to have been composed as an introduction or conclusion to the oracles about foreign nations in the book. In any case, the use of the figure seems to have been already established for the author of Zech. 12. In the Jeremiah passage it is only the general idea of the judgment of Yahweh to all upon the nations. In the passage from Second Isaiah this is already being reversed for Jerusalem, in that the judgment she has suffered is now to be dealt out by Yahweh to her former tormentors. Here there is identity of vocabulary in the use of root רעל, a use which seems to suggest that the prophet is here claiming that this prediction is about to be fulfilled. He takes the picture still a step further, however. Jerusalem herself is to be the 'cup of reeling' to these {209} peoples, although clearly it is Yahweh's work to make it so.

In none of these earlier passages, however, is the word סַף used. It has a double meaning, as 'threshold' or 'sill', but also a 'goblet' or 'basin'. It is occasionally used in a secular sense (as in Judg. 19.27; 2 Sam. 17.28; Zeph. 2.14), but much more often it is used, either of the threshold of the Temple, or of sacred temple vessels for cultic purposes.[14] One wonders whether, in view of that, there is a deliberate use of the term, evocative of the Temple, and the presence of Yahweh in the midst of his people of which the Temple was the sign. If so, it would provide another link with Proto-Zechariah, for whom this very sign was the assurance of Yahweh's deliverance of Jerusalem, two ideas explicitly related in Zech. 2.13ff. (9ff.), but connected throughout the earlier prophecy.

14. Of the threshold of the Temple, 2 Kgs 12.10 (9); 22.4; 23.4; 25.18; 1 Chron. 9.19, 22; 2 Chron. 3.7; 23.4; 34.9; Isa. 6.4; Jer. 35.4; 42.4; Ezek. 40.6, 7; 41.16; 43.8; Amos 9.1. Of sacred vessels, Exod. 12.22; 2 Kgs 12.14 (13); Jer. 52.19.

The other metaphor of Jerusalem as a stone of burden on which those who attempt to carry it off injure themselves, is often associated with the Greek sport of weight-lifting (so Dentan 1956: 1106; Horst 1964: 255; Driver 1906: 262). That might have played its part but again there is 'prophetic' tradition for the idea of Jerusalem as a 'stone' in the words of Isa. 28.16:

> Behold, I am laying in Zion for a foundation,
> a stone, a tested stone (אֶבֶן אֶבֶן בֹּחַן)...
> He who believes will not be in haste.

Remembering that this stone is 'righteousness' (v. 17) and that it occurs in a context of warning to wrongdoers {210} whose refuge of lies will be swept away by hail and whose shelter will be inundated with flood water, it is an interesting link with the emphasis on a renewed community in Jerusalem brought into a right relationship with Yahweh, to be found in Zech. 12ff., and suggests that there was at least an evocation of this earlier prophetic passage intended here. Of course, it is certainly developed further, as was the picture of Jerusalem herself being the 'cup of reeling' to the nations. Here the picture is of the nations trying to lift the stone. How much more starkly the folly of such action appears if the stone they are trying to remove is that which Yahweh himself has laid. Those who do so will 'be gashed' or 'gash themselves'. The verb is the niphal of שׂרט, whose basic meaning is 'to scratch' and hence 'to incise'. It could evidently be used of self-inflicted incisions as a sign of mourning, for its only other appearance in the Old Testament as a verb is in the qal at Lev. 21.5. Here it is forbidden to priests at a time of death. The noun form שָׂרֶטֶת also appears in the same verse, and again in the form שָׂרֶט in Lev. 19.28, where it is forbidden to all Israelites. The use of such a rare term may carry with it, therefore, a conscious allusion. Those who do attempt to dislodge Yahweh's 'stone' will indeed have cause to mourn in a way that marks them off from those, priests and people, who now {211} are 'holy' to Yahweh (Lev. 21.6).

However, one further possible antecedent to the idea of Jerusalem as a 'stone' needs consideration. In commenting on the phrase in 9.16, where it is said that Yahweh will make his people like 'the jewels of a crown' (אַבְנֵי־נֵזֶר), attention was drawn to the prominent part אֶבֶן plays in the oracles of Proto-Zechariah (F 1: {85ff.}, now pp. 59ff.). It is of interest that Saebø draws attention to the same point in his comments on 12.3.[15] In 3.9,

---

15. 'Zudem ist aber nicht zu übersehen, dass auch in Sach. 1–8, mid zwar an den

with the 'stone with seven facets', which, presumably, is that worn in the high-priest's turban (cf. Exod. 28.36ff.), the emphasis is on the cleansing of the community as Yahweh removes its guilt, Joshua presumably being called to an 'atoning function'.[16] This would accord well with the association of the 'stone' which, according to Isaiah, Yahweh would lay in Zion, namely, 'rightness'. It may, like the use of the word סַף, suggest a duly reconstituted priesthood, officiating in a sanctified Temple. In the light of our discussion of Zech. 11.4-17; 13.7-9, this would be significant. In Zech. 4.7 the term is again associated with the Temple and Zerubbabel's triumphant conclusion of its rebuilding. In 4.10, it is said that men shall rejoice to see הָאֶבֶן הַבְּדִיל in the hands of Zerubbabel.[17]

It would seem then as though in Proto-Zechariah the idea of Isa. 28.16 receives some re-interpretation, {212} in that the laying of the 'stone' of the Temple is Yahweh's accomplishment through Zerubbabel, and who also, in Joshua, provides a 'stone', i.e. a priesthood by which the community can be cleansed and renewed.

It seems, therefore, that the two pictures in Zech. 12.2ff. are not just arbitrarily chosen nor, in the second instance, is the reference primarily to Greek sports. Nor are they intended merely as assurances of military victory. There are good grounds for seeing in them a conscious re-interpretation and re-application of earlier prophetic motifs giving assurance of renewal and cleansing. In addition, there may not be wanting a hint that

theologisch wichtigen Stellen 3.9, 4.7, 4.9, 6.12f und Jes. 28.16, eine besondere Rede von "Stein" vorleigt' (Saebø 1969: 269 n).

16. So P.R. Ackroyd (1962a: 648; 1968a: 199). It should be noted, however, that a re-arrangement of the text proposed by NEB links the stone with seven facets of 3.9 with the explanation of 4.10, 'These seven are the eyes of the LORD, which range through the whole earth', in which the significance of it is found in the presence of Yahweh in his Temple from which he sees (and therefore controls) the whole earth. Even if this is right, however (and attempts to re-arrange even an unsatisfactory text are often arbitrary), the cleansed priesthood is closely related to the idea of Yahweh's presence in the Temple again and so the two ideas are by no means foreign to each other.

17. Unfortunately, the exact sense of הַבְּדִיל is not clear. Interestingly, the NEB takes it as the 'stone called Separation', linking it with the Levitical doctrine of separation as enunciated in Lev. 20.24-26. Normally it is taken to mean 'tin', that which is 'separated' from precious metal, and hence a 'plummet'. Even so, prophetic imagery would link this with that which is יָשָׁר or 'on the level' as our own idiom has it, and so 'true', 'right' or 'just' (cf. Amos 7.7ff.). For other views, see P.R. Ackroyd (1968a: 172 n).

this will be associated with a properly ordered cultus, effected by a truly consecrated priesthood of Yahweh's appointing, in a Temple which is again his dwelling place, resulting in a community of true righteousness.

Before we finally leave this, it is worthy of note that that which Yahweh makes Jerusalem, he makes her 'to all peoples' (לְכָל־הָעַמִּים). It was the covenant with 'all the peoples' which had been annulled by the prophetic action in 11.10. Does this suggest there is to be an ultimate reversal of this? The effect on the nations here appears to be one only of confusion and destruction. However, in Zech. 14 this can be seen to be directed against those who actively oppose the people of God, yet such idea not being felt inconsistent {213} with a remnant of the nations coming up to worship in Jerusalem. The apparent alternation between 'universalist' and 'exclusivist' conceptions in these chapters must receive fuller treatment.

Brief attention must now be paid to the motif which appears in v. 2b, following the first picture of Jerusalem as a 'cup of reeling'. Here for the first time the motif of Judah's part in all that is happening around Jerusalem is mentioned, a theme which is to recur in various ways in vv. 4b, 5, 6 and 7. These are widely held to be secondary, and to reflect some period of tension between the capital and the surrounding territory (so *BHS* and many commentators).

Yet, leaving aside v. 2b for the moment, whose rendering is uncertain and whose sense appears ambiguous, there is little to suggest in these verses open hostility between Judah and Jerusalem. Verse 4 contrasts the favour with which God will regard with open eyes the 'House of Judah' when, on the contrary, he confounds the mounts of the invading nations with blindness and panic, and their riders with frenzy. It is not really certain that the use of the title 'House of Judah' is meant to be contrasted with Jerusalem. When it is used in the Old Testament it is mainly its close *connection* with Jerusalem and, above all, the royal line of David which is being emphasized. After all, it was the men of the {214} 'House of Judah' who first supported David and then acclaimed him king (2 Sam. 2.4-10); in the Chronicler the term 'House of Judah' together with 'House of Benjamin' became an almost technical term for the ideal community of God's people, ideal because of their allegiance to the line of David, the Temple and the royal city in their midst. And here in Zech. 12.4bf., there is a mutual interaction between the two, the 'House of Judah' drawing faith and encouragement from God's work at the city.

It has often been pointed out that v. 4a is very close to Deut. 28.28 where these words are used to describe the panic, frenzy and blindness which will come upon the people of God if ever they are disobedient to the prescriptions of the code of law:

> The LORD will cause you to be defeated before your enemies: you shall go one way against them and flee seven ways before them, and you shall be a horror to all the kingdoms of the earth… The LORD will smite you with madness (שִׁגָּעוֹן), and blindness (עִוָּרוֹן) and confusion of mind (תִּמְהוֹן לֵבָב) (vv. 25, 28).

The first and third of these occur in Zech. 12.4a, while the second, affecting the horses, comes in 4b. In that the second and third of the terms occur only in these two places it would seem that a conscious allusion was in mind. Again, therefore, we have a kind of reversal of judgment. That which was threatened against God's own people if they were disobedient now becomes {215} the fate of the nations who set themselves against Yahweh's purposes for his own people. But why should reference be made to *this* passage? Deut. 28.26 may provide a clue:

> And your dead body shall be found for all the birds of the air, and for the beasts of the earth; and there shall be none to frighten them away.

In Ezek. 39.17ff., the destruction of God is followed by an invitation to be addressed

> to the birds of every sort and to all beasts of the field…

to come to

> …the sacrificial feast which I am preparing for you…
> you shall eat the flesh of the mighty…

This feature of the motif does not appear in Zech. 12ff., but it is possible that it is being alluded to by this reference to Deut. 28.

So just as Yahweh opens his eyes on the House of Judah,[18] so the eyes of the 'clans of Judah', are opened to see that Yahweh is the strength of the inhabitants of Jerusalem, and consequently, theirs as well (v. 5). Far from suggesting an antipathy between the two, it suggests rather a close relationship of mutual faith. The knowledge that Yahweh will not abandon his city means deliverance and safety for the whole land.

Thus the 'clans of Judah' will be empowered by Yahweh to take an

---

18. If the emendation proposed by BH were accepted (וּלְבֵית יְהוּדָה אֶפְקַח אֶת-עֵינוֹ), it would be tempting here to see an evocation of the Dothan incident recorded in 2 Kgs 6.15ff. The emendation lacks any support in the Versions, however, and must be rejected as arbitrary.

active part in the final denouement of 'salvation-history' ('On that day').
In so far as {216} they stand first in the way of the advance of the nations
on Jerusalem they go into action first. Yahweh makes them 'like a fire-pot
in a wood' (כְּכִיּוֹר אֵשׁ בְּעֵצִים). It is strange that this elsewhere in the Old
Testament refers mainly to a vessel for holding water, and particularly to
the 'laver', in the Temple (Exod. 30.18, 28, 31; 39.39; 40.7, 11, 30, etc.).
So, like סַף, this also has cultic associations and is linked with the idea of
cleansing. Perhaps behind the use of such a term here is the thought of the
cleansing of the land of its defilement by its pagan invaders, an idea also
prominent in Ezek. 39. (Certainly, the idea of fire as a form of theophany
is common to the Old Testament; see Exod. 3.2ff.; Pss. 73.3 [2]; 83.15
[14]; 97.3, etc.) The metaphor is extended further by saying that the clans
of Judah will become like a 'blazing torch among the sheaves' כְּלַפִּיד
אֵשׁ בְּעָמִיר, and that they 'shall devour to the right and left all the peoples
round about', so that, while all this is going on, 'Jerusalem shall remain in
her place', i.e. in security.[19] To some extent this recalls Samson's exploit
when he let loose the torches tied to the tails of 300 foxes in the harvest
fields of the Philistines (Judg. 15.1-5). He also took לַפִּדִים (v. 4), and dis-
patched them to burn up the standing 'stooks' of the reaped grain. Remembering that in Zech. 9.6 there had been the promise, 'I will make an
end of the pride of Philistia', an allusion might be intended here. {217}

It is v. 7 which appears to introduce some note of tension between the
city of Jerusalem and the people of Judah. Judah will be the first to experience victory so that 'the glory of the House of David and the glory of the
inhabitants of Jerusalem shall not be exalted over Judah'. Yet this verse
does not appear to be marked by great hostility towards the city. Nor does
its main thrust appear to be to exalt Judah. Its chief emphasis seems to be
that the victory is *Yahweh's* (וְהוֹשִׁיעַ יְהוָה אֶת־אָהֳלֵי יְהוּדָה). Victory is seen
to be his gift, not the result of any special claims his people have on him
by virtue of an historic Davidic covenant, their cultic observances or their
special piety. Indeed, for the House of David and the Jerusalem community generally, it is followed by an act of repentance for sin. Thus, the
special relationship of Yahweh with David and Jerusalem is not denied,
nor their special place in his purpose of redemption, but these are not
allowed to be the *basis* of his deliverance. This would seem to be the

---

19. It is interesting that a free quotation of this verse appears in the *War Rule* of the
Qumran Community: 'Thou wilt kindle the downcast of spirit and they shall be a
flaming torch in the straw, to consume ungodliness and never to cease until iniquity is
destroyed' (11.10, G. Vermes' translation).

purpose in stating that they will not be the first to experience victory. Such a statement would be wholly consonant with the views of a prophet or group which, as we have suggested, is to be seen elsewhere in these chapters, had a love for Jerusalem and a belief in its crucial place in the *Heilsgeschichte*, yet also a persistent belief that its present priesthood, cultus and leadership were not such as were pleasing to {218} Yahweh and must, therefore, be dispensed with or transformed by the cleansing of divine grace.

Indeed, the use of the noun תִּפְאָרָה elsewhere in the Old Testament lends support to such a view. More than once it is stressed that true 'beauty' or 'glory' come from Yahweh alone. In Ps. 89, a psalm celebrating the Davidic covenant and which recalls Yahweh's mighty acts of deliverance and the promises made to David in order now to appeal to him in faith at a time of distress and apparent disaster, it is said, in v. 18 (17),

> For thou art the *glory* of their strength:
> by thy favour our horn is exalted.

Or again in one of the 'Enthronement Psalms' (96), it is said, in v. 6,

> Honour and majesty are before him,
> strength and *beauty* are in his sanctuary.

It is, then, a divine attribute received by men only as a gift of divine grace. Other nations have claimed to have a תִּפְאָרָה of their own apart from Yahweh, but it proved to be an illusory and short-lived supposition, e.g. Isa. 10.12. Nor must Yahweh's own servants seek to magnify their glory as over against Yahweh's. So Deborah as she sends Barak on his way against Sisera says,

> Nevertheless the road on which you are going will not lead to your *glory*,
> for the LORD will sell Sisera into the hand of a woman (Judg. 4.9). {219}

All this would tend to show that the emphasis here is not upon Judah, as over against Jerusalem, but on the initiative and grace of Yahweh. Any תִּפְאָרָה of the House of David and the inhabitants of Jerusalem will be, not by any right of theirs, but by the divine gift, and will consist not only of victory, but also of transformation of heart and spirit, a transformation about to be described.

But we have not yet dealt with v. 2b which presents difficulties of a textual and exegetical nature. As the MT stands its literal rendering could be, 'And, moreover, it shall be upon (or against) Judah in the siege against Jerusalem'. The Versions have had difficulty with this. The LXX reads (or

simplifies?), 'and in Judah there shall be a siege against Jerusalem'; the
Hebrew preposition עַל does not normally bear the meaning 'in', so presumably either the LXX is interpreting, or it read a Hebrew MS with the
preposition בְּ. The בְּ before מָצוֹר is omitted. The Vulgate omitted the first
עַל, and took it to mean that Judah would also take part in the siege against
Jerusalem, a sense given by the Targum, 'the people compel Judah to fight
against Jerusalem'. Several commentators conclude that the text did
originally refer to a participation on the part of Judah in the general assault
on Jerusalem. They base their conclusions on the similar sense of 14.14
and that the 'in' Judah of the LXX and the 'compel' {220} of the Targum
look like attempts to soften the original difficulty of the text. On the other
hand, Marti and Otzen have both argued that what was meant was that
Judah took part in the siege objectively, not subjectively, suffering it rather
than inflicting it. The arguments cannot be conclusive. The first עַל is hard
to explain if the original text spoke of Judah taking part in the siege subjectively. Again, it is quite possible that it is Zech. 14.14 which has
influenced the textual tradition of this verse, and not *vice versa*. Nor is the
form of יִהְיֶה feminine as one would have expected if Judah had been the
subject. Perhaps the balance of probability lies with the view that a rider is
added to the effect that Judah will also suffer the attack directed against
Jerusalem. A very slight textual emendation would establish this sense if
we were to read וְגַם עַל־יְהוּדָה יִהְיֶה כַּמָּצוֹר עַל־יְרוּשָׁלַיִם the prepositions כ
and בְּ being very easily interchangeable. This would yield perfectly good
sense. 'Against Judah it will be like the siege against Jerusalem', even if
we may still suspect that the clause is additional and secondary to what has
preceded it.

The conclusions to which we come on these verses, then, must of
necessity be tentative and cautious. The motifs of the inter-relations
between Jerusalem and Judah may well be secondary elaborations. There
are {221} form-critical grounds for believing that we have here the final
result of an elaborate process of composite arrangement. Yet the text as it
now stands does not offer such very great logical and structural inconsistencies as have been sometimes alleged. Judah and Jerusalem are not put
into violent opposition to one another. They are certainly treated as distinct, but by no means unrelated elements in the tradition. Both alike are to
be mutual recipients of divine grace and initiative in Yahweh's act of
salvation. There is little here which is not in the spirit of such an earlier
prophet as Isaiah who 'saw oracles concerning Judah and Jerusalem' (2.1).
The most extreme examples of the fragmentizing approach are afforded by

Lutz (1968: 11ff.) who on literary grounds and on divisions of subject matter reduces it to a basic core of vv. 2a, 3a and 4a, and Saebø, who on a rigid application of form-critical principles insists that the phrase בַּיּוֹם הַהוּא introduces one group of oracles, while the fuller וְהָיָה בַיּוֹם־הַהוּא introduces another (Saebø 1969: 260ff.). It is highly questionable whether by the time of this material the older forms of oracular utterance, if ever they were as clearly defined as some critics would have us believe, still were used with such precision and accuracy as is claimed. We are at least justified in asking whether they had not by this time become catch-phrases from the earlier prophetic material whose use now was {222} conventional or a sign of reverence for the words which the earlier prophets had spoken.

A certain parallel between the action of Yahweh towards the inhabitants of Judah and Jerusalem can be observed in the text as it now stands, which suggests a greater degree of structure than either Lutz or Saebø have seen. The clans of Judah are first led to 'see' the strength of Yahweh of hosts, a knowledge mediated to them at this time of crisis through the inhabitants of Jerusalem (v. 5); such insight presumably leads them to a renewed trust in Yahweh for they are enabled by him to perform superhuman feats against their enemies as Samson had done long before. But vv. 8ff. speak of the same divine action towards the inhabitants of Jerusalem. They will be given supernatural strength (v. 8) and will be led to an act of repentance (vv. 10ff.). True, the order is inverted, but too much should not be made of this. There is no suggestion in the text that a kind of timetable of the last events is being drawn up here. All must be largely events contemporary with each other, since the images in vv. 2ff. suggest ideas of righteousness and holiness as we have seen, while in v. 5 the inhabitants of Jerusalem already know such a relationship with God as proves to be an example to their neighbours. These things give perhaps the surest indication that a number of originally independent concepts and sayings have been brought together, since to {223} some extent they are tautologous. Yet, if so, they have been combined into a coherent whole with a very clear sequence of thought. It is not altogether strange that the act of penitence is described *after* the miraculous work of Yahweh, since this is the very clear and significant order in Ezek. 36.24-31. Ezekiel is thereby stressing that the ground of Yahweh's action is not the repentance of the Israelites, but his own sole and direct initiative out of concern for his 'Name' of which the repentance is a result. Perhaps the same emphasis is being made here.

It is said that Yahweh will put a 'shield' (גָּנַן) about the inhabitants of Jerusalem (v. 8). This is the re-statement of older promises concerning

Jerusalem. In the tradition of the Sennacherib invasion found in Isa. 37, the divine word is recorded (v. 35): 'I will defend (וְגַנּוֹתִי) this city to save it, for my own sake, and the sake of my servant David', a promise repeated to Hezekiah in 38.6. Indeed, the verb figures prominently in Isaianic Zion traditions, for in Isa. 31.5 it is said,

> Like birds hovering, so the LORD of hosts
> will protect Jerusalem,
> he will protect and deliver it (יָגֵן ...גָּנוֹן וְהִצִּיל).

Two thoughts arise. Remembering how the doctrine of the inviolability of Jerusalem seemed (rightly or wrongly) to be sanctioned by the Isaianic use of the Zion/David traditions, a doctrine against which Jeremiah and Ezekiel {224} struggled, is this why the prophet goes on immediately here to stress the repentance, renewal and cleansing of the community in a way more in the tradition, to some extent of Jeremiah, and certainly of Ezekiel? The other point is whether the close link of the Isaianic words about the future of Jerusalem with the David tradition ('for the sake of my servant David') accounts for the strangely phrased promise concerning the transformation of the House of David which follows. This calls for some more detailed treatment of the thinking concerning the Davidic line revealed here.

Of course, both the ideas of the divine deliverance of Jerusalem, and of the cleansing of the community through its leadership, are already familiar from Proto-Zechariah, as we have seen. The promise here is of a divine strengthening of the 'feeble' (הַנִּכְשָׁל) among them. It recalls the promise of Second Isaiah,

> Even youths shall faint and be weary,
> and young men shall fall exhausted (כָּשׁוֹל יִכָּשֵׁלוּ),
> but they who wait for the LORD
> shall renew their strength (Isa. 40.30ff.).

As C.R. North has suggested (1964: 90) there may be the thought in the Isaiah passage that the 'young men' (בַּחוּרִים) who fall, by contrast with the 'faint' and 'those who have no strength' of v. 29, may be those who have confidence in their own unaided powers, as opposed to those whose trust is entirely in Yahweh. He cites Ps. 27.2. C. Westermann (1969: 60ff.) traces in detail the close similarity of the language here with {225} that of Psalms such as Ps. 33, especially vv. 16ff., which run,

> A king is not saved by his great army;
> a warrior is not delivered by his great strength...

The eye of the LORD is on those who fear him,
on those who hope in his steadfast love.

Verse 20 continues,

Our soul waits for the LORD;
he is our help and shield (עֶזְרֵנוּ וּמָגִנֵּנוּ).

Westermann concludes, 'In such language, familiar to his hearers from the hymns they had sung at worship in earlier days, the prophet speaks to the nation's heart' (61). Such a nexus of ideas may well lie behind this choice of word here, suggesting further, that not only military strength is offered by Yahweh, but a turning of his people, who had erred in finding their confidence in themselves, to a new and sole trust in him.[20]

The promise that such shall be 'like David' shows that this author is again drawing on the David tradition, as appears to have been the case in 9.9ff. It recalls the special place such tradition assigned to David and his relationship to Yahweh by virtue of divine choice (2 Sam. 7.8ff.; 23.2ff.).

In dealing with 9.9ff. a number of suggestions were put forward concerning the modification which this traditional messianic hope appeared to have undergone, and a number of questions were raised which had, at that point, to be left unanswered. It was argued that the figure of the Davidic Messiah was being 're-interpreted' {226} in the light of the figure of the 'Suffering Servant' of Second Isaiah, and this raised the question of whether it was being subjected to the same kind of democratization of the Davidic hope expressed in Isa. 55.3ff. The question was also raised as to whether anything of the Chronicler's modification of the hope was echoed there, namely, the seeing of it as being fulfilled not in political terms, but in the emergence of the whole cultic community of the Temple and Torah-centred people of Judaism. Finally, the role of the spoken word was noted which might also give rise to the question as to whether the democratization of the hope was seen as being fulfilled by a particular prophetic community.

We certainly cannot assume identity of authorship or traditional viewpoint lying behind 9.9ff. and 12.7ff., but a comparison of them is needful, so that we may see how far the latter passage helps us to answer, or to leave in doubt, the questions raised by the earlier.

One major argument against a democratizing tendency might seem to be

---

20. כשל often has the meaning 'to stumble', 'stagger', 'be unstable'. Thus it is not only parallel to the root עיף in some instances, but often to root נפל (e.g. Isa. 3.8; 31.3; Jer. 6.15, etc). The noun כָּשִׁיל ('axe'), suggests a link with the idea of 'felling'.

that he still gives a place for the 'House of David'. Not only was this apparently alluded to in 9.9ff. but immediately following now, we have the phrase, 'the House of David shall be like God, like the angel of the LORD, at their head', whereas the logical outcome of the democratization of the Davidic hope would surely be the disappearance of the Davidic line. This is what von Rad maintains has virtually happened with {227} Second Isaiah.[21]

We must then examine what is said of the House of David. The phrase that it shall 'be like God' is a startling one, and it is usually suggested that the additional phrase, apparently in apposition, 'like the angel of the LORD' is an attempt to soften its impact by someone who found it too startling.[22] The Versions show such attempts. The Targum reads, 'The House of David shall be like princes and shall flourish like kings'; the LXX has, 'like the House of God'; the Vulgate 'domus David *quasi Dei*'. All of this is a powerful argument for the originality of the more difficult reading. S.R. Driver (1906: 264) saw as a possible rendering, 'comparable even to a divine being'.

Is there any Old Testament precedent which could throw light on the choice of so strange a saying? It seems to take us beyond the David tradition as such, unless, in a general way, it is the aspect of the king's role of God's vice-regent on earth which is being stressed (Mowinckel 1962: I, 53ff.; Johnson 1958: 204-35; 1967: esp. 1-30). But this very striking phrase is used of Moses. In Exod. 4.16, after Moses has complained that he cannot speak fittingly, God promises that Aaron shall be his spokesman,

> He shall speak for you to the people; and he shall be a mouth for you, and you shall be to him as God (לֵאלֹהִים).

Whether Rylaarsdam (1952: 879ff.) is right in seeing here some attempt to {228} define the relative positions of prophet and priests, or not, it certainly seems to suggest a certain mutuality of function. Moses, by virtue of his special relationship with Yahweh, enables Aaron to speak and act authentically according to Yahweh's mind and purpose. Yet Aaron has a vital link in the accomplishment of this purpose, so that it is by both roles,

---

21. 'In thus "democratizing" the tradition, Deutero-Isaiah actually robbed it of its specific content. Indeed, the Messianic hope had no place in his prophetic ideas' (von Rad 1965: 240).

22. So Mitchell (1912: 326); R.C. Dentan (1956: 1107); P.R. Ackroyd (1962a: 654), *inter alia*. S.R. Driver, takes it to be a reference to the angel of Yahweh as powerful protector (Ps. 24.7) and leader (לִפְנֵיהֶם), Exod. 14.19, etc. (1906: 264).

under Yahweh, that eventually the hostile power of Egypt is neutralized and the deliverance of the Exodus takes place.

Is it possible that such a thought is implicit in Zech. 12.8? The House of David will be restored to its right relationship with God, and this will be part of God's renewal of the *whole* community. The House of David has its place and role in the new community, but it is no longer the *sole* mediator of his life. Then the thought would be not only of military might, but of that kind of relationship to God which mediates all that makes for 'life', as Psalms such as Ps. 72 suggest (Johnson 1967: 4, 7ff., 101ff., 134ff), and indeed, as the use of such a term as root כשל earlier in the verse was seen to suggest. Then right relationship to God and the deliverance of Yahweh are as closely associated here as throughout this section.

In support of such a view it has to be noticed that the Messianism of these chapters is muted. Certainly the rejection of existing leadership and the provision {229} of other leadership of divine appointment is prominent, as we have seen. But this is most often spoken of in general terms which suggests not only political leadership but that of priests and prophets as well. Here, the House of David figures in a special role but, as the act of penitence which follows shows, it is by no means an exclusive one. It is one amongst others, and, with them, needs penitence, cleansing and renewal. We have already seen that the 'Messianism' of 9.9ff. appears to have been strongly modified. Traditional 'Messianic' hope does not figure prominently elsewhere. It is nowhere mentioned, for example, in ch. 14. This hardly fits a lively expectation of a Messiah whose miraculous intervention makes him the agent of salvation for the community as a whole.[23]

Further, it is to be noted that the 'House of David' is distinguished in vv. 8 and 10, from the 'inhabitants of Jerusalem', which does not suggest a total 'democratization' of the Davidic concept here. But it has also to be seen that the 'House of David' has to join in the general repentance of the whole community. So in no way is it seen as an agent of the deliverance and transformation of the community in traditionally {230} Messianic terms. A Messiah who needs to join in the general repentance is not quite the figure of traditional Messianic hope.

It is interesting to note the comment of T. Chary (1955: 230) on 12.7ff.: 'Devant cette imprécision, l'on est tenté de croire que les espérances messianiques placées dans la dynastie royale sont devenues hésitantes. Les

---

23. We may leave aside for a moment 'messianic' interpretations of 12.10 to which we shall turn shortly. We have already suggested why it is doubtful if any messianic allusion is intended in 13.7.

promesses faites à David ne sont pas oubliées, mais leur realisation semple faire de plus en plus problématique'.

Our examination of the first section of Zech. 12.1–13.6, then, has given grounds for believing that the emphasis is not only on outward military victory, but that the terminology and pictures used lay emphasis also on spiritual and moral renewal. In any event this becomes explicit with vv. 10ff. Yahweh will 'pour out' (וְשָׁפַכְתִּי) on the House of David and the inhabitants of Jerusalem רוּחַ חֵן וְתַחֲנוּנִים. There is a difference of opinion as to whether this is a reference to the Spirit of Yahweh or, more generally, to the bestowal upon his people of a disposition or attitude of heart and mind marked by these qualities.[24] Rightly to answer this needs a closer examination of the qualities which result from this outpouring. Both words are related to the root חנן which means basically 'to show favour' or 'to be gracious', and whose subject may be God or man. Of men, it is often used of dealing {231} rightly with the poor, the needy, the orphan, but generally of giving to each man his due.[25] When God is the subject it is used generally of the bestowal of favours, but more specifically of granting redemption, whether from an enemy, from disaster or from sin (e.g. Gen. 33.11; Exod. 33.19; Pss. 67.2 [1]; 123.2ff.). Its frequent occurrence in the Psalter, especially in Psalms of Community and Individual Lament suggest that it became a particular part of the vocabulary of Israel's worship. The noun חֵן means 'favour' or 'grace'. It may refer to appearance or speech[26] but more often refers to favour and acceptance with God and with men. So in Exod. 3.21 it is said, 'I will give this people favour in the sight of the Egyptians', that is, by setting them free from Egypt Yahweh will demonstrate that the Israelites are the recipients of his favour. There is, therefore, both an objective and a subjective aspect to this term. Men show

24. E.g. S.R. Driver (1906: 265), 'It is not *the* Divine Spirit'. M. Delcor (1951b) argues similarly.

25. E.g. Pss. 37.21, 26; 109.12; Lam. 4.16, where one of the reasons given for the judgment of Jerusalem was that within it 'no favour was shown to the elders'.

26. Ps. 45.3 (2); Prov. 31.30. A detailed study of the root חנן has been carried out by D.R. Ap-Thomas (1957). Both nouns indicate the favour shown by a superior to an inferior, and he agrees that תַּחֲנוּנִים is prayer for חֵן, not just the set prayer on one occasion, but 'The outpourings of the troubled spirit, without set forms or procedure' (p. 137). In Zech. 12.10, he takes the waw linking חֵן and תַּחֲנוּנִים, to be *waw explicative* and renders, 'a spirit of favour, or *rather*, of suplication for favour'. He sees no alternative to this but emendation on the basis of LXX to רַחֲמִים, 'compassion'. But 'favour' and 'supplication for favour', while closely related, are not quite the same thing.

favour because they receive it from Yahweh, as the further references in Exod. 11.3 and 12.36 make clear. An interesting use of the word occurs in Zech. 4.7, where it is said that Zerubbabel will complete the building of the Temple by laying the top stone with the cry, חֵן חֵן לָהּ. This would seem to indicate appreciation of the beauty of the restored Temple in appearance, but it surely carries with it the overtones that it is so particularly because its restoration is the mark of God's favour on the community which has been thus enabled to accomplish {232} the task. Indeed, interestingly in the light of Zech. 12.10, the preceding verse in Zech. 4 has made clear to Zerubbabel that his accomplishments will not be by his own strength, 'but by my *Spirit*', says Yahweh of hosts (v. 6). Thus in Zech. 12.10, the חֵן which Yahweh will pour out on his people may refer to a subjective disposition which makes them favourable in men's eyes, but they are so because first they receive such 'favour' from Yahweh. Perhaps the Exodus references suggest, in addition, a mighty deliverance to be wrought on their behalf. But when one recalls that in Proto-Zechariah, such is the gift of Yahweh's Spirit, it certainly is shown to be no human accomplishment. Is there here an echo of the promise to the community through Zerubbabel? In Proto-Zechariah, the completion of the Temple was both the mark of Yahweh's power and deliverance, but also the restoration of the means of the continuation of the right cultic relationship between Yahweh and his people. It is possible that in the reference to the gift of חֵן by virtue of the outpouring of the Spirit here, ideas of Proto-Zechariah are being taken up and re-applied to suggest the restoration of right relationships with Yahweh for the renewed community as a result of the activity of the Spirit of Yahweh.

Such an impression is strengthened by the use of {233} the other term, תַּחֲנוּנִים, which the RSV and NEB render as 'compassion', but which basically means 'supplication for חֵן'. So in Jer. 31.9 we read,

With weeping (בִּבְכִי) shall they come,
and with supplications (וּבְתַחֲנוּנִים)
I will bring them back,

where the idea of moving contrition suggests not only a physical return from distant places, but a spiritual return in penitence to Yahweh (cf. Jer. 3.21). The cry for חֵן, then, seems to suggest a note of genuine repentance, of turning to Yahweh for true 'favour' which only he can give. We have already seen how in Ezekiel, Yahweh's work of deliverance is accompanied by the bestowal of his Spirit, by which a true repentance is effected (e.g. Ezek. 36.26, 31; 37). Such seems to be the sequence of thought here, and so there appear traditio-critical grounds for believing that all this is the work of *the* Spirit of Yahweh, that more is implied than a mere subjective change of attitude. The emphasis in Ezekiel, the connection of רוּחַ with the Spirit in Proto-Zechariah, the use in the prophets of the term תַּחֲנוּנִים, alike point to this conclusion. Even the use of the root שׁפך suggests it, linked as it is elsewhere with the bestowing of the Spirit of Yahweh (e.g. Ezek. 39.29; Joel. 3.1 [2.28]).

This change of attitude effected by the Spirit of Yahweh's action in bringing about a renewal of Yahweh's favour to them, and so of their 'favour', and of a spirit of 'supplication' or penitence, is marked by penitence {234} towards one whom they have 'pierced'. This introduces us to a notable *crux interpretum* in Zechariah studies.

The MT reads וְהִבִּיטוּ אֵלַי אֵת אֲשֶׁר־דָּקָרוּ. Three points arise which add to the difficulty of understanding who is meant and what action it is exactly which the people will mourn. Since the words occur in a first person speech of Yahweh, the use of the first person singular would seem to imply that they have 'pierced' him. But many commentators have found difficulty with the idea of people having 'pierced' Yahweh,[27] especially as it is said that their mourning for him is like that for a 'first-born'. The second is the abrupt transition to the third person, 'they shall mourn for him'. The third is the awkwardness of the Hebrew construction which has the preposition אֵת indicating the accusative case, immediately following the אֵלַי and itself followed by the relative אֲשֶׁר.

Only a brief summary of the many conjectures at textual emendation and ways of interpreting what is referred to can be given here.[28] Stade, and others since, have emended the אֵלַי to the third person singular אֵלָיו. This is the reading found in Jn 19.37. It obviates the difficulty of the abrupt switch of person, and is accepted by the RSV, for example, without even a marginal note referring to the {235} extant Hebrew text. It opens the way

---

27. E.g. Condamin (1910: 52ff.), '…c'est Iahvi. qui parle; comment peut-il se dire transpercé?', cited by Lamarche (1961: 80); Elliger (1964: 170), 'Zunächst scheidet die Möglichkeit aus, dass Gott sich selbst meinen könnte'. Lamarche also cites the view of Knabenbauer that Yahweh is being 'pierced' through the person of his representative by what they have inflicted on him: 'Aliud est dicere: qui vos spernit me spernit, et dicere: qui vos occidit me occidit; prius verum est et recte dicitur; alterum nonita'; cited by Lamarche (1961: 81n). The reference is from *Commentarius in Minores Propheetas*, II (1886: 373 [the writer has not had access to this work]).

28. Fuller surveys of the history of criticism of this verse are to be found in Lamarche (1961: 80ff.), who cites Condamin's survey (1910: 52ff.); Saebø (1969: 96ff.), and Delcor (1951b).

for a wide-ranging group of interpretations as to who this person was. Earlier Christian exegetes, for example, favoured a Messianic reference, but as Mitchell points out (1912: 330) the act of piercing appears to be in the past. Nor is the pierced one the *agent* of their deliverance. Other suggestions have included Josiah (in the light of v. 11), Uriah, Gedeliah, Jeremiah, and Sellin's thought of Zerubbabel,[29] Onias III and Judas Maccabaeus. Others again, have felt that a collective sense is implied. So Gaide (1968: 131), 'On peut donc appliquer au Transpercé de Za. 12 le concept de *Corporate personality* ou "personalité incorporant"'. Mitchell (1912: 331) says, in an important observation,

> One of the most attractive suggestions is that the object of consideration in the clause quoted is not a single unfortunate individual, but a considerable number of godly persons who have perished by violence. This interpretation is favoured by the striking likeness between the situation here outlined and that portrayed in Isa. 52.15–53.12, where the loyal remnant of Israel is represented by the servant of Yahweh.

Others also have sought to find a link between this figure and the 'suffering servant' of Second Isaiah.[30] Elliger (1964: 171ff.) veers towards some such connection between the guilt of the people and its cleansing with the death of this unnamed martyr, while leaving open the fact that the text does not explicitly say he was slain by his fellow-citizens, a point also rightly made by P.R. Ackroyd {236} (1962a: 654) and D.R. Jones (1962a: 161) who draw a specific distinction between them. C.C. Torrey found here one of a number of references in the Old Testament to the belief, usually assigned to later Judaism, in a 'Messiah ben Ephraim' who was destined to lead the armies of Israel triumphantly and to reign long and prosperously but who was eventually to fall in battle before the walls of Jerusalem.[31] Horst, who says there can be no connection between this pierced one and the good shepherd of 11.4-14 since the death of the latter brought chaos, sees a connection between the death of the pierced one as the sacrifice of an innocent for deliverance from enemies, and believes the reference may be to a myth concerning the last times otherwise unknown

29. All cited by Mitchell (1912: 330).

30. So, cautiously, Dentan (1956: 1108); Condamin (1910: 51ff.); Lagrange (1906: 76).

31. Torrey (1947: 253-77). Specifically of this passage he says it was so understood in later Jewish tradition, and he refers to the Babylonian Talmud (*Sukkah* 53a). It shows that the earlier Messiah died through no fault of his own, but because his people failed him.

to us.[32] Otzen finds here a connection with the cult of pre-exilic Jerusalem in which the king suffered for the sake of the people, now embodied in the fate of the people as a whole.[33] Others have sought refuge on the lee shore of safe agnosticism here.[34]

Not all those whose views have been touched on here depend upon the emendation of the text. The majority indeed favour reading the אֵלַי of the MT, since the אֵלָיו lacks any strong support in the Versions,[35] and since the MT offers the more difficult reading. Those who favour retaining the MT reading face the ensuing difficulties in various ways. Hitzig, followed {237} by Reuss, Kirkpatrick and von Orelli (all cited by Condamin 1910), say that Yahweh has been pierced *in the person of his representative.* Knabenbauer's objection to this has already been mentioned, namely, that Yahweh might be wounded by the maltreatment of his representative, but could hardly have been said to be killed by his death. Others follow Van Hoonacker who divided the phrase, 'They will look towards me. (As for) the one they have pierced they will lament for him'. This was based on the ingenious emendation of וְסָפְדוּ to יִסְפְּדוּ and possibly by adding וְ before the אֵת (Van Hoonacker 1902: 345f.; 1908: 683; Lagrange 1906: 75). Another approach has been that of M. Delcor (1951b). In an important article on the problems of this verse he argues that the verb root דקר can have a metaphorical sense. For example, in Lam. 4.9 it is used of those in Jerusalem who were injured by hunger, while in Prov. 12.18 the wounds inflicted by rash words are likened to those inflicted by the sword. Thus it would be fitting for Yahweh to speak of himself as being 'wounded' by

32. Horst (1964: 256); cf. R.C. Dentan (1956: 1107), who says it probably refers to 'some well-known eschatological legend'.

33. Otzen (1964: 179ff.). He cites Riesenfeld (1948: 15), 'It can therefore not be considered far-fetched to presume that the fate of the people in the cultic drama itself has also been interpreted, in analogy to the king's acting, as a kind of descent into death and a revivification'.

34. So S.R. Driver (1906: 256), 'The Passage is, however, one of those which our ignorance of the circumstances of the time makes it impossible to interpret as a whole satisfactorily or completely'; G. Gaide (1968: 131), 'Les connaissances que nous avons sur l'époque de la Restauration et la période grecque ne nous offrent personne qui réponde exactement à ces caractéristiques'. Such comments, however, do assume an historical basis for the reference to the 'Pierced one'.

35. Only the Lucian recension of LXX, and a group of late MSS have the variant, and it is not impossible that this was influenced by Jn 19.37. In these circumstances, the Johannine reading can hardly be taken as weighty textual evidence for the original reading.

the sins of the people. This is the sense given by the LXX which at this point reads κατωρχήσαντο, a word which means to dance in mockery or scorn before someone. The Vulgate clearly follows the LXX here in reading 'insultaverunt'. Long ago St Jerome suggested that this presupposed a reading of the Hebrew root רקד ('to stamp about'), rather than root דקר but Delcor says that it never has the sense of dancing in *scorn*, and {238} takes it that the LXX was rightly interpreting the general sense of the root דקר in its context here. Delcor shows how clearly Ezek. 36.16-28 lies behind the thought of this passage. There Yahweh says that by the action of his people his name has been 'profaned' (מְחֻלָּל) among the nations. He argues that one sense of the root חלל is to 'pierce', and that it is this motif which the author of the Zechariah passage is reproducing here, only he used the word דקר to broaden the concept to include the thought of 'moral injury' as in Lam. 4.9. The abrupt transition from first person to third, says Delcor, is a feature of the style of these chapters (Delcor cites Zech. 10.5ff., 7ff.; 12.6ff., 8ff.) and need occasion no difficulty.

With such a variety of scholarly opinion (and only a very broad outline has been attempted here) on so obscure a passage great care is needed. It is well to start with one or two general statements concerning the main emphasis of this passage which do appear with some clarity.

First, what is being described is a work of Yahweh, a work of regeneration and spiritual renewal following the military deliverance of Jerusalem and Judah. The order is the same as in Ezek. 36, and, as there, the aim is to result in the cleansing of the 'uncleanness' of the land, in both passages the same word (נִדָּה) {239} being used to denote this, a word indicating the menstrual uncleaness of a woman.

Second, this work is effected by the outpouring of the Spirit of Yahweh which appears as an act of unmerited grace. It *results* in, it is not occasioned by, repentance and grief for sin. The same is true in Ezek. 36 which speaks of a new heart and a new spirit being given (v. 26). Afterwards (v. 31) 'you will remember your evil ways and your deeds that were not good and you will loathe yourselves for your iniquities'. Both passages use the metaphor of water (Ezek. 36.25; Zech. 13.1) and both refer to idolatry as one form of that uncleanness (Ezek. 36.25; Zech. 13.2).

Third, since in both the emphasis is on a return to Yahweh and observance again of his commands, the words 'they shall look to me' seem right, not only on textual grounds, but because they are in keeping with the main thrust of the context. It is conversion and renewal which Yahweh is working, and so often the root נבט is associated with such a turning (e.g. Ps. 34.6 [5]; Isa. 5.12; 22.11; 42.18; 51.1).

Fourth, the weeping over the 'one they have pierced' (whoever that may be) is the result and consequence of that regeneration of Yahweh. It is not its cause. This means we have to be careful here in assigning a vicarious role to the death of this one in the manner of the king in the earlier Jerusalem cult, or the Suffering Servant of Isa. 53. We may not say categorically that {240} no such idea is present. But it is certainly not prominent. It is not by contemplating his sufferings that they are to be saved. They contemplate his sufferings with grief because they have been saved. T. Chary, speaking of the role of both the Messiah and the 'pierced one' says that each '…reste subalterne. C'est Yahweh lui-même qui est l'acteur central de toutes les transformations à venir' (Chary 1955: 230).

Finally, by way of these general observations, it can be seen that the detailed and marked emphasis on the grief which follows is something peculiar to Zechariah. It has only a general counterpart in Ezekiel who says, as we have seen, they shall 'remember their evil deeds' and 'loathe themselves' for them. Whatever is meant here appears to be something peculiar to this tradition, or a particular deed or evil act which ranks above all others, although it is related to idolatry and false prophecy, as 13.2-6 makes plain, and which, for this prophet or circle, assumes especial importance.

What follows can, by the nature of the case where so much is obscure, be put forward only tentatively and as a theory to be tested. Yet certain considerations from the text, as we shall see, can be brought forward in its support. We have already seen indications in these chapters that they may have come from a prophet, or from a circle, who saw the official leadership of {241} Jerusalem as corrupt and who disassociated itself from the worship of the Temple. If this is sound, we may well imagine that such a feeling would have been mutual, and something approaching a sect rigorously denounced and excluded by the official priesthood would have emerged, whether this led to actual maltreatment or not. Is it possible that this new element, this particularizing of an earlier general prophecy, reflects such an official reaction? It is of interest here to recall Mitchell's comments on the unknown person of v. 10b (Mitchell 1912: 235). In which case the sense here would be that when, by the gracious initiative of the outpouring of the divine Spirit, leaders and people are led to seek a true 'favour' or 'grace', and so look to Yahweh, they will suddenly realize that those whom they have all along opposed (whether 'pierced' metaphorically or literally persecuted) were his true spokesmen keeping alight the flame of genuine faith. So their 'looking' to God will result in such a radical re-assessment of their attitude to his true community that they will bitterly lament their earlier treatment of and attitude towards them. They will see their own worship as little better than idolatry and their own deeds as uncleannesses from which alone the grace of Yahweh can cleanse them. This would make a little more intelligible the abrupt switch between the use of the first person referring to Yahweh and the {242} third person referring to the prophet and/or his circle, whether we accept Van Hoonacker's emendation or not, when we recall how closely the true prophet felt himself to stand to Yahweh, related to him as his representative or mouthpiece, so that harm to the prophet was injury to Yahweh himself (cf. Jer. 26.19).

The description of the mourning in v. 11 provides a difficulty, examined in particular by M. Delcor in a detailed study of this verse and the history of its interpretation (Delcor 1953). A literal rendering of the MT would be,

> In that day the mourning in Jerusalem will be as great as the mourning (of) Hadad-Rimmon in the Plain of Megiddo.

Delcor shows how interpretations of this verse have fallen into two groups— those which have seen it to be the name of a deity and have hence found here an allusion to pagan cultic rites, and those which have seen Hadad-Rimmon as a topographical reference. Jerome was the first to find a place name here. P. Abel identified it with Rummane near to Ta'anak, the modern El Leggun, and many have followed him in this identification. On the basis of 1 Sam. 14.2, Van Hoonacker emended it to Rimmon in the valley of Migron, near Geba', for that verse refers to the pomegranate tree there (Hebrew, רִמּוֹן). In the absence of any reference to the cult of Rimmon there, however, and any other grounds for this identification, this has not found wide support. It is often assumed that, if the reference is to the Valley {243} of Megiddo, the mourning there particularly would be for the death of Josiah. The Targum made this point, specially placing the mourning for Ahab and Josiah alongside each other. G. Gaide, while recognizing that the Ugaritic discoveries made the reference to Hadad here most likely, yet suggests there is an overtone of reference to the death of Josiah, a reference itself closely linked with the thought that Josiah was 'pierced', representing the 'piercing' of the whole people at the hands of Nebuchadnezzar shortly to come. Others have pointed out, however, that Josiah was taken and buried in Jerusalem, and that it is hardly likely that a cult for the mourning of Josiah's death, if such ever existed, would have taken place at Megiddo.[36]

---

36. It has been said however, that 2 Chron. 35.25 does suggest a continuing lamen-

Since Wellhausen, many scholars have seen here rather a reference to
the cult of the deity, Hadad-Rimmon, already known by the time of Elisha
(2 Kgs 5.18). The Ras Shamra material has shown that Baal and Hadad
were identified, and that similar mourning rites took place in the name of
this deity as in the cult of Tammuz Adonis (Kapelrud 1965: 45ff.; Rowley
1945: 49). Delcor, in the article referred to above, however, argued against
this. He asks whether this author would have put on the same plane a
lamentation for Hadad with a lamentation for Yahweh. His arguments
were countered in a later article by J. Hoftijzer (1953). He believes that
Delcor's own view, that the original {244} reference was to a mourning
for Josiah, makes this even more difficult, for in that case he puts on the
same plane a lamentation for Yahweh and a lamentation for a *man*. But we
can ask, may it not be deliberate irony? If, in the eyes of this author, their
worship has been little more than paganism, an actual pagan cult affords
the comparison. Its intensity of grief at the death of its deity affords the
pattern for the grief and mourning they will know as they realize their
worship has been false, their zeal and devotion misplaced. Their former
religion has to die and be re-born by the action of Yahweh.

We suggest, therefore, that the reference here is to pagan cults, and may
be the author's contemptuous estimate of the worth of the worship now
being offered in Jerusalem by those whose knowledge of the will of Yahweh has become perverted. It would strengthen the suggestion implied by
the terms 'only son' and 'first-born', that they have become strangers to
the true community of Yahweh, and rejected the true Israel.

The catalogue-type style of the list of mourners which follows is
reminiscent of the Chronicler with his lists of those who returned from the
exile, took part in the rebuilding or were assigned their place in the cult.[37]

tation for Josiah, and associates the name of Jeremiah with it. This is interesting in the
light of Zech. 12.9-14, especially when the persistence of a tradition linking these
chapters with the name of Jeremiah in Mt. 27.29 is remembered. See Ackroyd (1973:
205).

37. There is, of course, a parallel in the use of the term מִשְׁפָּחוֹת in the lists of
1 Chron. 1–9 and in those of the Priestly Code. But it is in the purpose of the use of
such lists that a more significant relation may be seen to lie. Lists such as those in
1 Chron. 1–9; Ezra 2; Neh. 7; 11, seem designed to demonstrate the ideal constitution
of the people of God. Commenting on 1 Chron. 9.1, Ackroyd (1973: 43ff.) says that it
is to be seen as 'a résumé of the tribes of ALL ISRAEL—an important concept to the
author... The reference to the "Book of the Kings of Israel" might be analogous to the
concept of a "book of life"...in which God himself records those who are part of his
accepted community'. J.M. Myers (1965: 6) says of the lists of 1 Chron. 1–9, 'Authority

It is not clear what significance is to be attached to the names which are specifically mentioned. Most commentators have taken it to refer to royal and {245} priestly lines, 'the House of Nathan' being taken as descended from David's son of that name (2 Sam. 5.14). Shimei is spoken of as a descendant of Levi (Exod. 6.17, etc.) and in the Chronicler he is the head of a division of Levites (1 Chron. 25.17). This may, therefore, betoken a repentance and renewal of the leadership of the nation as a whole, seen, in the manner of Proto-Zechariah as being both the civil and priestly heads. It may be cast in the quasi-official record style of the Chronicler's lists to indicate that this will fulfill his view of the returned community, enumerated by its 'families' and 'divisions' as the nucleus of the true people of God, the renewed community now emerging the other side of the process of purification by judgment. But the emphasis seems to be on *totality*, what Mitchell calls the 'universality' of the work of divine renewal. All sections of leadership will be involved, and through them and their example, the whole community, for 'all the families that are left' will be caught up in the act of penitence and submission. Perhaps there is in this list a suggestion of the reversal of the earlier pre-exilic prophecy of judgment against, not only the 'House of Jacob' but against 'all the families of the House of Israel' (Jer. 2.4), a judgment already reversed in Jer. 31.1, 'I will be God of all the families of Israel, and they shall be my people', {246} a promise rooted in the context of covenant (so Weiser 1969: 274ff.; Cunliffe-Jones 1966: 193).

There is an interesting insistence that each family mourns *by itself*, and further, their wives *by themselves*. This may suggest a cultic background.[38] But, more, may it not suggest *individuality*? This was a feature of the new covenant as it was foreseen in Jer. 31.31ff., for, when God wrote his law in men's hearts and renewed the covenant relationship,

> ...no longer shall each man teach his neighbour and each his brother, saying, 'Know the LORD', for they shall all know me, from the least of them to the greatest, says the LORD; for I will forgive their iniquity, and I will remember their sin no more.

It may be this aspect of the new covenant which, in his own way, our author wants here to stress. This would be not altogether dissimilar to Joel

for (the Chronicler), rested upon family relationships and continuity, both of which were important to maintain the pure Israelite religious community in his day'. A similar purpose may lie behind the use of the list of 'families' in Zech. 12.12ff.

38. Wellhausen (1892: 191) thought this whole list reflected a background of processions.

3.1ff. (2.28ff.) where the pouring out of God's spirit comes upon all, old and young, high and low, men and *women*. This is not to suggest any direct link necessarily between Joel and Zechariah at this point, but both may bear witness of how the promises of earlier prophecy in this respect were interpreted and applied. In which case, these verses show both the *totality* and the *individuality* of the work of Yahweh's Spirit.

This penitential mourning, itself the result of the work of the Spirit of Yahweh, is accompanied by the {247} divine provision of cleansing, described as a 'fountain' (מָקוֹר) which is opened for the House of David and the inhabitants of Jerusalem (13.1). This is a picture met with frequently in the Old Testament. Apparently in the Jerusalem cult itself the presence of God in the midst of the city was likened to a 'river' (Ps. 46.5ff. [4ff.]; cf. Isa. 8.6). Again, Yahweh is described as the source of 'the fountain of life' (Ps. 36.10 [9]), a picture which Jeremiah used to denounce his people's desertion of Yahweh (2.13). As already mentioned, in Ezek. 36.25 the people are to be cleansed from all their uncleannesses and idols by the sprinkling of 'pure water' (מַיִם טְהוֹרִים). In Ezek. 47.1-12 there is an elaborately drawn picture of water streaming from its source in the Temple and becoming a river which flows to the east through the Arabah, so bringing fertility to it and sweetening the waters of the Dead Sea, so that trees growing on both banks bring a constant supply of fruit. There seem to be a number of motifs here including that of the presence of Yahweh in his Temple as a source of life for the whole land, and of the Paradise myth of the 'Tree of Life'. But the ideas of fertility and cleansing appear to be intermingled as well, for the fruit of the tree is for food, while the leaves will be for 'healing' (לִתְרוּפָה). Eichrodt's comment here is significant: {248}

> The river of paradise and the marvellous effects brought by it signify the transformation of this world into the garden of paradise, whence not only the hosts of earthly diseases, *but also sin and guilt* have been banished (1970: 585 [italics mine]).

This passage certainly seems to stand behind Zech. 14.8. But it may also form part of the rich heritage of this tradition in the Old Testament on which our author has drawn also to depict the work of redemption and new creation coming together by the renewed presence of Yahweh in the Temple in Jerusalem. He is the 'fountain of life' whose water brings both cleansing and newness of life. Again it would fit the picture of one who sees the need for this renewal in the renewed presence of God with his people at the very heart of their life, namely, the Temple cultus, a thing which seemed to him not to be a reality at the time at which these words were uttered.

That from which they are to be cleansed is sin (חַטָּאת)[39] and לְנִדָּה, the term for menstrual uncleanness which also occured in Ezek. 36.17, and which seems to afford another link between this passage and the general thought of Ezek. 36. The word is part of the priestly vocabulary of the cult, as its frequent occurrence in Leviticus testifies. Indeed, Num. 19.9 speaks of the waters for נִדָּה חַטָּאת, bringing together the very terms used in Zech. 13.1. The context here is the rite for cleansing following any {249} contact with the dead. Once or twice it becomes a picture in the Old Testament for contamination generally, but the application varies interestingly in at least two different traditions. In Lam. 1.8 it is used generally for the state of Jerusalem which has been so disgraced by judgment that she is the object of contempt among her neighbours. She has become a thing to be avoided in order to escape contamination. The Chronicler uses it in Ezra 9.11 in the prayer of Ezra who relates it to the Israelites inter-marrying with the occupants of the land. In his eyes they are a source of contamination. Ezekiel, however, applies it to idolatry.

> ...their conduct before me was like the uncleanness of a woman in her impurity. So I poured out my wrath upon them for the blood which they had shed in the land, for the idols with which they had defiled it (36.17ff.).

And again:

> I will sprinkle clean water upon you, and you shall be clean from all your uncleannesses and from all your idols (v. 25).

In this latter instance the word used is different (טֻמְאוֹתֵיכֶם), but the idea and the connection between 'uncleanness' and idolatry remain, and the same word occurs in Zech. 13.2b. It is an interesting example of how priest and prophet meet in Ezekiel. A mainly priestly term is made the vehicle of the prophetic word of denunciation against religious syncretism. It is of interest to note that the term was frequently {250} used by the Qumram Community to refer to the impurity of individuals within the community (Myers 1965: 75). The fact that in the final section, Zech. 13.2-6, 'unclean' is also explained as relating to idolatry suggests that the

---

39. The MT gives a construct form, לְחַטַּאת. Since Stade, this has usually been emended to לְחַטָּאת (cf. Mitchell 1912: 339). Otzen (1964: 265n), thinks this is not necessary, since there are instances of the first of two words linked by waw being in the construct.

Ezekiel tradition is source and inspiration here. Yet, is it merely slavish following? Or does it carry the suggestion that that from which the House of David and the inhabitants of Jerusalem need to be cleansed is little better than idolatry? It could well be another indication of the estimate of the official cult in Jerusalem of their day by those from whom these chapters came. In a sense what is envisaged would be parallel to the cleansing of Joshua, the High Priest, as representative of the whole community in Zech. 3. Presumably, 'House of David' is a way of referring to the leadership of the community generally, either because of the claim of its leadership at that time, or ironically, in line with the modified messianic expectation we saw to be reflected in 12.7ff.

What is of special significance here is to note the way in which it departs from its 'source', where it adds that which is peculiar to itself, or omits what was dominant in an earlier model, for here we get our rare glimpses of the particular outlook of those who gave us these chapters. This is certainly true of the statement that the prophets are to be removed from the land. {251} This corresponds to, and is parallel to, the removal of the idols as a mark of God's act of cleansing of the community. To remove the prophets is to remove the 'unclean spirit' (רוּחַ הַטֻּמְאָה). This may well be intended as a counterpart to the רוּחַ of 12.10 which Yahweh will pour out on all men.

This may afford a clue to understanding what is in mind here. The direct and immediate work of Yahweh will obviate the need for the mediated word. Indeed, if any person appears claiming to be the bearer of revelation or teaching from God, he would thereby show that he had had no part in the salvation Yahweh has worked. So Elliger (1964: 172) says rightly,

> So werden auch die Boten des göttlichen Wortes, die Propheten, als Mittler überflussig und können 'verschwinden' (2b), weil Gott ja unmittelbar gegenwärtig ist.

It is really another instance of the fulfillment of Jeremiah's new covenant that there will be no need for anyone to teach another saying, 'Know the LORD', for 'they shall all know me'. This idea receives very detailed elaboration in vv. 3-6 . Verse 3 seems to refer back to the law in Deut. 13.6ff., which says that even if a member of the family incites others to 'serve other gods' he must be put to death. He shall then be 'pierced' (דקר). One feels this can hardly be co-incidental. It seems also to be a counterpart to v. 10. The one who was 'pierced' there was so treated {252} wrongly. The action of piercing was an evil which needed to be repented of and mourned over. Here the false member of the renewed community is so treated rightly, the treatment reflecting the renewal of the community. Verses 4ff. seem almost to reflect Amos's apparent repudiation of his prophetic status[40] and are presumably to be read, not as a further effort to conceal the truth, but to underline the fact that prophets as such have no role in the community. Nevertheless, apart from the considerations adduced by Elliger to suggest that vv. 3-6 are secondary, their almost tedious elaboration of the point made in v. 2, their slight element of burlesque and the, at best, ambiguous reference to 'lovers' (מְאַהֲבָי) in v. 6, lead one to wonder whether behind them was some element of controversy with those of other groups who also claimed to speak authoritative words to the people of their time. Such an impression must be subjective and therefore remain in the realm of conjecture. But, if it were so, it would presumably come from the circle of tradition which preserved the prophet's words, and who would have been responsible for this polemical later expansion. {253}

---

40. Amos 7.14. For a discussion of this much-debated enigmatic verse, see Rowley (1947; 1965: 120n). It is not absolutely clear that the Amos passage is being recalled here, since the only words which coincide are לֹא נָבִיא אָנֹכִי and there cannot be so many ways of disclaiming prophetic status in Hebrew. Perhaps, however, in its rather different application of the phrase from that of the Amos passage, it is an instance of an early method of interpreting a saying which must have puzzled ancient readers of the text as much as modern exegetes.

Chapter 9

ZECHARIAH 14

Again one must recognize the force of much critical opinion which has found this chapter to be composite in origin, yet here also our main concern must be with the passage as it now appears before us. For the fact that it could be brought together and shaped into its present form indicates that, to some extent at least, the ideas appeared to some as congruous and relevant. As Saebø (1969: 282) has said, the chapter gives the impression of being, at least initially, a *traditio-unity* (*Überlieferungsganze*).

The account of the attack of the nations upon Jerusalem and Yahweh's deliverance of his city in vv. 1-5, raises severe problems for the relationship between this chapter and Zech. 12. For while ch. 12 spoke of an attack of the nations against Jerusalem this was only that Yahweh might realize his purpose of judgment against them by destroying them, so preserving Jerusalem in safety. In ch. 14, however, Jerusalem is depicted as having been conquered, its spoil divided in its midst by its captors who have been gathered by Yahweh himself for this purpose. Its buildings are plundered, its women raped, while half its population is carried away into exile, even although the rest of the population are not removed. Only after all this does the divine intervention take place, apparently aimed at judgment on the nations and the deliverance and renewal {254} of Jerusalem.

These differences have led many commentators to the conclusion that the two chapters cannot have been by the same author.[1] The most detailed

---

1. E.g. R.C. Dentan (1956: 1110); D.R. Jones (1962a: 170), 'It is certain that chs. 12 and 14 represent variant versions of the same tradition'; Horst (1964: 257), 'Man wird darum beide Abschnitte nicht vom gleichen Autor herleiten können'; Elliger (1964: 181), '…zwingt zu dem einzig möglichen Schluss, das Kap. 14 (wenigstens in seine Vorlage) ganz ohne Rücksicht auf Kap. 12f. entstanden ist'; Otzen (1964: 200) maintains that ch. 14 represents a fundamentally different eschatology. The fact that there are some similarities in chs. 12 and 14 must not mislead us. It is only because they have been shaped by the same cultic material. Bič (1962: 161) leaves the question

examination of the relation between the early parts of Zech. 12 and 14 has been undertaken by H.M. Lutz in his work, *Jahwe, Jerusalem und die Völker* (Lutz 1968), to which some brief reference has already been made. He believed that three basic motifs occur in these chapters drawn from earlier material in the Old Testament: the war of the nations against Jerusalem, which was derived from the pre-exilic cult of Jerusalem as represented in the 'Songs of Zion', itself an interpretation of the pre-Israelite Jerusalem cult of El Elyon; Yahweh's war against the nations, which derived partly from the old concepts of the 'Holy War', and which broadened out from the idea of battle against specific historical enemies to include the general idea of 'the Nations' in the oracles of Jeremiah and Ezekiel; and finally, the concept of Yahweh's war against Jerusalem, a direct reversal of the preceding theme which appeared first with Amos and after him in the teaching of most of the prophets. In ch. 12 it is the first of these three themes which appears alone, the war of the nations against Jerusalem which is repulsed by Yahweh. But in ch. 14 the remaining two elements have been combined as they had {255} already been in Isa. 29.1-8; Ezek. 38.1-9, 14–16; 39.1-5, in a way which suggests that the final deliverance of Yahweh can only be experienced by a remnant of the faithful, which emerges the other side of judgment. Such judgment against Jerusalem is seen as a process which Yahweh must first carry through by the agency of the nations he brings against her for this purpose (Lutz 1968: 64-84, 100-10, 147-204, esp. 203ff.).

This analysis is a helpful one and indicates clearly the kind of process of development the traditions represented in these chapters must have undergone, even if we cannot always be as clear about the stages of that process as Lutz suggests, and if some of his surgical approach to the various texts with which he deals appears too drastic. We shall return to Lutz's suggestion for the reasons for this different emphasis and treatment of tradition in chs. 12 and 14, and the source from which such differences of outlook may be presumed to have come. One thing does seem clear. Chapter 14 appears to reflect a more pessimistic and hostile attitude to Jerusalem than ch. 12.

The opening formula הִנֵּה יוֹם־בָּא לַיהוָה, is strongly reminiscent of the formula which occurs, with slight variations, in the early chapters of Joel.

---

open: while the difference between the chapters might lead us to suppose difference of authorship, it is not absolutely certain. Indeed, the question of authorship is not important, he maintains. The redactor had the opportunity to smooth out the contradictions. That he did not do so suggests he had something to proclaim even through them.

In 1.15 we read, כִּי קָרוֹב יוֹם יְהוָה and in 2.1 כִּי־בָא יוֹם־יְהוָה.[2] {256}

The first of these (1.15) occurs in a context of a call in vv. 4-14 to the priests to mourn and fast because 'cereal offerings are withheld from the house of your God' to which we have already had occasion to refer (above, F 1 {140}, now pp. 97ff.). This was because of the occurrence in v. 13 of the rather unusual prophetic designation of God as 'my God' which occurred in Zech. 11.4 and which, interestingly, is repeated in 14.5. We saw that this phrase seems to carry with it the suggestion that the speaker is putting himself over against those whom he addresses. Certainly, the reference in Joel does not appear to be uncritical of the cultic functionaries of the Temple, since v. 13bβ suggests that not all the zeal is being shown in approach to God that the seriousness of the occasion warrants (cf. my remarks on this passage above, F 1 {140}, now pp. 97ff.). Eissfeldt suggests that in Joel 1.15-30 the prophet is putting into their mouths a prayer of lamentation introduced by the words 'Alas for the day! For the day of the Lord is near' (Eissfeldt 1965: 392). In what follows, complaint is made,

> Is not the food cut off before our eyes;
> joy and gladness from the house of our God? (1.16)

The reference in 2.1 is to the coming Day of Yahweh in the context of a call to alarm over the menacing approach of a plague of locusts even to the city itself, and includes in vv. 12-14 a call to repentance. {257}

The dating of the Joel passages, as with the dating of the Zechariah passages, is too uncertain to be able to speak confidently about borrowing in one direction or another. Yet the close similarities in vocabulary and style in speaking of the Day of Yahweh, as well as the context of a threat to Jerusalem in particular, the recurrence in both of the unusual phrase 'the Lord *my* God', let alone the many parallels between Joel 4 and Zech. 14,

---

2.   Any thought that the book of Joel had any influence on these later chapters of Zechariah hinges on the much-discussed question of the date of the Joel oracles. It is often held that chs. 1ff. are descriptions of an actual plague of locusts, and that chs. 3ff. have been added, either by the author or another, as eschatological predictions in the light of such a catastrophe. It is difficult, however, to deduce that chs. 1ff. are early and chs. 3ff. later, since the phrase 'Day of Yahweh' is common to both, chs. 1f. bear evidence of late style and outlook, and there are other features common to both (Eissfeldt 1965: 391ff.). Simple 'borrowing' by one or the other cannot therefore be assumed when, to the uncertainty over the date of Joel, is added the uncertainty over the date of these chapters. Very strong connections between Joel 4 and Zech. 14 call for notice, however. The writer hopes to return to this theme in more detail than is possible in the present work.

to which attention must yet be given, suggest that they may have originated in circles which showed at least some aspects in common. Not
least of these, we have suggested, is an attitude which was critical of the
official cult and leadership of the Temple of their time with whom some
responsibility for the present is seen to lie. This should warn us at least to
be on the outlook for signs of a viewpoint in Zech. 14 similar to that which
we found in 10.3ff.; 11.4-17; 13.7-9 and 12.1–13.6. Has such a view
increased to the point where it is believed that the enormities of the
Judaism of its day are so great, that the city which is its official centre and
focal point must first be ravaged in judgment before the hoped for cleansing and renewal can take place?

Certainly Jerusalem is here to be judged. Spoil (שְׁלָלֵךְ) will be taken
from it and divided in the eyes of its inhabitants. This becomes a poignant
and dramatic reversal of the promise to the city in Proto-{258}Zechariah,
in 2.12 (8)ff., where Yahweh summons those who dwell in other lands to
flee (נֻסוּ) to Zion, for Yahweh sends his message to the nations who were
plundering his people (הַשֹּׁלְלִים) to announce that he will shake his hand
over them so that they shall become plunder (שָׁלָל) for those who serve
them. Now, not only will the people of Jerusalem provide spoil for their
captors, but half of them will be taken away into exile from a city which is
no longer secure, since its women are ravished and its citizens plundered.
Instead of gathering back the exiles from their dispersion, Yahweh will
now gather the nations in hostility to Jerusalem, and before long its inhabitants will be fleeing (if we so read the second and third occurrences of
וְנַסְתֶּם in v. 5) away from the city, not towards it. It is as though this circle
of tradition which so venerated and re-applied the promises of Zechariah
to their own time, now sees Jerusalem and its cult as so rotten as to be no
longer worthy of them without a process of refining by judgment. The
promises are not rescinded, but can now only be fulfilled the other side of
judgment of the present order. In this respect it is probably significant that
judgment and destruction will not be total. If half the city goes into exile,
'the *rest of the people* (יֶתֶר הָעָם) shall not be cut off from the city'. If the
judgment of 701 BC is repeated so will the divine mercy experienced then
be {259} renewed, a deliverance of which Isaiah could say, וְנוֹתְרָה בַת־צִיּוֹן
כְּסֻכָּה בְכָרֶם (Isa. 1.8), an act which was utterly the result of divine grace,
לוּלֵי יְהוָה צְבָאוֹת הוֹתִיר לָנוּ שָׂרִיד כִּמְעָט. The fact that such a sparing of half
the population of Jerusalem and reversal of her fortunes is also entirely a
work of Yahweh is stressed in v. 3, which introduces his appearance and
intervention against the nations in language traditional to the ancient

concept of the Holy War. Yahweh 'goes forth' (וְיָצָא יְהוָה), he fights 'as in
the day of battle' (כְּיוֹם הִלָּחֲמוֹ בְּיוֹם קְרָב).[3] Such traditional language had
already been taken up into the prophetic literature, probably by way of the
cult, for it appears often in the Psalms, so that in Second Isaiah it is said,
'The LORD goes forth like a mighty man, like a man of war he stirs up his
fury' (42.13), where the context is Yahweh's final judgment of the whole
earth and the deliverance from exile of his own people. Again, similar
language is found in the 'Isaiah Apocalypse',

> For, behold, the LORD is coming forth out of his place, to punish the
> inhabitants of the earth for their iniquity (Isa. 26.21).

This is particularly interesting with its preceding call to take cover while
the work of vengeance is going on: {260}

> Come, my people, enter into your chambers,
> and shut your doors behind you:
> hide yourselves for a little while
> until the wrath is past (v. 20).

This is a thought which stresses both the fact that this is Yahweh's work
alone with no human help, and the terror of the act. It may help to explain
the reference in Zech. 14.5b to the inhabitants of Jerusalem fleeing at the
appearance of Yahweh, not so much because the Isaianic verses themselves are being depended upon here, but as showing that such ideas did
become associated with the terrible final act of Yahweh's judgment.[4]

The phrase בַּיּוֹם־הַהוּא in v. 4, if it is not intrusive (so *BH* and *BHS*)
may introduce a section which is an expansion of vv. 1-3, but the contents
of the expansion, including details within it which may themselves be
secondary, are of great significance and, in any case, it is hardly possible
now to say at what stage such expansion was introduced. One must

---

3.   For such terminology, see Judg. 5.4; 2 Sam. 5.24; Ps. 18.8-16 (7-15), etc.; cf.
von Rad (1958: 9). F.M. Cross (1966) in an article, 'The Divine Warrior in Israel's
Early Cult', criticizes von Rad for setting the origin of the concept of the Holy War
entirely in the period of the Judges. He believes that its origins are to be found in the
history of the conquest as remembered and re-enacted in the cult, but that it also owed
something to mythological aspects of the divine 'Warrior-God'. In Israel, however,
myth served 'primarily to give a cosmic dimension and transcendent meaning to the
historical...' (p. 19).

4.   Such an idea may have had its origins in thought of the final judgment in the
light of the plagues against the Egyptians and the injunction of Exod. 12.22ff. Perhaps
Mt. 24.16-20 shows how such ideas develop in apocalyptic tradition.

therefore ask whether its thought is consistent with the rest of the chapter.

The theophany is to take place on the Mount of Olives. This mountain is so called only here and in 2 Sam. 25.30, describing David's sad ascent of the mountain on his departure from Jerusalem at the time of Absalom's rebellion. Its summit is described there (v. 32) as 'the place where God was worshipped'. However, there is to the east of the city, across the Kidron Valley, {261} a range of highland with three summits, and there are further references to this complex in the Old Testament. In 1 Kgs 11.7 it is said that Solomon built shrines for Chemosh, the Moabite god, and Milcom, the Ammonite god, 'on the mountain, east of Jerusalem' (בָּהָר אֲשֶׁר עַל־פְּנֵי יְרוּשָׁלָם), a phrase strikingly reminiscent of Zech. 14.4 which describes the Mount of Olives as עַל־פְּנֵי יְרוּשָׁלָם מִקֶּדֶם. In 2 Kgs 23.13, where Josiah's reform is being described, it is said that he defiled the high places that were 'east of Jerusalem' (עַל־פְּנֵי יְרוּשָׁלַם), 'to the south of the Mount of Corruption' (לְהַר־הַמַּשְׁחִית), so that although it is said that this was to the north of the high places destroyed by Josiah, yet it specifically links these with the sanctuaries built by Solomon for the foreign cults of his wives.

The reference to the appearance of Yahweh on this mountain, has often been linked with Ezek. 11.23 and 43.2.[5] In 11.23, Ezekiel, in vision, sees the glory of Yahweh depart from the midst of the city and stand upon 'the mountain which is on the east side of the city' (עַל־הָהָר אֲשֶׁר מִקֶּדֶם לָעִיר).

This marks the culmination of the vision in chs. 8–11 (11.14-21, with its promise of restoration and renewal being clearly intrusive at this point), in which Ezekiel sees the city as under judgment because of its idolatry (8.5-18), and the sins of its leaders (11.1-13), so {262} that the glory of Yahweh, understood as his visibly apprehended presence, removes first from the Temple and then from the city. Ezek. 43.2 seems to be the counterpart to that, where the glory of Yahweh re-enters city and Temple from the east.

Such a parallel to our Zechariah passage seems very likely and, if it has indeed provided the model and inspiration for this passage, it underlines our comments that the state of affairs existing within city, cult and leadership, prior to this divine theophany, were seen by the circle from which these chapters come to be such as had been abandoned by the presence of Yahweh. Then the use of the Ezekiel material here would show a belief that in the near future his promise of Yahweh's return to that Temple, with all its consequences, was about to be fulfilled.

---

5. So, e.g., Mitchell (1912: 343); Ackroyd (1962a: 655); D.R. Jones (1962a: 172); G. Gaide (1968: 145); Otzen (1964: 203ff.); Saebø (1969: 289ff.); M. Bič (1962: 162).

Yet one may wonder if there was a still deeper significance in the mention of the Mount of Olives at this point. J.B. Curtiss, in an examination of biblical and extra-biblical references to the Mount of Olives, sought to establish that the Mount of Olives had become the centre for the cult of the Akkadian death god, Nergal (Curtiss 1957). Morgenstern goes further into this (1960: esp. 179ff.) by a reference to a mural in the synagogue at Dura which brings Zech. 14 and Ezek. 37 together. It shows the dead rising from a cleft mountain, over which the hand of Yahweh is outstretched. It was, he maintains, Zech. 14 which gave {263} rise to the idea that the Mount of Olives was the place of entry and exit to the realm of the dead, an idea which finds expression in the Targum of 14.4, which says that when Yahweh stands on the mountain he takes and blows a trumpet to awaken the dead.

Such surmises must be treated with caution, yet the Old Testament references which do link the Mount of Olives chain with the cultic apostasy and abominations of earlier times, and notably with Solomon, may well be significant. For its mention here may well carry not only association with Ezekiel's vision of the return of Yahweh's glory to his renewed city, but also overtones of that divine theophany being a reversal of the cultic abuses which had brought the judgment of Yahweh on it, a divine and permanent fulfillment of that which Josiah's reform had achieved only transitorily. Indeed, if the Mount of Olives had been the scene of the departure of the broken-hearted, rightful ruler of Jerusalem, because long ago a usurper had snatched leadership to which he had neither legal, sacral nor moral right, may its mention here not suggest, not only a purging of the corrupt worship at the approach of Yahweh, but also the dispossession of a corrupt and improper leadership in order that its rightful leaders might be restored once more? Again, it would be a veiled reference, as such references in apocalyptic type literature usually are,[6] but would express exactly the kind of outlook which we {264} have seen reflected in Deutero-Zechariah, especially in chs. 11ff., since by such reference to earlier biblical literature it would be making its uncompromising comments on present leadership, temple and cult in Jerusalem.

This brings us to the very involved topographical description in vv. 4f. of what happens when Yahweh takes his stand upon the Mount of Olives. This description has perhaps been complicated by textual additions in v. 5, and certainly by the textual obscurity of the thrice-repeated נַסְתֶּם and by the apparent place names, גֵּי־הָרִים and אֶל־אָצַל.

---

6.   One has only to compare with the political references in the book of Daniel.

Verse 4 itself presents a straightforward and quite intelligible picture, it is, even in the choice of verb, root בקע, descriptive of the earth-quaking phenomena which traditionally accompany the theophany (e.g. Ezek. 38.19ff.; Mic. 1.4; Nah. 1.5; Hab. 3.6; Ps. 18.8 [7]; Judg. 5.5; 1 Kgs 19.11ff.). Indeed, the same verb, root בקע, occurs in Mic. 1.4 and Hab. 3.9. But if we go on to ask *why* the Mount of Olives is sundered so that an east–west valley opens up, is it possible that we hear an echo of Isa. 40.3ff., where the triumphal return of Yahweh to his city is facilitated by the fact that 'every valley shall be lifted up and every mountain made low'? Then 'the glory of the LORD (כְּבוֹד יְהוָה) will be revealed'. The Babylonian captivity of the city of Jerusalem will be at an end, and the expectation of Ezekiel that the corruption and false leadership which caused the departure of the 'glory of Yahweh' will be renewed by the return of that glory. {265}

It seems then that several earlier Old Testament references may have been woven together, and alluded to suggestively by the reference to the appearance of Yahweh on the Mount of Olives and its being split in two, but that all combined to make the same kind of points that are found in the preceding chapters. They combine a devastating assessment of the contemporary state of affairs in the capital city and its official cultus with a confident hope that all is about to be renewed by the advent of Yahweh to his city with its subsequent transformation and renewal. Such a view of v. 4 is further supported by two further references in the very obscure and uncertain v. 5.

Concerning the first half of v. 5 it is very difficult to arrive at any confident conclusions, why should the opening of an east–west valley through the Mount of Olives chain lead to 'the stopping up of the valley of my mountains'?[7] Some have concluded that it refers to the creation of a causeway across the Kidron Valley, thus continuing the triumphal highway into the city (so, e.g., Mitchell 1912: 343). On the other hand it has been objected that the blocking up of the stream Kidron is 'hardly a suitable opening to the New Age' (D.R. Jones 1962a: 173). Others have seen it as a divinely provided means of escape (Driver 1906: 274; Otzen 1964: 205). Otzen links it with Isa. 2.9ff., although it is not certain that the text of v. 5b speaks of flight. Wellhausen originally suggested the emendation of גֵּיא־הָרַי, or even גֵּיא־הָרִים to {266} גֵּיא־חִנֹּם, the Valley of Hinnom, and this has most recently been vigorously championed by Saebø (1969: 295ff.).

---

7. Reading the נַסְתֶּם of the MT as נִסְתַּם.

Having rejected Morgenstern's suggestion of cultic associations with the Mount of Olives in v. 4, he believes there is such association intended in v. 5. Its assurance that the Valley of Hinnom will be stopped up must be understood in the light of the associations of that valley with idolatry and uncleanness. Then, the reference to 'my mountains' can be kept, since they indicate the Temple mountain. So in Saebø's opinion also, a promise of a similar cleansing and sacral restitution is promised here to that which Ezekiel foretold. All attempted interpretations of v. 5a must, in the last resort, remain conjectual since the text is unsure, an uncertainty which also attaches to the topographical reference to the place where the valley is to reach.

This also applies to the same verb which occurs twice in v. 5b, for נסתם may be pointed either as the second person plural of the qal of root נוס, 'to flee', and so be rendered 'You shall flee', or as third person singular niphal of the root סתם 'to stop up', 'close', and be rendered '(the valley) shall be stopped up'. The Versions vary in their interpretation here.[8] One wonders whether the text, originally or subsequently, has been influenced at all by Jer. 31.38-40, the {267} concluding oracle of 'the Book of Consolation', usually assigned to a time later than Jeremiah.[9] Its promise that Jerusalem shall be rebuilt 'for Yahweh', however, suggests a date in the exile, or in the immediate post-exilic period. Two of the specific points mentioned to illustrate the dimensions of the rebuilt city are the Tower of Hananel and the Corner Gate, both of which also occur in Zech. 14.10, although each passage mentions places not found in the other and not all of which are known.[10] But the Jeremiah passage goes on to make what is usually taken to be a reference to the Valley of Hinnom by saying,

> ...the whole valley of the dead bodies and the ashes and all the fields as far as the brook Kidron, to the corner of the Horse Gate toward the east, shall be sacred to Yahweh.

8.   The Targum, for example, takes the first occurrence of the verb in v. 5 to mean 'blocked up', but the second two as 'to flee', while the LXX takes all three to mean 'blocked up' and renders 'The valley of my mountains shall be blocked, and the valley of the mountains will reach as far as Yasol, and it will be blocked as it was blocked in the days of the earthquake, in the days of Uzziah, king of Judah'. Josephus follows the LXX. Syriac and Vulgate follow the MT in reading all three as 'to flee'.

9.   E.g. Weiser (1969: 289). J. Bright expresses slight hesitation here (1965: 287).

10.   Just as no one is sure what is meant by the hill Gareb and Goah in Jer. 31.39, so no one can be certain as to the exact location of the king's wine presses in Zech. 14. It is usually assumed that in both places limits to the east and south of the city are being given since the known limits are those of the north and west.

This is followed, as in Zech. 14.11, by a promise of the final security of Jerusalem,

It shall not be uprooted or overthrown anymore for ever.

It is true that the unusual word for valley (עֶמֶק) has led some to question whether this was meant to be originally a reference to the Valley of Hinnom, but normally it is so taken,[11] and this, then, is presumably a reference to the cleansing, as well as to the rebuilding and final security of the city, from such cultic malpractices as have already been condemned by Jeremiah, in 2.23; 7.31. {268}

The question arises, then, whether the Jeremiah passage has influenced Zech. 14, either originally or in the course of its development, or whether both reflect dimly a current eschatological hope of a golden future for Jerusalem, stressing the extent of its ideal boundaries, its cleansing and its security. If so, it does tend to lend weight to the idea that it is the Valley of Hinnom which shall be 'stopped up', which would show how one group saw the promise of cleansing of the site of former cultic abuses, so that it should be 'sacred to the LORD'. But again, there can be no certainty here.

Yet, as has been said, two points of interest remain. The first is the reference to the earthquake 'in the days of Uzziah' (cf. Amos 1.1), a reference which can fit either the idea of fleeing or to valleys being 'blocked up'. There are indications that a tradition had grown up around Uzziah of some act of impiety which merited the divine disfavour. 2 Kgs 15.1-5 tells of the leprosy to which he becomes prey, and attributes it to his failure to remove the high places, and v. 5 suggests that Jotham, his son, acted as co-regent towards the end of his father's life.[12] However, the Chronicler gives another reason for the judgment of this illness. In 2 Chron. 26.16ff., it is said that when he was strong 'he grew proud to his destruction'. He usurped the role of the legitimate priesthood, and entered the {269} Temple to burn incense on the altar of incense. When opposed by Azariah, the chief priest, and 80 others, he became angry with them and, at the same moment, leprosy broke out on his forehead.

This, of course, was to judge him by the standards of a later time. There seems little doubt that in later years he contracted leprosy, and the general

---

11. So Weiser (1969: 290); Bright (1965: 283); J.P. Hyatt (1956: 1041ff.), and, tentatively, Cunliffe-Jones (1966: 203ff.)

12. So also J. Gray (1970: 559ff.). This may be why Azariah is not given what was presumably his court name, either in the king's account of Jotham's accession (2 Kgs 15.32) or in Isa. 6.1. For a different view, however, see G.B. Gray (1912: 569n).

abhorrence of the disease may have given rise to the speculation that he
had sinned in some way. So it is not hard to imagine how such a tradition
grew. If it grew early it would give added poignance to the temporal
setting of Isaiah's vision of the holiness of Yahweh and sinfulness of the
community 'in the year that King Uzziah died'.[13] But the tradition
obviously took the form that Uzziah had had some head-on clash of
interest with the official priesthood since it is known to Josephus (*Ant.*
9.10.4) who adds (possibly, of course, by derivation from Zech. 14) that
the outbreak was incurred by

> ...a great earthquake which shook the ground and a rent was made in the
> temple and the bright rays of the sun shone through it, and fell upon the
> king's face...

Josephus seems to follow the LXX, for no mention of flight is made but
only of obstructions because half of the mountain broke off and rolled four
furlongs. Yet the reference to the Temple seems to suggest some variant
of the tradition known to Josephus, yet independent of the Chronicler's
account. {270}

The existence of such a tradition is testified, therefore, and one wonders
whether the allusion requires us to see that the text spoke originally of
flight, or, with slightly greater probability, of valleys obstructed, in order
to recall the lesson of Uzziah, that Yahweh visits in judgment those who
falsely usurp their position in the Temple. From such, the rule will now be
taken away, as it was from Uzziah.

The final reference which calls for comment in v. 5 is the recurrence of
the phrase, 'Then the LORD *my* God will come', which also occurs in 11.4,
and which was discussed there. It was suggested that its significance was
that it differentiated the speaker from his hearers, who, by the use of the
term, sets himself over against them. The re-appearance in this chapter, of
so unusual a phrase, would again strengthen the impression that a similar
outlook is finding expression in this chapter as in ch. 11. The speaker sees
himself, or the group he represents, as in opposition to those who occupy
the Temple and leadership in Jerusalem, against whom every activity of
Yahweh will be directed at his coming.

But what of the 'you' (feminine singular עִמָּךְ) at the end of the verse?
This reads, 'The LORD my God will come and all the holy ones with you'.
This also is often emended, since the reference is taken to be to the angelic

---

13. Suggestions, however, that the accompanying phenomena of the vision were
those of the earthquake later attributed to this time are fanciful (Snaith 1946, II: 8).

hosts which Yahweh will bring with him.[14] Saebø, however, wonders whether the reference may not be {271} back to the address to Jerusalem in v. 1, in which case the term 'holy ones', 'refers rather to the community of the holy city' (Saebø 1969: 296). This is significant, for קְדֹשִׁים can, and does, refer to *people* and not only to angelic hosts of heaven. In the singular, it refers in Isa. 4.3 to the remnant left in a purified Jerusalem, 'everyone who has been recorded for life in Jerusalem when the Lord shall have washed away the filth of the daughter of Zion and cleansed the bloodstains of Jerusalem from its midst by a spirit of judgment and by a spirit of burning'.[15] This in itself can be a reflection of the often-repeated injunction of the Code of Holiness, 'You shall be holy (קְדֹשִׁים) because I, the LORD, your God, am holy' (Lev. 19.2, etc.). It is therefore by no means impossible that the reference here is to the fact that when Yahweh comes, he will make clean those who had remained loyal and true, that is 'holy' to him, the community, not of all Jerusalem as Saebø suggests, but the members of the circle of the writer, the community of the faithful. Then the עִמָּךְ is not addressed to God, still less does it require emendation. It is addressed to those now in position of honour and security in Jerusalem while the faithful have been driven underground. They will be 'with you' again, the implication being, to their great discomfort. Their days of secure but unworthy tenure of office will be over.[16] {272}

We may conclude our survey of 14.1-5 therefore, by saying that there are signs within it of an outlook which is very much akin to that of ch. 11 and 12.1–13.6. This outlook appears to be opposed to the existing official leadership of Temple and society in Jerusalem which it sees as corrupt and under sentence of divine judgment. It represents those who see themselves as the faithful community, rejected and even oppressed now, but to share

14. So LXX, Syriac and *BHS*; among moderns, Driver (1906: 274); Jones (1962a: 173); Gaide (1968: 147); Bič (1962: 163) takes the reference to be to the heavenly host, but keeps the MT as direct address to God; Lamarche (1961: 95) also keeps the MT and takes it to refer to God.

15. This passage is usually assigned to the post-exilic period (e.g. O. Kaiser 1972: 53ff.), but a direct dependence is not being suggested here, rather a similarity of idea and of a possible similarity in the sense in which the term קָדוֹשׁ is used.

16. For עַם in this hostile sense, see BDB: 767, and see, e.g. Ps. 94.16; Job 9.2 (3). It is true that such an interpretation might lead us to expect most naturally the plural form, עִמָּכֶם. But the writer might be thinking of them as collectively representing the city of Jerusalem and hence the use of the second person feminine singular. This is the more likely if his viewpoint is, even mentally if not literally, from 'outside' the present order of Jerusalem.

in the victory of Yahweh at his appearance and final victory. This will usher in a new age for Jerusalem and Judah in which the city will be cleansed, its society renewed under true leadership (although any emphasis on human leadership appears to be falling further and further into the background), and made everlastingly secure, its enemies of every kind, external and internal, destroyed. The greatest divergence between what has preceded ch. 14 is the latter's more pessimistic and drastic view of what must first befall Jerusalem before the promises of Ezekiel and other earlier prophecy, not least that of Proto-Zechariah, are fulfilled. To this difference we must return later.

There follows in vv. 6-11 a section on the consequences of the final victory of God. Verses 6ff. present us with a textual problem, since a literal rendering of the MT would yield, 'And it shall happen on that day that there shall not be light, precious things shall congeal'. However, the *Qere* changes the initial yodh of יְקָפאוּן {273} to a waw, intending it to be read, 'and ice'. The Targum follows the *Qere* of the MT. The LXX has changed the initial yodh of the first יְקָרוֹת to a waw, and so renders, 'and cold and ice', and in this is followed by Syriac, Latin and Symmachus. Some take the verse as it then stands, 'There will not be light, but cold and ice', so that the whole becomes a warning of darkness and doom, perhaps coloured by traditional ideas of the Day of Yahweh as a day of darkness.[17] Others emend the אוֹר to עוֹד (so Mitchell, 1912: 346) reading, 'There shall not be any more cold and frost', which seems then to fit more closely with a context which is usually seen as hopeful. A choice is not really helped by further obscurity in v. 7, which yields the literal meaning, 'and there shall be one day (known to Yahweh), not day, nor night, but it shall come to pass at the time of evening it shall be light'. Does this mean then, that the Day of Yahweh will be one of utter darkness, of chill terror, but that when things are at their darkest the light (of salvation) will break through? In this respect, is it somewhat akin to Joel 3.3f. (2.30f.)? Or, is the whole a promise of constant light and fruitful warmth? The text alone does not make this clear, although the context, as it continues in v. 8 to speak of a miraculous transformation of the land, suggests the latter. Perhaps the reference to light in the evening is a deliberate {274} reference to the 'joy cometh in the morning' theme familiar from the cultic setting of the Psalms, such as Ps. 30.6 (5).[18]

17. Lamarche (1961: 95ff.), e.g., adopts this reading and says that other versions show obvious attempts to avoid a difficult reading.

18. E.g. J. Ziegler (1950). Ziegler argues that there are three roots for the idea: (a)

Again, the apparent allusion to the terms of the Noachic Covenant, bringing together as it does in Gen. 8.22 cold and heat, day and night, seems significant:

> While the earth remains, seed time and harvest, cold (וְקֹר) and heat, summer and winter, day and night, shall not cease.

This allusion is strengthened in that 'summer and winter' are also mentioned in v. 8.

How far does this represent a conscious re-adaptation of the terms of the Noachic Covenant? The answer, to some extent, hinges on the sources behind the thought of v. 8 which depicts an unceasing flow of 'living waters' (מַיִם־חַיִּים) from Jerusalem, half of which flows east to the Dead Sea, and half to the west, to the Mediterranean. Inevitably, we are reminded of Ezek. 47.12. Here the phrase is simply that 'water' issued and it issued specifically from the Temple, then flowing to the Dead Sea and the Arabah, bringing fertility to that arid region. Fertility is not its only function, however, for in Ezek. 47.12 it is said that the leaves and the fruit of the trees which grow by the stream will not fall with the passing seasons but will be constantly renewed, and 'their fruit will be for food, and their leaves for healing'.

Is there significance in the heightening of the {275} imagery of Ezekiel in Zech. 14 by the doubling of the stream so that it flows both east and west? If one remembers that the notorious thing about the region of the Dead Sea was not merely its aridity but that it had once been laid under a divine curse (Gen. 19.23ff.; cf. Isa. 1.9; Jer. 49.18; Lam. 4.6; Amos 4.11, etc.) does this suggest by the fact that the stream flows in both directions through the land that the whole land had become contaminated and needed cleansing? One could expect the circles which preserved such traditions to have taken seriously the threat of cursing for disobedience to the word of Yahweh and forsaking of the covenant in Deut. 29.22ff.

But there is a line of tradition behind the Ezekiel picture of the land being supplied by a constantly renewed source of fertility and healing. It was a concept already familiar from the cult of the pre-exilic Jerusalem, as

the imagery of the sun putting to flight the fears of the night; (b) the fact that morning was the time of judgment (e.g. 2 Sam. 15.2ff.); (c) the historical occasions when tradition reported the help of God coming in the morning, as in the Passover night, the drowning of the Egyptians in the Reed Sea, the deliverance of Jerusalem from Sennacherib, etc. Ziegler rejected Schmidt's view that the idea originally grew from a night incubation period in the Temple.

Pss. 46 and 48 make clear, the life-giving waters of the presence of Yah-weh himself in the city. But already in the Paradise narrative there was the river which divided into four and made the whole region fertile. Some have suggested that this concept is related to Zech. 14.10ff. where the whole land, except for Jerusalem, becomes a plain, that is, it is sunk to the level of the Arabah, to be watered by the stream issuing from the capital city (Saebø 1969: 300ff.). In which case, vv. 6ff., taken together, might be held to indicate a return to the state of affairs which existed before the sin of man spoiled Paradise and led to judgment of the {276} flood. The promise of the Noachic Covenant, the regulation of nature for the providential care of even fallen man, will be superseded. Redemption, while it is pictured in this-worldly terms, leads to a renewal of the realm of creation, a return to the conditions of Paradise.[19] A similar idea, which may either have influenced Deutero-Zechariah, or be itself the product of a similar line of tradition and interpretation of older concepts is found in Isa. 60.9ff.

The lines of tradition behind this concept appear, then, to be many-layered and several aspects of salvation are suggested by it. The use made of it appears to be similar to that in Joel 4.18 (3.18). But the mention of the last passage raises one more point of difference between the Zechariah passage and its counterpart in Ezekiel, and certainly in the Songs of Zion. The Temple is not mentioned as the source of the stream (as it is in Joel 4.18) but the more general term 'Jerusalem' is substituted. Is this difference significant?

An answer must remain tentative, but one clue may be afforded by the use of the phrase מַיִם־חַיִּים. It may mean simply 'running water' as, for example, in Lev. 14 where instructions are given for the cleansing of a leper, and in Num. 19.17, for the cleansing of someone contaminated by contact with a corpse. But this easily lends itself to illustrate the satisfaction to be {277} found in relationship with God, as in Ps. 36.8 (7)ff., 'with thee is the fountain of life (מְקוֹר [מַיִם] חַיִּים)'.[20] It is not surprising then to find it passing into oracles of such a prophet as Jeremiah in judgment on the people who had forsaken this relationship:

19. This is substantially the view of Otzen (1964: 205ff.), '…er soll zu dem paradiesischen Zustand, wie er vor dem Sündenfall da war, zurückkehren'. He speaks of an '*Aufhebung* der gottgegebenen Naturgesetz' (Otzen 1964: 205ff., italics mine). Saebø (1969: 304) objects, and says rather that, 'die kommende Lichtoffenbarung (über Jerusalem) eine neue heilsgeschichtliche *Überbietung* der vorhandenen Schöpfungsordnumg zu meinen'. The distinction appears a nice, if not a false one.

20. For a comment on this passage in the context of the whole concept of 'Life' in the Old Testament, see Johnson (1964: 105).

They have forsaken me, the fountain of living waters (מְקוֹר מַיִם חַיִּים)
(Jer. 2.13; cf. 17.13).

It is possible then that the change made in Zech. 14 indicates that it comes from those who do not wish to exclude the Temple from the general restorative work of Yahweh (cf. vv. 16ff.), but are anxious to stress, in the light of the grievous compromise of Temple worship in Israel's history, and perhaps again in their own time, that it will be by the presence of Yahweh himself and by living relationship with him, that the blessings of salvation will be realized, not by any automatic guarantee offered by the presence of the Temple alone. And indeed, there is not wanting even in v. 21 the suggestion that the Temple and its cult, while central, will enjoy no monopoly of holiness.[21]

We must notice also that Zech. 14 diverges significantly, not only from Ezek. 47 but, in this particular respect, from Proto-Zechariah. The picture of the idyllic prosperity of the land consorts well with Zech. 3.10 and 8, together with the exaltation of Jerusalem, but nothing akin to the eagerness associated with the rebuilding of the Temple of those chapters is {278} found here. Absent also is any of the Messianic hopes that were attached to Zerubbabel, while the silence concerning the priestly personnel of the Temple reflects none of the enthusiasm that attached to Joshua as the second in a kind of dyarchy. Such omission could well be explained by a deep sense of disillusionment over the character and performance of these men's successors and the quality of worship in the restored Temple.

In fact, v. 9 does take up the issue of leadership, but in order to stress the kingship of Yahweh himself. Such an emphasis is not necessarily in contradiction to thoughts of human leadership as well. For example, Zech. 2.14 (10)ff., anticipates 14.9 remarkably closely, in a context of the highest hopes for Zerubbabel and Joshua. Nevertheless, the absence of any reference to human leadership can hardly be coincidental, especially in the light of 9.9ff. To this we shall have to return in our attempt to summarize the thought of Deutero-Zechariah.

It has often been suggested that v. 9 is intrusive at this place, and that

---

21. Saebø (1969: 305) also mentions this strange contrast, both with the Ezekiel passage and with the eager expectation connected with the rebuilding of the Temple in Haggai and Zechariah, and he follows Kraus (1966) in suggesting disappointment in those earlier eschatological hopes as a cause. The view expressed in this work is that it was due, not just to general disappointment over future hopes as such, but to bitter disillusionment with the life of the reconstituted Temple and the quality of its leadership.

the leveling of the territory of Judah, except for Jerusalem, to the level of
the Arabah, was related to the flow of waters in v. 8, and perhaps even to
the seismic upheaval of v. 5.[22] However, the theme seems to be closely
related to what has preceded and what follows by the themes long since
common to the Enthronement Psalms with their joyful {279} cultic cry,
מָלַךְ יְהוָה. With these must be associated the closely related Songs of Zion.
The idea of the elevation of Jerusalem, for example, which follows in
v. 10 is linked with the victory of Yahweh celebrated in Ps. 48; the thought
of Yahweh's victory over his enemies is the theme of Pss. 93 (where it is
the cosmic floods of chaos which he has subdued), 97 (where not only are
his adversaries burned up so that the mountains melt before him, but 'all
worshippers of images are put to shame', for 'he is exalted above all
gods', who 'bow down before him', the theme of Zech. 14.9b), in 96.10ff.,
and 98 (where the joy and prosperity of the earth are assured by his
victory). In the light of such parallels associated with the kingship of Yahweh there seems little doubt that the כָּל־הָאָרֶץ of v. 9 suggests a cosmic
sweep of consequences to the reign of Yahweh in his city again. The echo
of the Deuteronomistic creed (the 'Shema' of Deut. 6.4) in the phrase, 'the
Lord will be one and his name one', suggests a cleansing from idolatry
among the redeemed community, the subjugation of idols and their
worshippers as in Ps. 97. Gaide (1968: 150) links this with Zech. 13.2, the
promise that the people will be cured of idolatry in a return to a true
allegiance to the Deuteronomic theology and worship. It is yet another
indication of the assessment of the state of the {280} nation's life and
worship by the circles from which this chapter came.

The cosmic sweep of כָּל־הָאָרֶץ may have had its counterpart in v. 8
where the thought of the land being watered by the rivers which flow
through it seem to echo the Paradise motif. That is, by virtue of the divine
deliverance of Jerusalem all the earth will return to the conditions of

22. So Mitchell (1912: 347), who finds this verse not only out of immediate context
but out of harmony with the thought of the rest of the chapter. Horst (1964: 257, 259)
finds it intrusive in vv. 6-11, but related in thought more to vv. 16-19. Saebø (1969:
302ff.) says that the theme of v. 9 is quite separate from its immediate context and the
expression כָּל־הָאָרֶץ refers to the cosmos, whereas in v. 10 it refers only to Judah. The
twice-repeated אֶחָד suggests a traditio-link with the יוֹם־אֶחָד of v. 7a. On the other
hand, Elliger (1964: 179, 182ff.) finds that v. 9 expresses the theme, not only of this
section but the whole passage, and that it is v. 10 which is secondary. Indeed, its
reference to 'the whole earth' shows that it belongs with the basic core of this section.
Otzen (1964: 207ff.) finds v. 9 to be the central point in a chapter, constructed on the
pattern of the former New Year Festival Enthronement ceremony.

Paradise before the fall.[23] At first sight, the narrowing of this concept to the terrain of Judah in v. 10 appears to be contradictory and to support those who find the connection between vv. 9 and 10ff. to be artificial. But it seems more probable that the reference to the reduction of the level of Judah to that of the Arabah is neither the main emphasis of vv. 10ff., nor linked with the stream of v. 8 (against Saebø). Rather, it is on the *elevation* of Jerusalem. Amidst the topographical details therefore, a tradition of cosmic significance is being drawn on here. It is the tradition which finds expression in Isa. 2.1-4 and Mic. 4.1-4:

> It shall come to pass in the latter days that the mountain of the house of the LORD shall be established as the highest of the mountains, and shall be raised above the hills.

But this is in order, not only that Jerusalem may be more secure, but the more fitted to play a cosmic role, the conspicuous goal of the nations' quest for religious enlightenment and true worship: {281}

> ...and all the nations shall flow to it,
> and many peoples shall come and say:
> 'Come, let us go up to the mountain of the LORD,
> to the house of the God of Jacob:
> that he may teach us his ways
> and that we may walk in his paths'.
> For out of Zion shall go forth the law,
> and the word of the LORD from Jerusalem.

Just such a significance is seen in Zech. 14; an elevated (v. 10), cleansed and secure (v. 11) Jerusalem will be the centre of all the survivors of the nations (vv. 16ff.), a connection which is all the clearer if the intrusive vv. 12-15 did not interrupt the sequence of thought.

Thus, in main thrust at least, there is no return in vv. 10ff. to a limited, parochial outlook which contradicts the universalism of v. 9. Verses 10ff. can be seen as depicting the consequences for Jerusalem, and Judah, and so for the whole world, of the universal kingship of Yahweh.

Verse 11 says that the elevated Jerusalem shall never again know the חֵרֶם. This term, particularly at home in the concept of the Holy War, signified that which was 'holy' or 'tabu' for private use, since it was dedicated to the deity. In Deut. 7.1ff. the rationale for applying חֵרֶם to all the former inhabitants of the land (an idea which existed only in the purist

---

23. So, very strongly, Otzen (1964: 207), following Aalen (1951: 27). (The writer has not had access to this final work).

theory of the Deuteronomists' minds, never to any great degree in practice) is because they were hostile to Yahweh and 'would turn away your
sons from following me, to serve other gods'. This must be the concept
here. There will {282} be nothing in the restored Jerusalem which would
be contrary or opposed to the sole worship of Yahweh and therefore merit-
ing his judgment. It is yet another picture of the *cleansing* of Jerusalem
and therefore yet another estimate of the need for cleansing which is seen
to be the viewpoint of this chapter. It is somewhat akin to the idea expressed
in the appendix to the book of Malachi, that Elijah *redivivus* will

> ...turn the hearts of the fathers to their children and the hearts of the
> children to their fathers, lest I come and smite the land with חֵרֶם (Mal. 3.6
> [4.6]).

J.M. Powis Smith's suggestion that this refers not only to a general social
disintegration but a conflict with elders because 'the younger generation
has taken up with some new philosophy or cult or political course' is an
interesting one here.[24]

The security of the new Jerusalem is also stressed in v. 11, for it 'shall
dwell in security (לָבֶטַח)'. This not only echoes 12.6, but takes up another
theme of Proto-Zechariah (2.9 [5]; 8.3ff.) which itself repeats the theme of
Ezek. 28.26.

It is hard to believe that vv. 12-15 are not intrusive. The sudden return
to the battle against the nations of v. 3 which appeared to have been settled
by the divine theophany and followed by the restoration of nature, and of
Jerusalem and Judah is made without apparent reason or logical order, but
with a great deal {283} of irrelevant detail. Further, it interrupts what
appears to be a close connection between the elevation, cleansing and
security of Jerusalem in vv. 10ff., and the pilgrimage of the nations to it in
vv. 16ff, ideas which were linked in the tradition of Isa. 2.1-4. Even the
inner unity of the section is hard to maintain. Verses 12 and 15 appear to
be connected by their references to the plague which falls upon the nations
and their animals, and the phrase 'a plague like this plague' in v. 15
assumes a connection with v. 12.[25] Verse 13 introduces the apparently
different theme of destruction, not by a plague, but as a result of the
divinely wrought panic, perhaps inspired by 12.4, while v. 14a appears to

---

24. J.M. Powis Smith (1912: 83). He sets this in the Greek period when the spread
of Greek ideas would have produced just such a state of affairs.

25. So Driver (1906: 279). He takes vv. 13ff. to have been inserted by a later writer
from the point of view of ch. 13.

derive from 12.2. Verse 14b introduces yet another aspect, the bringing in or tribute from the defeated nations, a theme taken, perhaps, from Zech. 1.7; 2.13 (9), but which is also a theme common elsewhere in prophecy (e.g. Isa. 60.5, 11; 61.6). It is thus difficult to avoid the justice of P.R. Ackroyd's (1962a: 655) suggestion that the section looks like 'a collection of independent sayings'—independent that is, of each other, but each related to earlier themes of prophecy, though without the creative originality and variety of allusiveness that usually marks the treatment of such material in these chapters. For this reason, and because they scarcely advance the thought further, they need not be subjected to minute or extended scrutiny here. {284}

The main stream of thought is resumed in v. 16, where the idea of the pilgrimage of the nations is given a distinctively special interpretation, an idea related to the elevation of Jerusalem in vv. 10ff., as in Isa. 2.1ff., and already a major theme of Proto-Zechariah in 8.20ff. It is not quite certain whether the 'everyone that survives' (כָּל־הַנּוֹתָר) of the nations is meant to imply more than a literal piece of harmonizing with the earlier part of the chapter, or is meant to indicate a doctrine of a 'remnant', applied to the Gentiles. If it is this latter, there would appear to be an echo of 9.7 where the Philistines, it was said, would be a 'remnant of our God' (root שאר) perhaps typifying the Gentiles as a whole. In any event, the promise would now seem to be extended to all the nations. Certainly the niphal participle of the root יתר is twice used in Isaiah in a more than literal sense:

> And he who is left in Zion and remains in Jerusalem will be called holy, everyone who has been recorded for life in Jerusalem (Isa. 4.3);

> For every one that is left in the land will eat curds and honey (Isa. 7.22b).

We cannot be confident enough of the dates of either of the Isaiah passages to assume that they have influenced Deutero-Zechariah here, but they do show us how in certain circles נוֹתָר could be understood in terms of a 'remnant'. If it is so intended here, it is a remarkable extension of the universalism of Proto-{285}Zechariah which shows that such nations come not only to learn, but to worship, and so share in the 'holiness' of the redeemed cultic community (vv. 20ff.).

In any event, those who come, do so not in attack, nor even as passive witnesses of the salvation of the Israelites, but as fellow-worshippers. Unique to Deutero-Zechariah is the thought that they come to share in the worship of the Feast of Booths. The question naturally arises as to why it is *this* festival they come to observe.

G. Gaide has said that this one act is intended, by metonymy, to stand
for the whole of the religious life (1968: 154: 'Ici, comme en 9,7, un acte
désigne par métonymie toute la religion'.). While that may be so, it could
hardly have been expected that foreigners would make the pilgrimage to
Jerusalem more than once a year. If their taking part in the Feast of
Tabernacles is used to designate their whole new relationship to Yahweh,
the question remains, Why is this the cultic festival chosen to represent
this truth?

It is generally agreed that the Feast of Tabernacles, mentioned only in
the later religious calendars and texts which depend on them (e.g. Deut.
15.13, 16; Lev. 23.34), is to be equated with the early Feast of Asiph, or
'Ingathering', a feast which celebrated the harvesting of the vintage crops
and hence was an occasion of much joy (e.g. Judg. 21.19; 1 Sam. 1.3;
1 Kgs 8.2, 65ff.; 12.32f.; Ezek. 45.25; also de Vaux 1961: 495ff.). Not
only so, but it figured so prominently in the cultic year that it could be
called '*the* Feast'. {286} Thus, at the very least, for the 'remnant' of the
nations to share in this, would be to share in the high point of Yahweh
worship and to be involved in its most joyful occasion.

Further, as is made clear in these verses, the gift of rain was closely
linked with the due observance of this feast. Nor is this the least surprising
when one recalls that it had always been an essentially agricultural festival, intimately connected with the idea of the fertility of the land, fertility
so dependent on the gift of rain (Snaith 1947: 62ff.). Rain, therefore,
signified a blessing from God which brought life and fertility, and so was
itself tantamount to a sign of salvation (e.g. Deut. 11.13ff.; 28.12; 1 Kgs
8.35). The king, by his right relationship to Yahweh, could ensure such
blessing for his people (Ps. 72.6) and from that it is hardly surprising that
one passes over into expectation of Yahweh's future salvation and
blessing.[26] Already in Deutero-Zechariah, men have been summoned to
that seeking of Yahweh (in contrast to idols) which shall bring rain (10.1).
Apart altogether, then, from any disputed theories concerning the relation
of the Feast of Tabernacles to the New Year Enthronement Festival of
Yahweh, we see that the significance of the coming of the nations to
participate in it is not only to admit them to the highest point of Yahweh
worship, to its greatest expression of joy, but is a sign that they will seek
the means of life, no longer from their idols, but from Yahweh. {287}
They will participate in all the blessings of the future salvation.

---

26. Hos. 6.3; Isa. 30.23. Such a concept is already found in Proto-Zechariah, 8.12ff.

If the findings of many scholars can be justified, and this was already before the exile closely associated with a New Year Enthronement Festival which, after the Babylonian pattern, celebrated the kingship of Yahweh by virtue of his subduing of the elemental waters of chaos, a kingship manifested in his control of the powers of nature to guarantee fertility for the coming year, of which the 'Enthronement Psalms' were the liturgical expression, then the relation of this to the theme of the kingship of Yahweh in this chapter becomes all the more striking. The issue is too complex for discussion here, especially since sufficient importance attaches to its mention as the festival to which the nations come, to underline the significance of its mention independently of the validity of such theories or not.[27]

Perhaps one more significance of the Feast of Tabernacles should be mentioned. It cannot be overlooked that the Chronicler records its observance on two occasions which must have seemed of the utmost importance to the Jewish community. It was observed, according to him, immediately after the return to Jerusalem from exile, after the altar was rebuilt, under the leadership of Joshua and Zerubbabel.[28] Again, it is said to have been observed following the reading of the law by Ezra (Neh. 8.13-18). {288}

27. For a fuller discussion of the New Year Enthronement Festival, see Mowinckel (1962: I, 106-89); Johnson (1967: but esp. pp. 58ff. in relation to Zech. 14). For differing viewpoints, see Snaith (1947) where the view is expressed that it was only after the exile that the concept of the kingship of Yahweh was associated with the New Year Festival; and de Vaux (1961: 502ff.). Gray (1961: 20, 22, 23ff.) makes a strong claim that Zech. 14 demonstrates a connection with both the pre- and post-exilic New Year Festival.

28. Ezra 3.4. There are many difficulties raised by Ezra 3.1-7. The only date given is that of the 'seventh month', and the reader is left to assume that it is in the first year of Cyrus, after the return. Rudolph (1949: 29) thinks this is too early, and that two or three years must have elapsed. Brockington (1969: 67ff.) thinks the phrase has been borrowed from the account of the reading of the Law in Neh. 8. Indeed, the reference in Neh. 8.17 that it had not been celebrated since the time of Joshua indicates that the whole account is the Chronicler's invention. However, not only is the supposition that the returned exiles would have felt the need to build a new altar a very likely one, so that they might resume what they would have regarded as legitimate cult practices, but the very contradiction with Neh. 8.17 suggests as more likely that the Chronicler was bound by accepted tradition than that he was freely inventing. The other difficulty relates to the part of Joshua and Zerubbabel in the work of rebuilding the altar and in such an observance, for they are assigned by the books of Haggai and Zechariah to the time of Darius II. Whether the mention of them is an error at this point, or whether they had been active for some time already by 520 BC is not of moment here.

Of course, the relative dates of the final form of the Chronicler's work and Zech. 14 need not concern us here. There are indications (notably the contradiction between Neh. 8.17 and Ezra 3.4) that the Chronicler was, at least in part, utilizing traditions concerning the history of the Feast of Tabernacles which were already current. If, in the mind of the restored community, it had become associated with two critical points in their history, their return from exile to the land of promise, and the adoption of the law as constitutive of the true people of God under the leadership of Ezra, the second Moses, does this not suggest a further possible significance in its mention in Zech. 14? The next great stage of renewal, the next decisive step forward in the life of the people of God, will be when Gentile nations also come to acknowledge the kingship of Yahweh and to worship him, and this too will be marked by the observance of the Feast of Tabernacles.[29] Neither the strong admonitory note of the statement warning of the consequences of failure so to acknowledge Yahweh as king, nor the pedantic and laboured addition concerning Egypt whose land would not suffer from the witholding of rain, should blind us to the nobility of the concept nor the courageous new sweep of faith expressed here. A radical transformation of the make-up of the people of God by the addition of faithful Gentiles is being envisaged. It is a promised fulfillment of the {289} noble hope with which the oracles of Proto-Zechariah ended (13.20ff.). There, however, it was said that men of other nations will come for instruction but here it is being said that instruction has passed into enlightenment. It is the realization of Isa. 2.2-4 (=Mic. 4.1-4), the fulfillment of the purpose of the elevation of Zion.[30]

The final verses speak of the holiness of the renewed Jerusalem and Judah, of both its secular life and its Temple cult. Elliger (1964: 186) finds this to be a later addition which, over against the universalism of the preceding passage, seeks to emphasize the holiness of the people of God themselves, so that there is no danger of the border lines between them and the 'nations' becoming blurred. On the other hand, Saebø (1969: 307)

---

29. A very interesting example of how, still later, the Feast of Tabernacles came to assume an even greater importance, is attested in 2 Macc. (1.9, 18; 10.5ff.). The historical work of Jason of Cyrene which formed the basis of this work is dated by Eissfeldt (1965: 581) towards the end of the second century BC, the work of the summarizer a generation or two later, and the final reviser in the second half of the first century BC.

30. For other expressions of this thought, see Pss. 22.28 (27)ff.; 47.8 (7)ff.; Jer. 3.17; Zeph. 3.9f.; Isa. 61.6ff.; 66.18ff. Also Mowinckel (1959: 146ff. nn).

says it is not too sharply to be distinguished from what has gone before, for all its emphasis on the cult, whereby the sanctity of the community is grounded in the Temple. Such an emphasis on the renewal of Jerusalem and the community would be wholly in keeping with what we have found in these chapters. Nor should the attention paid to *ritual* aspects of holiness lead us to see here in any way a falling away from the strong prophetic influence we have found in them. Haggai and Zechariah both stood in the line of earlier prophetic ethical teaching, but insisted on the due restoration of the Temple and the order of its cult. This was to be the evidence of their {290} inner response to God's claims, as Ezekiel had seen it before them. This, then, would remain quite within the influence of Proto-Zechariah as seen in Zech. 3; 5; 6.13ff.; 8.1ff. and 8.18ff.

Horses, which once were symbols of human might used in rebellion against, and independence of, God, will now bear the same inscriptions as the High Priest's diadem, and thus all secular power shall be brought under the dominion of Yahweh (cf. Exod. 28.33ff.; Horst 1964: 260; Ackroyd 1962a: 655). In the same way, even the ordinary pots for the Temple will be fit to use for the same purposes as the sacred bowls used at the altar to collect the blood of the sacrificial victims. Perhaps there is the overtone here, that so many people will be coming to sacrifice that all such vessels will have to be pressed into service for such use. But the emphasis seems to be on the holiness rather than their material[31] or their size.[32] Even pots in common, secular use will be fit to be used in this way. Far from this being a weakened, entirely ritual view of the renewal of the community, it is a not unworthy statement that it will be so much open to God that, by metonymy, even its humblest implements can be used in his service. The whole of life, religious and secular, will alike reflect the covenant relationship with him their temple worship both expressed and effected. It is not yet quite the same idea as expressed in Rev. 21.22, where the relationship is said to be such that the Temple can {291} be dispensed with altogether, but it is not far from it.

As it is, the Temple will be cleansed and renewed. That seems to be the force of the promise that there will be no כְּנַעֲנִי in it. It can scarcely mean only that, when all is holy, there will be no need for trading in the

---

31. Ackroyd (1962a) makes the suggestion that it is their golden material which is receiving emphasis.

32. So Dentan (1956), following Wellhausen (1892: 194), and other older commentators.

exchange of 'holy' vessels.[33] D.R. Jones (1962a: 180) has said, with some force, that there is likely to be a play on the word 'trader' here. In the prophets and in Deuteronomy the Canaanite 'had become a symbol of apostasy and idolatry', and hence 'it was impossible that a Jew, brought up on the law and prophets, should not see here a picture of the perfect and comprehensive cleansing of the Temple'. Horst (1964: 260) saw a possible reference to the Samaritans to be intended, from whom, the writer is saying, one must be now and for ever separated. Elliger (1964: 186), in making the same point, has some comments to make which are significant in the light of our discussion in these chapters. He points out that the word כְּנַעֲנִי has this two-fold meaning, and yet can hardly apply to traders since they, and all their wares, have become holy! Is the double meaning therefore deliberate? It seems, he says, to refer to some group in Palestine, who in the time of the author had the opportunity of dealing in the Temple. He believes that such a group would have been the Samaritans. But in what way would the Samaritans have had opportunity to deal in the Temple? And what {292} of the universalism of the preceding verses?

The question therefore arises whether this is a final, veiled allusion to the priesthood in the Jerusalem Temple at the time of the writer, from whose ministrations he, and the circle from which he came, saw the need for the Temple to be utterly cleansed as a prelude to the final act of divine renewal and salvation. Might not the shady transactions which certainly went on at some periods such as the time of Antiochus IV, whereby the High Priesthood went to the highest bidder, to the one who was prepared to 'sell' (as they would have seen it) the true interests of their people, suggest that the term 'trader' was a most appropriate one in both its senses? They showed the cultic apostasy of Canaanites, they showed the greed for gain of traders. There would be no room for them in either capacity in the Temple in the renewed community of the era of salvation.[34]

---

33. So Mitchell (1912: 357), who refers to Joel 4.17 (3.17), 'And Jerusalem shall be holy, and strangers shall never again pass through it', and finds a reference to Canaanites as such to be irrelevant here. Ackroyd (1962a: 655) maintains that the exclusion of Canaanites would be contrary to the universalism of the previous verse (also Dentan 1956: 1114; Driver 1906: 282).

34. The article of van Seters (1972), is of relevance here. He argues that not every reference to them in the Old Testament is to be taken historically literally, and certainly not as indicating antiquarian origin for the passage in question. He summarizes, 'The "nations" are archetypal and even seem to move in the direction of representing super-human evil' (p. 81). It may be that the term 'Canaanites' could be treated in the same way.

If we now survey the chapter as a whole, the question arises as to its relation with what has preceded it. As has been shown before, it is often taken that the different form of the tradition concerning the attack of the nations upon Jerusalem betokens different authorship, as do the more developed apocalyptic features of the chapter. But some who recognize the variations allow more weight to the parallels which do exist. D.R. Jones, for example, has said, '...ch. 14 is not to be understood {293} as the completion and climax of chs. 12–13, but as a collection of prophecies which illustrate the same theme from a different viewpoint'. But he also adds, 'The unknown prophet would have belonged to the same prophetic school as Haggai and Zechariah and the prophets of chs. 9–11' (Jones 1962a: 171).

There are in fact significant parallels between ch. 14 and 12.1–13.6. Both speak of the future work of Yahweh as involving not only the physical security of Jerusalem but also its spiritual renewal. Both see the renewal of mind and spirit as expressing itself in cultic terms in ritual mourning and abolition of idol worship in chs. 12ff., and in observance of the Feast of Booths in ch. 14. Both speak of new springs of waters. While ch. 14 shows a universalistic outlook which does not come to expression in chs. 12ff., it is found elsewhere in Deutero-Zechariah, notably in 9.7. While the doctrine of the kingdom of Yahweh is made explicit in ch. 14, the whole theme and spirit of chs. 12ff., with Yahweh's arbiting of the fate of the nations, suggests it. Both show similarly the thought and influence of Proto-Zechariah, as we have seen. The idea of rain as symbolic of the blessings of salvation finds a counterpart in 10.1ff., and perhaps lies behind 13.1. While the reference in chs. 12ff. to the Davidic line is conspicuous by its absence in ch. 14, it remains true that Messianic thought, apart from the debatable 9.9ff., does not figure prominently {294} in these oracles. Above all, we have traced in both chs. 12f. and ch. 14 a similarly and strikingly negative attitude to the existing leadership, cult and state of affairs generally.

It is this which calls for more detailed comment, especially in the light of Plöger's (1968) important work, *Theocracy and Eschatology*. Plöger's thesis is that, in post-exilic Judaism, there are two main movements to be discerned. One is represented by the official priesthood and all those who found in the rebuilding of the Temple and the resumption of its cultus the fulfillment of the former prophetic promises concerning Yahweh's renewing work of salvation. To such, the theocratic state of Judaism was the end of the divine purpose for his people. Such is the view of the Priestly writers and the Chronicler. God's presence was mediated through the cult, and so eschatological expectation begins to fall away. The prophets then come to be seen as supremely interpreters of the law. While such a community may have to be judged from time to time, to be cleansed and refined, any radical overthrow is unthinkable, since that community is itself the goal of God's redeeming purpose, its cult the guarantee and mediator of the divine life in its midst.

But, argues Plöger, there is evidence in the apocalyptic literature that there were groups within this theocracy who were not content that this represented the {295} final fulfillment of the divine promises given through the prophets, but looked for a more radical break with the existing order, and complete renewal in the future. In an examination of Isa. 24–27; Zech. 12–14 and Joel, he sees an emergence of this more radical outlook which reached its climax in the book of Daniel, when these groups threw in their lot with the Maccabaeans. So, in Zechariah is to be found a traditional eschatology which saw the fulfillment of the old prophetic promises of the time of the David-orientated hopes of the pre-exilic period fulfilled in the restoration of the people from exile. In 12.1–13.6 there is some extension of this, a greater degree of eschatological expectation in the idea that Israel must go through the judgment of God. But in Zech. 14 (together with what Plöger sees as its introduction in 13.7-9) a much more radical view still has appeared, namely, that a ritual lament within the context of the present cult such as was thought adequate in 12.10ff. no longer meets the situation. Historical Jerusalem must be laid in ruins and its cultus disrupted so that a new remnant may emerge as a result of the dramatic theophany in a climax of crisis. The break between 'then' and 'now' becomes complete.

Such a treatment is most significant, especially in the light of the present examination of Deutero-Zechariah. Its suggestion that the apparent homogeneous unity presented by post-exilic Judaism was in fact divided {296} by internal tensions and among schismatic groups both answers to other investigation[35] and to the inferences that have been drawn from the

35. Here, an important article by R.J. Coggins is relevant (1968). In this it is argued that the simple view of 'Judaism vs. Samaritanism' offers too facile a view of post-exilic Judaism. 'The very existence of the Qumran Community should warn us (that)… it is too narrow a view which sees all the divisions within Judaism simply in terms of Jews and Samaritans' (pp. 44ff.). On the one hand, Coggins argues for a much stronger link between the Samaritans and official Judaism and that the break between them came finally much later than has been suggested; and, on the other hand, that there

outlook expressed, especially in Zech. 11ff. here. The old single Jew/ Samaritan schism begins to appear less and less able to answer all questions and dispose of all evidence. A group rejecting the official cultus as identifiable with the prophetic promises of salvation; steeping itself in the work of the older prophets; re-interpreting it and applying it to the contemporary situation; seeing in themselves the faithful remnant who would emerge the other side of radical and drastic judgment as the nucleus of the new, redeemed and purified community answers exactly to what we have found to be the viewpoint expressed in these chapters of Deutero-Zechariah.[36] Two differences are outstanding in our conclusions.

The first is that the evidence put forward here seems to suggest a more radical break with a more complete hostility to the official Judaism of its day than Plöger allows for.

The second is the finding in Zech. 14 of a markedly different view from that found elsewhere in these chapters to the point that ch. 14 is a correction to and rejection of 12.1–13.6. For all Lutz's enthusiastic acceptance of this latter interpretation, this part of Plöger's work must be decisively rejected in the light of the studies undertaken here. It fails, in the first place, {297} to allow sufficiently for the radical nature of the renewal of Jerusalem described in 12.1–13.6. To describe the mourning of the community as mere cultic lamentation within the existing framework is to fail to realize that it is in response to an inner renewal by the outpouring of the divine Spirit every bit as radical as that promised in Joel, and leads to a rejection of the old cult (13.2-6) which is complete. The significance of it must be seen against the background of the older biblical material to which it makes allusion and which it seeks to re-interpret for its own time. Again, Plöger's treatment fails to detect the attitude of hostility to the official Temple and cult which we have found to run through Zech. 11; 12.1–13.6; and 14 (if not in 10.1ff. also). Indeed, it is significant that Plöger pays scant attention to the Shepherd Allegory of ch. 11 and divorces 13.7-9 from all that has gone before and attaches it to ch. 14 so that it may sharpen the attitude of total renunciation he finds there, but not elsewhere. In fact, vocabulary, ideas and mood all lead the other way for

---

were more diverse views within Judaism itself than one dissident group to be labelled 'Samaritans'. 'All this suggests a far richer diversity within Judaism than is sometimes recognized' (p. 45). The significance of this for the discussion here will be readily appreciated.

36. The main lines of the results of the present examination of the chapters of Deutero-Zechariah had been laid before Plöger's work became known to me.

13.7-9. It remains our opinion, that chs. 11–14, at least, for all their diver-
gences, evince just such a 'schismatic' outlook and radical rejection of the
established cultic community of their time, as Plöger finds in ch. 14 alone,
and all share alike a belief in a drastic rejection of the existing order and
hope for its renewal by a divine {298} intervention from beyond history.

And so the question of the differences between 12f. and 14 remains.
How are the different, more drastic fate of Jerusalem and the absence of
any reference to the Davidic king to be explained? The answer is probably
to be found in a lapse of time, although how long a lapse cannot possibly
be estimated. Chapter 14 seems to date from a later time than 12.1–13.6
and to represent a later stage in the relations between this traditionist circle
and the official leadership of their day. Had the opposition by this time
grown more intense? Had the sense of the futility and wickedness of
leadership become so much more marked by what they saw, that by now it
seemed that only through judgment 'as by fire' could there come the kind
of purification that Isaiah had foreseen in 1.21ff.?[37] Is that also why all talk
of human leadership of any kind has fallen into the background? Is that
why the divine rule alone is exalted? Nor, must it be forgotten, that both
chs. 12 and 14 share alike an identical view of what the outcome of the
battle around Jerusalem will be, deliverance and safety for Jerusalem, and
its cleansing and renewal.

As with so much else in these chapters the answer is not plain beyond
doubt. But such a view as outlined above would both give weight to the
connecting lines {299} which run from one section to another and so
support the view of D.R. Jones that they represent different viewpoints on
the same theme which nevertheless emanate from similar traditionist
circles, and yet give due weight to the otherwise strange differences of
detail and emphasis between them. {300}

---

37. This is very close to the view of Stade (1881: 94). Explaining the relationship
between chs. 11–14 and 9ff., all of which he assigns to one author, he too comments on
the greater pessimism in the last chapters. He also suggests that a lapse of time has to
be assumed to explain this, but also, chs. 9ff. told of the future that could be expected,
had it not been for the sins of his contemporaries which are the subject of 11.1-17 and
13.7-9, and which mean that first the events of chs. 12ff. and 14 have to be suffered.
Chapter 14 relates to chs. 12ff. as chs. 11ff. generally, relate to chs. 9ff. (Stade 1881:
96).

We must now return to the questions which were raised at the outset in the Introduction, and attempt to summarize briefly the findings of this investigation. These questions concerned: (i) the principles of exegesis of earlier biblical material in these chapters in the hope that they might afford some clue concerning (ii) the place of the author or group responsible for their final form in the developing traditio-history of the community of post-exilic Judaism which, it was suggested, might even if indirectly, throw some light on (iii) more traditional problems relating to date, authorship and unity.

Concerning the first issue it can fairly confidently be concluded that Stade and others have been right to find here considerable dependence upon earlier biblical material, particularly, although not exclusively, upon the major prophetic collections. It was suggested that, while great caution has to be shown in too quickly assuming that a certain verse or reference has been inspired by this particular text or that, there is a cumulative weight to a great number of probabilities which in the end proves decisive. The final verdict must therefore be that these chapters reveal an outlook {301} which is steeped in the prophetic word of the past and which believes that the great prophetic hopes are about to be fulfilled.

The caution is always necessary since Deutero-Zechariah scarcely ever quotes directly or exactly. The nearest approaches to such quotations are in 9.10b to Ps. 72.7 (8)f., but even here the 'quotation' is not verbatim and, as was suggested in discussing the passage, there may well be a common original to both in the language of the cult. A direct quotation from Amos 7.14 occurs in 13.5, but even here only the first part coincides and, while it is probable that the Amos saying is being recalled, particularly in the context of controversy, yet, significantly it is being re-interpreted in a different way and applied in a new context, namely, that of the fulfilment of the eschatological hope in which the role of the one who predicts that fulfilment will have disappeared.

Nevertheless, within the wider boundaries of fluid and free adaptation of earlier material, it is still quite clear that certain passages have formed the original for what is now being said. In 9.1-8, the oracles of Ezekiel concerning Tyre and those of Amos concerning the Philistines are clearly evoked by the use of phrases and words which are taken over, but altered, or freely adapted in new groupings or attached to different subjects, but within a context of the same {302} general theme as the original, which justifies our seeing in such coincidence of vocabulary and phraseology a real allusion to the earlier material. The echo of Jeremiah's attacks against the 'shepherds' in 10.3 and also, in the same context, of Ezek. 34 by the use of the word עַתּוּדִים, occurs where the same general teaching of the earlier prophets is being emphasized, shown particularly by the promise here as there that Yahweh will himself act as 'shepherd'. We have seen also how significant is the echo of Jeremiah's words by the use of the phrase צֹאן הַהֲרֵגָה, when set in the context of the Jeremiah passage in which it occurs, for the understanding of the passage in Deutero-Zechariah. There are other instances where the use of a phrase or term may serve to recall a whole prophetic theme.

This leads us to remark that often there is what may perhaps best be described as 'allusive word-play'. An instance of this would be the use in 13.1 of Ezekiel's special word for 'uncleanness' (נִדָּה), which occurs in a section in which much of the whole emphasis of Ezek. 36.16-36 is being newly applied, the concept of cleansing by water, of the gift of a new attitude of heart, and a new repentance by the whole community. Enough examples of this have been shown in the course of the study to be able to maintain that this is a method of exegesis used in these chapters, {303} whatever questions we may have to ask over individual instances of its application.

Mention of this last example brings another point to the fore, however, for there is no slavish following of Ezekiel. The tradition is modified. Ezekiel's 'sprinkling with clean water' has become a 'fountain' in which, it was suggested, a related but distinct tradition from the Zion theology and liturgy has been introduced. So to the freedom over the use of the vocabulary and phraseology of the original must be added a freedom by which its teaching can be adapted and modified, often by the selection of material from another source or relating to a different tradition. Thus original sources can be subject to re-interpretation, so that while often the main emphasis of the original text is kept, often it is modified. Instances of such re-interpretation and re-application are to be found in 9.7, where Amos's threats of judgment against the Philistines are given a universalist 'twist' which develops much further an idea perhaps implicit in Amos 9.7, but nowhere made explicit in the Amos tradition. Again, largely 'traditional' messianic ideas have, in 9.9f., been modified in a way unknown to the main stream of messianic hope and, although the messianic expectation of these chapters is not always as clear as we could wish, if indeed it is a single expectation and not a compound of differing elements (cf. F 1: {58ff., 225ff.}, now pp. 42ff., 155ff.), {304} enough has been said to show that traditional Davidic hopes have been severely modified, as 12.7–13.1 and, possibly, 10.4 show. Such a process is not unique of course to these chapters; within the Old Testament we have other such modifications, for example, in Second Isaiah and in the Chronicler's work. One more example may suffice. The tradition of the exaltation of Zion and the pilgrimage of the nations to receive instruction is modified and extended to include the idea of a 'converted' heathendom coming actively and fully to participate in the worship of Yahweh. It is possible that the Isaiah/Micah theme, itself related to the Old Jerusalem cult and Zion theology, has been developed here still further by the influence of the concluding oracles of Trito-Isaiah, just as the Messianic hopes, as has been argued here, have been modified by taking into account the thought of Second Isaiah and even some theological outlook akin to that of the Chronicler. Such 're-interpretation' of biblical themes therefore, as far as the present examination has been able to discover, demonstrates still a dependence upon earlier biblical themes and tradition, and yet at the same time a 'freedom' towards them which betokens a creative and distinctive outlook, and which means that there is far more in these chapters than mere slavish and mechanical imitation. {305}

Such freedom is shown by a still more radical principle of exegesis, that of 'reversal'. Thus at times earlier prophetic judgments and hopes are announced as about to be reversed in the purpose and activity of Yahweh. One example is the reversal in 11.7-14 of the symbolic act of Ezek. 37.15-23 by which the promise of the reunion of the sundered kingdoms is about to be 'reversed' and becomes instead a threat of the disruption of the community in judgment. Other examples may be found in 9.12 where, as in Second Isaiah, a threat of 'double punishment' becomes a promise of 'double restoration'. Or again, another symbolic act of Ezekiel's (ch. 5), which originally announced the completeness of Yahweh's judgment of his people, becomes 'reversed' in Zech. 13.8f. to show that such judgment will be purifying in purpose and that from it a remnant of one third will emerge. That such a process seems already to have begun within the Ezekiel material hardly lessens the boldness of the concept here. Yet, even such 'reversals', still take place within the broad lines of prophetic tradition. There is still dependence in the broadest sense. And this leads us to what is of chief importance and interest for our study of Zech. 9–14. Is all this process of quotation, adaptation, re-interpretation and even reversal carried out in the light of any detectable, consistent lines of tradition? Does the treatment of {306} earlier biblical material afford any clue as to the outlook and stance of its author(s)?

The investigations here have shown two such broad lines of tradition to emerge with some consistency and clarity.

The first is that there is a very strong continuity of tradition between Proto- and Deutero-Zechariah. Details of this have been sufficiently drawn out in the course of the discussion to make only the barest summary necessary here. The lines of continuity can be seen most clearly in the centrality of Zion and God's deliverance and protection of it, and his presence within it; the divine provision of leadership as a sign of the new age; the cleansing of the community to enable it to fulfill its mediatorial role, and, above all, the note of universalism. The greatest modification has taken place in the understanding of the nature of the leadership which Yahweh will provide. There has been a tendency towards a greater 'collectivisation' or 'democratisation' of the hope. This is only to be expected, however, in the light of historic developments by which messianic hopes attaching to Zerubbabel, and perhaps to Joshua as well, were disappointed. Enough remains impressively to suggest a similar continuity of tradition between Proto- and Deutero-Zechariah as that which is often held to have run from Isaiah of Jerusalem {307} to Second Isaiah.

The second main line of tradition which has emerged has suggested that these chapters emanate from a prophet or group in increasing opposition to the official leadership of the Judaism of their time. They believed that its corruption was affecting the life of the whole community which would therefore need to come under the judgment and cleansing of God, a process which was seen in terms of increasing severity. While this conclusion relies on arguments of cumulative force it is suggested here that a view which sees these chapters as the product of such a group with such an outlook gives them a coherence, an inner unity and a developing and continuing line of theological thought without which they so easily fall into a scattered and diverse group of unrelated units. The oracles in chs. 9–10 would then have formed almost the 'eschatological hymnbook' of such a group expressing their hopes that the fulfilment of the old prophetic promises, as they collected, interpreted and expounded them, are about to be fulfilled. Even within these there are not wanting indications of a detached and critical outlook on the existing state of affairs. The prophet, whom we can only call Deutero-Zechariah, exercised a ministry of urgent pastoral exhortation to the community (10.1f.) which was already seen to be in need of such a pastoral call because of the influence of its corrupt leadership (10.3). {308} The rejection of the prophet and failure of his ministry is reflected in 11.4-17, leading to his total rejection of the official leadership and Temple worship (13.7-9), a rejection which is perhaps hinted at in 12.10ff. This last occurs in a context of eschatological hope with a deepening content. Yahweh's work, the hoped-for final victory, will have to be one which includes first inner cleansing and renewal as well as outward deliverance. Chapter 14 would then represent a later and still more pessimistic appraisal of how radical and severe this final work will need to be, but the glory of the original hope, not only for Israel, but for all men, is not lost. It shows more brilliantly at the close than anywhere else in these chapters.

The thought of a schismatic group, withdrawn from the Temple and community of contemporary Judaism, regarding the official priesthood and leadership as corrupt and under sentence of divine judgment, strongly eschatological in outlook, treasuring and searching the literature of the prophets which it re-interprets and applies to its own time and situation, with its collection of eschatological hymns, envisaging a final cosmic conflict, taking its rise from a leader who was repudiated by the Judaism he attacked, all this inevitably invites thoughts of Qumran. Any attempt at a comparison of the two has been avoided here, however. This is partly because the writer has no special qualification to deal {309} in detail with the Qumran material, but partly also because one has to be careful not to 'read back' what one already knows of such a community into these last chapters of the book of Zechariah. In any case, no facile equating of the two could be considered for a moment. The differences are immense. Qumran has none of the universalist outlook of these chapters, and they evince none of the Qumran community's concern with matters of priestly orders (12.11ff. can certainly not be pressed into this service), ritual lustrations and internal community organization. The existence of such a group, however, would be interesting as showing, as has already been increasingly suggested in several quarters, that there was considerably more diversity within post-exilic Judaism than the blanket term 'Samaritan schism' suggests, and that groups existed which demonstrate the kind of atmosphere and outlook from which the Qumran community and others could nourish their roots and draw their life.

These two main lines of tradition suggested here as characterizing these chapters might appear to be inconsistent in the conclusions to which they lead. If there is continuity of tradition with Proto-Zechariah, one would tend to look for an earlier date in the Persian period. On the other hand, the emergence of a schismatic 'splinter-group' from within Judaism would appear to {310} indicate a later stage, at least in the Greek period, when the kind of tensions and difficulties which were to give rise to the Maccabean upheavals were being increasingly felt. A resolution of these apparently contradictory tendencies is indicated, however, by the work of Beuken on the books of Haggai and Zech. 1–8 to which reference has already been made. His suggestion that these, as we now have them, represent the form of the tradition of these two prophets as it took shape within a traditio-context closely akin to that of the Chronicler's is a plausible one. This, however, would mean, that in their final form, they could well be dated around 300 BC, and it might well be that Zech. 9–14 belongs within such a continuing stream of tradition or one which emerged from it. This would account both for the strong continuity of theme and theological outlook, but also for the indications within them of a later internal situation within Judaism.

So we turn to our last question. Does this line of approach throw any light on the vexed questions of date, authorship and unity? In fact it offers disappointingly little. Indeed, in one way, it makes the darkness more obscure since it suggests that so-called 'historical' allusions and references, as for example in 9.1-8, the 'sons of Jawan' of 9.13, references to Ephraim, etc., may not be intended as literal 'historical' {311} references at all, but are chosen rather for their echo of earlier biblical material and represent 'typical' examples from that literature now intended to refer to some event in the contemporary situation. On the positive side, however, one or two things may be said. It would seem as though the process of compiling the major prophetic collections was far enough advanced for something akin to their present form to be available to and known by the author. This is said with great caution, remembering the fact that the dates of both are unknown factors as has been said before, but the number of cumulative citations and examples suggest that we are on the way towards the completion of the process which must have been finished by the time of Ben Sirach. That would mean these chapters cannot be dated too early. In particular, if we are right in suggesting that Zech. 1–8 reached its final form around 300 BC, then a date earlier than that is precluded, and one at least 50 years later is by no means unreasonable, since there have been occasions when we have shown that even the order of oracles in Proto-Zechariah appears to have had its significance in these chapters. The rejection of the official leadership of the time could perhaps well be accounted for by the kind of bargaining and worldly jockeying for power by rival priestly families in the Greek period, but we know too little of the internal history of Judaism in that period, and the {312} allusions in Zech. 9–14 are too imprecise to allow us to locate them with confidence. It is possible that 12.1ff., and even more ch. 14, could reflect a sense of danger growing from the Seleucids in the north, but again, the references are too general and seem to owe too much to earlier biblical themes and imagery for us to be sure. In any case, are all these oracles to be dated at one time? And this raises the vexed questions of authorship and unity.

Here, too, there appears to be conflicting evidence which can well account for the great divide in critical opinion on this point. There are differences of theme, style and even atmosphere between chs. 9–10 and 11, let alone between chs. 12 and 14, details of which have been mentioned in the earlier discussion on these chapters. Yet, on the other hand, everywhere we have found the same kind of attitude to earlier biblical material, the same methods of exegesis and even evidence of the same lines of tradition. It would seem then, although this can only be a suggestion based on subjective impression after study of these chapters (we lack clear, objective evidence), that we have to posit a 'Deutero-Zechariah', whose preaching and ministry are recounted in only obscure outline, in 10.1f.; 11.4-17; 13.7-9 and 12.10. Such a prophet almost certainly would have gathered around him a group who learned to share his attitude of veneration for the prophets and his methods of under-standing {313} and applying them, and who shared his conviction that their fulfilment was shortly to be brought about. Such a group collected and expressed their eschatological hopes, first in the collection of oracles in chs. 9–10, some of which might have been originally independent (even pre-exilic?) oracles, but which, if they did not compose all of them, they certainly modified to express their own particular interpretation of scripture, their own distinctive tradition and outlook. As time passed, however, and the gulf between this group and the official Judaism of their time widened, their eschatological hopes became more radical, as if seen against a darker background. The contrast between the 'now' and the 'then' began to savour more of the outlook of apocalyptic. So, perhaps after the death of the prophet (?), 12.1–13.6 were added and, still later, ch. 14, each representing greater modification of earlier hopes, but which still came from within the same traditio-circle. This would account to some extent for both differences and agreements. Thus we have to speak both of a Deutero-Zechariah but also of a traditio-circle as being responsible for the final form of these chapters.

Such conclusions remain, at best, however, tentative. What is not in doubt is that these chapters, for all their difficulties and obscurity, testify to the fact that the Word of God which once spoke in living tones through the great prophets of Israel's history, did not fall {314} silent and inactive when the era of the written word began to replace the living voice of prophecy. As men collected the words of these prophets, and pondered the Word which had spoken through them, it proved to have continuing vitality and relevance to address them as they were challenged, judged and stirred by it to hope and faithfulness in successive generations and widely differing circumstances.

Not the least noble expression of such an encounter and commitment is that expressed in Zech. 9–14. These chapters show us that during this 'dark' period such a living process of re-interpretation continued and that the vital pulse of Israel's faith continued to throb.

There could be few more fitting tributes to 'Deutero-Zechariah' than the words attributed to Jesus in Mt. 13.52:

> Therefore every scribe who has been trained for the kingdom of heaven is like a householder who brings out of his treasure what is new and what is old.

Part II

RESPONSES

ZECHARIAH 9–14: METHODOLOGICAL REFLECTIONS*

David L. Petersen

The *raison d'etre* for this paper is a colloquy devoted to discussion of 'inner biblical allusion', with special focus on Zech. 9–14 and the contributions that Rex Mason has made to this arena of inquiry. Mason's dissertation, 'The Use of Earlier Biblical Material in Zechariah IX–XIV: A Study in Inner Biblical Exegesis', was accepted by the University of London in 1973. Since that time, sea changes have worked their way through the field of biblical studies. The methodological perspectives regnant at the time, most especially form criticism, tradition history, and redaction criticism, have been supplemented by attention to literary and social world studies. Moreover, those same three decades have seen biblical scholars increasingly attend to the Persian period, which, prior to the last third of the twentieth century, had received relatively little attention, and which was most likely the time during which Zech. 9–14 was written. Mason's dissertation was, therefore, something of a harbinger of changes that were afoot in the field. The critical literature in the field is now replete with phrases such as 'inner biblical allusion' (Nurmela 1996), *traditionsgeschichtliche Hintergründe* (Tai 1996), and *innerbiblische Schriftauslegung* (Schmid 2000).

The careful reader of the previous paragraph will have noted a difference between the title of the dissertation and the title of the colloquy. The dissertation refers to 'inner biblical exegesis', the colloquy to 'inner biblical allusion'. That difference in vocabulary betrays a significant difference in method. In this paper, I would like to explore differences in method and perspective that lurk behind this and other related distinctions in critical vocabulary. Put in interrogative form: What method or perspectives are appropriate when one is interested in exploring the relation of Zech. 9–14

* As noted above in the Preface, this paper and some of the others in this volume were originally produced for a colloquy held at the annual meeting of the Society of Biblical Literature in Denver, Colorado, on 18 November 2001.

to other (and presumably prior) biblical literature? In order to pursue this question, I will offer thumbnail sketches of several different methods. In addition, I shall contend that diverse critical vocabulary—for example, allusion, exegesis, intertext, and tradition—reflects diverse interpretive claims, which in turn represent the use of different methods.

At the outset, one should recognize that Mason's dissertation itself used a diverse analytical vocabulary. In the introduction, he referred to 'allusion', 'reference', 'direct quotation', 'reinterpretation', and 'principles of exegesis'. He was following in the line of Stade, who, among others, had noted the 'connectedness' between Zech. 9–14 and other biblical literature. Mason's interest was, therefore, not new. He was, however, not interested in simply cataloguing such connections. Rather, he wanted 'to examine the use of earlier biblical material in Deutero-Zechariah in the attempt to see what principles of exegesis, if any, can be detected in such use, and, above all, to see if this affords any clue to the place of the author, or authors, in the developing traditio-history of the community of post-exilic Judaism' (Mason 1973: ii). After reading this sentence, one may observe that the dissertation involved three distinct tasks: (1) identifying a 'connection'; (2) classifying or analyzing it; and (3) placing it in a socio-religious context. The enterprise was not a purely literary one (unlike the work of some who have followed him).

Mason's conclusions were several. Indeed, Mason observed that Zech. 9–14 draws on earlier biblical, especially prophetic material. He also saw that the connections are broad, extending far beyond those between Zech. 9–14 and Zech. 1–8. Mason identifies what he termed 'allusive word play'; for example, a reference to 'uncleanness' (נִדָּה) that apparently depends upon Ezekiel. In such allusion, Zech. 9–14 modifies that which Ezekiel had written. Mason notes that Zech. 9–14 attests a remarkable freedom in handling earlier texts; for example, the motif of the pilgrimage of the nations turns in the direction of conversion for the nations. Such freedom even involves 'reversal' (Mason 1973: 305). Here, however, Mason seems to move away from the language of allusion and into the arena of tradition history, which does not necessarily include explicit claims about textual dependence. That move to tradition is significant (and will reappear in the work of Nurmela) and prompts the question: What method should one use when comparing various elements in Zech. 9–14 with other and (presumably) prior texts?

1. *Diversity in Analytical Vocabulary and Method*

During the past five decades, scholars interested in the 'connections' between one biblical text and another have used various critical vocabularies. I think it fair to say that at least four terms or phrases occur prominently: inner biblical allusion, inner biblical exegesis, intertextuality, and tradition. I shall proceed to discuss each term or phrase, along with reference to at least one representative work, and the relevant method.

a. *Inner Biblical Allusion*

Scholars often maintain that one biblical text alludes to another. However, they frequently do not define what they mean by 'allusion'. Some presume that an allusion is not a quotation of the generating text but more of a reference to it. What, then, would count as an allusion, and what would be its significance, should an allusion occur?

Benjamin Sommer has recently published a study of allusion as it occurs in Isa. 40–66. In that volume he offers, following Earl Miner, this definition of 'allusion' as it is used in the discourse of literary criticism: 'tacit reference to another literary work, to another art, to history, to contemporary figures, or the like' (Sommer 1998: 10). As Sommer explores this notion, he argues that allusion involves the notion of influence, one text (and its author) having been influenced by an earlier one. Allusion involves a source text and an alluding text. Still, influence may not be equated with allusion.[1] Sommer proceeds to distinguish between allusion, influence, echo, and exegesis—all of which are to be viewed as something distinct from an intertext.

According to Sommer, influence is a more general notion than allusion. One author, work or even tradition might influence another author. However, there may be no specific allusion from one text to another. Echo, in contrast, involves a specifiable link between two texts, but the presence of the echo in the derivative text does not constitute a consequential reuse of the earlier text. It is more of a literary fossil than a living entity in the new text.

Having distinguished allusion from influence, echo, and exegesis, Sommer identifies three ways in which the alluding text may relate to the source

---

1.   Sommer also uses the phrase 'inner biblical allusion and exegesis', suggesting that the act of allusion involves an exegetical move. I am not sure such is the case. An allusion can be suggestive, an exegetical move is more definitive.

text: 'explicit citation (e.g. "as it is written in the Teaching of Moses",
1 Kgs 2.3), implicit citation (Mal. 1.6–2.9 as it relates to Num. 6.23-27),
and inclusion (the explicit citation of earlier material in a later work, viz.,
the Chronicler's quotation of material found in Kings)' (Sommer 1998:
21-22).

Let me offer an example apart from the book of Zechariah. Ezek. 14.14
identifies three individuals: Noah, Dan'el and Job. The argument that
Ezekiel is making requires there to be some fundamental similarity that is
shared by these persons. The Dan'el attested in the biblical book, though
preternaturally righteous, never saves anyone other than himself, which is
the motif that Noah and Job share. However, the Dan'el attested in the
Ugaritic Tale of Aqhat is apparently able to revivify his slain son. One
might, therefore, claim that Ezekiel alludes to the Dan'el of Aqhat. More
specifically, and using Sommer's typology, it would appear to be an implicit citation. In sum, Sommer has developed a useful typology to help us
conceptualize various types of inner biblical allusion.

Risto Nurmela has explicitly used the language of 'inner biblical allusion' in analyzing the relation of Zech. 9–14 to other biblical texts—
principally, though not exclusively, Zech. 1–8 (Nurmela 1996). Though
Nurmela discusses the nature of allusion, he is especially concerned with
identifying and then deploying the criteria to determine if one text 'depends' on another. He uses a four-fold process, which involves:

1.   Assertion of the internal dependence between a passage in
     Zechariah and in another book;
2.   Establishment of the direction of the dependence;
3.   Establishment of the allusion and the degree of it (sure, probable
     or possible);
4.   Establishment of the character of the allusion (concordant, etc.)
     (Nurmela 1996: 37).

In this research program, Nurmela focuses on 'expressions' (i.e. words and
phrases) which occur in Zechariah and another book in the Old Testament,
but do not occur frequently—or at all—in other Old Testament books
(Nurmela 1996: 27). Nurmela does not, however, contend that simple
verbal correspondence permits a claim for the existence of an allusion. For
example, one might presume that Zech. 3.2, 'a brand snatched from the
fire', alludes to Amos 4.11, 'like a brand snatched from the fire'. However,
Nurmela thinks that both passages probably refer to a common expression
in ancient Israel. Similarly, though some have claimed that Zech. 13.5 ('I

am not a prophet') alludes to Amos 7.14 ('I am not a prophet'), both texts are simply making a rudimentary claim that is difficult to express in any other way.

In order to refine his work, Nurmela classifies the kinds of 'similarities' that appear between texts:

> Expressions which in the entire Old Testament only occur in Zechariah and one other book are registered as *exclusive verbal similarities*. Expressions that occur in Zechariah and another book but also occur in the rest of the Old Testament are registered as *verbal similarities*. Furthermore, *synonymic similarities* and, when similar themes are dealt with in different words, *thematic similarities* are registered. (Nurmela 1996: 28)

Nurmela utilizes these categories when discussing the similarities between Zech. 9–14 and other Old Testament texts. For example, he observes the phrase 'from the sea to the sea and from the river to the ends of the earth' in both Zech. 9.10 and Ps. 72.8 (Nurmela 1996: 195-96). Since this phrase appears nowhere else in the Old Testament, it may be viewed as an exclusive verbal similarity. Moreover, since both texts refer to the extent of the royal domain (in Ps. 72, that of the human king; in Zech. 9, that of the divine king), Nurmela deems the two texts to be 'concordant'—that is, 'expressing the same idea', which is even stronger than a 'thematic similarity'. The fact that the allusion is so strong, that is, that it is really a quotation, does not enter into Nurmela's analysis.

Unlike some recent literary studies of Zech. 9–14, Nurmela offers proposals about the formation of Zech. 9–14. Once he has observed that both Zechariah 1–8 and 9–14 depend significantly on Isaiah, Jeremiah, and Ezekiel, he goes on to offer some redaction critical judgments. For example, Zech. 9–14 is related in a significant way only to Isa. 1–11 and 29–31, and not to later parts of that book. Further, 'there is no dependence of Zech. 9–14 on books which could be dated later than Zech. 1–8' (Nurmela 1996: 234). These judgments would sustain a date of composition for Zech. 9–14 that is earlier than some would suppose. Nurmela thinks that Zech. 9–13 is roughly contemporaneous with Zech. 1–8.

However, arguments on behalf of allusion might work in a different and more purely literary fashion. If one were to accept the notion that Zech. 11.1-3 alludes to Jer. 25.34-38, as Nurmela maintains, what might be the function of such an allusion? Both poems share vocabulary, though the words often have different referents. For example, in Jeremiah 'lion' refers to Yahweh, but in Zech. 11.3 'lions' does not; and the 'lords' in Jer. 25.36 are probably to be identified with the previously mentioned shepherds, whereas the 'lords' in Zech. 11.2 are trees (Petersen 1995: 79-85; Nurmela 1996: 133-36). Jeremiah would seem to be the earlier text. Having said that, one might ask what the author of Zech. 11.1-3 has accomplished by picking up elements of an earlier poem. What is the literary function of the allusion?

At the outset, it is important to observe that the theme of Jer. 25.34-38 is very different from that of Zech. 11.1-3. The former poem creates a metaphoric world involving pasture, sheep and shepherds in order to speak about the destruction that Yahweh (as lion) will wreak on Judah. The destruction is localized, focusing on the pasture. Only in Jer. 25.38 does the world become larger: 'their land has become a waste', that is, something beyond the pasture has been destroyed. In contrast, Zech. 11.1-3 offers a broader horizon, from the coast of Lebanon to the banks of the Jordan. Moreover, the agricultural world in Zechariah is more inclusive, moving from arboriculture to animal husbandry. If the author of Zech. 11.1-3 had such a different purview, why might that author have alluded to Jeremiah? I suggest that the later poet found it useful to appropriate a Jeremianic poem that had already integrated the discourse of lament with the world of agriculture. The later poet was then able to broaden the earlier imagery—by expanding the geographic horizon, by introducing toponyms, and by referring to trees as well as sheep. Moreover, the earlier text might resonate with some readers of Zech. 11, were they familiar with the emerging prophetic corpus/canon. The author of Zech. 11 might have intended that resonance to address something that was left ambiguous in the later poem—namely, the agent who was responsible for this destruction in Syria-Palestine. Yahweh as punitive agent is not identified in Zechariah, whereas Yahweh the lion is the destroyer according to Jer. 25.38.

When working with inner biblical allusions, one may do more than identify the allusion. It is possible to use such evidence to hypothesize about the formation of the literature, that is, the work of redaction criticism. Further, one may enter the allusive world of Jer. 25.34-38 and Zech. 11.1-3. In so doing, the reader moves beyond stating that an allusion exists and attempts to explore the ways in which the later text might deploy the imagery, form, and so on, of the earlier text. The primary method at work in such an exercise is literary criticism.

b. *Inner Biblical Exegesis*
Like the notion of inner biblical allusion, that of inner biblical exegesis involves a claim about a relation between texts. Now, however, the earlier

text has an authoritative, even quasi-canonical character. The later text
is thought to comment, reflect on or explicate the prior text. Hence, the
claim that texts are related in an exegetical manner is, in some measure, a
'stronger' claim than that of an allusion. The notion of inner biblical
exegesis has been explored in a particularly fruitful way by Michael
Fishbane (1988).

Fishbane makes the case on behalf of inner biblical exegesis and proceeds to classify its various manifestations. When introducing the conceptual framework of the volume, he appeals to the analytical vocabulary of
traditum and *traditio*, which he borrows from the work of Douglas Knight.
Fishbanc writes, 'The content of the tradition, the traditum, was not at all
monolithic, but rather the complex result of a long and varied process of
transmission, the traditio' (Fishbane 1988: 6). It is interesting that the
method to which Fishbane implicitly appeals is 'tradition history'. However, he wants to distinguish between tradition history, which he deems to
focus on oral materials, and study of inner biblical exegesis, which involves written materials. 'Inner-biblical exegesis...takes the stabilized
literary formulation as its basis and point of departure' (Fishbane 1988: 7).
Whereas tradition history works with a fluid *traditum* (e.g. the multiple
enumerations of the plagues), inner biblical exegesis works with one text
and its later interpretation.[2] Fishbane discerns three basic modes of this
activity: legal exegesis, aggadic exegesis, mantological exegesis.

Fishbane's work poses a fundamental question: What are the hallmarks
of an exegetical allusion? Put another way, even if there is a *traditum* in
the form of a stabilized text, does any reference to it count as 'inner biblical exegesis'? Could a later author not simply 'allude' to the earlier text
without 'exegeting' it? We may examine the way Fishbane addresses this
issue by focusing on his analysis of texts from Zech. 9–14. He discusses
most extensively Zech. 9.9 and 12.4. Let us examine these two examples
in turn.

(1) Fishbane maintains that Zech. 12.4 'reuses' Deut. 28.28 (Fishbane
1988: 501). He clearly appeals primarily to shared vocabulary. Deut. 28.28
reads:

> Yahweh will strike you (יככה) with madness (שגעון),
> blindness (עורון) and confusion of mind (תמהון לבב).

Zech. 12.4 features some of this same vocabulary:

---

2.   With regard to the plague traditions Fishbane cites Exod. 7–11and Ps. 78, and I
would add Ps. 105.

On that day, says Yahweh,
I will strike (אכה) every horse with panic (תמהון),
and its rider with madness (שגעון).
But on the house of Judah
I will keep a watchful eye,
when I strike every horse of the peoples with blindness (עורון).

The shared lexical stock is clear: one verb and three nouns. Deuteronomy is almost certainly the earlier text. Hence, one may legitimately ask whether Zechariah depends on it. Here things become complex and one may posit several possible responses. First, the texts are related since they both reflect the language of curses. We know that many of the curses in Deuteronomy (and throughout the Hebrew Bible) reflect a trove of curses known through the ancient Near East. Zechariah and Deuteronomy may both be drawing on such a tradition; that is, Zechariah may not be referring to the literary form of the curse in Deuteronomy, but rather to another form of that curse tradition, particularly one involving horses, which is a prominent motif in the book of Zechariah. Second, one might claim that Zechariah does indeed reuse the vocabulary of the curses as the author of Zech. 12.4 knew it from Deut. 28.28. However, the reuse is not exegetical, but rather allusive. Third, following Fishbane, one might claim that the author of Zech. 12.4 read Deut. 28.28 with an interpretive eye, and wanted to change the object of the curse—from Israel/Judah to the 'peoples'. If such is the case, does this change in object function as an exegetical move? The answer is not clear. In sum, the similarites in vocabulary do not easily permit one to identify Zech. 12.4 as a case of inner biblical exegesis of Deut. 28.28.

(2) The second putative case of inner biblical exegesis involves Zech. 9.9 as a 'reflex' of Gen. 49.10-11 (Fishbane 1988: 501-502). The similarities here are, in my judgment, less clear than in the previous case. (In this regard, it is interesting that Nurmela does not identify Zech. 9.9 as an allusion to Gen. 49.10-11.) Here is the text of Gen. 49.10b-11a:

Until he comes (יבא) to Shiloh...
And that he will hitch (אסרי) his ass (עירה) to the vine
And the progeny of the she-ass (בני אתנו) to a bramble.

Zech. 9.9 has similar vocabulary and imagery:

Behold your king will come (יבוא) to you,
Triumphant, his victory won,
Riding on an ass (חמור), on a colt (עיר), the foal of a she-ass (בן־אתנות).

Apparently, Fishbane also thinks that the use of אסר in Zech. 9.11—'I will set free (אסיריך) your prisoners'—involves a 'return' to the text of Gen. 49.10-11. However, since the use of the triliteral root is so different in Genesis and Zechariah, tying up the ass vs. setting prisoners free, this is a very difficult case to sustain.

How, then, might one think about the relation of Zech. 9.9 to Gen. 49.10-11? There seems to be a clear reference to a royal figure who will 'come'. His arrival is associated with an animal, the donkey. Both texts refer to that animal using two parallel nouns. However, the first and controlling noun is different: עירה in Genesis and חמור in Zechariah. It is difficult to understand why, if the second text is a reflex of the first one, that noun would not be the same. One might speak of a motif, of a king riding on or arriving with a donkey, that is shared by both texts, but an argument on behalf of literary, much less exegetical, dependence is less convincing.

The real issue that this case raises is how one determines when one text is exegetically related to another. In this instance, the similarites might be explained in an entirely different way. Both Gen. 49 and Zech. 9 are poetic texts. They obviously use the dominant trope of Hebrew poetry, parallelism. Since there is an ancient Near Eastern tradition according to which kings rode on donkeys (e.g. Dan'el in the Tale of Aqhat), the authors of both biblical poems naturally drew on numerous words for donkeys and mules in order to refer to these animals in parallel lines. From the literature from ancient Ugarit we know that '*r* could stand in parallelism with *atnt* (Dahood 1972: 303). Put another way, the presence of similar words for mule is hardly surprising in poems that speak of a royal figure riding on an animal.

That inner biblical exegesis exists, I do not question. However, not all instances in which one text alludes to another involves an exegetical impulse. Based on the cases that Fishbane adduces, it is not clear that the book of Zechariah offers any instances of inner biblical exegesis.

c. *Intertextuality*
The notion of intertextuality is fraught with ambiguity, since the notion has been used in such diverse ways. It is possible to identify a semiotics-based form of intertextuality (e.g. Draisma 1989; Clayton and Rothstein 1991) and a less technical approach (e.g. Fewell 1992; Nielsen 2000). The key here is the relationship between texts as perceived by readers, not putative directions of influence as intended by authors.

Edgar Conrad has recently offered a commentary devoted to the book of Zechariah which was informed by, among other elements, the perspective of intertextuality. He writes:

> Both the inception and reception of texts are influenced by and are, in some sense, a mimesis of other texts, which authors and readers bring to their writing and reading. My reading of the Twelve from an intertextual perspective means that I do not require one text to be prior to the other but understand the relationship between texts synchronically as a way of aiding the interpretive process. (Conrad 1999: 18)

One critical test for such work will, accordingly, be the extent to which the reader relates Zech. 9–14 to other texts.

In this regard, it is interesting to compare the cases of intertexts identified by those interested in inner biblical allusion or inner biblical exegesis with Conrad's intertextual approach. One may take the case of Zech. 9.9-10, a text that Fishbane related to Gen. 49. Conrad makes no such identification. Instead he suggests that the humility of the king (9.9) recalls a scene earlier in the book of Zechariah. Zerubbabel's victories have not been due to martial power but rather to the empowering spirit of the deity (Conrad 1999: 160). Or, one may look at the way in which he analyzes 11.1-3. Here Conrad does adduce texts outside Zechariah, but only in an illustrative fashion.

> The imperatives to the 'cypress' and the 'oaks of Bashan' to wail sustains the image of the trees as symbols of ruling power (see Isa. 2.3 and Judg. 9.8-15) and communicates the grievous ruin of what the NRSV renders as 'glorious trees' (11.2). The word used to refer to trees here metaphorically suggests majestic kings (cf. Ps. 136.18), powerful nations (cf. Ezek. 32.18), and in one instance, leaders who are also called shepherds of the people (cf. Jer. 25.34-36). (Conrad 1999: 171)

With his use of the oblique language of 'cf.', we have no reason to think that Conrad claims there is an important relation—an intertextual connection—between any of these non-Zecharian texts and those in Zechariah. The former may exemplify similar linguistic usage, but no more.

Conrad's intertextual reading is interested primarily in finding coherence within the book of Zechariah, and less between Zechariah and other biblical books, especially those beyond the boundary of the Book of the Twelve. Conrad deems the Book of the Twelve to be the 'macro-context' for Zechariah whereas Haggai and Malachi comprise its 'micro-context' (Conrad 1999: 22, 39). Yet, one might ask why the potential connections between Zechariah and literature beyond the Book of the Twelve should not count in an intertextual reading. Both those who use the language of allusion and those who use the vocabulary of inner biblical exegesis explore potential connections between Zechariah and the rest of the Hebrew Bible. In theory, so might an intertextual reading. But Conrad has not offered that sort of approach.

d. *Tradition History*

As I noted at the outset, reflection about traditions and the way they work themselves out over time was present in Mason's dissertation. Moreover, those who have worked with the language of allusion have, on occasion, turned to the explicit language of tradition history. Nurmela (1996) is obviously interested in discussing relations between texts, even when they did not involve an allusion. In an 'Excursus: Jerusalem in Zechariah and Other Old Testament Books', Nurmela speaks primarily in terms of tradition history. In these pages, he focuses on what others would describe as 'the Zion tradition'. Here he discusses the general notion of Zion as a place that Yahweh will elect and that will serve as the dwelling place of the deity. Nurmela contends that such a view 'is shared by four other Old Testament writings: Isa. 1–39, Micah, Joel, and the Psalms' (Nurmela 1996: 174). This judgment, and the analysis that led up to it, do not depend upon identifying specific allusions, but upon noting more general claims about the place of Zion and/or Jerusalem in the divine economy. (To use the aforementioned language of Knight, he has focused on the *traditum*, the content of the tradition, but not necessarily the precise form of its textualization.)

Nevertheless, tradition history as such was not the method of choice for Nurmela. It has been for others, most notably Lutz (1968), to a lesser degree Saebø (1969), Person (1993), and most recently Tai (1996). Lutz examined the relation of Zech. 12.1-8 and 14.1-5 to earlier biblical material. In his judgment, these two texts drew on the Zion tradition. After comparing these two texts to other biblical literature, he concluded that one could identify different forms of a Zion tradition that are now present in Zech. 9–14. In particular, the role of the nations seemed to vary.

Nicholas Tai (1996) has taken up this line of research with special concern for clarity of method. He, too, wants to address tradition history, but he also wants to integrate attention to specific allusions (*Stichwörter*). He differs most from Lutz by including explicit attention to form-critical issues (here he incorporates the perspectives of Saebø).

It is instructive to examine the way Tai addresses a text, since it is quite different from many of his contemporaries. When working on Zech. 9.9, he does not treat the verse in isolation (Tai 1996: 37-51). Rather, he delimits and categorizes the text of which it is a part. He judges that Zech. 9.9-10 is to be the pericope and thinks that it should be construed as a hymn. He then poses the question: Is this hymnic piece in Zechariah designed to praise the earthly or the heavenly king? To answer this question, he turns to tradition history. He uses both the presence of similar vocabulary and similar form-critical features to identify the first set of related texts (Zeph. 3.14; Zech. 2.14; Mic. 4.7-8). Finally, he turns to the traditions about kings attested in the Psalms, especially Ps. 72. Based on these comparisons, Tai concludes that Zech. 9.9-10 does indeed refer to the earthly Davidide, not to the divine king.

When one compares his analysis and conclusions to those of other scholars, it becomes clear that the use of different methods or perspectives results in very different conclusions. For example, when Fishbane looked at Zech. 9.9, his eyes were drawn primarily to the similarity in vocabulary (the words for 'donkey'). For Tai, however, form-critical and traditio-historical considerations meant that, for him, the psalmic genre and royal traditions were of primary importance, issues never mentioned by Fishbane.[3]

e. *'Literature in the Second Degree'*

With the exception of those who claim to work in an intertextual fashion, most scholars who relate the literature of Zech. 9–14 to other biblical texts are interested in, among other things, directions of influence and the relative chronology of the literature. And yet, as we have seen, they have adopted various critical vocabularies and methods, often apparently unaware of other (and sometimes competing) options available to them. In my judgment, what is now required is not only clarity about these differences, but also a conceptual scheme by means of which to relate them.

As for the former, Timothy Beal has facilitated the search for such clarity by offering capsule definitions of some important analytical terms. Allusion, echo, inner biblical exegesis, intertextuality, intertext, intratextuality, poetic influence, and trace comprise his roster (Beal 1992). As noted above, Sommer has attempted to distinguish influence, intertextuality, allusion and exegesis, even moving to the important question of what an allusion is designed to accomplish (Sommer 1998: 6-31). But what we really need is a systematic overview of the ways in which liter-

---

3.   Tai refers once to the similarity between Zech. 9.9 and Gen. 49.11 (1996: 41), but these data are essentially unimportant for his work.

ature can be related—and to what ends. And such an overview will need to take seriously the notion of earlier and later texts, and not simply appeal to the web of all texts, regardless of their respective dates of composition.

Gerard Genette has offered such a thoroughgoing proposal in a book entitled *Palimpsests: Literature in the Second Degree* (1997).[4] Though I do not want to endorse Genette's program as *the* way to conceptualize the relations between various literatures, I do want to commend the comprehensive character of the program, which includes many of the topics that have just been addressed. He has offered a remarkable inventory and set of assessments about literary relations. Terms like echo, pastiche, caricature, parody, antinovel, parody, antiromance, imitation, plagarism, digest, condensation, amplification, supplement, versification, prosification, quotation, and allusion suggest that the typical universe of analytical categories which biblical scholars have been using might well be enhanced.[5]

Genette theorizes that the study of literary relations may be subsumed under the general rubric of *transtextuality*. By that he means 'all that sets the text in a relationship, whether obvious or concealed, with other texts'. He discerns five basic types of transtextual relations:

(1) *Intertextuality*. With this term, Genette refers to various 'copresences' between texts. Such copresence can take various forms, including quotation, plagiarism, and allusion.

(2) *Paratextuality*. Paratextuality involves the text, in a limited sense, and its relation to the totality of a literary work. Paratextual elements include elements like a title, terminal notes, chapter headings, marginalia, forewords, and the like.

(3) *Metatextuality*. Here Genette uses the word 'commentary' as an equivalent, but it is not the kind of commentary to which biblical scholars are accustomed. Such a commentary 'unites a given text to another, of which it speaks without necessarily citing it (without summoning it), in fact sometimes even without naming it'. For example, Hegel's *The Phenomenology of Mind* is a commentary on Diderot's *Le Neveu de Rameau* (Genette 1997: 4).

(4) *Hypertextuality*. This is the primary focus of Genette's volume. 'By hypertextuality, I mean any relationship uniting a text B (which I shall call the *hypertext*) to an earlier text A (I shall, of course, call it the *hypotext*), upon which it is grafted in a manner that is not that of commentary'. For an example, he adduces Virgil's *Aeneid* and Joyce's *Ulysses* as hypertexts

---

4. I am indebted to Dennis MacDonald for this reference.
5. On quotation in prophetic literature, see Schultz (1999).

drawing on Homer's *Odyssey*. However, as hypertexts, they are very different. Joyce's directly transforms the *Odyssey* from ancient Greek to twentieth century Dublin, whereas Virgil tells 'an entirely different story', even while 'imitating' the earlier hypotext. These two paradigms—simple transformation and imitation—become crucially important analytical categories throughout the volume.

(5) *Architextuality*. Genette thinks here of a 'silent' relationship. It might be the relationship between the individual text and its type. For example, the rubric 'novel' might appear on cover of a book, but the text might not declare itself as a novel. (One might think of a psalm, which in its paratextual preface is termed a מַשְׂכִּיל, to have an architextual relation to that data.)

This or some comparable conceptual framework might prove very useful to the biblical scholar. Rather than search immediately for an allusion, commentary or intertext, the scholar might draw back and reflect initially about the diverse ways in which texts (and traditions) are related. Further, such a framework offers a refined set of analytical vocabulary. For example, many biblical scholars have claimed that Zech. 9–14 draws on earlier texts. Those chapters are, to use Genette's term, hypertexts. What then is the hypotext? Moreover, is the use of the hypotext one of imitation or transformation?

Obviously, to adopt such a scheme or to use such critical vocabulary creates no panacea for the methodological problematics to which I have pointed. Nonetheless, even if only for heuristic purposes, to explore such a system introduces the biblical scholar to a larger horizon than the discourse of inner biblical allusion or exegesis regularly offers.

2. *Conclusions*

Let me conclude. First, claims about the relations between Zech. 9–14 and other biblical texts have been made in various ways. Such arguments are replete with diverse analytical vocabulary: allusion, exegesis, intertext, and tradition are the most prominent ones. I have assayed recent representative studies and contended that they reflect different methods: literary criticism, intertextual studies, and tradition history appear to have pride of place. The methodological underpinnings for claims about the existence of inner biblical exegesis are less clear. Second, I have argued on behalf of the need for a comprehensive theory to discuss such relations. Beyond the pale of work on Zech. 9–14, Sommer and Beal have made some significant contributions to the discussion of some of these notions—Sommer especially on allusion, Beal on intertextuality. What we now need is a comprehensive theoretical map to address what Genette has termed 'literature in the second degree'. The data presented by Zech. 9–14 are amenable to more than one approach—literary criticism, intertextual studies, and tradition history (and for that matter, form criticism and redaction criticism) have important roles to play, depending upon the texts in question and upon the questions being asked.

Deutero-Zechariah and Types of Intertextuality

Michael H. Floyd

Here I would like to recognize Rex Mason's contribution to the study of Zechariah, particularly in his dissertation, 'The Use of Earlier Biblical Material in Zechariah IX–XIV: A Study in Inner Biblical Exegesis'. His results were summarized in later articles (Mason 1976, 1982), but the full discussion has remained largely unavailable until its belated publication in this volume. Though completed in 1973, Mason's dissertation still deserves attention. It marks a turning point in the study of the relationship between Proto- and Deutero-Zechariah and in the study of so-called inner biblical exegesis, beyond which we have not progressed very far. I will attempt to show what is distinctive about Mason's work, arguing that we can now advance the discussion by following his lead.

First, some terminological clarifications are in order. Although Mason was not very systematic in the vocabulary with which he described Deutero-Zechariah's use of earlier biblical material, he was most invested in the term that appears in his title, 'inner biblical exegesis'. In characterizing Deutero-Zechariah as 'exegetical', he certainly did not mean what modern biblical scholars have usually intended by this word. He did not mean that Deutero-Zechariah explicitly discusses the original meaning of other biblical texts, but that the message of Deutero-Zechariah was a reinterpretation of already authoritative texts, which entailed applying them more or less analogously to the time of the writer. If so, his usage can be seen as generally consistent with Michael Fishbane's more recent and widely influential standardization of the term. To explain the fact that some biblical texts are reminiscent of others, modern scholarship has generally supposed that some pre-textual traditions were historically influenced by others. Fishbane argued that in many cases this phenomenon is better explained as the reinterpretation of one text by the writer of another, in ways that include but are not limited to the way Mason supposes Deutero-Zechariah to be a reinterpretation of other texts. The interpretation of received texts regarded as holy Scripture did not wait until the finalization of the biblical canon, but was rather a factor in the development of the canon (Fishbane 1985).

As the term 'inner biblical exegesis' came to be used with greater precision, the whole field of investigation was simultaneously complicated by the advent of 'intertextuality'. Initially, those who used this term were opposed to investigating the various ways that writers could draw upon previously existing texts. They were instead interested in the various ways that readers could find meaningful connections among texts with or without any intrinsic interconnection (van Wolde 1989; Fewell 1992; Sommer 1998: 6-10). This has been a helpful correction to an overemphasis on historical influence at the expense of other kinds of textual relationships. However, it is unjustifiably arbitrary to exclude historical influence from the field of intertextual relations—just as it is to exclude the diachronic aspect of language from even a primarily synchronic approach to linguistics. Under the theoretical rubric of 'intertextuality' it is possible, and arguably even necessary, to include both the production and reception of texts (O'Day 1999; cf. Schmid 2000). In any case, this essay is concerned only with the former aspect of intertextuality as it relates to Deutero-Zechariah, the question of how the writer of Deutero-Zechariah might have drawn upon previously existing texts. The other aspect, which deals with connections resulting from the juxtaposition of texts by readers, lies beyond our scope. We will nevertheless work within the category of 'intertextuality', rather than 'inner biblical exegesis', because it allows for a wider range of possibilities (Eslinger 1992). The term 'exegesis' has traditional connotations above and beyond the rather narrow sense imposed upon it by historical critical scholarship, but it nevertheless implies a deliberate attempt to explicate the meaning of a received text. When our question about Deutero-Zechariah is approached from the more broadly conceived perspective of intertextuality, it is evident that one text can be reminiscent of another for various reasons.

For example, the resemblance may not be deliberate. Writers can replicate expressions that have become part of the common cultural domain of their time, without necessarily making any direct or intentional connection with the texts from which these expressions originally came. The term 'echo' has gained recognition as a name for textual connections of this sort (Hollander 1981). Even when writers make deliberate connections with previously existing texts, such connections may serve more to create connotations for the newly written texts than to explicate the meaning of the previously existing ones. Moreover, deliberate connections between texts can be established in a variety of ways. One text may be tightly connected to another by verbatim quotation, or loosely connected by a less precise repetition of vocabulary or motifs. Whether tight or loose, some connections are marked by explicit references to their sources. Others are left unmarked in the expectation that readers will recognize them without any such signals. The latter are 'allusions' in the technical sense (Abrams 1993: 8).

These are just some of the basic possibilities to be considered when the question of Deutero-Zechariah's relationship with other biblical texts is approached in terms of a general theory of intertextuality. Mason reckoned with some of these possibilities, but without a conceptual framework in which to consider them systematically. My goal here is to show the potential usefulness of such a conceptual framework for advancing the discussion, and to take a preliminary stab at describing Deutero-Zechariah in terms of such a theory. Heading toward this goal, a review of Mason's work is the point of departure.

Mason carefully identifies significant verbal parallels, with regard to terminology and topoi, between Zech. 9–14 and Zech. 1–8 on the one hand, and between Zech. 9–14 and other prophetic texts on the other hand. For example, in his analysis of Zech. 9.1-8—the pericope that I will use here as an example—Mason identifies the following parallels:

(1) In Zech. 9.1 the ambiguous phrase דמשק מנחת resonates with the use of the same root נוח in Zech. 6.8. The description of Yahweh's spirit being 'at rest in the land of the north' (i.e. Babylon) is analogous to his having a 'resting place' in Damascus. In both cases the locus of Yahweh's involvement in human affairs is a foreign country. In Amos 5.27 Yahweh takes Israel into exile toward the region 'beyond Damascus' (לדמשק מהלאה), but in Zech. 9.1-8 the movement is from the region beyond Damascus— Hadrach and Hamath—back toward the Temple in Jerusalem.

(2) Zech. 9.2b-4 resonates with the prophecies against Tyre in Ezek. 26- 28. In both cases the hubris of Tyre is at issue. More specifically, the description of Tyre's having 'built' (ותבן) a rampart (Zech. 9.3) corresponds with Ezekiel's pronouncement that 'you shall never be rebuilt' (לא תבנה, Ezek. 26.14). Similarly, the description of Tyre's silver being cast out 'like dust' (כעפר) corresponds with Ezekiel's pronouncement that the Babylonians 'will cast your dust (עפרך) into the midst of the waters' (Ezek. 26.12).

(3) In Zech. 9.4b-7 the consequences of Yahweh's activity are traced

from Phoenicia through Philistia along a route that resembles the one in
Amos 1.6-9. In both cases the action progresses from Gaza to Ekron by
way of Ashkelon and Ashdod. The divine agency is described as punish-,
ment by fire (Zech. 9.4b; cf. Amos 1.7) and the areas of Ashkelon and
Ashdod become uninhabited (Zech. 9.5b; cf. Amos 1.8a). The remnant
concept also figures in both texts, but in different ways. In Zech. 9.7 the
Philistines will 'become a remnant (נשאר) for our God', but in Amos 1.8
'the remnant (שארית) of the Philistines shall perish'.

The distinctiveness of Mason's work lies not in the identification of
such parallels. Other studies before and since have amassed far more
examples (Delcor 1952; Willi-Plein 1974; Person 1993; Larkin 1994;
Schaefer 1995; Nurmela 1996; Tai 1996). Mason does not really explain
how he has chosen the points at which to look for verbal parallels, but
from comparison with the explanations of other scholars who have undertaken a similar task it is evident that he often searches where there seems
to be ambiguity in the relationship between the main sections of the text.
He then uses these parallels to explicate this ambiguity, so that readers can
better understand the text's line of thought. For example, how are we to
understand the opening statement in Zech. 9.1 that 'the word of Yahweh is
in the land of Hadrach, and Damascus is its/his resting place'? Does this
mean that Syria is included in the punishment that is subsequently proclaimed for Phoenicia and Philistia? Or does it describe Syria as the locus
of Yahweh's activity from which the punishment of these other lands
proceeds? In terms of rhetorical structure, what is the relationship between
vv. 1-2a and vv. 2b-7? The inconclusive scholarly debate shows that this
question cannot be resolved on a purely philological basis. The parallels
adduced by Mason (see above) show not only that other prophetic texts
use the same terminology as Zech. 9.1, but also that these earlier texts use
this terminology to describe the locus of Yahweh's activity in foreign
lands, sometimes in order for Yahweh to judge other nations and sometimes in order for Yahweh to judge his own people. This fact does not in
itself conclusively resolve the question in favor of the latter alternative,
but it shows the possibility that prophetic insights from earlier times are
being reapplied to a later time, and are being reinterpreted for a particular
purpose.

By analyzing all of Zech. 9–14 in this way, Mason showed that there are
often illuminative parallels with earlier prophetic texts at such points of
rhetorical ambiguity. From this result he drew two major conclusions.
First, the possibilities for reading Deutero-Zechariah are not exhausted by

the conventionally posed alternatives. Some scholars have maintained that this text should be historically understood, so that it proclaims Yahweh's judgment of foreign nations and the salvation of his people with reference to particular events which—in view of the many divergent and unsuccessful attempts—we must now admit that we can no longer identify with certainty. Other scholars have maintained that this text should be eschatologically understood, so that it proclaims Yahweh's judgment of typical rather than historically particular enemies and the salvation of his people at some unspecified future time. Mason saw that the phenomenon of parallels with earlier prophetic texts does not in itself preclude either of these alternatives, but the recurrence of such parallels at points of rhetorical ambiguity gives rise to yet a third possibility. The ambiguity could be intentionally allusive word-play, in which case the reinterpretation of earlier prophetic material would have served a distinctively paranetic or homiletical purpose. Such an allusive text would have proclaimed Yahweh's judgment of any opposed to him and his salvation of any allied with him, whether they be Judean or foreign. The prospect of earlier prophecies again being fulfilled would have motivated hearers to become allies rather than opponents of Yahweh. Read in this way, Zech. 9–14 would have been occasioned by a particular historical situation sometime in the Second Temple period but not formulated so as to refer to that situation alone.

After dealing only with Zech. 9.1-8, Mason arrives at his hypothesis concerning the authorship of Zech. 9–14 as a whole, a hypothesis that is sustained by his analysis of all the subsequent pericopes:

> This would suggest, then, a prophet or circle who: (i) venerated the teaching of the earlier prophets and not only recalled them, but expounded them for their own preaching, announcing their imminent fulfilment in their own time and echoing the teaching of those prophets; (ii) a prophet or circle which seems to have been particularly influenced by the teaching of Proto-Zechariah and bearers of that tradition; and (iii) possibly a prophet or circle who had…a critical evaluation of some elements in the Jewish community, and who were perhaps particularly critical of the leadership of that community and saw the need for renewal within the Temple itself. (Mason 1973: 35)

For present purposes it is interesting that, at the end of his investigation, Mason has no less of a basis on which to propose this hypothesis and no more of a basis on which to confirm it. On the one hand, he has discovered that the same kinds of parallels are all-pervasive. On the other hand, he must still reiterate the same qualifications noted at the outset regarding the tentative nature of such evidence. He notes that none of these parallels consists of verbatim repetition, and that they can be regarded as reinterpretations of earlier prophecies only if such reinterpretation is defined so as to include radical modification and even complete reversal of what the earlier prophecies said. Nevertheless, because the parallels are so prevalent Mason can only conclude that the writer of Zech. 9–14 is in the business of homiletically expounding older prophetic texts: 'Enough examples of [allusive word-play] have been shown…to be able to maintain that this is a method of exegesis used in [Zech. 9–14], whatever questions we may have to ask over individual instances of its application' (Mason 1973: 302-303).

Scholarship in this area has not moved far beyond the impasse evident in Mason's conclusion. Quantitatively, we have more than enough evidence that whoever wrote Zech. 9–14 was steeped in Second Temple Judaism's growing corpus of canonical Scriptures. Qualitatively, we have few if any well-developed criteria for determining how this text relates to the other texts with which it seems to be connected. To begin with, we cannot really tell whether the many demonstrated parallels in terminology and topoi happened by coincidence or by design. Are they subconscious echoes of texts with which the writer(s) of Zech. 9–14 had some familiarity, or are they deliberate allusions? Mason readily admits this problem, but maintains on quantitative grounds that such a high occurrence of parallels suggests some kind of intentional 'exegetical' activity. To realize how problematic this suggestion is, one need only think of the way in which newspaper articles covering a particular development often repeat the same terminology and topoi day after day. Each article extensively echoes previous articles, but this hardly shows that its aim is to exegete them. Even when there is a very high incidence of verbal parallels, this sort of deliberate allusion is not necessarily the most probable explanation.

Moreover, even if we could be relatively sure that at least some parallels have happened on purpose, so that one text could be regarded as a probably deliberate 'reinterpretation' of another text, we have no well-developed categories for describing the various kinds of intertextual relationships that this might entail. To what extent, and in what way, is a connecting text constituted by the text with which it connects? Or, to put it another way, what is the strategy of the connecting text *vis-à-vis* the precursor text? Mason assumes that Zech. 9–14 alludes to other texts in an 'exegetical' way, that is for the purpose of homiletical exposition. This is a plausible (even if highly protestant) assumption, given what we generally know about the function assumed by canonical Scriptures and how they came to be interpreted in the Second Temple period, but there may be other possibilities. For example, the typological correspondence between the Flood and baptism in 1 Pet. 3.20-21 does not so much reinterpret the story of Noah in Gen. 6–9, as it uses the symbolism of the Flood to interpret the significance of baptism. Even though preaching on scriptural texts gradually became a definitive feature of Jewish worship in the Second Temple period, we cannot assume that writers of that time would have alluded to sacred texts only in order to preach them.

Although Mason's investigation of the use of earlier biblical material in Deutero-Zechariah reflects problems that are still endemic to much work on this subject, two distinctive features of his approach also point beyond this impasse. First, Mason generally makes rhetorical ambiguities his point of departure in trying to understand how Deutero-Zechariah is related to Proto-Zechariah and other earlier prophetic texts. This suggests that we pay greater attention to the rhetorical structure of Deutero-Zechariah, or of any text that supposedly reinterprets other texts. Terminological and thematic parallels can show *that* texts are interrelated, but they in themselves—as we shall see—cannot show *how*. If one text has designs on another, this could well be reflected in the overall shape it takes. How one text connects with another may be evident in how it is designed to do so.

Second, in his use of the term 'inner biblical exegesis', Mason has in mind a particular kind of interpretive activity. He presupposes that parallels between Zech. 9–14 and earlier prophetic texts reflect the homiletical reactualization of prophecies previously addressed to an earlier historical context. Such preaching would have tacitly claimed that these prophecies were being fulfilled, albeit in ways that bear very loose symbolic correspondence to their original referents. This is richly suggestive and certainly plausible (Mason 1984, 1990), but it begs the question of whether there might be other kinds of interpretive activity. Deutero-Zechariah does not resemble other texts that more obviously reflect the kind of preaching presupposed by Mason—the apostolic sermons in Acts, for instance. If these two very different kinds of texts belong to one and the same family of homiletical exposition, we must then suppose that the sermonic reinterpretation of canonical Scriptures could follow widely varying models indeed. And might there not be types of scriptural reinterpretation that are not particularly sermonic? Mason's assumptions about the 'exegetical' nature of the relationship between Zech. 9–14 and earlier prophecies show the need to extend categories of reinterpretation and define more systematically the range of possible relationships between texts.

Those who wish to pursue the issue of Deutero-Zechariah's relationship with Proto-Zechariah and other earlier prophetic texts would do well to focus on two questions highlighted by the foregoing review of Mason's work. First, does the rhetorical structure of Deutero-Zechariah show any signs of its having been designed to reinterpret other texts? And second, if so, where does Deutero-Zechariah fall along the range of possible relationships between texts? For scholarship to shed much light on the question of what Zech. 9–14 is saying *vis-à-vis* earlier prophecies, I believe that it should now follow Mason's lead.

To demonstrate how the discussion might proceed, we will first explore the range of deliberate intertextual relationships and then ask whether the rhetorical design of Deutero-Zechariah shows it to belong somewhere along this continuum. There are well-developed general theories of intertextuality that may eventually prove useful in the study of texts like Zechariah (e.g. Genette 1997; cf. Sommer 1998: 10-28), but they are too complicated and technical for our present purposes. For now, it is enough just to show the potential usefulness of such theories, and to that end there follows a rough sketch of the hypothetical range of possibilities using only four examples: (1) Gerard Manley Hopkins's poem, 'Thou Art Indeed Just, Lord'; (2) Tom Stoppard's play, *Rosencrantz and Guildenstern Are Dead*; (3) John Donne's Second Prebend Sermon; and (4) Martin Luther's *Commentary on St Paul's Epistle to the Galatians*.

Hopkins's poem, written in 1889, is brief enough to quote in full:

> Thou art indeed just, Lord, if I contend
> With thee; but, sir, so what I plead is just.
> Why do sinners' ways prosper? And why must
> Disappointment all I endeavor end?
> Wert thou my enemy, O thou my friend,
> How wouldst thou worse, I wonder, than thou dost
> Defeat, thwart me? Oh, the sots and thralls of lust
> Do, in spare hours more thrive than I that spend,
> Sir, life upon thy cause. See, banks and brakes
> Now leavèd how thick! lacèd they are again
> With fretty chervil, look, and fresh wind shakes
> Them; birds build—but not I build; no, but strain,
> Time's eunuch, and not breed one work that wakes.
> Mine, O thou lord of life, send my roots rain (Hopkins 1918: 69-70).

The first two lines and most of the third—down to the end of the question 'Why do sinners ways prosper?'—are quoted from Jer. 12.1. The phraseology does not closely match the King James Version, nor the Douay-Rheims version with which Hopkins, as an English convert to Catholicism, might have felt some affinity. The metric translation appears to be his own, based on the Vulgate, the Latin text of which is prefixed as an epigraph to most editions of the poem. This device shows that the reference to the biblical text is deliberate, and that Hopkins thus invites readers to compare Jeremiah's sense of God-forsaken failure with the complaint of the poem's protagonist, who also vainly spends his life in God's cause while sinners prosper.

Although the allusion is certain, there is no explicit indication that the Latin epigraph is from Jeremiah, or even that it is a biblical passage. The author evidently hopes that readers will bring to the text some familiarity with Jeremiah's 'confessions', and thus enrich their reading with the many connotations that emerge from comparing the poetic persona with the prophetic persona. However, it is important to note that the poem is a self-standing text that does not depend upon this association to convey its message. Its overall design remains largely unaffected by the allusion. It has a conventional prosodic shape, as a sonnet in iambic pentameter, with a rhyme scheme of *abba abba* in the octet and *cd cd cd* in the sestet. Even if readers did not recognize the connection with Jeremiah, the poem would be accessible to them as a sonnet, and its main point would not be lost on them. The complaint of divine mistreatment would be no less sarcastic and no less poignant.

In contrast, Tom Stoppard's play, *Rosencrantz and Guildenstern Are Dead*, has a more direct relationship with another text, namely, William Shakespeare's *Hamlet*. In Shakespeare's play, Rosencrantz and Guildenstern are secondary characters, courtiers commissioned by King Claudius of Denmark, Hamlet's stepfather, to find out the underlying reason for the prince's ostensibly disturbed behavior. Hamlet quickly detects their insincerity and uses them in his scheme to reveal that Claudius is his father's murderer—beginning with a none-too-subtle court drama that re-enacts a crime suspiciously like Claudius's before his own eyes in order 'to catch the conscience of the king'. As the enraged Claudius tries to get rid of Hamlet, Hamlet manages to get revenge. Claudius orders Rosencrantz and Guildenstern to accompany Hamlet to England, bearing a letter that will get Hamlet executed upon his arrival, but Hamlet discovers their plan and alters the letter so that they get executed instead. In the meantime, he escapes and returns to Denmark where he eventually meets his own death.

In Stoppard's play, Rosencrantz and Guildenstern are the main characters. He tells the story from their perspective, letting them speak on center stage at those points when in Shakespeare's version they are offstage or peripherally involved in the dramatic action. From the perspective of *Hamlet*, Stoppard begins in *medias res* with Rosencrantz and Guildenstern's being summoned by King Claudius. There are only occasional retrospective references to the first part of Shakespeare's narrative in which Hamlet becomes suspicious of his stepfather. And Stoppard ends with the report of Rosencrantz and Guildenstern's death, accompanied by a sudden flash-forward to the final scene in Shakespeare's tragic denouement, where Hamlet and three other main characters lie dead. Stoppard's own narrative, from Rosencrantz and Guildenstern's initial involvement with Hamlet's stepfather to their own demise, is interwoven with explicit excerpts from the directly corresponding parts of *Hamlet* and threaded with more oblique references to the parts with which there is no direct correspondence.

Despite such extensive dependence upon *Hamlet*, the audience needs only the vaguest impression of Shakespeare's play in order to make sense of Stoppard's. The interaction between Rosencrantz and Guildenstern involves matters that could but do not necessarily pertain to the dramatic events that frame it. Their dialogue has been aptly compared with that of Estragon and Vladimir in Samuel Beckett's *Waiting for Godot*. For example, in the initial scene the two courtiers toss coins and muse upon the implications of a seemingly impossible run of heads over tails, introducing a visual motif and a theme of improbability that reappear from time to time throughout the play. Verbal exchange often plays upon the humorous absurdity of language, in a style that smacks of *Monty Python*:

> GUIL: What does it all add up to?
> ROS: Can't you guess?
> GUIL: Were you addressing me?
> ROS: Is there anyone else?
> GUIL: Who?
> ROS: How would I know?
> GUIL: Why do you ask?
> ROS: Are you serious?
> GUIL: Was that rhetoric?
> ROS: No. (Stoppard 1968: 42-43)

Although such dramatic action and dialogue are framed by the plot of *Hamlet*, they sit rather loose to this context. One could perhaps say that the superstructure of *Rosencrantz and Guildenstern Are Dead* directly mirrors the central dramatic action of *Hamlet*, but that its own dramatic action consists of much other stuff. To enjoy the former, the audience need not have read or seen the latter. They could probably get by with just an inkling of why someone named Hamlet was moved by the sight of a skull to utter that oft-repeated (and oft-satirized) line: 'To be or not to be...'.

The third of our examples is John Donne's Second Prebend Sermon, preached at St Paul's in London on 29 January 1625. His text was Ps. 63.7: 'Because thou hast been my help, therefore in the shadow of thy wings will I rejoyce'. After making some summary remarks on the Psalms in general, Donne puts this verse in context by relating it to the superscription of Ps. 63, and on this basis outlines a three-part structure for his remarks:

> The key of the psalme (as S. *Hierome* calls the Titles of the psalmes) tells us, that *David* uttered this psalme, *when he was in the wildernesse of Iudah* There we see the present occasion that moved him; And we see what was passed between God and him before, in the first clause of our Text; (*Because thou has been my helpe*) And then we see what was to come, by the rest, (*Therefore in the shadow of thy wings will I rejoyce.*) So that we have here the whole compasse of Time, Past, Present, and Future; and these three parts of Time, shall be at this time, the three parts of this Exercise; first, what *Davids* distresse put him upon for the present; and that lyes in the Context; second, how *David* built his assurance upon that which was past; (*Because thou hast been my help*) And thirdly, what he established to himselfe for the future, (*Therefore in the shadow of thy wings will I rejoyce*). (Donne 1967: 95)

Donne then moves systematically through each of these three parts of the homiletical 'exercise', concluding with an extensive exhortation to joy. He mentions with understatement the occasion for concluding in this way, an epidemic of plague which had two weeks earlier left large parts of the city desolate and subject to looting:

> God hath accompanied, and complicated almost all our bodily diseases of these times, with an extraordinary sadnesse, a predominant melancholy, a faintnesse of heart, a chearlesnesse, a joylesnesse of spirit, and therefore I returne often to this endeavor of rasing your heart, dilating your hearts with a holy Joy, Joy in the holy Ghost, for *Vnder the shadow of his wings*, you may, you should, *rejoyce*. (Donne 1967: 111-12)

Finally, Donne gives a cosmic and death-transcending scope to his treatment of joy:

The true joy of a good soule in this world is the very joy of Heaven; and we
goe thither, not that being without joy we might have joy infused into us,
but that as Christ sayes, *Our joy might be full,* perfected, sealed with an
everlastingnesse; for as he promises, *That no man shall take our joy from
us,* so neither shall Death it selfe take it away...[and] in the agonies of
Death, in the anguish of that dissolution, in the sorrowes of that valediction,
in the irreversiblenesse of that transmigration, I shall have a joy, which
shall no more evaporate, than my soul shall evaporate, A joy, that shall
passe up, and put on a more glorious garment above, and be joy super-
invested in glory. *Amen.* (Donne 1967: 113-14)

With regard to the relationship between this sermon and the scriptural text
that it expounds, there are two things to be noted. First, as this example
shows, a sermon is not a self-standing text, but one that exists in a symbiotic relationship with a scriptural text. The preaching of the sermon is a
liturgical event that presupposes the liturgical reading of the text which it
expounds. In our time it is conventional for the sermon to be based on a
text that is read when the sermon is preached. In Donne's time, too, this
was often so, but it was also common for the sermon to be based on a text
not read on the same occasion. This was particularly the case with respect
to preaching on the Psalms. In the liturgy of the Church of England the
entire Psalter was recited each month, a portion every morning and a
portion every evening. Preachers might choose a text from the psalm
appointed for the day, but they might also choose a text from any psalm on
the assumption that the entire Psalter was always being read. In the case of
Donne's Second Prebend Sermon, it is unlikely that Psalm 63 was recited
when he preached on it, but this does not obviate the fact that sermons presuppose the liturgical reading of the texts they expound. This is generally
the case despite considerable historical and cultural variation in the
practice of preaching and in the selection of scriptural texts for liturgical
reading.

Second, this interdependence between the scriptural text and sermon is
evident in the design of the sermon. Again, there is tremendous variation
in this regard. In general, however, the main parts of the sermon correspond to the main points construed in the exegesis of the text. In the case
of Donne's sermon, the three sections in its main body correspond with the
three aspects of the psalm text that Donne has chosen to draw out: (1) the
relation of v. 7 to Ps. 63 as a whole, taking the superscription as the key to
the context; (2) the causative clause in the first part of v. 7, and (3) the
result clause the second part of v. 7. The correspondence between the
preacher's parsing of the text and the shape of the sermon is not always

this neat, but in a sermon that purports to expound a scriptural text there is usually some connection between the way the text is construed and the sermon's overall design.

Finally, for our fourth example we take Luther's *Commentary on St Paul's Epistle to the Galatians*. This text was not actually written by Luther himself. It was based on lectures he delivered—in Latin, of course—at the University of Wittenberg in 1531. He spoke from outlines and never wrote out his remarks in full, but several of his devoted students took notes. By 1535 they produced a transcript for publication, which was reviewed by Luther and for which he wrote a Preface. Although patristic and medieval commentaries were typically written by the commentators themselves, not by students or other surrogates, they often originated as notes for teaching and therefore reflected the rhetoric of the oral catechetical or academic exposition of Scripture. In this respect, Luther's commentary on Galatians was pretty conventional.

The work takes a rather simple shape. First, there is an overview of Paul's argument in Galatians. Next comes the exposition, in which a brief segment of text is quoted and then discussed. The individual segments of text occasionally contain as much as a verse or two, but they are usually much smaller and often consist of only a word or phrase. For example, the first verse in the main body of the letter (1.6) is broken down into five segments: (1) 'I marvel'; (2) 'that so soon'; (3) 'ye are removed away'; (4) 'from him that hath called you in the grace of Christ'; and (5) 'unto another gospel' (Luther 1953: 57-64). Each of these phrases gives rise to several paragraphs of comment. Occasionally, the discussion seems to abandon Paul's argument and take up Luther's own arguments concerning contemporary doctrinal or ecclesiastical issues. In subsequent editions he gave these sections distinctive headings, not to suggest that such application was regarded as a secondary rather than an integral aspect of exposition, but simply to show that at these points the application was debatable.

In this commentary, we have perhaps the most extreme example of one text's symbiotic relationship with another. As is true of commentaries in general, the interpreting text is not self-standing but can only be read in close connection with the interpreted text. In this particular case, because nearly every section of commentary is appended to some quoted segment of Galatians, one cannot read the commentary at all without also reading the text of Galatians simultaneously.

Even commentaries that do not quote the entire text they expound, however, must be read in tandem with that text. Commentaries do not exist in their own right, but only to help readers make sense of other documents.

These four examples can provide us with an approximate indication of some cardinal points along the continuum of deliberate intertextual relationships. On one extreme, we have a poem that alludes to a biblical text but can be understood without recognizing the allusion. On the other extreme, we have a commentary that makes no sense unless it is read in close connection with the text it explicates. Hopkins's poem does not necessarily assume prior knowledge of the Jeremiah passage to which it alludes, but Luther's commentary entails a close reading of Galatians. Along the middle of the continuum we have, on the one hand, a play explicitly premised on the plot of another play, but whose own plot often goes its own way. And on the other hand, we have a liturgical oration expounding a text that the audience is assumed to have heard in the same or some similar ritual context. Both the play and the sermon presuppose at least some familiarity with the texts they reinterpret, but different kinds of familiarity, neither of which is particularly close. Informed by nothing more than a casual awareness of *Hamlet*'s reputation, an audience can enjoy *Rosencrantz and Guildenstern Are Dead*. Most of the audience for Donne's sermon, however, would have directly experienced the entire text of Ps. 63 as a liturgical reading.

As we move along this continuum there is a progression with respect to the dependence of the interpreting text upon the interpreted text. On one end, the interpreting text ('Thou Art Indeed Just, Lord') is relatively independent, definitely alluding to the interpreted text (Jer. 12.1) but capable of being understood without explicit reference to it. On the other end, the interpreting text (Luther's commentary) is completely dependent on the interpreted text (Galatians), explicitly referring to it at every turn and incomprehensible on any other basis. In between these two poles, *Rosencrantz and Guildenstern Are Dead* is more dependent on *Hamlet* than Hopkins is on Jeremiah, but less dependent on *Hamlet* than Donne is on Ps. 63.7, and so on. There is also a progression in the extent to which the genre of the interpreting text is defined in terms of a reinterpretive function. Sonnets and plays may be more or less allusive, but neither is necessarily so. In contrast, sermons are typically informed by both direct and allusive references to scriptural texts. There can be considerable variation in the extent to which sermons consist of interaction with Scripture, but nearly all sermons do so to some degree. And commentaries are of course defined in terms of continuous explicit reference to scriptural texts.

From this rudimentary illustration of some types of deliberate intertextuality, we can draw two conclusions relevant to the present study of Zechariah. First, judging from these examples, the frequency of direct quotation and/or other verbal parallels is not a very significant index of the extent to which, or the way in which, one text serves to reinterpret another. In all four examples, a relatively high proportion of the interpreting text consists of direct quotes from the interpreted text, and yet there is extreme variation in the dependence of the former on the latter—ranging from the rather tangential relationship between Hopkins's sonnet and Jer. 12.1 to the virtually parasitical relationship between Luther's commentary and Galatians. Of course there must be some verbal parallels in order for there to be a deliberate intertextual relationship of any sort, but neither the sheer quantity of verbal parallels nor the extent to which they are verbatim is particularly telling with regard to the nature of the intertextual relationship. This suggests that much of the work done thus far on verbal parallels between Deutero-Zechariah and other prophetic texts needs to be complemented by other kinds of analysis that can put the results in a larger literary perspective.

Second, if verbal parallels suggest that Deutero-Zechariah serves to reinterpret other texts, it may be worthwhile to raise the question of the genre of Deutero-Zechariah, and of whether its genre is defined in terms of a reinterpretive function. As noted above, Mason concluded that Deutero-Zechariah was sermonic material and that it reinterpreted earlier prophetic texts homiletically. This remains a possibility, but one would have to show more fully that Deutero-Zechariah has the form of a sermon, and that it interacts with other texts in the same ways that, say, Peter's sermon in Acts (2.14-36) and Donne's sermon interact with other texts. As shown by our rudimentary demonstration of the range of types of intertextuality, one would also have to allow for other possibilities and consider what they might be. In the remainder of this essay, I would like to explore one other possibility.

Elsewhere I have argued, following Richard Weis, that the *maśśā'* is a prophetic genre defined in terms of its reinterpretive function, and that Zech. 9–14 and Zech. 12–14 have the term *maśśā'* as their superscription because they are texts belonging to this generic category (Floyd 2000, 2002). This hypothesis may well be debatable, but I do not intend to defend it here. I would rather use the concept heuristically to show the kind of literary analysis that is appropriate in light of what we have learned from comparing four representative types of intertextuality. This provides a good example of the role that form criticism can play in intertextual analysis.

According to Weis, *maśśā'* texts have a rhetorical pattern with three definitive elements. First, an assertion is made, directly or indirectly, about Yahweh's involvement in a particular historical situation or course of events. Second, this assertion serves to clarify the implications of a previous revelation from Yahweh that is alluded to, referred to or quoted from. And third, this assertion also provides the basis for directives concerning appropriate reactions or responses to Yahweh's initiative, or for insights into how Yahweh's initiative affects the future. Oracular speech of Yahweh is also a definitive feature, but its occurrence does not follow any particular pattern. Defined in rhetorical terms, *maśśā'* means something like 'prophetic reinterpretation of a previous revelation'. It is thus a genre defined in terms of a reinterpretive function (Weis 1986, 1992).

In three cases—Nahum, Habakkuk, and Malachi—the term *maśśā'* applies to the composition of the book as a whole, and the reinterpreted revelations are contained within the main body of each book. In the case of Zechariah, however, the term applies not to the book as a whole, but to the relationship between each of the two appendices (chs. 9–11 and 12–14) and the preceding material. Each appendix contains the first and third elements of the *maśśā'*, an assertion about Yahweh's involvement in a particular situation and a directive regarding the appropriate response. The preceding sections of the book constitute the second element of the *maśśā'*, the previous revelation(s) that the assertion serves to clarify. The conceptual basis for such a relationship is established in the introduction (1.1-6), as it develops the theme of prophecy's significance above and beyond the historical circumstances to which it was originally addressed. The function of the appendices is to reinterpret what the prophet Zechariah discerned regarding Yahweh's involvement in the restoration of Yehud in the early Persian period, elaborating on its implications for the discernment of Yahweh's involvement in the events of a later time. Here I will illustrate these generalizations only with respect to the relationship between Zech. 1–8 and Zech. 9–11, but similar observations could be made about the relationship between Zech. 1–11 and Zech. 12–14.

The basic prophetic claim of the book of Zechariah is that Yahweh intends for his people to resume their rightful place among the nations. By means of the Persian Empire he is reconfiguring the world order so that his people's homeland can be reconstituted as the imperial province of Yehud. By means of Zechariah's prophetic role he is reconfiguring the local polity of his people as a community centered around the restored royal temple in Jerusalem, an institution maintained by the imperial governor and administered by the high priest (1.7–6.15). This new arrangement calls for a different form of religious life in which the people renew their commitment to the ideals of their covenant with Yahweh in a new calendar of cultic observances (7.1–8.23). The main body of Zechariah (1.7–8.23) describes the formative events of the early Persian period in terms of two basic elements: first, Yahweh's initiative on the worldwide as well as the local scene (1.7–6.15); and second, the kind of response that the people are thereby called to make (7.1–8.23). In chs. 9–11, typological correspondences are drawn between the early Persian and early Greek/Hellenistic periods with respect to these same two basic elements.[1]

The first *maśśā'* appended to Zech. 1–8 begins with an assertion of Yahweh's intention to secure a place among the nations for his people and his temple (9.1-8), followed by a call for Yahweh's people to rejoice because of the peace he is establishing through a new imperial order (9.9-10). This pattern of Yahweh's initiative and the people's response is then reiterated. Yahweh has freed the captives (9.11); and consequently they are to return (9.12a). Yahweh has restored the territorial integrity of his people, enabling them to resist foreign enemies (9.12b-17); and consequently they are to ask for rain, thus beginning the process by which they attain economic prosperity, sound local leadership, and the reunification of all Israel (10.1-12). Yahweh's intentions are thwarted, however, by an alarming local leadership crisis (11.1-3). He attempts to bring this crisis to a head, raising up a leader so bad that the present order will self-destruct (11.4-17). In 9.1–11.17 the replacement of Persian by Greek/Hellenistic imperial hegemony is analyzed theologically in light of a typological contrast with the replacement of Babylonian by Persian imperial hegemony in the time of Zechariah. Yahweh intended for the Greek/Hellenistic imperial order to provide for his people advantages analogous to those provided by the Persian restoration, and it initially promised to do so. In view of the problems that emerged, however, Yahweh came to regard the whole arrangement instituted under the Persians—that is, imperially legitimated temple authorities with local jurisdiction—as constitutionally deficient.

If we assume for the sake of argument that this reading of Zech. 9–11 as a *maśśā'* is viable, then this text would fall on our continuum somewhere

---

1. Although I hold that Zech. 9–11 and 12–14 were composed in the Greek/ Hellenistic period, the claims that Zech. 9–11 is related to Zech. 1–8 as a *maśśā'*, and that Zech. 12–14 is related to Zech. 1–11 as a *maśśā'*, do not necessarily entail this dating. These appendices could conceivably serve to draw typological correspondences between the early Persian period, as described in Zech. 1–8, and any later time.

between Stoppard's play and Donne's sermon. *Rosencrantz and Guilden-stern Are Dead* assumes the basic plot of *Hamlet* and singles out the central dramatic action as a pretext on which to elaborate. Zech. 9–11 similarly assumes the basic structural progression of Zech. 1–8 and singles out the main rhetorical elements as a pretext on which to elaborate. Just as Stoppard's work is a separate play, but one that nevertheless presupposes the existence of another play, Zech. 9–11 is a separate section of the prophetic book of Zechariah, but one that nevertheless presupposes its being appended to the previous material in the book.[2] The main difference is that the genre of *Rosencrantz and Guildenstern* as a play is not defined in terms of a reinterpretive function, but the genre of Zech. 9–11 as a *maśśā'* is. In this respect Zech. 9–11 more closely resembles Donne's sermon. Donne assumes that his audience has participated in a liturgical reading of the text reinterpreted in his sermon, and that they tacitly know what the sermon is doing with it. The writer of Zech. 9–11 similarly assumes that its readers have studied the text that this *maśśā'* reinterprets, and that they tacitly know what the *maśśā'* is doing with it. The main difference is that the sermon is permeated with explicitly marked direct quotes of Ps. 63.7, but the *maśśā'* has only indirect connections with Zech. 1–8. The only explicit indication of the reinterpretive function of Zech. 9–11 is the use of this genre term in its superscription.

When Zech. 9–11 is viewed as a *maśśā'*, the significance of the verbal parallels between it and other biblical texts is relativized. Such parallels are no longer the basis on which the reinterpretive function of Zech. 9–11 is established. This text can be seen as a reinterpretation of Zech. 1–8, not because the former repeats certain terms and topoi found in the latter— although it does repeat them—but because Zech. 9–11 recapitulates the distinctive rhetorical structure of Zech. 1–8. The two basic rhetorical elements of both texts are: (1) prophetic description of what Yahweh is doing to save his people; and (2) prophetic exhortation directing the people to make an appropriate response. Zech. 1–8 consists of a section (1.7–6.15) in which prophetic description of Yahweh's initiatives pre-dominates over directives concerning a response (e.g. 2.10-17), followed by a section in which prophetic exhortation to respond appropriately (7.1–8.23) predominates over description of Yahweh's initiatives (e.g. 8.1-8). Zech. 9–11 similarly consists of sections in which prophetic description of

---

2.   A *maśśā'* can be a self-standing document that contains the prophecy it reinterprets, but in this case it is an appendix to the reinterpreted prophecy.

Yahweh's initiatives predominates (9.1-8, 11, and 12b-17), followed by sections in which prophetic directives to respond predominate (9.9-10, 12b, and 10.1-12). These rhetorical parallels show that the pattern of divine action and human response first described in relation to Zechariah's time corresponds typologically with the pattern of divine action and human response subsequently described in relation to a later time. The reverse of these elements in ch. 11, where the human response (11.1-3) precedes the divine action (11.4-7), shows that this typological correspondence has been turned inside out (for details see Floyd 2000: 440-92).

Although the verbal parallels between Zech. 9–11 and various other texts are not the basis of its reinterpretive function, they are stylistically significant. Parallels with Zech. 1–8 serve to reinforce the reinterpretive function of Zech. 9–11 *vis-à-vis* Zech. 1–8. Parallels with other texts connotatively enrich the reinterpretation of Zech. 1–8 by Zech. 9–11. In this regard it does not matter much whether they are allusions or echoes— if we could ever tell the difference. In either case, they reflect the kind of setting in which texts like Zech. 9–11 were produced. These parallels are not typical of the kind of textual familiarity that preachers of sermons assume on the part of their audience, which consists of memorable expressions and images imparted through liturgical reading. They are typical of the kind of textual familiarity that scribal writers assume on the part of scribal readers, which consists of a loaded vocabulary resulting from their close study of previously existing texts. Documents like Zech. 9–11 were written by scribes steeped in prophetic writings for fellow scribes who were similarly steeped in the same prophetic writings. When such texts were subsequently read to the congregation and preached upon, preachers might draw out any verbal parallels that they as educated readers could recognize. But although verbal parallels might in this way become the subject of preaching—as they actually did in both the rabbinic and patristic homiletical traditions—they were not a product of preaching. They were a by-product of mantic scribal activity.

In this essay I have attempted to build upon Mason's work concerning the relationship between Proto- and Deutero-Zechariah, putting it into a theoretical framework afforded by recent scholarship's more systematic approach to intertextuality. Even this rudimentary representation of various types of intertextuality has provided a better idea of the possibilities and the criteria for identifying them. In light of this preliminary analysis, Mason's basic hypothesis of Deutero-Zechariah as a reinterpretive text is confirmed, but with major modifications. The definitive feature no longer appears to be verbal parallels, and the main function no longer appears to be homiletical. Whether or not the particular arguments presented here hold, I hope I have at least managed to demonstrate that this approach is the way to go, and that Mason has pointed us in this direction.

THE GROWTH OF THE BOOK OF ISAIAH
ILLUSTRATED BY ALLUSIONS IN ZECHARIAH

Risto Nurmela

1. *Introduction*

This article is based on the research done in connection with my doctoral thesis, 'Prophets in Dialogue: Inner-Biblical Allusions in Zechariah 1–8 and 9–14' (Nurmela 1996). As the title indicates, I studied the dependence of the book of Zechariah on the rest of the Old Testament writings, and it is no wonder that the book of Isaiah occupies a central position in this connection. To be sure, I am not the first one to address this topic. On the contrary, the very first critical contribution to the research of Zechariah dealt with the relation between Isaiah and Zechariah. The first article of the first issue of *Zeitschrift für die alttestamentliche Wissenschaft* in 1881 was 'Deuterosacharja: eine kritische Studie' by Bernhard Stade. He argued in favour of dating chs. 9–14 of Zechariah later than chs. 1–8. At that time, chs. 9–11 were thought to have originally belonged to Jeremiah and thus to be earlier than chs. 1–8. Stade corroborated his theory with a comparison of themes in Zech. 9–14 and the rest of the Old Testament, which showed that these chapters are postexilic, that is, later than the book of Joel.

Following Stade numerous studies have been made, which take as their starting point the similarities between Zechariah and other Old Testament writings. The first to be mentioned are those by Mathias Delcor (1952) and Paul Lamarche (1961). Then the doctoral thesis of Rex Mason (1973), with the subtitle 'A Study in Inner Biblical Exegesis', demonstrated how Old Testament writings are interpreted in Zech. 9–14. Following Mason, Raymond Person (1993) and Katrina Larkin (1994) have written theses that aim at connecting Zech. 9–14 with the deuteronomistic school and Wisdom Literature, respectively. Janet Tollington has investigated Zech. 1–8 from the same viewpoint in her thesis (1993).

I am critical of all these studies as to the method of tracing similarities.

This is of vital importance, as the similarities are used to demonstrate the parts of the Old Testament on which Zechariah is dependent. If you want to do this, you should also be able to prove that there are not some other similarities that would indicate a dependence at least as strong on other parts of the Old Testament. Zechariah could, of course, be dependent on several different parts of the Old Testament, but not too many. If the writings on which Zechariah is thought to be dependent cover more or less the entire Old Testament, what would the research then have proved? It would have demonstrated that everything in the Old Testament is dependent on everything else, which is true but too trivial to be presented as a result of serious scholarship. In other words, there are themes that are more or less common to the entire Old Testament.

In fact, none of the above-listed studies provides us with an answer to the question of how similarities are detected. The similarities are presented as if they had always been known. Confused by the numerous proposals considering dependence in various directions, I wanted to have an objective criterion, and this can only be the vocabulary. The first thing to be done is a careful study of concordance: Are there words and phrases that outside Zechariah occur in only one Old Testament book? In fact, there are quite a lot of such words and phrases, which justifies an analysis of these connections exclusively on this basis. I refer deliberately to 'Zechariah'. For more than 100 years the focus has been on Zech. 9–14 in a rather one-sided way. The division between chs. 8 and 9 is hardly so sharp as to preclude an investigation of the entire book of Zechariah.

When dealing with words and phrases as indicators of dependence, one should be careful not to register them uncritically. For instance, many scholars regard לֹא נָבִיא אָנֹכִי ('I am no prophet') in Zech. 13.5 as an allusion to the identical phrase in Amos 7.14 (e.g. Rudolph 1976: 229; Meyers and Meyers 1993: 380-81; Reventlow 1993: 120; Petersen 1995: 127; Redditt 1995: 135-36). In my judgment, in both passages somebody denies that he is a prophet, but on highly different grounds. In both passages this is said in the most elementary way, and therefore the similarity can be merely due to chance. This is also pointed out by Mason in his doctoral thesis (Mason 1973: 395-96 n. 90).

When the significance of the vocabulary for studies of literary dependence is underscored, it should not be forgotten that verbal similarities are of course not the only thing that can indicate a dependence. In his review of my thesis Mason wrote: 'Nurmela believes that demonstrations of inner biblical allusions are valid only when they are based on *verbal* points of contact, and this leads him to make short shrift of the work of those who have preceded him in the study of this aspect of the Book of Zechariah' (Mason 1997). However, this was not exactly what I meant. What I wanted to say was that an analysis of Zechariah, which takes its starting point in the vocabulary, results in conclusions that are in some respects radically different from those based on other methods. As the other methods are less objective and less verifiable, analyses based on verbal similarities should be preferred in the face of contradictory results.

In 1996, Nicholas Ho Fai Tai published a book based on his doctoral thesis, 'Prophetie als Schriftauslegung in Sacharja 9–14: Traditions- und kompositionsgeschichtliche Studien'. His approach is very close to mine. Tai also underscores the significance of verbal similarities. However, his study demonstrates a problem that must be overcome when performing an investigation like this. If two Old Testament writings are connected by a verbal similarity which is so strong that dependence is indicated, the question of its direction still remains: Which passage is dependent on which? At first sight one might answer the question by dating the passages. The later passage is dependent on the earlier one. This is what Tai does; but, in fact, he does not offer any argument concerning the parallels to Zech. 9–14 that he studies. Instead, he apparently takes it for granted that they all are earlier (Tai 1996: 3). Person first recapitulates a number of methods of dating Zech. 9–14, and then declares briefly that he relies on the one presented by Andrew Hill: 'The validity of his dating is assumed in this work' (Person 1993: 18). However, most of the Old Testament books are the result of a redaction that may have taken hundreds of years. The argument should thus not be based on the dating of Old Testament writings in their final form. Instead, the short passages involved should be individually dated. Nevertheless, if the direction of an assumed dependence is to be established on the basis of the dating of the passages, the questions of dating, or at least a *terminus ante quem*, should be decisively settled. Within Old Testament exegesis this is seldom the case. This problem is illustrated by Tollington's observation: 'Psalm 109 is frequently assigned to a postexilic date, though the evidence offered in support of this is inconclusive; thus it would be unwise to claim any dependence on it by Zechariah' (Tollington 1993: 118).

For this reason, I have completely given up the idea of establishing the direction of the dependence on the basis of dating. Instead, I have analyzed the integration of the verbal element shared by Zechariah and other Old Testament writings in their respective contexts. When an expression is taken from one context and used in another in order to make an allusion to the former, it usually forms some kind of contrast to its new context. An allusion can also consist of a quotation of a fragment of a longer passage. Or an expression can be cited but not quite literally, and in such a way that it can be explained how one form emanates from another but not the other way around. For instance, Zech. 4.10 and 2 Chron. 16.9 are connected by an expression which contains the word צין ('eye'). In Zech. 4.10 the word is masculine, as it is in only one other place in the entire Old Testament (Zech. 3.9); otherwise צין is always feminine (Albrecht 1896: 75). This indicates that the Chronicler alludes to Zechariah, as it appears unlikely that the gender of an unambiguously feminine word would be changed into masculine in an allusion, whereas the reverse is totally understandable. Something very uncommon is 'normalized'. This could be characterized as an application of the *lectio difficilior* rule of textual criticism.

One of the results of my study was that throughout the book of Zechariah a dependence on the book of Isaiah can be demonstrated. As for Zech. 9–14, this is nothing new. Both Stade and Mason have pointed it out. However, the connections of chs. 1–8 have not been investigated as thoroughly.

2. Examples of Similarities between Zechariah and Isaiah

In the following examples I am going to deal with the similarities between the books of Zechariah and Isaiah, which I have traced by an analysis of the vocabulary.

a. *Zechariah 2.14 and Isaiah 12.6*
The imperative of the verb רנן ('shout with joy') addressed to Zion occurs in the Old Testament only in Isa. 12.6, Zeph. 3.14, Zech. 2.14 and Lam. 2.19. In Isa. 52.9 the imperative of this verb is addressed to the ruins of Jerusalem, the only case in the Old Testament of an expression that parallels those previously mentioned. In Lamentations רנן is used with a meaning different from the one that it has in the rest of these passages. Zion is exhorted to 'moan'. In the first three passages it is also said that God will be in the midst of Zion. Verbally, Zechariah and Zephaniah are most similar; but as for the structure, Zechariah and Isa. 12 are most similar. In both passages there is an exhortation to Zion followed by a clause introduced by כי ('because'), whereas the structure of Zeph. 3.14

differs considerably. In my judgment, Zeph. 3.14 is dependent on both Zech. 9.9 and Isa. 12.6 (Nurmela 1996: 214-16). I will thus focus on Isa. 12.6 and Zech. 2.14. It should be noted that besides רנן, the rare verb צהל ('shout'—eight occurrences in the Old Testament) is used in Isa. 12. Moreover, the exhortation to Zion is actually directed to ישבת ציון ('she who lives in Zion'), an expression that besides this passage occurs only in Jer. 51.35. In Zechariah, however, the common verb שמח ('rejoice') is used besides רנן, and also in Zechariah the more common בת־ציון ('daughter Zion') is used instead of ישבת ציון. It is more likely that Zechariah replaced the uncommon expressions with more commonplace ones than that Isaiah alluded to Zechariah using very rare expressions. This is thus an example of dependence on Isaiah in Zechariah.

b. *Zechariah 2.15 and Isaiah 14.1*

The verb לוה in niphal ('join, attach oneself') occurs in the Old Testament 12 times, including Isa. 14.1 and Zech. 2.15. The subject is גר ('foreigner') in Isaiah and גוים רבים ('many nations') in Zechariah. Moreover, according to Isa. 14.1 Yahweh will elect Israel, whereas in Zech. 2.16 he will elect Jerusalem. The phrases are otherwise identical: ובחר עוד בישראל/בירושלם. In Isaiah the wider context (ch. 13 and its sequel in ch. 14) is Yahweh's judgment upon Babel, a theme that is also included in Zech. 2.10-11. In Isa. 14.2 a promise is made to Israel whereby it will receive the nations as a possession and as slaves, but according to Zech. 2.13 God will fight against the nations who have plundered Israel and make them the booty of their Israelite slaves. Also Zech. 2.16 possibly reflects Isa. 14.2. According to Isaiah, Israel will take over possession (והתנחלום) of the nations, whereas in Zechariah, Yahweh will take possession (ונחל) of Judah in the holy land. Furthermore, in both passages the land is referred to by אדמה (Isaiah: אדמת יהוה; Zechariah: אדמת הקדש), which is far less common in this sense than ארץ.[1]

In Isaiah, the verb ספח in niphal ('attach oneself') is used as a parallel to לוה. There are only five occurrences of this verb in the Old Testament, the only one in niphal being here. It might appear plausible that Zechariah dropped this strange word when alluding to Isaiah. Moreover, נחל in hithpael, used by Isaiah, occurs only seven times in the Old Testament, including two instances in the prophets, whereas the qal form of the verb used by Zechariah is far more common. The qal form could also have been

---

1. Against Tollington (1993: 237), who asserts that Isa. 14.1 does not bear any marked resemblance to the prophecies of Zechariah.

used in Isaiah (cf. Zeph. 2.9). Thus it is more likely that Zechariah has altered the hithpael form into qal than the other way around. Zechariah is thus dependent on Isaiah.

c. *Zechariah 7.11, 14 and Isaiah 6.10, 11*

The phrase אׁזן הכבד ('make the ear dull') occurs in the Old Testament only in Isa. 6.10 and Zech. 7.11. Besides these two passages, כבד in hiphil occurs in this meaning only in Exodus, where it is used four times to describe Pharaoh's heart. In Isaiah, the prophet is told to make the people's ears dull, whereas in Zechariah the people are blamed for having made their ears dull. In the following verses in Zechariah the result of the disobedience of the people is described. The land was made נׁשמה ('desolate'), so that nobody was going or coming there, and turned into שׁמה ('what is horrible', v. 14). Also in Isa. 6 the desolation is described: the cities will be made desolate so that nobody lives in them, Yahweh removes the people and the land becomes שׁממה ('sinister desolation', v. 11).

　　In Isa. 6.10 אׁזן הכבד is included in a chiastic construction:

> (a) Make the *heart* (לב) of this people unreceptive
> 　　　　(b) *make their ears dull* (ואזניו הכבד)
> 　　　　　　　(c) keep *their eyes* (עיניו) shut
> 　　　　　　　(c) lest they see *with their eyes* (בעיניו)
> 　　　　(b) and hear *with their ears* (באזניו)
> (a) lest *their heart* (לבבו) perceive.

Thus the expression is so tightly integrated with its context that it can hardly be regarded as dependent on Zech. 7.11, for it does not appear obvious that this chiastic construction would be an elaboration of ואזניו הכבד, which in turn would refer to Zechariah, particularly as this expression does not introduce the chiasm. However, if it is assumed that Zechariah is dependent on Isaiah, one might ask why just this expression has been picked up. This might be due to there being an allusion to Jer. 6.10, 17-19 in the very same verse in Zechariah, dealing precisely with the people's unwillingness to *listen* (Nurmela 1996: 72-75).

　　The word order אׁזן הכבד is uncommon. As for Isaiah, it can be explained by the fact that 'ears' and 'eyes' form a natural couple, whereas the verbs כבד and שׁמע appear as mere appendages to the nouns. Also, in Zechariah אׁזן הכבד is followed by two expressions in which the object is placed first, but these are לב ('heart') and תורה ('law'), which do not form a couple as natural as 'eyes' and 'ears'. It thus appears that Zechariah has taken over the uncommon word order from Isaiah.

d. *Zechariah 8.3 and Isaiah 1.26*

ונקראה ירושלם עיר־האמת ('Jerusalem will be called the faithful city') in Zech. 8.3 is strongly reminiscent of Isa. 1.26: יקרא לך עיר הצדק קריה נאמנה ('you will be called a righteous town, a reliable city'). In both Zechariah and Isaiah the oracle is addressed to Jerusalem. Moreover, it can be noted that in both passages Yahweh's action is necessary for there to be a righteous city (Petersen 1984: 299). In Isa 1.26 the expressions clearly refer to v. 21, where קריה נאמנה and צדק are also used when Jerusalem's moral qualities in the past are contrasted with her present sinfulness. In vv. 25 and 26, Yahweh promises to cleanse Jerusalem and restore it morally, and therefore it will again be called a righteous town and a reliable city. In Zechariah the description of the Israelites' disobedience at the end of ch. 7 could also be regarded as such a background, but no verbal connections like those in Isaiah can be pointed out. Therefore it is clear that the present expression in Isaiah is better integrated in its context than the similar expression in Zechariah, and that Zechariah is thus dependent on Isaiah.

e. *Zechariah 8.20-23 and Isaiah 2.2-4*

In both Isaiah and Zechariah there is a vision of the nations' pilgrimage to Zion. The vision of Isaiah has an almost word-for-word parallel in Micah. There are a number of connections between Isa. 2.2-4/Mic. 4.1-3 and Zech. 8.20-23: עמים רבים ('many nations'), גוים עצומים ('strong nations'), and the cohortative of the verb הלך ('go'), נלכה. Moreover, the formulation לכו ונעלה ('come, let us go up') in Isaiah and Micah is very close to נלכה הלוך ('let us go') in Zechariah. The context of ונעלה is an exhortation to 'go up to the mountain of Yahweh', while that of נלכה הלוך is an appeal to 'go to entreat the favour of Yahweh'.[2]

The oracle in Isaiah and Micah is characterized throughout by strict *parellelismus membrorum*:

> In days to come the mountain of Yahweh's house shall be established as the
> highest of the mountains,
> and shall be raised above the hills;
>
> all the nations shall stream to it,
> many peoples shall come and say,

---

2. Against Tollington (1993: 236), who asserts that the only textual connections between Zech. 8.20-23 and Isa. 2.2-4/Mic. 4.1-3 are עמים and גוים.

'Come, let us go up to the mountain of Yahweh,
to the house of the God of Jacob;

that he may teach us his ways
and that we may walk in his paths'.

For out of Zion shall go forth instruction,
and the word of Yahweh from Jerusalem.

In Zechariah the parallelism is far less strict:

Thus says Yahweh of hosts: Peoples shall yet come,
the inhabitants of many cities;

The inhabitants of one city shall go to another, saying,
'Come, let us go to entreat the favour of Yahweh,
and to seek Yahweh of hosts; I myself am going'.

Many peoples and strong nations shall come
to seek Yahweh of hosts in Jerusalem,
and to entreat the favour of Yahweh.

The direction of the dependence is hard to decide in this case. This calls seriously into question whether the passages actually are mutually dependent. Both might instead be dependent on a third source unknown to us. This, however, does not rule out the possibility that one of them has been composed on the basis of the other. Given the classic style of Isa. 2/Mic. 4, there is no doubt regarding which section could be an imitation of which. Zechariah is thus to be considered dependent on Isaiah and/or Micah rather than the other way around.

Up to this point I have been referring to Isaiah *and* Micah. On which of them is Zechariah dependent? In fact, גוים עצומים ('strong nations') is not used in Isaiah and thus forms a connection only between Micah and Zechariah; Isaiah reads עמים רבים in the corresponding clause. Nevertheless, since the oracles in Isaiah and Micah agree almost word-for-word, it would not be wise to assume that גוים עצומים had never been in any connection with the oracle in Isaiah. On the other hand, if the present oracle at that time was included in early versions of both Isaiah and Micah, why would the author of this section in Zechariah have been aware of Micah but not Isaiah, especially as there are a number of allusions to Isaiah in Zech. 1–8? Of course, one might ask whether it is correct to speak in terms of 'either Isaiah or Micah', instead of simply dealing with the oracle regardless of its canonical framing. Nevertheless, I find it unlikely that such a short oracle would have been known apart from a connection with any larger collection. Another question is whether Isaiah might be dependent on Micah at this point, or vice versa. In this regard it should be noted that the oracle in Micah is followed by two significant verbal similarities: וישבו איש תחת גפנו ותחת תאנתו in Mic. 4.4a repeats almost literally 1 Kgs 5.5 (a similar expression occurs nowhere else in the Old Testament), while כי פי יהוה צבאות דבר in Mic. 4.4b (a *hapax legomenon*) should be compared to כי פי יהוה דבר, which occurs only in Isa. 1.20, 40.5 and 58.14. The fact that the present oracle is immediately followed by further verbal similarities to other writings indicates that the oracle itself is a quotation of Isa. 2 (cf. Blenkinsopp 2000: 190-91). In sum, I consider Zech. 8.20-23 an allusion to Isa. 2.2-4.

f. *Zechariah 1.16, 17 and Isaiah 52.8, 9*

There is also an example of reverse dependence. In Zech. 1.16 and 8.3, as well as in Isa. 52.8, Yahweh 'returns' (שוב) to Zion/Jerusalem. According to both Isa. 52.9 and Zech. 1.17, he will comfort his people or Zion. In both passages the verb for 'comfort' is נחם in piel. Moreover, 1QIs^a 52.8 is one word longer and ends in ברחמים ('in compassion'), which makes the stich still more reminiscent of Zech. 1.16: שבתי לירושלם ברחמים.

Yahweh's return to Zion is described in a very vivid manner in Isaiah: עין בעין יראו בשוב יהוה ציון ('Eye to eye they will see Yahweh return to Zion'). This appears as an intensification of the prophecy in Zech. 1.16, where it reads simply: שבתי לירושלם ('I am returning to Jerusalem'). This indicates that Isaiah is dependent on Zechariah at this point. Moreover, the text of 1QIs^a with ברחמים is clearly overloaded. The MT reads:

קול צפיך נאשו קול יחדו ירננו
כי עין בעין יראו בשוב יהוה ציון:

1QIs^a reads:

קול צפיך נאשו קול יחדו ירננו
כי עין בעין יראו בשוב ציון יהוה ברחמים

Because 1QIs^a is clearly overloaded, the MT is to be preferred. However, this addition can be explained by the fact that ברחמים occurs also in Zech. 1.16. The connection between Isa. 52.8 and Zech. 1.16 also exerted an influence on the textual tradition.

Nevertheless, the similarity between these passages might also be due to the same issue being discussed in both of them. Neither שוב יהוה ציון nor שבתי לירושלם is indeed a very peculiar wording.[3] It is thus possible that there is no allusion on this point, except in 1QIs^a.

---

3. I am indebted to Rainer Albertz for this observation.

g. *Zechariah 9.8 and Isaiah 29.3*

We will now move on to Zech. 9–14. The verb חנה ('encamp') in the first person singular occurs in the Old Testament only in Isa. 29.3 and Zech. 9.8. In both passages God is the subject, the verbal form is exactly the same (וחניתי) and the setting is one of war. In Isa. 29.1-4, God threatens with an attack on Ariel (Jerusalem), whereas in Zech. 9.5-7 a desolation of Philistine cities is predicted. In Isaiah, חנה refers to an act hostile to Jerusalem (God will encamp against the city), in connection with two other military terms (מצב, 'siegewall'[?]; and מצרת, 'siege-mounds'). In Zechariah the warlike context refers to the foreign cities, whereas חנה depicts God's protection of his house.

The word חנה is almost exclusively used in two meanings in the Old Testament: (1) of the Israelites—to 'encamp' (especially in Numbers) or even 'live' (Neh. 11.30) in a non-military meaning; (2) of military troops—to 'encamp' in order to encounter a hostile army in battle or to attack it, or to 'besiege' a city. Isa. 29.3 belongs to the latter group. The only exceptions to the use of חנה in these ways are Zech. 9.8 and Ps. 34.8. In the latter passage the angel of Yahweh encamps around those who fear him and saves them, whereas in Zechariah God encamps in order to protect his house. The possibility that Zech. 9.8 is dependent on Ps. 34.8 is contradicted by the closer similarity between Isaiah and Zechariah: the same verbal form, the same subject (God himself, in the first person, not the angel of God in the third person, as in Ps. 34) and the warlike setting. Since חנה is used in Isaiah in one of its common meanings, whereas the meaning, which occurs in Zechariah, is only paralleled by Ps. 34, it appears more likely that חנה in Zechariah is dependent on Isaiah than vice versa. Zechariah alludes to an oracle of judgment in Isaiah, thereby reversing it into an oracle of salvation.

h. *Zechariah 9.15; 12.8 and Isaiah 31.5*

The verb גנן ('fence in, protect') occurs in the Old Testament only in the Isaiah legends (2 Kgs 19.34; 20.6; Isa. 37.35; 38.6) and in Isa. 31.5, Zech. 9.15 and Zech. 12.8. In all of these passages God is the subject, in the Isaiah legends in the first person, in the remaining instances in the third person. Besides Zech. 9, where the object in plural obviously refers to the Israelites, the object is consistently Jerusalem. Since Zech. 9.15 and 12.8 are thus most similar to Isa. 31.5, a dependence between these passages appears most likely.

The expressions that include גנן are not very well integrated in their context in Zechariah. In Zech. 9.14 and 15 the line of thought is, in fact, interrupted:

> The Lord Yahweh will sound the trumpet and march forth in the whirlwinds of the south. *Yahweh of hosts will protect them*, and they shall devour and tread down the slingers...

The same can be said about Zech. 12.8. Even if the line of thought is not interrupted as markedly, the clause that includes גנן sounds unexpected in the context (vv. 7 and 8):

> And Yahweh will give victory to the tents of Judah first, that the glory of the house of David and the glory of the inhabitants of Jerusalem may not be exalted over that of Judah. *On that day Yahweh will shield the inhabitants of Jerusalem* so that the feeblest among them on that day shall be like David...

This does not mean that the clauses with גנן should be deleted; this is not textual criticism. Instead, they should be regarded as parenthetical comments in the form of allusions, which may very well stem from the same author as the rest of the context. Such problems, however, are not connected with Isa. 31.5. The entire context deals with God's protection of Jerusalem. This indicates that Zechariah is dependent on Isaiah and not vice versa.[4]

i. *Zechariah 10.8-10 and Isaiah 5.26; 7.18*

The verb שרק ('whistle') in the meaning 'call', occurs only in Isa. 5.26, Isa. 7.18 and Zech. 10.8, and in all these passages the subject is God. In Isaiah, he whistles in order to call the nations against Israel, whereas in Zechariah he does it in order to call the Israelites home from their exile. In all other passages where שרק occurs it expresses the fright of those who face desolation. However, Isa. 5.26 and 7.18 also deal with future desolation. Thus only in Zech. 10.8 is שרק used in an oracle of salvation. Isaiah's oracles of judgment are thus reversed into their opposite. Without this

---

4. Wildberger (1982: 1450-51) calls attention to the use of the formula אלהי דוד אביך in Isa. 38.5. This formula occurs besides the parallel passage in 2 Kings only in 2 Chron. 21.12 and 34.2. The passage must stem from circles that hoped for the restoration of the throne of David and hoped for salvation from him, possibly circles in which prophets like Haggai and Zechariah were met with sympathy. The argumentation of Wildberger contains an interesting aspect. If he is right, then the redaction of Isaiah has at least at some level had a close connection with the activity of the prophet Zechariah. And as גנן makes a connection between Zech. 9–14 and Isa. 1–39, the verb also makes a connection between the circle in which Zechariah was acting and Zech. 9–14, though it does not appear in Zech. 1–8.

explanation it would be difficult to understand why שׁרק is used in an oracle of salvation. This shows that Zechariah is dependent on Isaiah (cf. Tai 1996: 102-103).

j. *Zechariah 12.1 and Isaiah 51.13*

The phrase נטה שׁמים ויסד ארץ ('the one who stretches out the heavens and establishes the earth') occurs in Zech. 12.1 and Isa. 51.13, and nowhere else in the Old Testament. This terminology, however, is very typical of Deutero-Isaiah (cf. Isa. 40.22; 42.5; 44.24; 45.12; 48.13; 51.16). There is thus no reason to think that Isa. 51.13 is dependent on Zech. 12.1, and not the other way around.

k. *Zechariah 13.7-9 and Isaiah 1.21-26*

Zechariah 13 and Isa. 1 are connected by a rather terse transition from judgement to the deliverance of a purified rest. In Zech. 13.8, 9 it is described like this:

> In the whole land, says Yahweh, two-thirds shall be cut off and perish, and one-third shall be left alive. And I will put this third into the fire, refine them as one refines silver, and test them as gold is tested. He will call on my name, and I will answer him. I will say, 'He is my people'; and he will say, 'Yahweh is my God'.

In Isa. 1.24-26 a similar transition is described like this:

> Therefore says the Sovereign, Yahweh of hosts, the Mighty One of Israel: Ah, I will pour out my wrath on my enemies, and avenge myself on my foes!
> I will turn my hand against you;
> I will smelt away your dross as with lye and remove all your alloy.
> And I will restore your judges as at the first, and your counselors as at the beginning.
> Afterward you shall be called the city of righteousness, the faithful city.

In both passages the expression והשבתי/אשׁיבה ידי על ('I will turn my hand against') occurs (Isa. 1.25; Zech. 13.7). Similarly, the image of refining precious metal and the verb צרף ('smelt, refine') occur in both Isa. 1.25 and Zech. 13.9 (cf. Tai 1996: 226-31). The integration of the first mentioned expression in Zechariah is somewhat awkward in its immediate context, since God does not otherwise speak in the first person in vv. 7 and 8 but addresses, for instance, the sword. The transition from judgment to deliverance appears unnaturally terse in Zechariah—not even a ו connects v. 9b with v. 9a. The transition from plural in v. 9a to singular in v. 9b should also be noticed. Again, such problems are not connected with the corresponding transition in Isa. 1. Verse 25 depicts the cleansing from impurity, v. 26a describes the restoration of the social justice, and v. 26b claims that Jerusalem will be called a righteous city, a faithful town. Thus Zech. 13.7-9 is dependent on Isa. 1.25, and not vice versa.

l. *Zechariah 10.6 and Isaiah 41.17*

Also in Zech. 9–14 there are two examples of reverse dependence. The clause כי אני יהוה אלהיהם ואענם ('for I am Yahweh, their God, and I will answer them') in Zech. 10.6 is strongly reminiscent of the similar clause in Isa. 41.17: אני יהוה אענם ('I, Yahweh, will answer them'). There is also a synonymic similarity between לא־זנחתים ('I had not rejected them') in Zechariah and לא אעזבם ('I will not abandon them') in Isaiah.

In Isa. 41.17 the present clause interrupts the line of thought in the first stich of the verse, which then continues in the following verses. Its linkage to the preceding stich is also linguistically awkward; an introductory ו or כי seems to be lacking. In Zechariah the clause has a connection to the preceding one, which at least cannot be said to be awkward, as it offers an explanation as to why it will be 'as if I had not rejected them'.[5] Thus on this point Isaiah appears to be dependent on Zechariah and not vice versa.[6]

m. *Zechariah 14.12, 16 and Isaiah 66.23, 24*

Zech. 14.16 and Isa. 66.23 are connected by several verbal similarities: והיה ('and it will happen') introduces both of them; מדי שנה בשנה ('year after year') in Zechariah, מדי־חדש בחדשו ומדי שבת בשבתו ('new moon after new moon and sabbath after sabbath') in Isaiah; להשתחות ('in order to worship') in both. The following verse in Isaiah, v. 24, is connected with Zech. 14.12 by a thematic similarity, the punishment of the sinners in Isaiah and that of the soldiers who have fought against Jerusalem in Zechariah. This punishment is described in a most distasteful manner: 'Their flesh shall rot while they are still on their feet; their eyes shall rot in their sockets, and their tongues shall rot in their mouths'. Trito-Isaiah's assertion, 'their worm shall not die', appears to be an allusion to the drastic imagery in Zechariah. Claus Westermann notes that the intention in

---

5. Meyers and Meyers (1993: 210) point out that the parallelism of the preceding two lines of Zech. 10.6 certainly does not continue here. However, the poetic quality of this chapter does not adhere to 'classical' (the Meyerses' quotes) standards, and the formal variation alone should not disqualify this line from being original to the verse.

6. Against Tai (1996: 94), who regards Zech. 10.6 as a quotation of Isa. 41.17.

Isa. 66.23 appears to go even further than Zechariah, since in Zechariah the survivors of the judgment of the nations come up to Jerusalem year by year, but in Isaiah 'all flesh' will worship Yahweh every new moon and sabbath. He also points out that the word דראון ('abomination') only occurs in Isa. 66.24 and Dan. 12.2, which suggests a very late addition in Isaiah (Westermann 1970: 339-40). Again, Isaiah is dependent on Zechariah.

3. *Conclusions*

There are five examples of dependence on Isaiah in Zech. 1–8, and six examples in Zech. 9–14. A closer look at the passages alluded to in Zechariah shows that all allusions in Zech. 1–8 refer to passages in Isa. 1–39. Moreover, there might be an allusion to Zech. 1–8 in Deutero-Isaiah. As regards the six allusions to Isaiah in Zech. 9–14, five of them refer to Isa. 1–39 and one to Deutero-Isaiah. In addition, there is one allusion to Zech. 9–14 in Deutero-Isaiah and one in Trito-Isaiah. This might indicate that both parts of the book of Zechariah can be dated to a period when the book of Isaiah did not yet include Deutero-Isaiah. To establish this, however, is not significant, since we do not know when Deutero-Isaiah was connected with the book of Isaiah. The fact that there is an allusion to Deutero-Isaiah could be negated by saying that one single instance is not sufficient to prove any dependence. Nevertheless, it should also be noted that the expression, which seems to allude to Deutero-Isaiah, bears all marks of being a secondary addition. Some scholars regard the heading formed by Zech. 12.1 as an introduction to a third part of the book of Zechariah, so-called 'Trito-Zechariah', but I do not share this view (Nurmela 1996: 167-77). The verse reads: משא דבר־יהוה על־ישראל נאם־יהוה נטה שמים ויסד ארץ ויצר רוח־אדם בקרבו ('The word of Yahweh concerning Israel: Thus says Yahweh, who stretched out the heavens and founded the earth and formed the human spirit within'). This heading might very well have been expanded, so that at least נאם־יהוה and its sequel were added later, and thereby an additional allusion to the book of Isaiah, which in the meantime had been expanded with Deutero-Isaiah.

The passages of Isa. 1–39 alluded to in Zech. 1–8 are found in chs. 1, 2, 6, 12, and 14. In chs. 1, 2, and 6 we are dealing with oracles that could all be pre-exilic (Wildberger 1972: 80; 1982: 1554; Blenkinsopp 2000: 181), whereas the same can hardly be said about ch. 12, or the verses alluded to in ch. 14 (Wildberger 1978: 525; Kaiser 1981: 254; Kilian 1986: 92; 1994: 101-102; Blenkinsopp 2000: 270, 281). Nevertheless, the allusions to the latter chapters might very well belong to a later level in Zechariah, as they follow each other at the end of Zech. 2 and are included in a section (vv. 10-17) that interrupts the chain of visions in an enigmatic way.

As for the passages in Isa. 1–39 alluded to in Zech. 9-14, they are found in chs. 1, 5, 7, 29, and 31. They all, except ch. 1, belong to the core of Isa. 1–39, that is chs. 2–11 and 28–31 (Wildberger 1982: 1557-59; cf. Jensen 1984: 14; Blenkinsopp 2000: 90-91), and the verses referred to in ch. 1 are hardly very much later, either.[7] The results of an investigation of the connections of Zech. 9–14 thus correspond more or less exactly with the theories of the successive growth of Isa. 1–39, although the latter are not based on studies of literal dependence. I find this all the more remarkable, since the core of Isaiah now consists of two separate units; and my observations concerning Zech. 9–14 'respect' the gap of 17 chapters between them. Nothing between Isa. 11 and 29 is involved.

Moreover, the passages outside of the core of Isaiah referred to in Zech. 1–8 are found in sections very close to that core, namely, chs. 12 and 14. This could indicate that the consciousness of the connections between the books of Zechariah and Isaiah prevailed for some time, so that the redactors who added allusions to Zechariah used material in the immediate context of sections already alluded to. In fact, I previously made a similar observation concerning Isa. 52.8, possibly an allusion to Zechariah, namely, that 1QIs[a] 52.8 has been expanded with one additional word from Zechariah. The allusion in Zech. 12.1 deals with a passage that cannot be said to be very close to those referred to otherwise (Isa. 51.13), but actually this allusion is more likely a later addition than any of the other ones.

The allusions to Zechariah in Deutero-and Trito-Isaiah are, to be sure, too few to form the basis of any theory of dependence. Nevertheless, these examples are interesting, as the dependence of Zechariah on the latter parts of Isaiah seems to be negligible. Moreover, I have not registered any allusion to Zechariah in Isa. 1–39.[8]

---

7. Sweeney writes on Isa. 1.21-26: 'The metaphorical use of foundry imagery in this passage is characteristic of Isaiah and indicates that the prophet is the author' (1996: 85).

8. In my thesis I have registered allusions to Isaiah, which are not listed in this article. Here I have applied stricter criteria for the similarities required to indicate an allusion, and therefore some of the allusions dealt with in the thesis have been dropped.

SOME OBSERVATIONS ON THE RELATIONSHIP
BETWEEN ZECHARIAH 9–11 AND JEREMIAH

Eibert Tigchelaar

1. *Introduction*

The classic studies of Delcor (1952), Mason (1973) and Willi-Plein (1974) all discussed the use of earlier biblical material in Zech. 9–14. Yet they did not tackle the question of the distribution and frequency of allusions to other biblical books. Delcor did mention that Deutero-Zechariah mainly uses Ezekiel, Second Isaiah and Jeremiah, but he did not pursue this matter any further.

Some monographs of the 1990s, for example Person (1993), Larkin (1994), and Tai (1996), do comment to some extent on the statistics of the correspondences. All scholars refer to similarities between Deutero-Zechariah and Jeremiah, but this phenomenon is approached in different ways, and these studies do not draw the same conclusions. Nowadays, with little consensus on method (diachronic and synchronic), as well as the character and date of prophetic texts and collections, no study should completely neglect theoretical aspects. I cannot refrain from some methodological issues, but on the whole I wish to focus on one specific issue, namely, the relationship between Zech. 9–14, in particular chs. 9–11, and Jeremiah.

2. *Correspondences between Zechariah 9–14 and Jeremiah*

It is not necessary to discuss all the correspondences between Zech. 9–14 and Jeremiah *in extenso*. Many cases have been discussed by Mason. Other scholars present lists, charts, tables or summaries of correspondences with earlier biblical material in general, or Jeremiah in particular. See, for example, the remarkably short and astonishing list of Delcor (1952) . He omits correspondences observed by all other scholars, but includes 'sources' which no one else recognizes as such. Or one may consult Willi-Plein's concise but valuable study, which has had too little impact outside of

Germany, and her lists of correspondences between Zech. 9–14 and prophetic texts. More recent overviews include Meyers and Meyers' (1993) charts of examples of intertextuality, Person's inventories of deuteronomistic language in Zech. 9–14, Larkin's cases of mantological exegesis, or Tai's study on tradition in Zech. 9–14, including a survey on the use of Jeremiah.

It should be noted that the correspondences listed in these works are of different sorts. Delcor includes both correspondences of language and of content, whereas most other scholars focus on the former. Larkin only discusses alleged examples of mantological exegesis in Deutero-Zechariah. On the other side of the spectrum, Person lists many instances of Deuteronomic language found both in Jeremiah and Deutero-Zechariah. In the latter case, it is not at all clear whether the authors or editors of Zech. 9–14 'used' (a version of) the book of Jeremiah. To a lesser extent, the same goes for the examples of intertextuality. Here, Mason's introductory remarks with regard to 'dependency' still apply: 'It is all too easy…to assume that one passage is dependent upon another, forgetting that both may have had a common origin, for example, in the language of worship in the cult, or in common everyday usage, and so be only indirectly, if at all, related to each other' (1973: iv).

I shall not present here a full discussion of all the proposed, real or alleged correspondences with Jeremiah. It should suffice to give a selective list of proposals of either correspondence, exegesis, or intertextuality, presented by Delcor (D), Mason (M), Willi-Plein (W-P), Meyers and Meyers (M&M), Larkin (L), and Tai (T). Person's cases of Deuteronomic language in Deutero-Zechariah are not included in this list because his examples of 'Deuteronomic passages that significantly parallel II Zechariah' include the most important Jeremianic passages (either Deuteronomic or not) mentioned by other scholars (1993: 105-17).

Some correspondences are referred to by all scholars, but other similaritieonly by one or two authors. This suggests a certain degree of subjectivity. Also, not each alleged correspondence is indicative of dependency. Presumably Meyers and Meyers would not claim that each case of intertextuality also implies a direct relationship. Some of Delcor's cases are of a very general nature and, in my opinion, not relevant at all. I disagree with several of the listed suggestions. For example, I am not at all convinced that Jer. 2.13 is used in Zech. 13.1 or 14.8; nor do I see any reason why Zech. 14.10 should be dependent on Jer. 31.38-40. Likewise, I question suggestions about the use of Jer. 5.20-25 in Zech. 9.5 and 10.1, or Jer. 30.14 in Zech. 13.6.

Table 1. *Alleged Correspondences between Zechariah 9–14 and Jeremiah*

Zechariah	Jeremiah
9.5	5.20-25 (T)
9.5-6	25.20 (M&M)
9.9	23.5; 33.5 (M&M)
9.11-17	31.10-20 (W-P)
9.11-12	38.6 (M, M&M)
10.1	5.20-25 (T)
10.1-2	14.1–15.4 (M); 14.15 (W-P); 14.14, 22 (L); 14.14; 27.9-10; 29.9-10 (M&M)
10.3–11.3	2.8; 3.15-18; 10.20; 12.10; 22.22-23; 25.36-38; 23.1-6 (M, W-P, T); 30.21; 33.3 (M)
10.3-12	31 (T)
10.4	30.21 (W-P)
10.6	31.18, 20 (L)
10.8	31.27; 30.19; 31.3b; 31.11 (D); 23.3 (M&M)
10.10	50.19 (D)
10.11	51.42, 55 (W-P)
11.1-3	25.34-38; 49.19 (W-P)
11.3	25.36 (D); 25.3 (M&M)
11.4	7.32; 19.6 (D); 12.3 (M, W-P); 25.34-38 (W-P, M&M)
11.5	50.7 (D)
11.7	14.19 (D)
11.8	22 (D)
11.9	15.2 (D, M&M)
11.17	50.35-38? (W-P, L)
12.1	10.12; 51.15 (M&M)
12.2	25.15-31; 49.12 (M&M)
12.10	6.26 (M&M)
13.1	2.13 (W-P)
13.3	20.9; 26.16; 29.23; 44.16 (M&M)
13.6	30.14 (T)
13.9	7.23; 31.33 (M&M)
14.2	4.5-8; 25.1-21, etc. (M&M)
14.8	2.13 (W-P); 8.13 (M&M?, a typographical error?)
14.10	31.38-40 (D, M, W-P)
14.11	25.9; 43.28 (W-P)

Whatever one's judgment on the nature of each of these listed correspondences, a comparison of all alleged cases of use and intertextuality shows that the most extensive and verbal correspondences between Zech. 9–14 and Jeremiah are found in Zech. 9–11, in particular in 9.11 (or 9.17)–11.4, and perhaps in 11.17. These correspondences are also those on which most scholars agree. The density of correspondences with Jeremiah in these few chapters may perhaps be attributed to the common shepherd motif employed both in Zech. 10–11 and throughout Jeremiah. Yet a more penetrating analysis is called for, for example, to explain the wealth of correspondences with Jeremiah in Zech. 10.1–11.4, and the relative lack of such correspondences in the body of the Shepherd Allegory.

a. *Zechariah 10.3-12*
In my thesis (Tigchelaar 1996: 89-109) I proposed an interpretation of Zech. 10.3-12 which was partially based on the studies of Saebø (1969), Willi-Plein (1974), and van der Woude (1984), especially on their distinction between divine oracles (Zech. 10.3a, 6, 8-10, and perhaps 12) and prophetic comments (Zech. 10.3b-5, 7, 11). All scholars mention the many correspondences between Zech. 10.3-12 and Jeremiah, but no scholar, apart from Willi-Plein, has explicitly referred to the fact that the clear correspondences with Jeremiah are found in the divine oracles, and even she does not pursue the point. The structure of Zech. 10.3a, 8-10 reflects the order of Jer. 23.2-3, 7-8, and most corresponding phrases are found either in Jeremiah 23 or in Jeremiah 31. Other correspondences can be found in Jer. 12.15; 22.6; 30.10; and 51.50. There may perhaps exist a correspondence between Zech. 10.12 and Jer. 9.22-23, if one accepts the emendation וּגְבָרְתָּם (*ûgburātām*) for MT וְגִבַּרְתִּים (*wᵉgibbartîm*), and the LXX and 4QXIIᵍ reading variant of MT יתהלכו. Both LXX (κατακαυχήσονται) and 4QXIIᵍ 104.2 (לו נאם יהוה) suggest the reading יתהללו instead of יתהלבו. On the other hand, one may also argue that Jer. 9.22-23 provoked the variant reading יתהללי.

Most of the correspondences consist of words expressing 'having mercy', 'saving', 'gathering', 'redeeming', 'bringing back', and 'bringing' of the returnees. More specific are other correspondences: 'sowing', 'multiplying', 'remembering from afar', and perhaps the names of 'Gilead', and 'Lebanon'. But other typically Jeremianic words, such as הפּיץ, 'scatter', and נדח (H-stem), 'disperse', have not been used.

In contrast, there are few correspondences with Jeremiah in the prophetic comments. Zech. 10.3b פקד את reminds one of Jer. 23.2, but it may also be influenced by Zech. 10.3a, and Zech. 10.4 may be compared to Jer. 30.21 (ממנו) and יצא, with possibly a connection between נוגש and ונגש). Many scholars have commented on the close phraseological correspondence between Zechariah chs. 9 and 10. In part this may be due

Table 2. *The Divine Speech in Zechariah 10.3-12 in Relation to Jeremiah*

Jeremiah		Zechariah 10.3-12: 'divine speech'	
23.2	על הרעים	על הדעים חרה אפי	10.3a
23.2	הנני פקד עליכם	ועל העתודים אפקוד	
		וגברתי את בית יהודה	10.6
30.10	הנני מושעך מרחוק	ואת בית יוסף אושיע	
31.7	הושע יהוה את עמך		
12.15	ורחמתים והשבתים	והושבותים כי רחמתים	
		והיו כאשר לא זנחתים	
31.18	כי אתה יהוה אלהי	כי אני יהוה אלהיהם ואענם:	
23.3	ואני אקבץ	אשרקה להם ואקבצם	10.8
31.11	יקבצנו		
31.11	כי פדה יהוה	כי פדיתים	
23.3	ופרו ורבו	ורבו כמו רבו:	
31.27	וזרעתי את בית ישראל	ואזרעם בעמים	10.9
31.10	ממרחק	ובמרחקים יזכרוני	
51.50	זכרו מרחוק את יהוה		
30.10	ושב יעקב	וחיו את בניהם ושבו:	
31.8	קהל גדול ישובו		
31.17	ושבו בנים		
23.3	והשבתי אתהן	והשיבותים מארץ מצרים	10.10
23.7	מארץ מצרים		
23.3	ואני אקבץ...מכל הארצות	ומאשור אקבצם	
23.8	הביא	ואל ארץ גלעד ולבנון אביאם	
31.8	הנני מביא אותם מארץ צפון		
22.6	גלעד אתה לי ראש הלבנון		
		ולא ימצא להם:	
9.22	ואל יתהלל הגבור בגבורתו	וגברתים (? וגברתם) ביהוה	10.12
		ובשמו יתהלבו (? יתהללו)	

to the common martial language, but there are also expressions which are found nowhere else in the Hebrew Bible except for these two sections (הבה בים, and כמו יין, קשת מלחמה). Again, few scholars apart from Willi-Plein have observed that these agreements are restricted to the prophetic comments.

In short, the divine oracle verses are closely related to Jeremiah, whereas the prophetic comments show some correspondences with Jeremiah, but mainly share the vocabulary of Zech. 9. I argued that the author of the prophetic comments adopted this divine oracle because it dealt with the unfulfilled part of Zech. 9, namely, the return of the Northern exiles (Tigchelaar 1996: 109).

Table 3. *The Prophetic Speech in Zechariah 10.3-12 in Relation to Zechariah 9*

Zechariah 10.3-12 'prophetic speech'		Zechariah 9	
כי פקד יהוה צבאות את־עדרו את־בית יהודה	10.3b		
ושם אותם כסוס הודו במלחמה:		סוס	9.10
		ושמתיך כ	9.13
ממנו פנה ממנו יתד ממנו קשת מלחמה	10.4	קשת מלחמה	9.10
ממנו יצאכל נוגש יחדו:		נגש	9.4
והיו כגברים בוסים בטיט חוצות במלחמה	10.5	טיט חוצות	9.3
		גבור	9.13
ונלחמו כי יהוה עמם			
והבישו רכבי סוסים:		רכב	9.9
		הביש	9.5
והיו כגבור אפרים	10.7	אפרים	9.10, 13
ושמח לבם כמו יין		כמו יין	9.15
ובניהם יראו		תרא אשקלון	9.5
ושמתו		ותירא	
יגל לבם ביהוה:		גילו מאד	9.9
ועבר בים צרה והכה בים גלים	10.11	והכה בים חילה	9.4
והבישו כל מצולות יאר		הביש	9.5
והורד גאון אשור ושבט מצרים יסור:		גאון...והסרתי	9.6b-7a

In my thesis I considered the possibility that the divine oracle of Zech. 10 was an already existing prophecy, which was taken up and commented on in later times. Yet the structure of the divine speech section indicates that this oracular section is dependent on Jeremiah, and perhaps also Ezekiel. Zech. 10.3 begins with an oracle against the shepherds, but the divine oracles in ch. 10 do not discuss these shepherds anymore. This is different from both Jer. 23 and Ezek. 34, which are concerned with the 'shepherds', that is, human leadership of the nation. Instead, Zech. 10 deals with God's saving acts by which he will bring the exiles back. In other words, the threat against the shepherds in Zech. 10.3 does not have a function within the divine speech section. The most likely reason for its appearance here is that it derives from another text. That text may be Jer. 23.1-4, or perhaps a similar text that has not been preserved.

With the exception of a few words and expressions like שרק ('to whistle'); זנח ('reject'); and גבר (D-stem, 'make mighty', or rather 'restore, repatriate', as in Arabic *jabara*); חיה (D-stem, 'to raise'); and בית יוסף ('the house of Joseph'), all the words and phrases in the divine oracle are Jeremianic (i.e. either typically Jeremianic, or in any case attested in Jeremiah). One may perhaps dismiss this correspondence as happenstance, or resulting from the common subject matter. Yet it is in contrast to the prophetic comments on this oracle, and remarkable when compared to several other sections, the language of which is hardly or not at all Jeremianic. One may therefore consider the question why some sections refer extensively to Jeremiah, and others hardly, or not at all.

b. *Zechariah 9.17–10.2 and 11.1–4, 17*

The delineation of literary sections in Zech. 9–11 is disputed, especially the place, function, and origin of the small poems in 9.9-10, 10.1-2, 11.1-3 and 11.17. Even though these poems are form-critically and prosodically distinct, they have connections to the preceding and following sections, and are 'link passages between larger blocks of material' (Larkin 1994: 91). This is most obvious in the case of 10.1-2, which is linked by the motif of fertility with 9.17, and by the sheep and shepherd motif with 10.3. Likewise, 11.1-3 shares some terms with 10.10-12, but it is also indirectly linked to 11.4.

The latter case is most instructive. In itself, Zech. 11.1-3 shows many correspondences to Jer. 25.34-38, but this may in part be attributed to the use of the same literary form. Zech. 11.1-3 is also closely related to 10.3-12, especially 10.10-12, in sharing the catchwords 'Lebanon' (10.10 and 11.1) and גאון ('pride' or 'thicket', 10.11 and 11.3). In addition there are some indirect correspondences. Jer. 50.19, which corresponds in part to Jer. 23.3 (which in turn corresponds to Zech. 10.8, 10), links Bashan (Zech. 11.2) to Gilead (Zech. 10.10); but then, the association of such names need not be literary at all, but could be based in geography. Another link between Zech. 10.10 and 11.1-2 is furnished by Jer. 22.6-7 which has the same geographical names (Gilead and Lebanon), and a few other correspondences, namely, 'cedars', 'fire', and the use of נפל. Compare also Bashan and Lebanon in Jer. 22.20.

On the other hand, Zech. 11.1-3 is also connected with 11.4-17. Stade already pointed out that Zech. 11.3 and 11.4 correspond to vv. 5 and 3 of Jer. 12, respectively. The phrase 'the pride [or: jungle] of Jordan' is found only in Zech. 11.3 and in Jeremiah, twice connected with a 'lion' which threatens the flock (Jer. 49.19; 50.44), and once more in Jer. 12.5. Again, הרגה, 'slaughter', is found only in Zech. 11.4 and 7, and in Jeremiah: twice in the phrase גיא ההרגה (Jer. 7.32 and 19.6), but also in Jer. 12.3, where it is related to יצא, just as in Zech. 11.4. Many scholars call this correspondence 'striking' (e.g. Mason 1973: 143), and it is sometimes presented as an intentional authorial or editorial linking of the passages. However, apart from these two correspondences there is little else in Jer.

12 which corresponds with Zech. 11.1-3 or 4-17. An indirect connection is found in the word לטבחה (cf. also Jer. 11.19, לטבוח), which reminds one of לטבוח in Jer. 25.34, the section that has many verbal correspondences with Zech. 11.2-3. However striking these connections may seem, they could still be coincidental; but if they are intentional, they suggest that an author or editor deliberately used allusions to Jeremiah in order to link 10.3-12 to 11.4-17.

The place of Zech. 10.1-2 is even more complicated. Zech. 10.1 is linked to 9.17 by the fertility motif, whereas 10.2 is linked to 10.3 by the shepherd and flock motif. The themes of Zech. 10.1-2, YHWH as the giver of fertility and the condemnation of divination, are linked in the Jeremiah/ Deuteronomist tradition (Mason 1973: 73-79), and Jer. 14.14-22 is probably the source passage of Zech. 10.1-2 (Larkin 1994: 86-90). Yet, apart from these links there is also a link between Zech. 9.17 and the divine oracles of Zech. 10.3-10. The present text of Zech. 9.17 corresponds to Jer. 31.12-14. Both texts have the words טוב ('goodness'); דגן ('grain'); תירוש ('new wine'); בחורים ('young men'); and בתלות/בתלה ('young woman', or 'women'); whereas, the immediately preceding verses, Jer. 31.10-11, but also vv. 7-8, display numerous idiomatic correspondences with the divine oracles of Zech. 10.3-12.

Zech. 11.17 is not a real transition poem like the other ones, but it relates to the preceding, and it 'appeals to the tradition of Jeremiah' (Larkin 1994: 138). A correspondence consisting of חרב על and the verb יבש ('dry up'), is found in Jer. 50.35, 38, and Zech. 11.17. Larkin suggests that Zech. 10.1-2, 11.1-3, and 11.17 have possibly been composed to stand where they are (Larkin 1994: 138; Tigchelaar 1996: 93-94).

In short, three of the transition poems as well as the divine oracles in Zech. 10.3-12 seem to allude to Jeremiah. The same pertains to the very end of the first section (9.17) and the beginning of the third section (11.4) of Zech. 9–11. This is in contrast to the rest of Zech. 9 and the Shepherd Allegory of Zech. 11.4-16 (17) which hardly refer to Jeremiah, and certainly not in the same clear way as the transition poems and the divine oracles.

I would therefore argue that there are three major sections in Zech. 9–11. The first is Zech. 9.1-16, which has few correspondences to Jeremiah (with the possible, but disputed, allusions to Jeremiah in 9.11, אין מים בו; and 9.12, תקוה). The second is the Shepherd Allegory of 11.4-17, which does not have correspondences with Jeremiah apart from the very beginning (11.4) and end (11.17). The third consists of 9.17; 10.1-2; 10.3-

12; 11.1-3; 11.4, and 11.17, which are all linked, and which correspond with Jeremiah, even to some extent the prophetic comments in 10.3-12 that refer to Zech. 9. The Jeremianic phrasing in 9.17, 11.4, and 11.17 may be coincidental, or perhaps intentionally used by an editor to link these passages to 10.1-2, 10.3-12 and 11.1-3. But then, one may wonder whether this editor could not be the same as the author of 10.1–11.3. That is, the author of 10.3-12 was also responsible for the composition of 10.1-2, and 11.1-3, and for the composition or rephrasing of 9.17 and 11.4. In that case the Shepherd Allegory should be regarded as an already existing text which was included by means of 11.17 and a rephrasing of 11.4, into the text which is now Zech. 9–11. One might even consider the possibility that some of the alleged additions to the text, such as אֵין מַיִם בּוֹ in Zech. 9.11, or Zech. 11.6 with כִּי לֹא אֶחְמוֹל עוֹד, were added by the editor on the basis of Jer. 38.6 and 13.14.

In short, a focus on the correspondences between Deutero-Zechariah and Jeremiah suggests that the genesis of the text was a complex process, in which an author–editor reflected on Zech. 9 by means of adding prophetic comments to a divine oracle. The same author–editor also incorporated Zech. 11.4-16 and linked all these sections together by means of transitional poems. It may also be added that the absence of such transitional poems in Zech. 12–14, as well as the paucity of correspondences with Jeremiah in those chapters, suggests that the authors–editors of Zech. 12–14 were not identical to those of Zech. 9–11.

3. *A Relation with Which Jeremiah?*

The large number of correspondences with Jeremiah in Zech. 9–11 raises the question about the relation of the authors–editors of Deutero-Zechariah to the book of Jeremiah. First of all one should observe that even though sections of Deutero-Zechariah seem to draw upon the language of Jeremiah, there are extremely few cases where a phrase from Zech. 9–11 is identical to one found in the book of Jeremiah. The rare cases include common phrases such as נְאֻם יהוה, but also עַל הָרֹעִים and מֵאֶרֶץ מִצְרַיִם as a supplement of a form of הֵשִׁיב. It is tempting to interpret some of the correspondences between Deutero-Zechariah and Jeremiah as allusions or even exegesis, but there is no clear evidence that the authors–editors of Zech. 9–11 read and interpreted some form of Jeremiah. Can one, for example, say with Willi-Plein that the author of Zech. 9.11-17 used Jer. 31.10-20? Or, with Larkin, that Zech. 10.1-2 alludes to Jer. 14.14, 22?

Willi-Plein makes things even more complicated when she regards some of the correspondences with Jeremiah as late editorial glosses. On the other hand, she claims that most correspondences do not result from dependency, but are due to the use of similar literary forms.

Second, there is no consensus about either the development of the text of Jeremiah or the date of Zech. 9–11, and many relationships are conceivable. Person argues that Deutero-Zechariah was produced by a Deuteronomic redactor belonging to the same school as the early post-exilic Deuteronomic redactors of Jeremiah, and that Deutero-Zechariah was significantly influenced by several Deuteronomic passages in the Deuteronomic History and Jeremiah. Yet it is not clear to me how one should understand this 'influence'. Did the redactor of Deutero-Zechariah read Jeremiah, or was there a common Deuteronomic language which was used both in Jeremiah and Zechariah? Carroll's much-disputed model of an ongoing growth of the text in postexilic and exilic times, with a date of Jer. 30–31 in the fifth or fourth century (Carroll 1986: 72) would not be incompatible with a model in which the editor of Deutero-Zechariah belonged to the circles that wrote Jer. 30–31, though these circles need not be termed deuteronomistic. Or one may date Deutero-Zechariah in Hellenistic times and argue for a reinterpretation or rewriting in that period of earlier, in this case Jeremianic, prophecy. Here one is dealing with diverging models, rather than with different interpretations of the concrete data.

Third, the correspondences between Deutero-Zechariah, in particular Zech. 9–11, and Jeremiah, suggest a complex relationship. Zech. 9.17–11.4, 17 corresponds to many different verses and sections (not only deuteronomistic ones!) from Jeremiah, which would seem to suggest a knowledge of some form of the book. Yet, there are two Jeremianic sections in particular which correspond to Zechariah, namely, Jer. 23.1-8 and Jer. 30–31. Above I argued that the divine oracles of Zech. 10.3-12 would be dependent on Jer. 23.1-8 or a similar text. The dates of both Jer. 23.1-8 and of Jer. 30–31 are disputed, with most scholars thinking that some parts of these sections may be quite late. It should be noted that many of the correspondences with Zechariah are found in these alleged late parts of Jeremiah, for example, Jer. 31.10-14, which has correspondences with both the divine oracles in Zech. 10.3, 8, 9, 10, and Zech. 9.17. Most interestingly, these correspondences also concern words which are not typically Jeremianic at all, for example, פדה in Jer. 31.11 (cf. also Jer. 15.21) and פדיתים in Zech. 10.8; and דגן and תירש in Jer. 31.12 (nowhere else in Jeremiah) and Zech. 9.17. The easiest conclusion would be that since Zech. 9–11 corresponds with both Jer. 31.10-14 and other, older, parts in Jer. 30–31, the author–editor of Zech. 9–11 must have had access to a more or less final version of Jer. 30–31. For a similar kind of argument see Unterman (1987: 45-46), who argues that Isa. 35 uses the vocabulary and thoughts of Jer. 31.7–9, 10-14, which would suggest an early joining of the different sections of Jer. 31. Yet one cannot but speculate on other possibilities too. If one departs from the idea of ongoing revisions of and additions to prophetic texts in postexilic circles, couldn't it be possible then that the author–editor of Zech. 9–11 belonged to one of these circles that added to the book of Jeremiah? In other words, some of the correspondences with Jeremiah would result from the author–editor's knowledge of the book of Jeremiah, whereas other correspondences with Jeremiah may result from the fact that the circles from which the author–editor of Zech. 9–11 stemmed also revised the book of Jeremiah.

DEUTERONOMIC TOPONYMS IN SECOND ZECHARIAH

Raymond F. Person, Jr

In his 1973 dissertation Rex Mason suggested that the community that produced Second Zechariah (Zech. 9–14) stood within the 'Jeremiah/Deuteronomist tradition' (1973: 96-97). The following two quotes demonstrate the close connection Mason observed between Second Zechariah and 'the Jeremiah/Deuteronomist tradition':

> [Second Zechariah] is setting his own prophetic word deliberately in the spirit of the Jeremiah/Deuteronomist tradition from which he draws, in order to apply the same spirit of polemic against the false spiritual direction in terms of the situation of the community of his own day, as he sees it. (1973: 97-98)

> Some striking similarity of thought in particular to that of the circles amongst whom the words and traditions of Jeremiah received expansion can be detected. (1973: 131)

Although Mason was not explicit about what he meant by the phrase 'Jeremiah/Deuteronomist tradition', he refers favorably to the work of J. Philip Hyatt (1956) and Ernest Nicholson (1970), both of whom argue for a Deuteronomic redaction of Jeremiah (Mason 1973: 364 n. 40, 374 n. 19, 415, 418).

Building upon previous work suggesting Deuteronomic influence in the book of Jeremiah, Hyatt (1956, 1984a, 1984b) was the first to propose a Deuteronomic redaction of Jeremiah. Nicholson (1970, 1973) expanded upon Hyatt's understanding of a Deuteronomic redaction of Jeremiah by arguing that not only the 'prose sermons' (source C), but also the prose biographical narratives (source B) were Deuteronomic. Since Mason refers to the work of Hyatt and Nicholson, we can assume that he understands the 'Jeremiah/Deuteronomist tradition' to refer to the Deuteronomic scribes that redacted the book of Jeremiah.

In my own dissertation (Person 1993), I adapted the method used by Hyatt and others in arguing for a Deuteronomic redaction of the book of

Jeremiah to examine the redaction of the book of Zechariah.[1] Due to the prevalence of Deuteronomic language and themes, I concluded that the prose in Second Zechariah was Deuteronomic prose analogous to that in the book of Jeremiah. That is, Second Zechariah is the product of the Deuteronomic school reinterpreting Zech. 1–8 for a later historical and theological context just as, for example, the 'prose sermon' in Jer. 7 is the product of the Deuteronomic school reinterpreting earlier materials from the Jeremiah tradition. Thus, the conclusion I reached in my dissertation can be understood as a further exploration of Mason's observation that Second Zechariah was a reinterpretation of Zech. 1–8, which also stood within the 'Jeremiah/Deuteronomist tradition'.

Below I assume the validity of my conclusion that Second Zechariah is the product of a Deuteronomic redactor and explore further the implications of this conclusion as they relate to some of the toponyms found in Second Zechariah.[2] In fact, Mason himself noted close similarities between some of these toponyms and their use in the Deuteronomic 'prose sermon' of Jer. 31 (Mason 1973: 266-67).

1. *Deuteronomic Toponyms in Second Zechariah*

The following discussion of the toponyms is arranged according to the order in which they appear in Second Zechariah. As we will see, some of the toponyms used in Second Zechariah appear to be Deuteronomic ways

---

1. Some scholars have misinterpreted the emphasis in my dissertation on the relationship of Second Zechariah to Deuteronomic literature as suggesting that I did not recognize the influence of other books on Second Zechariah. In fact, I agreed then and continue to agree with Mason's observation that Second Zechariah was significantly influenced by the books of Isaiah, Jeremiah, and Ezekiel (Person 1993: 22-24). The influence of these other books on Second Zechariah does not create a problem for my thesis of Deuteronomic redaction, since it is quite possible, if not likely, that Isaiah and Ezekiel were considered authoritative literature by the Deuteronomic school (Person 1993: 168-75). Of course, since most scholars limit the Deuteronomic school to the exilic period, I had to first argue that the Deuteronomic school's redaction of the Deuteronomic History and the book of Jeremiah continued into the postexilic period (Person 1993: 39-78). I have expanded this argument significantly in later studies (most extensively in Person 2002).

2. Although toponyms play a role in my argument for a Deuteronomic redaction of Zech. 9–14, they certainly are not the most important elements of the argument. The argument begins first and foremost with Deuteronomic phraseology that occurs in Zech. 9–14. See especially Person (1993: 84-97).

of referring to certain locations, some of which differ from other contemporaneous descriptions of the same locations.

The phrase 'the House of Joseph' as a way of referring to the northern
kingdom is found primarily in Deuteronomic literature (Josh. 17.17; 18.5;
Judg. 1.22, 35; 25.19, 21; 1 Kgs 11.28; Amos 5.6; Obad. 18; Zech. 10.6).

The phrase 'the thickets of Jordan' appears only in Jeremiah (12.5;
49.19; 50.44) and Second Zechariah (11.3). This phrase is used to describe
the dangerous wilderness of the Jordan, often in connection with lions on
the prowl (Jer. 49.19; 50.44; Zech. 11.3).

The toponym 'the Mount of Olives' is found only in Second Zechariah
(twice in 14.4), where it clearly refers to the mountain 'before Jerusalem
on the east'. However, in 2 Sam. 15.30 the mountain just outside of Jerusalem where David flees is uniquely referred to as 'the Ascent of Olives'.
These two toponyms appear to be describing the same mountain outside
of Jerusalem and, since these are the only two references to a 'Mount/
Ascent of Olives' in the Hebrew Bible, this suggests a possible connection
between them.

The next four toponyms discussed are all found in Zech. 14.10 in the
eschatological description of Judah and Jerusalem. They are 'from Geba to
Rimmon', 'the Gate of Benjamin', 'the Corner Gate', and 'the Tower of
Hananel'.

The phrase 'from Geba to Rimmon' occurs only in Second Zechariah
(14.10), but has some indications of Deuteronomic influence. The influence of Deuteronomic style is suggested by the cumulative effect of the
following observations. (1) Although the structure of 'from [toponym] to
[toponym]' appears throughout the Hebrew Bible, the only other occurrence of Geba in this structure is in 2 Kgs 23.8 ('from Geba to Beersheba'). (2) The phrases 'from Geba to Beersheba' (2 Kgs 23.8) and 'from
Dan to Beersheba' (Judg. 20.1; 1 Sam. 3.20; 2 Sam. 3.10; 17.11; 24.2, 15;
1 Kgs 4.25) are distinctively Deuteronomic ways to refer to Judah and all
of Israel, respectively. This is especially clear when we note that these
phrases do not occur in Chronicles, with two exceptions (1 Chron. 21.2 [=
2 Kgs 24.2]; 2 Chron. 30.5) where the order of the names is reversed
('from Beersheba to Dan'). (3) Rimmon, situated near Beersheba, was
closely related to Beersheba (see Josh. 15.28-32) and was repopulated in
the postexilic period (Neh. 11.29) while Beersheba was not. The change in
circumstances from the pre-exilic to the postexilic period, therefore,
necessitated the change from 'Geba to Beersheba' to 'Geba to Rimmon' as

the Deuteronomic manner of referring to Judah in the postexilic period.[3] (5) The toponym 'Geba' occurs more frequently in Deuteronomic literature (Josh. 20.17; 18.24; Judg. 20.10, 33; 1 Sam. 13.3, 16; 14.5; 2 Sam. 5.25; 1 Kgs 15.22; 2 Kgs 23.8; Zech. 14.10) than other literary corpora (Isa. 10.29; Ezra 2.26; Neh. 7.30; 11.31; 12.29; 1 Chron. 6.45 [= Josh. 20.17]; 8.6; 16.6). Given all of these observations, the phrase 'from Geba to Rimmon' in Zech. 14.10 probably represents a development of the distinctively Deuteronomic phrase 'from Geba to Beersheba' to refer to Judah with the necessary change required by the new circumstances of the postexilic period—that is, Beersheba was no longer inhabited, but its closely related sister-city Rimmon was.

'The Gate of Benjamin' is mentioned only in Jer. 20.2; 37.13; 38.7; Ezek. 48.32; Zech. 14.10, and may be a Deuteronomic name for this gate. This possibility is strengthened further by the observation that the roughly contemporaneous descriptions of the Jerusalem walls and gates in Neh. 2.11–3.32 and 12.27-43 omit 'the Gate of Benjamin', probably referring to the same gate by a different name.[4] In fact, the omission of 'the Gate of Benjamin' in Nehemiah has led to various attempts to identify it with a gate mentioned in Nehemiah, assuming that the description in Nehemiah used another name for the same gate. For example, Mitchell (1912: 350) identified 'the Gate of Benjamin' with 'the Sheep Gate' (Neh. 12.39), Cohn (1986: 141) identified it with 'the Fish Gate' (Neh. 12.39), and Williamson (1985: 210-11) has suggested the 'Muster Gate' (Neh. 3.31).

Other than in Zech. 14.10, the toponym 'the Corner Gate' appears only four times in the Hebrew Bible. The first reference is in the Deuteronomic History (2 Kgs 14.13), which has influenced its use in Chronicles (2 Chron. 25.23 [= 2 Kgs 14.13]; 26.9). The other reference is in Jeremiah

---

3.   Although they did not conclude that 'Geba to Rimmon' is Deuteronomic, the following commentators argued that 'Geba to Rimmon' expresses the northern and southern limits of Judah as does 'Geba to Beersheba' in 2 Kgs 23.8: Dentan (1956: 1112); Elliger (1950, II: 172); Mason (1977: 129); Mitchell (1912: 348); Schaefer (1995: 84).

4.   *Contra* Redditt (1994: 676), who argues that the 'the Gate of Benjamin' and 'the Corner Gate' simply were in the northern wall that was completely destroyed by the Babylonians and, therefore, these gates were not rebuilt by Nehemiah. However, the toponyms 'the Sheep Gate' and 'the Fish Gate' would then need to refer to two gates in the same northern wall that were built where no previous gate existed. This is less likely than 'the Gate of Benjamin' and 'the Corner Gate' referring to the same two gates as 'the Sheep Gate' or 'the Fish Gate'.

(31.38).[5] Therefore, all of the references to 'the Corner Gate' may have their origin in a particular Deuteronomic way of referring to this gate. This observation is strengthened in that the roughly contemporaneous descriptions of the Jerusalem walls and gates in Neh. 2.11–3.32 and 12.27-43 omit 'the Corner Gate', probably referring to the same gate by a different name. In fact, the omission of 'the Corner Gate' in Nehemiah has led to various attempts to identify it with a gate mentioned in Nehemiah, assuming that the description in Nehemiah used another name for the same gate. For example, Smith (1972, I: 201-202), Avi-Yonah (1954: 240), Mitchell (1912: 350), and Williamson (1985: 204-205) all have identified 'the Corner Gate' with 'the Old Gate'/'the Mishneh Gate' (Neh. 3.6; 12.39).

'The Tower of Hananel' is mentioned only four times in the Hebrew Bible (Jer. 31.38; Zech. 14.10; Neh. 3.1; 12.39). In each of these books, this name is found in the description of the limits of the city wall of Jerusalem (Jer. 31.38; Zech. 14.10; Neh. 12.39). Given the close similarities between Zech. 14.10 and the book of Jeremiah concerning 'the Gate of Benjamin' and 'the Corner Gate', 'the Tower of Hananel' may also be a Deuteronomic name for this tower as reflected in Jer. 31.38.[6]

We can now reach some conclusions concerning toponyms in Deuteronomic literature, including Second Zechariah. First, it appears that due to the long span of time during which the Deuteronomic school redacted its literature, the Deuteronomic school by necessity revised some of its ways of referring to places. The most obvious example would be the change from the phrase 'from Geba to Beersheba' to the phrase 'from Geba to Rimmon' as a way to refer to Judah due to the fact that Beersheba was not rebuilt in the postexilic period. Second, Deuteronomic toponyms sometimes differ from toponyms used by others who may have been roughly contemporaneous. The most obvious examples would be the toponyms 'the Gate of Benjamin' and 'the Corner Gate' in Zech. 14.10, which may refer to gates mentioned in Nehemiah even though these toponyms are not present there.[7]

---

5.   Mason (1973: 266-67) also noted the close connection between Zech. 14.10 and Jer. 31.38-40 on the basis of 'the Corner Gate'.

6.   Mason (1973: 266-67) also noted the close connection between Zech. 14.10 and Jer. 31.38-40 on the basis of 'the Tower of Hananel'.

7.   The difference in toponyms between Zech. 14.10 and Nehemiah may suggest the dating of Second Zechariah to the period between the prophetic careers of Haggai and Zechariah and Nehemiah's mission—that is, the Deuteronomic school continued to use the toponyms from pre-exilic Jerusalem but when Nehemiah rebuilt the walls of

2. *Implications*

In my monograph *The Deuteronomic School* (Person 2002) I have argued that the Deuteronomic school probably returned to Jerusalem under Zerubbabel to support the restoration of the temple cult with its scribal duties. After the temple was rededicated, many of the hopes placed on its rebuilding went unfulfilled. The further the Deuteronomic school got from the rededication of the temple the more the Deuteronomic school became disenfranchized with its participation in the Persian-controlled Jerusalem administration. This unfulfillment of hopes and the resulting disillusionment led to an increasingly eschatological perspective. This disillusionment and increasingly eschatological perspective probably led to the Deuteronomic school's demise. Most likely the Persian imperial administration became increasingly concerned about the changing attitude of the Deuteronomic school and reasserted its control over the Jerusalem administration in the missions of Ezra and Nehemiah, two more loyal Jewish subjects who reformed the Jerusalem administration. It is in the context of this increasing conflict between the Deuteronomic school and the Persian imperial administration that I place the Deuteronomic composition of the prose in Second Zechariah (Person 1993: 166-68, 177-81).

The foregoing discussion of toponyms demonstrates the connection between Second Zechariah and earlier Deuteronomic literature, on the one hand, and the difference between Second Zechariah and Nehemiah, on the other hand. Thus, the above discussion provides some qualified support to my arguments for the Deuteronomic composition of the prose in Second Zechariah as well my reconstruction of the history of the Deuteronomic school. All of these arguments have been influenced by Mason's observation that Second Zechariah draws from 'the Jeremiah/Deuteronomist tradition'.

Jerusalem new toponyms were used. If so, then this would lend qualified support to the dating of Second Zechariah by linguistic criteria as done by Andrew Hill (1982), who dated Second Zechariah to the time period between Haggai and Zechariah's prophetic careers (520 BCE) and Ezra's mission (458 BCE).

READING BETWEEN THE LINES:
ZECHARIAH 11.4-16 IN ITS LITERARY CONTEXTS

Mark J. Boda

1. *Introduction*

When Rex Mason embarked on his study of inner biblical exegesis in the early 1970s, his focus was unabashedly historical. As he noted in his Introduction, the aim of his work was to identify 'principles of exegesis' and 'above all' to see if such principles afford 'any clue to the place of this author, or authors, in the developing traditio-history of the community of post-exilic Judaism' (Mason 1973: ii).

Mason's aims were natural for a scholar working within the parameters of the historical-critical paradigm, but even in his own day a hermeneutical shift was already underway. This shift would move the focus from authorial intention to reader impression and redefine (or at least supplement) the methodologies used for the study of the Hebrew Bible. The recognition of this hermeneutical shift and its implications for the study of intertextuality can be discerned in two recent works that focus on the book of Isaiah.

Benjamin Sommer introduces his book on allusion in Isa. 40–66 by orienting his readers to the academic discipline of intertextual studies (1998: 6-14). Sommer wisely identifies two main streams of scholarship, distinguishing between those focused on 'influence/allusion' and those focused on what he calls 'intertextuality'.[1] According to Sommer (1998: 6), the approach of the former group is diachronic in character, 'asking how one composition evokes its antecedents, how one author is affected by another, and what sources a text utilizes'. In this way it is focused on the author–text relationship. The approach of the latter is synchronic in

---

1.   See also the essays in Draisma (1989), especially those by Vorster, Voelz, Delorme, and van Wolde; and the essays in Fewell (1992), especially those by Fewell, Beal, and Miscall. Both Snyman (1996) and Hatina (1999) note the fundamental difference between intertextuality and historical studies.

nature, focusing 'not on the author of a text but either on the text itself (as part of a larger system) or on the reader'. This synchronic method 'interprets signs in the text by associating them with related signs in the reader's own mind' (Sommer 1998: 7).

Although presenting the two approaches fairly, Sommer adopts the diachronic approach of influence/allusion to guide his study of Isa. 40–66 because 'some authors call attention to their own allusivity; they seem to insist on their relation to earlier texts'. An exclusive intertextual approach 'would lead a critic to overlook an important aspect of the text at hand' (1998: 9).[2]

Similar to Sommer, Richard Schultz, in his recent volume on 'verbal parallels' in prophetic material, also identifies these same two aspects of intertextual analysis. For Schultz, the *diachronic* phase of analysis examines the 'historical factors which may have produced or influenced the use of quotation' (1999: 229). This phase demands attention to the identification of the source and its context and also the determination of the historical context that prompted the quotation. His *synchronic* phase shifts attention to the function of the repeated language within texts to examine its literary impact on the reader (1999: 232-33).

In contrast to Sommer, however, Schultz encourages an intertextual approach that incorporates both diachronic and synchronic analyses.[3] By incorporating both approaches into his interpretive framework, Schultz avoids the extreme of an intertextual analysis that merely catalogues connections to earlier texts (diachronic extreme) as well as the extreme of an intertextual analysis that only explores the musings of the postmodern mind (synchronic extreme).

Following Schultz's lead, this article will build on the previous work of

2.   See further the vigorous debate between Eslinger and Sommer. Eslinger (1992) advocates an abandonment of traditional inner biblical exegesis in favour of a synchronic ahistorical approach. Sommer maintains a place for both diachronic and synchronic studies, although wary that at times the synchronic 'masks an abdication of critical rigor' (1996: 488). Similar debates are underway in New Testament studies; cf. Hays and Green (1995) and Litwak (1998). This is displayed vividly in the debate between Beale (1999, 2001), Moyise (1999), and Paulien (2001) over the book of Revelation. Two recent collections, Marguerat and Curtis (2000) and Moyise (2000), reveal enduring variation in intertextual approaches within the biblical guild.

3.   One should not forget that Sommer does see a place for synchronic approaches, as the previous note asserted. It should also be admitted that Schultz's 'synchronic' analysis is not concerned with the discovery of further intertexts, but rather how the intertexts identified diachronically impact the reading process.

Rex Mason by analyzing Zech. 11.4-16 both diachronically and synchronically.[4] A diachronic analysis will identify connections between Zech. 11.4-16 and two prophetic pericopae in the book of Ezekiel (chs. 34 and 37) and interpret Zech. 11.4-16 within its historical context in light of these connections. Then with synchronic sensibilities it will identify the way that this interpretation impacts the reading of Zech. 9–14 as a whole. For full bibliography see Boda (2003a, 2003b).

2. *Zechariah 11.4-16*

a. *Delimitation of the Text*
Although part of the larger literary complex of Zech. 9–14, Zech. 11.4-16 is a discrete unit. That it is a distinct unit from the preceding text unit in 11.1-3 is clear not only from my form-critical analysis, below, which will highlight the sign-act form in 11.4-16, but also from the initial phrase of 11.4, כה אמר יהוה אלהי. Although it is possible that subsequent textual unit, Zech. 11.17, is merely the conclusion to the sign-acts,[5] two of its features suggest that it is a separate unit.[6] First of all, on the formal level, 11.17 contrasts vv. 4-16 with its sign-act form by employing the 'woe' oracle common in prophetic literature (see especially Isa. 5). This form is the declaration of curse and judgment on those who have met the disapproval of God.[7] Typically it includes three elements: the declaration 'woe', the identification of the recipient of judgment, and then usually details of the judgment or accusation (see Floyd 2000: 649). Second, in terms of content, 11.17 announces disaster for a shepherd, contrasting vv. 4-16, which has enacted judgment on the flock.

---

4. In doing so I am risking the displeasure of van Wolde, who has attacked recent studies for using 'intertextuality as a modern literary theoretical coat of veneer over the old comparative approach' (1989: 43). One should not overlook the work of Schaefer (1992, 1993a, 1993b, 1995) who considers the allusion technique of Zech. 14 in depth as part of a larger study of the overall shape of the book of Zechariah.

5. So Mason (1973: 167) and Petersen (1995: 99). These scholars argue from Ezek. 24.1-14 that a 'woe' oracle can be inserted into a larger form unit. However, in this example the 'woe' oracles are introduced by messenger formulae (כה אמר אדני יהוה), unlike Zech. 11.17.

6. Many have treated 11.17 as part of 11.4-16; e.g. Cook (1993) and Redditt (1993). Others have tried to connect 11.17 to 13.7-9, even rearranging the text to accomplish this; e.g. Mitchell (1912: 314-19). This is offensive to the redactor's purpose in Zech. 9–14, see further below.

7. As opposed to the use of 'woe' as a cry of lamentation (see Ezek. 2.10).

b. *Genre*

Zech. 11.4-16 contains the elements of a prophetic form displayed throughout the books of Jeremiah and Ezekiel, the prophetic sign-act.[8] This form, also evident in Zech. 6.9-15 (Boda 2001), has three basic elements: exhortation, execution, and explanation. God first commands the prophet to perform an action (exhortation) and this action is reported by the prophet (execution) and interpreted by God (explanation). Although the exhortation is always the first element, the order of the others can vary and sometimes one of these elements is absent.[9]

Zech. 11.4-16 contains three sign-acts introduced by the three exhortations: רעה את־צאן ההרגה (11.4), השליכהו אל־היוצר (11.13), and קח־לך כלי רעה אולי (11.15). The following chart lays out the basic elements of these sign-acts:

Sign-Act 1	Sign-Act 2	Sign-Act 3
Exhortation: 11.4-5[10] Explanation: 11.6 Execution: 11.7-12[11]		
	Exhortation: 11.13a[12] Execution: 11.13b	
Execution: 11.14[13]		
		Exhortation: 11.15 Explanation: 11.16

Although this does indicate three sign-acts, it appears that the second sign-act is incorporated into the execution section of the first. The resulting

---

8. So also Floyd (2000: 489-90). For the details of this form see Fohrer (1952); Fohrer (1968); Stacey (1990); and especially Friebel (1999, 2001).

9. Thus, in Jer. 13.1-11, some elements are repeated: exhortation (v. 1), execution (v. 2), exhortation (vv. 3-4), execution (v. 5), exhortation (v. 6), execution (v. 7), explanation (vv. 8-11). In Ezek. 5, the execution is not reported: exhortation (vv. 1-4), explanation (vv. 5-17). Notice how in Ezek. 5 the exhortation also contains some foreshadowing of the explanation (vv. 2b, 4b).

10. Verse 5 extends the exhortation by building the picture almost in allegorical style.

11. Verse 10b acts like an explanation, although different than the usual form because the prophet is speaker rather than God; v. 11 acts like a prophetic confirmation formula (knew it was the word of the Lord).

12. Prompted by the execution in v. 12 of Sign-Act 1.

13. Verse 14b, like v. 10b, acts like an explanation although the prophet is speaker rather than God.

structure indicates two basic sign-act reports—one focused on a good shepherd and the other a foolish shepherd.[14]

Some have suggested that this passage represents an allegory or parable, rather than a sign-act.[15] Indeed, Zech. 11.4-16 does transform and expand the sign-act form at points. In v. 5, the image introduced by the exhortation in v. 4 is expanded to include buyers, sellers and shepherds. Although the exhortation is limited to the simple imperative, רעה את־צאן ההרגה, the execution is very detailed (taking two staffs) and includes the reaction of the flock to the fulfilment of the exhortation. The interpretation in v. 16, continues the shepherd motif introduced in the sign-act, rather than reveal its referent in reality (as v. 6). Finally, contrary to the earlier prophetic sign-acts, it is uncertain whether this sign-act was ever acted out by the prophet. These expansions and transformations in the form may be reason enough to conclude that here we find an allegorical use of the sign-act form.[16]

c. *Content*

In typical sign-act fashion, the passage begins with an exhortation in the imperative mood as the prophet is to assume the role of a shepherd. Some have assumed this is a reference to the prophet as shepherd (e.g. Mason 1973: 140; Larkin 1994: 114), but roles laid on the prophet in sign-acts are usually not related to the vocation of a prophet, but rather merely function as a vehicle for communication. In this case, the prophet as shepherd is representing God's appointed leadership of his people.[17]

The first indication that this sign-act will not be positive for the people comes in the initial line as the flock is described as the flock of slaughter

14. So, e.g., Cook (1993: 456) and Petersen (1995: 100-101); *contra* Redditt (1993), who sees both shepherds as evil/foolish. Redditt fails to see that the sign-act is directed at the community not at leadership, that the first shepherd pledges to care for the weak of the flock, and that he removes three shepherds as part of this protection.

15. See the discussion in Meyer (1977: 225-27) and Petersen (1995: 89). Although Larkin stresses the allegorical/parabolic genre, she does note closeness stylistically to the prophetic sign-act (1994: 132-34).

16. Nevertheless the suggestion by some that this is a prophetic commissioning is untenable considering the lack of elements from that genre (see Petersen 1995: 89).

17. This need not refer to royal leadership exclusively. See the debate in Meyer (1977), Redditt (1993) and Cook (1993). Sweeney (2000: II, 678-79) has recently suggested that the shepherd here is a reference to a priest who had care for the temple flocks for sacrifice, but this does not fit the image of the shepherd who was to protect the sheep from slaughter.

(הרגה). This slaughter is immediately linked to activities connected with the business of agriculture with people buying and selling sheep as the shepherds stand by. Slaughtering sheep for food was obviously the purpose of raising sheep in ancient societies, but this purpose is not part of the positive form of this metaphor in the Hebrew Bible where good shepherds protect their sheep from destruction while bad shepherds neglect their duties by not caring for the injuries of the sheep and allowing them to be eaten.[18] In Zech. 11, however, the indictment is not against the shepherds, but rather against the flock. Zech. 11.6, which functions as the explanation in the sign-act form (here a foreshadowing), reveals that it is God who is responsible for this slaughter of the ישבי הארץ. The people will be oppressed by their fellow human (רעהו)[19] as well as by those over them (מלכו).

Zech. 11.7-14 represents the execution of the first sign-act, signalled by the switch into autobiographical style. The shepherd is concerned for the עניי הצאן, a sign of good leadership in Israel, especially for the royal house which was commissioned to care for the oppressed (Ps. 72.2, 4, 12).[20] Furthermore, the names of the two staffs (נעם and חבלים) suggest a positive role for this shepherd.[21]

The positive picture of 11.7, however, is soon spoiled. The appointed shepherd must rid the flock of three shepherds. The verb כחד (hiphil) is used to speak of the annihilation of the Canaanites (Exod. 23.23), of the house of Jeroboam (1 Kgs 13.34), of the Assyrian army (2 Chron. 32.21), and of Israel as a nation (Ps. 83.5), suggesting that the shepherd did more

18.   *Contra* Petersen (1995: 91), who identifies the problem as the slaughter of the entire flock, and Sweeney (2000: 678-79), who links the flock to temple sacrifice. The problem here is *any* slaughter.

19.   Some have repointed the vowels of the Hebrew term רעהו, which translates 'neighbor', in order to produce the reading 'shepherd'; cf. Mitchell (1912: 304), Petersen (1995: 87) and Hanson (1979: 340). Although possible, it appears that v. 6 has moved to the interpretation phase of the sign-act, thus leaving the shepherd motif.

20.   Redditt's textual emendation at this point (1993: 684) is inappropriate.

21.   There is some debate over the precise meaning of these two implements. The names associated with the two staffs in Zech. 11 are נעם and חבלים. The staff called נעם which is linked to בריתי אשר כרתי את־כל־העמים (v. 10), is most likely a reference to God's use of the nations to bring blessing upon Israel, especially as seen in the Persian period with the restoration of the community in Yehud. The staff called חבלים which is linked to the האחוה בין יהודה ובין ישראל (v. 14) is most likely representative of the peaceful redistribution of the land in the restoration from exile (cf. Josh. 17.5, 14; 19.10; Ezek. 47.13). Cf. Boda (forthcoming).

than just 'fire' the shepherds.[22] Numbers are used here symbolically to refer to totality (three shepherds) and brevity (one month).[23] This removal of the shepherds is probably the cause of the tension that then arises between the shepherd and his flock. The phrase ותקצר נפשי is used elsewhere to refer to one's inability to endure a particular state of affairs.[24] The shepherd's impatience is matched by the flock's disgust (בחלה).

This mutual rejection has serious repercussions for both parties. The shepherd announces his intention to resign and describes the impact of this decision on the community as a whole (11.9). This verbal notice is followed by two symbolic gestures linked to the two staffs identified earlier. By breaking the first staff (11.10) the shepherd revokes his relationship with כל־העמים, a reference to the buyers and sellers of 11.5. Before breaking the second staff (11.14), the shepherd reports his request for payment of wages. The request for payment is addressed to העמים at the end of 11.10. The shepherd, however, follows the command of God by throwing the payment into the temple, symbolizing his rejection of the payment while linking the payment of the nations to temple personnel. With the payment the first symbolic gesture is completed, signalling the end of the covenant with the nations. In 11.14 the shepherd proceeds to break the second staff and with it shatter the hopes of a united kingdom.

Zech 11.15-16 represents the final sign-act and with it the complete ful-filment of the word of Yahweh in 11.6. The removal of the good shepherd in 11.9 represented the first instalment of the fulfilment of 11.6 (אנכי ממציא את־האדם איש ביד־רעהו). The prophet assuming the role of a fool-ish shepherd represents the fulfilment of the second warning (וביד מלכו). The prophet is to take the equipment of a foolish shepherd. This equip-ment is not necessarily the staffs which were broken in the first sign-act, since the word עוד does not modify the imperative קח, but rather the introductory statement ויאמר יהוה אלי.[25] The folly of this shepherd is

---

22. Of course, this is a metaphorical context, so even the use of a death motif does not necessarily mean that the appointed leader killed other leaders.

23. For a review of the various attempts to identify these shepherds see Redditt (1993). Recently Sweeney (2000: II, 678) has suggested Cyrus, Cambyses, and Darius.

24. The people's impatience in the wilderness (Num. 21.4); Job's impatience over his sorry state (Job 21.4); Samson's inability to endure Delilah's nagging (Judg. 16.16); and God's inability to endure Israel's misery (Judg. 10.16).

25. For this see the form in Isa. 8.5, where clearly 'again' (עוד) refers to God's speech; cf. Ezek. 8.13; Hos. 3.1. Notice that in 2 Kgs 4.6 'again' (עוד) refers to the exhortation it follows it.

detailed in 11.16 where, in contrast to the good shepherd (11.7), this shepherd refuses appropriate care for the vulnerable of the flock (הנכחדות, הנצבה, הנשברת, הנער[26]) while devouring the healthy sheep.

These sign-acts in 11.4-16 speak of two situations involving two leaders within the community. The first situation involves the rejection of a leader appointed by God over the people, and the second God's raising up of a replacement leader who would destroy the people. The first leader is appointed by God, although in covenant with the nations who are intimately related to temple personnel. He begins his commission with good intentions, equipped with the appropriate tools for leadership and with a sensitivity to his people. Due to tension between the leader and his people, however, the covenant with the nations is terminated. This rejection of the leader and demise of the covenant with the nations puts an end to hopes of the renewal of a unified people. The second leader is also appointed by God. The designation 'foolish' is appropriate for in contrast to the first leader he has ill intent for his people, insensitively forsaking his obligation to protect the vulnerable while abusing the community for his own benefit.

3. *Diachronic Analysis: Zechariah 11.4-16 and Ezekiel*

a. *Connections*

For those familiar with the book of Ezekiel, it is difficult to ignore several key links to this earlier prophet, in particular Ezek. 34.1-31 and 37.15-28 (Mason 1973: 150-53; 1982: 349; Meyer 1977; Hanson 1979: 228-40, 343-47; Witt 1991: 60; Nurmela 1996: 136-46). Ezek. 34 contains a prophetic message to the leadership of Israel employing an extended metaphor of shepherd and flock imagery. God attacks the shepherds for feeding on the flock, promises to personally shepherd them, gathering them from the nations to their own land, appointing David as their רעה אחד (34.23), and renewing covenant with the people (34.31). Ezek. 37 contains a prophetic sign-act in which two sticks with names on them are fused, representing the promised union of Israel and Judah. As in Ezek. 34, the focus is on gathering the people from the nations, returning them to their

---

26. The fourth category, הנצבה, is a niphal participle from the root נצב ('to take one's stand', 'to stand') referring collectively to 'the firm-standing' or 'the healthy'. If this is correct it would be a unique occurrence in the Hebrew Bible. Some have suggested another root which would render 'exhausted ones' and fit the list better; see Petersen (1995: 86); Holladay (1988: 243).

own land, appointing David as king over them as רועה אחד (37.24), and renewing covenant with the people (37.23, 27).

Several elements in Zech. 11.4-16 betray reliance on these two passages. First, on the formal level, 11.4-16 represents a fusion of allegorical and sign-act forms, probably due to reliance on Ezek. 34 with its extended metaphor and Ezek. 37 with its sign-act.

Second, and more importantly, on the rhetorical level, 11.4-16 employs similar imagery and vocabulary. The characteristics of the foolish shepherd in Zech. 11.15-16 echo Ezekiel's description of shepherds in ch. 34. In Ezek. 34.3-4, Ezekiel paints a dark portrait of the 'shepherds of Israel' only to contrast it in 34.16 with that of God's compassionate care for the flock (בריא, Ezek. 34.3; Zech. 11.16; cf. Ezek. 34.20; אכל, Ezek. 34.3; Zech. 11.16; רפא [piel], Ezek. 34.4; Zech. 11.16; קום [hiphil] + רעה, Ezek. 34.23; Zech. 11.16; נשברת, Ezek. 34.16; Zech. 11.16; also cf. דרש, Ezek. 34.11, 16; בקש, Zech. 11.16).[27] Furthermore, both Ezek. 37.13-23 and Zech. 11.4-16 focus attention on the unity of the community by picturing two sticks that are connected to the northern and southern tribes and given names.[28]

b. *Reuse*

Having first established these links between Zech. 11.4-16 and these two prophecies in Ezekiel, we must now consider the way in which Zech. 11 is reusing them in a new context. Ezek. 34 declares judgment on the leadership of Israel who have not cared appropriately for their flock during the exile. God offers hope to the community by promising to assume this role himself and gather the scattered exiles. Ezek. 37 also offers hope to the exiles, a hope that the scattered tribes will be reunited in the land of Israel.

Zech. 11.4-16 reverses the hope expressed in these two Ezekiel passages.[29] Whereas Ezek. 34 promises the judgment of the shepherds and care by God, Zech. 11 promises God's judgment on the sheep through abandonment of the flock by the good shepherd and appointment of an inadequate evil shepherd. Whereas Ezek. 37 promises the union of the tribes, Zech. 11 promises disunity.

---

27. Mason (1973: 167); Witt (1991: 60); Nurmela (1996: 136-46).

28. Zech. 11.4-16 creatively intertwines these two passages from Ezekiel by transforming the sticks into staffs. This forces the reader to reflect on both passages simultaneously.

29. See Mason (1973: 150-53): 'Here the meaning of the sign in Ezekiel is exactly reversed'.

So far, my analysis has been limited to points of contact between Zech. 11.4-16 and Ezek. 34 and 37. But a closer look at these two Ezekiel passages reveals points of contact that they share which should shape our reading of Zech. 11.4-16.[30]

The points of contact that have been highlighted so far have been elements shared between Zech. 11 and Ezek. 34 exclusively from elements shared by Zech. 11 and Ezek. 37. The only point of contact shared by all three passages is the use of the motif of shepherd for human leadership. Zech. 11 gives little indication as to the identity of the shepherds. But in the light of the fact that it is reversing the expectations of Ezek. 34 and 37, do these earlier prophecies offer any insight into the identity of the shepherds?[31]

Although very different in genre and vocabulary, Ezekiel 34 and 37 intersect at two key points: 34.22-31 and 37.23-28. At these two points we

30. As per the encouragement of Schultz: 'A quotation is not intended to be self-contained or self-explanatory; rather a knowledge of the quoted context also is assumed by the speaker or author' (1999: 224). Ben-Porat (1985) has noted this technique in her presentation of the fourth stage of allusion: 'The reader activates the evoked text as a whole to form connections between it and the alluding text which are not based on the markers and marked items themselves' (cited in Sommer 1998: 12). Earlier she had said that 'the marker—regardless of the form its takes—is used for the activation of independent elements from the evoked text. Those are never referred to directly' (Ben-Porat 1976: 108-109). This has often been observed by New Testament scholars such as Dodd, who notes New Testament authors' technique in citing 'particular verses or sentences...as pointers to the whole context' so that 'it is the *total context* that is in view, and is the basis of the argument' (1952: 126). So also Wright (1996: 584) who speaks of writers in Second Temple Judaism 'conjuring up a world of discourse with a word or phrase'. An excellent example of this is the work of Schaberg on the genealogy of Jesus in Mt. 1, in which she shows how the allusions to the four women from the Old Testament are designed to prepare the reader for a fifth woman 'who becomes a social misfit in some way; is wronged or thwarted; who is party to a sexual act that places her in great danger; and whose story has an outcome that repairs the social fabric and ensures the birth of the child who is legitimate or legitimated' (1990: 32-34).

31. This raises the question of the identity of the shepherds in the passage. Although Cook (1993, 1995) argues for civil leaders, and Meyer (1977) argues for the royal house, many have considered this is a metaphor for the priestly establishment of the Persian period (see Hanson 1979; Redditt 1989). Floyd (2000: 487) suggests a 'quasi official group', similar to the counsellors to Joshua the High Priest (Zech. 3.8) who in turn advised the governor (Zech. 6.9-15). Petersen, however, warns against such precision because the texts are 'perspectival' rather than 'particular' reporting. 'Yahweh's general response to and perspective on the international scene (as in the first report) and the Judean scene (the second report)' (1995: 100-101).

find identical motifs and vocabulary: God will save his people (הושעתי, 34.22; 37.23) and set his servant David over them as prince (עבדי דוד נשיא, 34.23; 37.24) who is called 'one shepherd' (רעה אחד, 34.23; רועה אחד, 37.24); this is followed by a renewal of relationship as God makes a covenant of peace with them (כרתי להם ברית שלום, 34.25; 37.26) so that they will be his people and he their God (34.24, 31; 37.23). The good shepherd is identified as a Davidic descendant who will be רעה אחד, uniting the tribes of Israel once again.[32]

This evidence from the broader context of Ezek. 34 and 37 suggests that the good shepherd in Zech. 11.4-16 is a Davidic descendant. The foolish shepherd must then be someone from outside the Davidic line, evidence of the reversal of the promises of Ezek. 34 and 37.

c. *Historical Context*

In the light of this evidence from Ezek. 34 and 37, the good shepherd in Zech. 11.4-16 would be a Davidic descendant who led Yehud in the early Persian period. The primary candidate would be Zerubbabel who functioned as governor in the early part of Darius's reign.[33] Some have suggested that Sheshbazzar, who is called פחה in Ezra 5.14-16 and הנשיא ליהודה in Ezra 1.8, was of Davidic descent, but the evidence is not convincing.[34] The only other Davidide involved in leadership in Yehud was Zerubbabel's daughter Shelomith (1 Chron. 3.19), who ruled in a co-regency with her husband Elnathan after the rule of Zerubbabel.[35] Although it is possible that Shelomith could be in view in Zech. 11, it would be a stretch for an ancient community to connect a Davidic woman with the promises of

32. Although Ezek. 34.22-31 does not explicitly discuss the issue of the unity of the tribes (as does Ezek. 37.23-28), the reference to 'one shepherd' implies this theme.

33. There is no reason to question Zerubbabel's Davidic lineage as, for example, Pomykala does (1995: 46). Haggai and Zechariah both use language closely associated with the Davidic line and action; cf. Boda (2001, forthcoming).

34. See Japhet (1982), Lust (1987) and Bianchi (1994). Berger (1971) has refuted attempts to equate Sheshbazzar with the Davidic Shenazzar mentioned in 1 Chron. 3.17, while Ben-Yashar (1981) undermines the attempt of Bartel (1979) to equate Sheshbazzar with Zerubbabel. Williamson (1985: 17-18) has argued convincingly that the title הנשיא ליהודה used of Sheshbazzar in Ezra 1.8 is a traditio-historical allusion to the gifts of the הנשאים of the various tribes in Num. 7.

35. Cf. Meyers (1985; 1987: 509-10); Meyers and Meyers (1987: xl, 12-13); Williamson (1988: 75-77); Kessler (1992: 73); Carter (1999: 50-52). See also Ackroyd (1982) for his evaluation of debate over the order and names of governors in the early Persian Period.

Ezek. 34 and 37, especially since she ruled in tandem with a non-Davidide. Most likely, then, Zech. 11.4-16 reflects the transition of leadership at the end of Zerubbabel's tenure as governor. The fact that the good shepherd is paid by the owners and then throws this money into the temple precincts, not only reflects the accountability of the governor to the Persian over-lords, but also possible collusion between the temple and the Persians in the demise of political influence for the Davidic line.

There have been many theories as to the fate of Zerubbabel. According to Haggai and Ezra 2–5, he was instrumental in the rebuilding of the temple precincts, but record of his participation is silent after the foundation-laying ceremony of Hag. 2.10-23 (reflected also in Ezra 3; Zech. 4.6b-10a; 8.9-13). It may be significant that although he is mentioned in Ezra 5.2, once Tattenai, governor of Trans-Euphrates, enters the picture in 5.3, there are no more references to him. Is this absence significant?[36] Is it possible that Zerubbabel resigned from his post due to Persian policies in the wake of Babylonian and Egyptian revolts and Jewish political intrigue in the province of Yehud?[37]

In any case, in the light of the great expectations afforded Zerubbabel within the Zechariah tradition (Boda 2001), it is not fantastic to suggest that the end of his tenure would spark debate over the Davidic promises. In the light of Ezek. 34 and 37, Zech. 11.4-16 represents a prophetic inter-pretation designed to explain the waning influence of the Davidic line. The text traces this threat to the people's rejection of the Davidic shepherd and identifies the present inappropriate leadership as judgment from God, giving the people the kind of leadership they deserve.

4. *Synchronic Analysis: Zechariah 11.4-16 within Zechariah 9–14*

Although a discrete unit within Zech. 9–14, possessing unique origins, 11.4-16 has been placed into the larger complex of Zech. 9–14 where it

36. There is a reference to a 'governor' in Ezra 6.7 alongside the 'elders of the Jews', but Zerubbabel's name is not mentioned. This may be an intentional excision by the redactor of Ezra 1–6 who places greater focus on the elders, priests and prophets and avoids Zerubbabel's Davidic connection.

37. Many scholars have avoided this conclusion after Ackroyd's (1958) critique of Waterman (1954). However, see more recently Stern (1984: 72). For an excellent review of dating questions related to this issue see Kessler (1992). In contrast to Waterman's theory, Zech. 11.4-16 does not indicate a revolution led by Zerubbabel, but it may suggest a resignation due to frustration with certain elements within the Yehud community with links to Persian authority.

plays a significant role in our reading of its final form. Having read Zech. 11.4-16 diachronically my intention now is to allow these insights to influence our reading of the final form of Zech. 9–14.

The complex of prophetic pericopae which constitute Zech. 9–14 are distinguished from the remainder of the book of Zechariah by the absence of the superscription style used in Zech. 1.1, 7 and 7.1, and the appearance of the superscript משא דבר־יהוה.[38] This superscription, which appears at 9.1 and 12.1, is a redactional marker which in the final form of the text signals rhetorical divisions.[39]

The first two major pericopae (9.1-17 and 10.3b-12) show affinity through their positive tone, concern for Judah and Ephraim and focus on the return from exile. The first pericope depicts God as divine warrior re-capturing his palace/sanctuary and then defending, saving and prospering his people (9.1-8, 14-17).[40] In the midst of this depiction appears an address to Zion (placed strategically between vv. 8 and 14, in the transition between God's return to the sanctuary and his salvation of the people) which celebrates the arrival of the king[41] and the return of the exiles from Judah and Ephraim who will become God's weapons (9.9-13). The second pericope (10.3b-12) shows affinity with the qualities of ch. 9, both on a stylistic level (switching between first and third person), as well as on a thematic level (with reference to Judah, Ephraim and restoration). These two pericopae share key themes:

1. Restoration is inaugurated by the action of God, who breaks into Israel's history to instigate and complete redemption (9.1-8, 14-17; 10.3b, 6, 8-10, 12).

---

38. This does not mean that Zech. 9–14 are unrelated to Zech. 1–8 as they represent the enduring tradition of Zechariah. See Boda (2001, 2004).

39. Although this section is focused on the rhetoric of the final form of Zechariah 9–14, I agree largely with the redactional sensibilities of Redditt (1989, 1994, 1995).

40. The switch between first and third person in 9.1-8, 14-17 is not odd. One can see this in 9.1-8 where there is a move from third person (9.1-4) to first person (9.6-8) and then (in 9.14-17) back to third person.

41. The exact identity of this king here is difficult to discern. With God's statement of his arrival at his house and protection of it, one may surmise that this is thus an announcement to Zion of God's arrival as king. However, v. 10 seems to distinguish between 'I' (God) and 'he' (the king). Thus, this is probably a reference to a royal figure in Jerusalem, which, coupled with evidence of connections to the promise to Judah in Gen. 49, suggests an allusion to the restoration of Davidic kingship, *contra* Leske (2000).

2. Restoration is envisioned for both Judah and Ephraim as they are
    rescued from foreign bondage, although Judah has the leading
    role to play in this restoration (9.11-13, 16-17; 10.6-11).

3. The people are described as God's flock, a term emphasizing
    God's personal and caring leadership with the people (9.16;
    10.3b).

These two sections in chs. 9–10 contrast the two dominant pieces found in
chs. 12–14. A key structural marker throughout the two oracles in 12.1–
13.6 and 14.1-21 is the phrase ביום ההוא which appears at regular intervals
(12.3, 4, 6, 8, 9, 11; 13.1, 4; 14.4, 6, 8, 9, 13, 20, 21). Rather than Judah–
Ephraim, 12.1–13.6 and 14.1-21 focus on a different pair, Judah–Jerusalem, with no mention of Ephraim (12.2, 4-5, 7-8, 10; 13.1; 14.14, 21).

Whereas chs. 9–10 depict God's return to his sanctuary-city and subsequent rescue of his people from the nations, 12.1–13.6 and 14.1-21 picture
the attack of Jerusalem by all the nations of the earth, a battle in which
God intervenes on Jerusalem's behalf, defeats the nations, and makes Jerusalem a sanctified space (cleansed, holy).

Although each pericope has its unique internal logic and message, this
study has highlighted clear affinities within chs. 9–10 and 12–14. But to
this point I have not discussed several smaller pieces within Zech. 9–14,
namely, 10.1-3a; 11.1-3; 11.17, and 13.7-9. Each of these stands out
from the surrounding text by employing imperatival/attention vocabulary,
using a negative tone, and presenting the shepherd motif. Each of them
focuses on God's displeasure with shepherd leaders. There is a progression
between the various pieces, from the Lord's anger (10.1-3a), to the prophecy of destruction (11.1-3), to a curse (11.17), to the execution of judgment (13.7-9).

These smaller units that appear at regular intervals throughout Zech. 9–
14 display close affinity with the sign-acts of 11.4-16. Both use the
shepherd motif, depict a frustrating leadership situation, and highlight the
impact of such leadership on the community as a whole. The difference
between the two, however, is that while the smaller shepherd-units direct
judgment against the shepherds, 11.4-16 directs it against the flock.

In its central location in the rhetorical complex of Zechariah 9–14, 11.4-
16 transitions the reader from chs. 9–10 to 12–14. This is displayed most
vividly in the account of the breaking of two staffs. The breaking of the
first staff signifies להפיר את־בריתי אשר כרתי את־כל־העמים (11.10). The
breaking of the second staff signifies להפר את־האחוה בין יהודה ובין ישראל
(11.14). These two actions of breaking correspond to two key discon-

tinuities between the oracles in chs. 9–10 and 12–14, especially seen in the focus on God's destruction of 'all the nations' (העמים, 12.2, 3, 4, 6; 14.12, הגוים, 12.9; 14.2, 3, 14, 16, 18, 19), and the absence of reference to Israel in chs. 12–14.

Thus, Zech. 11.4-16 serves a crucial role in its final position in Zech. 9–14 by transitioning the reader from the expectations of chs. 9–10 to those of chs. 12–14. Hopes of reunification of the restored tribes under Davidic leadership are dashed because of the community's rejection of this leadership, and such rejection prompts God's promise of inappropriate leadership. God takes direct control of the leadership of the nation in chs. 12–14, even though a future hope for the Davidic line remains.

5. *Conclusion*

This study of Zech. 11.4-16 has attempted to demonstrate a balanced intertextual approach. Such an approach flows from the diachronic to the synchronic. It demands careful delineation of the sources of ancient texts and interpretation of any transformation to these sources in their new context. It also, however, involves the description of the impact of such allusion on the reading of the final form of the text, especially within the broader context of the literary corpus in which it presently resides.

By honing diachronic and synchronic sensibilities the interpreter is able to 'read between the lines' of the present text. Diachronic analysis brings into focus the various intertexts that inhabit the gaps 'between the lines' of the ancient text.[42] As we have discovered, these intertexts are more than just the limited words or phrases that are shared between the passages, but extend to the larger context in which these words or phrases are embedded. But it is not enough merely to bring the various intertexts 'between the lines' into focus, cataloguing their references and trans-formations. One must then reflect on the impact that such intertext has on the reading of the final form of the text embedded in its larger context.

---

42. A complementary image is that of the palimpsest, in which ancient text appears in the background; cf. Genette (1982, 1997), even if I do not embrace his approach to intertextuality.

ZECHARIAH 13.7-9 AS A TRANSITIONAL TEXT:
AN APPRECIATION AND RE-EVALUATION OF THE WORK OF REX MASON

James D. Nogalski

Nearly 30 years ago, Rex Mason's dissertation, 'The Use of Earlier Biblical Material in Zechariah IX–XIV: A Study in Inner Biblical Exegesis',
anticipated several of the developments that would take place in the study
of the Hebrew Bible in the coming decades. These issues include inner
biblical exegesis, the use of allusion and citation, and an emphasis upon
explaining the final form of the text (even when recognizing the composite
nature of that text). One of the passages to which Mason devotes special
attention is Zech. 13.7-9. Mason argues that this passage originally formed
the conclusion to 11.4-17. This paper will summarize Mason's arguments
for Zech. 13.7-9; it will survey how scholarship since Mason has reacted
to the views he expresses; and finally, it will suggest refining the model to
explain the similarities and differences noted by various scholars.

1. *Mason's Treatment of Zechariah 13.7-9*

Mason joins those who believe that Zech. 13.7-9 originally concluded the
shepherd passage of Zech. 11.4-17. So confident is he of this function that
he places his treatment of 13.7-9 after the chapter on 11.4-17 and before
the chapter on 12.1–13.6. The association of 13.7-9 with 11.4-17 also
underlies Mason's treatment of the imagery of 13.7-9, since much of the
discussion of the three-verse unit develops as a continuation of the chapter
on 11.4-17. Still, Mason does not merely assume that the two units are
related. He focuses heavily on the tradition-historical background of significant phrases in 13.7 and the formulation of the remnant motif in 13.8-9.

In an earlier chapter, Mason documents numerous points of contact
between the Shepherd Allegory of Ezekiel 37.15-28 and Zech. 11.4-17
(1973: 135-67). In his chapter on 13.7-9, Mason examines the tradition-
historical background of six words and phrases from 13.7. He concludes

that the prophetic tradition behind this verse, which is reflected in its imagery, continues the judgment announced in 11.4-17. Mason first explores the background of the use of 'sword' as a metaphor of divine judgment that has significant parallels, including Isa. 34.5-6; Jer. 47.6, and Ezek. 21. He next delves into the problem of identifying the background of the shepherd, siding with those who see the term used ironically to refer to an unworthy leader. Third, he cautiously concludes that the word גבר may carry messianic connotations, but, if so, they too are utilized ironically. Fourth, Mason finds the ironic use of the rare word 'neighbor' (עמית) in prophetic texts to be significant since the word normally appears in the legal codes of Leviticus. Finally, Mason finds similar reasons for judgment against the leaders in the 'smiting' of the shepherd, which leads to the scattering of the flock. He argues that all of these terms portray a decidedly negative attitude toward the leadership of Judah, one that is quite consistent with refutation of the current leadership in 11.4-17 (1973: 168-79).

Mason sees the formulation of the remnant motif of Zech. 13.8-9 as another point in which Zech. 13.7-9 connotes an outlook similar to Ezekiel traditions (1973: 180-87). He argues that the three-group division of the people destined for judgment reflects an affinity to Ezek. 5, where one third of the population will be killed inside the city, one third will be cut down around the city while trying to flee, and the remaining third will be scattered and then killed by Yahweh's sword. Mason notes that Ezek. 5 appears to have experienced a revision in Ezek. 5.3-4, which reinterprets the scattering to allow for a remnant of the third group to survive. It is this additional action against the final third that solidifies the impression, for Mason, that Zech. 13.7-9 draws upon Ezek. 5. He also notes that Ezekiel also uses the metaphor of smelting to connote total judgment in 22.17-22.[1] Mason notes that Ezekiel's own use of the smelting, however, differs from Zech. 13.8-9 in that Ezekiel's use of the imagery of smelting depicts complete destruction, not the creation of a remnant (1973: 184). Finally, Mason suggests that another combination of motifs strengthens the association of the broader context of Zechariah to Ezekiel. Mason notes that the smelting imagery of Ezek. 22.17-22 is followed by a message of judgment against the leadership, judgment whose sign is the lack of rain (Ezek. 22.23). He believes that the movement from smelting to rain exhibits parallels with the role of cleansing water in the broader context of Zech. 9–14 (cf. 10.1; 13.1; 14.8, 17). For Mason,

---

1.   The issue of the intratextuality of the smelting imagery will be raised again in the third section of this paper.

The gift of water symbolises God's cleansing of the community from a corrupt and tainted leadership. It is yet another indication that the section before us belongs to that stream of tradition which sees the re-emergence of a redeemed community following the cleansing process which strikes down the false leadership of the old age. (1973: 185)

Thus, for Mason, the judgment and remnant motifs of Zech. 13.8 draw upon Ezekiel traditions because they are so closely related to Zech. 11.4-17.

The situation changes somewhat with Zech. 13.9, as Mason notes, which emphasizes the newness following the cleansing. Mason sees more influence from earlier prophetic traditions in 13.9. He singles out the similarity of Zech. 13.9 with Hos. 2.25, but also Ezek. 37.23, 27 and Zech. 8.8. In the end, it is not entirely clear whether, for Mason, Zech. 13.9 is citing Hos. 2.25 or whether he sees the Hosea text merely as one of several examples of an ongoing line of tradition.[2] At any rate, Mason correctly sees in Zech. 13.9 the renewal of covenant language that is only possible because of the judgment which has purified the community.

Mason concludes his treatment of 13.7-9 by observing its relationship to the context of 11.4-17 and to a lesser extent 12.1–13.6. He contends that similarities in language, structure, and especially theme create a striking similarity between 13.7-9 and 11.4-17. Mason notes five points of similarity (Mason 1973: 186):

1.　Both texts utilize shepherd imagery.
2.　Both texts mention the place where the sword will strike the shepherd.
3.　Both texts allude to smelting.
4.　Both texts draw upon covenant concepts.
5.　The metrical structure from 11.17 continues in 13.7.

It is these similarities that motivate Mason to discuss 13.7-9 immediately after the chapter on 11.4-17. However, Mason also notes thematic contacts with the tradition block of 12.1–13.6. He notes that both 12.1–13.6 and 13.7-9 refer to a time of general suffering that serves as a prelude to salvation. This suffering will be directed toward the removal of corrupt leadership and those parts of the community that have followed that

---

2.　On the one hand, Mason states that the renewed covenant language of 13.9 is 'strongly reminiscent of Hos. 2.25' (Mason 1973: 185). On the other hand, Mason goes on to discuss Ezek. 37.23, 27 and Zech. 8.8 before saying that 'It is such *a line of tradition* [emphasis mine] which seems to lie behind Zech. 13.8f.' (Mason 1973: 86).

leadership. At this point Mason suggests in passing the idea that the (re)location of 13.7-9 may not be the result of an accidental misplacement. He notes that while he has focused upon the similarities between 13.7-9 and 11.4-17, he also sees a general connection between 13.7-9 and 12.1–13.6 that 'indeed may vindicate its positioning where we find it'. Mason does not elaborate how the similarities between 13.7-9 and 11.4-17, on the one hand, and 13.7-9 and 12.1–13.6, on the other hand, could be explained; but he implies the possibility that the relationship is not accidental (1973: 186-87).

In the intervening period since Mason wrote his dissertation, several studies have appeared that have a direct bearing upon his work. A brief review of four of these works will help to sharpen the issues involved in understanding Zech. 13.7-9. While these works show that, in some ways, many of the debates noted by Mason continue unresolved, bringing these four treatments into conversation with Mason also allows one to create a springboard that helps to reconceptualize the model by which one relates 13.7-9 to the broader context.

2. Recent Treatments of Zechariah 13.7-9

The works of Redditt (1989, 1993, 1995), Cook (1993), Meyers and Meyers (1993), and Petersen (1995) may be utilized in a constructive dialogue with Mason. Redditt argues that Zech. 9–14 reflects two significantly different blocks of material, namely, chs. 9–11 and 12–14, each of which had a separate redaction history.[3] Redditt deduces that the process by which these blocks were brought together can be detected as the work of a redactor who has combined no fewer than six collections of material: (1) a futuristic section with a pro-Davidic empire perspective in 9.1-10; (2) a pro-union section demonstrating great concern for the exiles in 9.11–10.1 and 10.3b-12; (3) an anti-union collection consisting of shepherd materials now appearing in 10.2-3b, 11.1-17, and 13.7-9; (4) a pro-Jerusalem collection in 12.1-4a, 5, 8-9; (5) a collection that downplays Jerusalem's elevation over Judah and anticipates a purification of Jerusalem in 12.6-7 and 12.10–13.6;[4] (6) a pro-Jerusalem collection in 14.1-13, 14b-21 that

---

3.   Redditt draws upon the insights of Childs (1979) and Radday and Wickmann (1975).

4.   Here following Redditt's later delineation of this unit as stated in his commentary (1995: 103). The delineation of this block in his earlier article cites the

anticipates an attack on Jerusalem by the nations, an attack that is more debilitating for Jerusalem's inhabitants than the one depicted in ch. 12 (Redditt 1989: 636-38). Redditt later clarifies his argument to indicate that collections three and five in reality supplement existing material, making them better understood as the work of the redactor responsible for the basic shape of Zech. 9–14. While collection five comments upon the core of ch. 12 with a decidedly more negative attitude toward Jerusalem, the shepherd materials of collection three exhibit a negative attitude toward the leaders in a more general sense. They are the only group of texts noted by Redditt that crosses both chs. 9–11 and 12–14. Redditt argues that 'the redactor of 9–14 assembled the four collections and revised them by means of the supplements of 12.6-7, 12.10–13.6 and the shepherd materials' (1995: 103). For Redditt, the redactor of Zech. 9–14 serves as compiler, arranger, and author who displays a decidedly more pessimistic attitude than the core texts which the redactor also includes. For Redditt, this negative attitude also points to the redactor as a member of a community who probably lived in the Judean countryside outside Jerusalem (1989: 638-40).

Redditt's work has implications for Mason's presentation. Rather than seeing 13.7-9 as text that has been relocated from its original setting, Redditt argues that the author of 11.4-17 and 13.7-9 was also the editor who placed 13.7-9 in its current context to incorporate the idea of a purging into the cleansing discussed in 12.1–13.6 (1995: 136). Mason hints at the possibility that the placement of 13.7-9 functions meaningfully in the context of 12.1–13.6, but Redditt takes this idea a step further. This contextual function also comes into play in the works of Cook, as well as Meyers and Meyers, to explain the verses in their context. However, they take significantly different stands on how 13.7-9 relates to the context.

Cook counters Redditt's claim that the shepherd of 13.7-9 derives from a marginalized community or that the shepherd of 13.7-9 should be interpreted as a negative figure in its *current canonical* context (1993: 454, 456-57). Cook shapes his arguments in three parts. In part one, he acknowledges that 13.7-9 originally formed the conclusion of 11.4-17, when the shepherd narrative circulated independently.[5] Cook, however,

material as 12.6-7, 10-12 and 13.6, but later implies that 13.2-6 is also part of this collection (1989: 638).

5.   Since Ewald in 1840, a significant portion of scholars have argued or assumed that 13.7-9 has been *accidentally* dislocated from the end of 11.4-17 and somehow managed to be placed after 13.6 (Cook 1993: 454, esp. nn. 3 and 4).

notes that 13.7-9 does not flow as seamlessly when read with 11.4-17 as most people assume. The poetic style is not the same in 13.7-9, and 13.8 begins with a new introductory formula (וֹהיה) that makes it quite likely that one may understand 13.8-9 as a 'supplementary elaboration' to 11.4-17 (1993: 455-56). He believes, however, that this elaboration occurred while 11.4-17 still circulated as an independent tradition block. Cook also argues that the prophet of 11.4-17 actually portrays two shepherds: one good, the other evil (1993: 456). It is, according to Cook, to this latter figure that 13.7-9 is addressed.[6]

In part two of his article, Cook argues that the relocation of 13.7-9 radically changes its original meaning so that the shepherd figure of 13.7-9 ceases to be an evil figure when the verses are relocated to its new context of Zech. 12–14. Cook argues that in this new context the 'broad chiastic pattern', which he finds to be the structure of Zech. 12–14, now supercedes the original meaning of the text (Cook 1993: 460):

A. The eschatological war and the final victory (12.1-9).
    B. Descriptions of purification and return to God (12.10–13.1).
        C. Cleansing of idolatry and false prophecy (13.2-6).
    B´ Descriptions of purification and return to God (13.7-9).
A´ The eschatological war and the final victory (14.1-21).

More important than the pivotal involvement of 13.7-9 in this structure, according to Cook, is his claim that 13.7-9 'now mediates the logical contradictions between the descriptions of the eschatological battle at the outer extremes of the Trito-Zecharian chiasm' (1993: 461). As appealing as this simplistic chiastic structure might appear to be at first glance, its broad outlines hardly justify Cook's claim that 'the shepherd of 13.7-9 is now to be interpreted not as the anti-David in 11.15-17, but as a figure within the context of a more positive messianic expectation (as in Zech. 3.8, 6.12-14, 9.9-10, 10.4)' (1993: 461). Mason's tradition-historical treatment of the shepherd imagery offers a needed corrective to the Cook's retrofitting of 13.7-9 with the hermeneutic of the New Testament Gospel writers, a move that becomes explicit in the third portion of Cook's article.[7]

---

6. For the inherent problems of this interpretation, see Mason's chapter on 11.4-17 (1973: 135-67).

7. Cook's argument is even implicit in his headings: 'The New Messianic Meaning of Zechariah 13.7-9' (1993: 461-63) and 'The Use of Zechariah 13.7-9 by Mark and Later Interpreters' (1993: 463-66). Cook essentially contends that the New Testament writers correctly interpreted the messianic overtones from the context of Zechariah.

Nevertheless, Cook makes two significant observations regarding 13.7-9, which should not be overlooked. First, his analysis of the uneven quality of the relationship between 13.7-9 and 11.4-17 illuminates a significant problem for understanding 13.7-9 as an original ending to 11.4-17. He bases his arguments upon stylistic and formal markers (especially in 13.8-9). These arguments raise questions that require further consideration. Second, Cook underscores the possibility, already implied by Redditt, that the (re)location of 13.7-9 is not the result of accidental misplacement, even though his own explanation of a radically different meaning for 13.7-9 fails to convince.

In their commentary on Zech. 9–14 Carol and Eric Meyers offer several observations regarding the character of 13.7-9 as a piece better suited to its current canonical context than to 11.4-17 (1993: 384-97, 404-406). They state several rationales for relating 13.7-9 to the context of Zech. 13 (1993: 384-85). First, they argue that the fate of the shepherd differs between 13.7 (where the sword of Yahweh will slay the shepherd) and 11.17 (where the sword is only used against the eye and arm of the shepherd). The language of intimacy is also more appropriate for a king than a prophet. Second, they argue that the shepherd of 13.7-9 presumes a ruler (as in Jer. 23.1-6 and Ezek. 34.1-23), not a prophet (as in 11.4, 15, 17). Finally, they argue that 13.7-9 functions with 13.1 as part of the thematic frame for ch. 13. They note that Zech. 13.1 begins a new section, forming the first of three subunits. Zech. 13.1 introduces a theme of *royal* leadership, a theme to which 13.7-9 returns after the discussion of 13.2-6, that has no 'direct thematic links' with the framing material on either side (1993: 385).[8] They recognize that 13.2-6 concerns the removal of false prophets, but it presents this removal in a concrete fashion that is at odds with the abstract notion of the sword of Yahweh. By contrast, the frame of the chapter (13.1, 7-9) relates to the cleansing of the Davidides and the subsequent scattering of the people. Meyers and Meyers conclude that 13.7 provides a historical allusion to the end of the monarchy that leads to ultimate restoration of the people:

---

8.   Meyers and Meyers do note elsewhere, however, that 13.2-6 contain 'striking lexical connections' to 13.7-9 (1993: 398) which help to fashion a subtle cohesion through the idea of the removal of impurities: 13.1 addresses the cleansing of the leadership through a fountain; 13.2-6 speaks of the removal of the impure spirit of the false prophets (cf. 13.2); and 13.7-9 speaks of the purification of the remnant who survive the judgment of devastation and exile.

This image of the slain shepherd and the consequent scattering of the flock is best understood as retrospective language used to anticipate the future age when the suffering and hardships undergone by the scattered flock will at last prove to have been efficacious in the formation of a new order—a renewed covenant with Yahweh. (Meyers and Meyers 1993: 388)

Thus, the pronouncement of the smiting of the shepherd in 13.7 begins a process of purification for a remnant that will be tested and found pure.

Meyers and Meyers, like Cook, provide a logical framework for understanding 13.7-9 in its current canonical context. Unlike Cook, they argue against 13.7-9 having originally circulated with 11.4-17. Meyers and Meyers also differ from Cook in that they see the relationship of 13.7-9 focused more narrowly upon ch. 13 than upon chs. 12–14. Also, they see the reference to the shepherd in historical and eschatological, not messianic, terms. In this sense, they concur with Mason's conclusion that this shepherd is not a positive figure. How strong are the arguments of Meyers and Meyers that 13.7-9 are formulated for the immediate context without any strong connection to 11.4-17? To be sure, they illustrate several tensions between 13.7-9 and 11.4-17 that call for serious reflection about the nature of the relationship between these two passages. However, the fact that so many scholars have related 11.4-17 and 13.7-9 to one another makes one wonder if recognition of these tensions is enough to overshadow the powerful connections seen by so many between these passages. Meyers and Meyers argue, for example, that the condemnation of the prophets in 13.2-6 nowhere expresses the idea that the prophets are to be considered as shepherds. For example, they argue that 13.7 begins a new subunit, in part because 13.2-6 condemns false prophets but does not explicitly associate these prophets with shepherds (Meyers and Meyers 1993: 385). By contrast, they see in 13.7 a direct connection to the royal figures of 13.1, even though 13.1 also lacks any specific reference to shepherds. The subtle connections argued by Meyers and Meyers for the cohesion of 13.2-6 with 13.1 and 13.7 also do not appear to override the sense that 13.7-9 draws upon 11.4-17 when seen in light of the concrete connections noted by Mason and others. The work of Meyers and Meyers also requires that one re-evaluate the nature of the relationship between 13.7-9 and 11.4-17.

Another work deserves mention at this point, namely, the commentary of David Petersen (1995). It also challenges the view that 13.7-9 inherently belongs to 11.4-17. Like Meyers and Meyers, Petersen expresses doubt that 13.7-9 is an original ending to 11.4-17 on form-critical and literary

grounds (Petersen 1995: 88-89). Form critically, Petersen notes first that
11.4-17 can be seen as a unit without 13.7-9, and second, that 11.4-17 is a
narrative report of symbolic actions while 13.7-9 betrays a poetic style that
does not fit this genre. Petersen also observes that 13.7-9 not only draws
upon a different genre, but merely mentions the shepherd in passing before
moving on to a different focus (1995: 129). These observations lead Petersen to argue that 13.7-9 functions 'as a proleptic—and mildly sanguine—
summary of the events that are described in greater detail in chap. 14'
(1995: 129). He sees the verses as a poetic transition that involves a se-
quencing of events to answer the question: Will anyone survive the coming judgment of Yahweh? The sequence to which Petersen refers is the
sequence of destruction, refining, and restitution. In other words, for Petersen, these verses do not originally function with 11.4-17. Instead, they
point the reader forward by introducing Zech. 14.[9]

The comparison of more recent presentations with Mason's has elicited
several sources of similarity. To be sure, several points of contention remain. It is doubtful that unanimity will ever be achieved for this passage.
Still, many of Mason's conclusions continue to carry weight. The shepherd
figure is generally viewed as negative. The passage is most often viewed
as relating to the theme of the castigation of Judean leadership in some
form. The passage is taken by some to reflect a community's concern to
place themselves in contradistinction to the leadership of their day. The
sense that Zech. 9–14 draws extensively upon other biblical texts has certainly been enhanced. Finally, the relationship of 13.7-9 to 11.4-17 continues to play a major role in the discussion of the passage, even though
this relationship must now be viewed more complexly. This complexity of
the relationship between 11.4-17 and 13.7-9 appears to be the area of the
most significant challenge to Mason's presentation, especially with regard
to the need to explain the *current* function of 13.7-9 when it is separated
from 11.4-17 by the material in 12.1–13.6. Mason anticipates this question
by raising the possibility that the *placement* of 13.7-9 may appear after
13.6 for a reason. Four different presentations have been reviewed in this
paper. Redditt sees the shepherd material as a major redactional thread for
the tradition units of all of Zech. 9–14. Cook argues that the relocation of
13.7-9 to its current location radically altered its meaning. Meyers and

---

9.   Redditt (1993: 685) makes this point differently. While he focuses more on the
relationship between 13.7-9 and 12.1–13.6, he also notes that striking the shepherd and
scattering the people prepares the reader for the attack of the nations (14.2) and
Yahweh's intervention (14.9).

Meyers argue that the literary tensions between 11.4-17 and 13.7-9 force one to consider the latter as part of ch. 13 without significant reference to 11.4-17. Petersen sees the primary function as an introduction to ch. 14. At the risk of muddying the waters even more, the remainder of this study will consider a slightly different model for understanding 13.7-9, one that can help to account both for many of the similarities and for the tensions noted by others between 13.7-9; 11.4-17, and 12.1–13.6. This model will explore the implications of viewing 13.7-9 as a redactional composition created for its context in Zechariah *and* in the Book of the Twelve.

3. *Zechariah 13.7-9 as a Redactional Composition with a Broad Literary Horizon*

In most discussions of Zech. 13.7-9, two points often receive only minimal notice, if any at all. However, these neglected characteristics open the door for understanding 13.7-9 from a different perspective that can perhaps alleviate some of the long-standing issues. These items are the transitional function of these verses and the broad literary horizon they exhibit. In the case of the transitional function, all four of the recent presentations discussed above have suggested that these verses function meaningfully in the current context; nevertheless the emphasis tends to be placed upon the manner in which they comment upon, or are involved with, different portions of Zech. 11–14.

When viewed in totality, it is striking how consistently scholarship of the last 30 years has interpreted 13.7-9 as significantly related to the three major tradition blocks near it. Some (e.g. Mason and Redditt) see the primary and/or the original focus of 13.7-9 with 11.4-17. Some (e.g. Cook plus Meyers and Meyers) see 13.7-9 in relationship to all or parts of 12.1–13.6. And some (e.g. Petersen and Redditt) note that 13.7-9 introduces the material to come in ch. 14. All of these perspectives, divergent though they may be, are rooted in textual and contextual observations. The similarities to ch. 11 focus on the shepherd and sword connections in 13.7. The connections to 12.1–13.6 focus on the rejection of the leadership in general, or the royal house in particular, implicit in the smiting of the shepherd in 13.7. The connections to ch. 14 rely upon the introduction of an implicit attack in 13.8 or the remnant motif in 13.8-9.

Perhaps the biggest problem lies in the assumption that an either/or relationship best explains the relationship of these verses to their context. Each of the arguments tends to relate the *primary focus* of these verses to one of the major tradition blocks (11.4-17; 12.1–13.6, or 14.1-21). In reality, these verses have points of connections to *all* of the blocks in the vicinity. It seems plausible in the light of the arguments presented that we need to conceptualize 13.7-9 as a redactional transitional text composed to provide direction for combining the three major blocks around it. Redditt, I believe, comes very close to arguing this point, but he seems to maintain that 13.7-9 originally concluded 11.4-17, a position that Meyers and Meyers as well as Petersen show to be problematic. Conversely, just because 13.7-9 is not original to 11.4-17, does not mean that scholars such as Mason as well as Redditt do not see connections to 11.4-17 that were intended by the author of 13.7-9. I would suggest that Zech. 13.7-9 takes up the imagery of the shepherd *from* 11.4-17 through its allusions to the shepherd and the sword, but not as an original conclusion to 11.4-17. The same can be noted for its thematic connections with 12.1–13.6, on the one hand, and with 14.1-21, on the other. The three-verse unit stands out from its context on formal and stylistic grounds, but it also provides a connecting point on lexical and thematic grounds. As such, it guides the reader from the condemnation of the leadership and the annulment of the covenant (11.4-17) to the purification of the leadership (12.1–13.6) and the anticipation of the renewed covenant for the remnant following the day of Yahweh (14.1-21).

Regarding the second point about the character of 13.7-9, the literary horizon of these verses is not limited to Zech. 11–14. Rather, I would suggest that the redactional processes involved in combining the latter portions of Zechariah take place in a scribal prophetic milieu that has the coherence of the entire prophetic canon in its purview. The impetus for this argument derives from several observations, especially with respect to the formulations of the remnant motif and the covenant renewal of 13.9. Several of the scholars surveyed have noted that the covenant language recalls Hos. 2.25 (23), among other texts (Mason 1973: 185; Redditt 1995: 136; Meyers and Meyers 1993: 396; Petersen 1995: 132). However, most of these discussions have assumed that the connection to Hos. 2.25 derives solely from tradition-historical similarities. Close inspection of Hos. 2.25 and Zech. 13.9 suggests that the latter is alluding *specifically* to the former. While it is true that several texts rely upon the association of calling on the name of Yahweh to express the covenant idea, none of these other texts share their formulation to the extent that 13.9 and Hos. 2.25 do.

> And I will say to Not-my-people, 'You are my people'. And he will say, 'my god'. (Hos. 2.25 [note ענה in 2.23-24])

> He will call on my name and I will respond (ענה) to him. I will say, 'He is my people', and he will say, 'Yahweh is my god'. (Zech. 13.9b)

These are the only two verses in the Hebrew Bible in which the speech of Yahweh alternates with the speech of a prophet to express this idea. Further, this formulation is introduced with 'respond' (ענה), a verb used five times in the two verses preceding Hos. 2.25. The context of Hos. 2.25 is the renewal of the covenant (cf. 2.20 [18]) with the children of the prophet introduced in Hos. 1–2, the first explicit reference to 'covenant' in the Book of the Twelve. It is noteworthy that Zech. 13.9b alludes to Hos. 2.25.

It is equally noteworthy that Zech. 13.9a alludes to the passage containing the last reference to 'covenant' in the Book of the Twelve, namely, Mal. 3.1. Fewer scholars have noted this allusion, probably because so many have seen the refiner language in Zech. 13.9a as part of the continuation of the interplay between Zech. 11.4-17 and Ezekiel.[10] However, the coalescence of vocabulary and concepts between 13.9a and Mal. 3.1-3 suggests Zech. 13.9 alludes to Malachi. Both texts combine images of refining (בחן/צרף in Zech. 13.9; טהר/צרף in Mal. 3.3), with the concepts of Yahweh's day of judgment and the covenant playing significant roles in the surrounding verses.

Further relationships between Zech. 9–14 and other prophetic texts suggest these chapters draw upon other prophetic writings with enough regularity to see this as a central part of the character of these chapters. Given that Zech. 13.7-9 anticipates Zech. 14, as noted by Petersen, and that Zech. 14 is a pastiche of sayings concerning the day of Yahweh, it is not surprising that Zech. 14 contains its share of allusions and parallels to other prophetic texts. Chief among these would be Joel 4, as noted by Mason and others, and Isa. 66 (the beginning book of the Latter Prophets).[11] The end of Malachi also contains an editorial ending that has been seen in recent years as a text that alludes back to the beginning of Joshua (the beginning of the Former Prophets). Mason also notes briefly a similarity between the outpouring of the spirit in Joel 3.1 (2.28) and Zech. 12.10.[12]

10. Mason sees 13.8-9 in relationship to Ezek. 5.3-4 and 22.17-22 because of the division of the fate of the people into three groups in the former and the smelting imagery in the latter (Mason 1973: 182-84). However, the smelting imagery of Ezek. 22.17 uses another word.

11. I have discussed these canonical allusions elsewhere (Nogalski 1996: 123-24). See also how Meyers and Meyers explain the differences in Zech. 13.9 and Mal. 3.3 with respect to the metallurgical processes to which they allude (1993: 394-95).

12. Mason explains this similarity in tradition-historical terms, but in light of Joel's function as a literary paradigm for the Book of the Twelve, this relationship needs further exploration (see Nogalski 2000: 91-109).

In short, Zech. 13.9 is not the only verse in Zech. 9–14 that suggests a broader horizon than the immediate context, a horizon that likely has the entire prophetic corpus in its sights.

Thus, Zech. 13.7-9 should be viewed as a redactional text composed to create a literary transition between pre-existing tradition blocks. It speaks of the initiation of a process of refinement that begins with Yahweh's judgment upon the leadership, which in turn leads to judgment upon the leader and the people, before a small minority survives to continue the covenant relationship. This sequence reflects the themes of the context of ch. 11, 12.1–13.6 *and* ch. 14, which goes a long way toward explaining the function of 13.7-9 as a redactional and transitional unit.

It is becoming clear that one of the major functions of Zech. 9–14 as a whole is its recasting and its dependence upon other prophetic texts. The work of Rex Mason has played no small part in understanding this function of Zech. 9–14. If some of his conclusions have been modified over time, it is significant that he was asking many of the right questions long before the discipline as a whole.

ZECHARIAH 9–14: THE CAPSTONE OF THE BOOK OF THE TWELVE

Paul L. Redditt

Literary texts do not simply materialize out of thin air; they are the products of reflection, writing, and editing. That statement can be true even of simple texts, ostensibly written by one person. It is certainly true of the Book of the Twelve, ostensibly a collection of sayings by, and occasionally even narratives about, twelve prophets. Modern scholarship recognizes the voices of even more 'prophets' than those named, comprised of a whole series of anonymous editors or scribes, who collected, copied, arranged, modified, and eventually canonized that book. This study will examine primarily one anonymous (or perhaps pseudonymous) portion of it: Zech. 9–14. The thesis is that a redactor, possibly the redactor of Second Zechariah, inserted those chapters between First Zechariah and Malachi, not just to explain the failure of the hopes expressed in Zech. 1–8 to materialize, but also to provide a perspective for reading Malachi. As a consequence of capturing the end of the Book of the Twelve, the redactor articulated a reassessment of prophetic hopes in various places throughout the Twelve, and imposed upon the Twelve his sober reassessment in the process. In that sense, Zech. 9–14 not only was the last collection to enter the Twelve, but also was its capstone.

In arguing this case, I will first review the scholarship of Rex Mason and Raymond Person, scholarship that demonstrates a use of common themes in First and Second Zechariah. Second, I will review recent scholarship pointing to intertextual relationships between Second Zechariah and other biblical traditions. One conclusion that may be drawn from the first two sections is that Second Zechariah stands closer intertextually to First Zechariah than to anything else in the Book of the Twelve. Third, I will then focus on the Twelve by reviewing recent scholarship on the Twelve that advocates reading the composition as a whole and attempts to describe its rise. I will describe that rise in general terms and discuss the addition of Second Zechariah after the Twelve 'prophets' had been selected and brought together. Finally, three implications of this thesis will be examined.

1. *Connections Between Zechariah 1–8 and Zechariah 9–14*

The place to begin is the observation that Zech. 9–14 was appended to a previously existing, edited work, Haggai–Zech. 1–8. To be sure, three recent scholars have read Zech. 9–14 as a continuation of Zech. 1–8. First, Conrad (1999: 151-52) reads Zech. 9–11, 12–14 and Malachi as literary oracles to Bethel, from where messengers came asking questions in Zech. 7.1-2. The backdrop of Zech. 9–14 is, thus, the question about the future in Zech. 8.6. By this reading strategy, Conrad combines the two parts of Zechariah, and the book of Malachi as well. Second, Sweeney (2000: II, 566) sees the overall structure of Zechariah as 1.1-6 (introduction), 1.7–6.15 (visions), and 7.1–14.21 (oracles or pronouncements), each introduced by the putative date when the visions or oracles came to the prophet. Sweeney points to the use of the first person singular in Zech. 11.4-17 as a warrant for reading the passage (and, hence, the entirety of Zech. 9–14) as the proclamation of Zechariah. Third, Moseman (2000: 487-98) also reads Zech. 9–14 as added collections introduced by the word מַשָּׂא. Whatever the merits of these readings, and those merits are many, Conrad, Sweeney, and Moseman do not challenge the consensus that the chapters were added to Zech. 1–8. This article, then, will begin with that consensus and build upon it

It is no accident that Zech. 9–14 was placed behind Zech. 1–8. The two sections of Zechariah share a number of themes, suggesting that they belong together,[1] and Haggai already preceded chs. 1–8. Besides, chs. 9–14 clearly presuppose a functioning temple (11.13; 14.20-21; and probably 9.8), whereas in Haggai–Zech. 1–8 it stood in ruins. Hence, Zech. 9–14 could only follow Haggai–Zech. 1–8. Mason (1976; 1977: 78-79) studied the relationship between the two 'Zechariahs', finding five shared themes. They consist of the following: (1) the centrality of Jerusalem and a common sharing of the Zion tradition (e.g. 9.8, 9-10; 12.1–13.1; 14.1-21; cf. 1.12-16; 2.1-13);[2] (2) the cleansing of the community as part of God's final act (e.g. 10.9; 12.10; 13.1-2; 14.20-21; cf. 3.1-9; 5.1-11); (3) a universalism which sees a place for all nations in God's kingdom (e.g. 9.7, 10; 14.16-19; cf. 2.22; 8.20-23); (4) an appeal to the authority of the

---

1.   As will be seen shortly, Person (1993) argues that Zech. 9–14 was compiled for its place after Zech. 8—and he may well be correct.

2.   Starting from Zech. 8, Gowan (2000: 4-16) argues that the centrality of Jerusalem is the center for eschatology in the First Testament.

earlier prophets (implied by the reuse of older prophetic documents combined with the rejection of contemporary prophets in 13.3-6; cf. 1.2-6; 7.12);[3] (5) a concern with the problem of leadership as one sign of the new age (e.g. 9.9-10; 10.1-2; cf. the emphasis on Joshua and Zerubbabel in Zech. 1–8). These shared themes seem to Mason to tie the two parts of Zechariah together, despite their obvious differences in style, genre, and time of origin. Consequently, he suggests (1976: 238) that something like a school of Second Zechariah emerged to nurture and add the final six chapters.

Person (1993: 142) accepts Mason's conclusion and tries to describe the nature of that school. He finds it to have been imbued with Deuteronomic theology, so he called it the 'Deuteronomic School'. He thinks the school consisted of a group of scribes active in the exilic and postexilic periods (and possibly even in the pre-exilic period) that reinterpreted proto-Deuteronomy and Jeremianic poetry (1993: 13). He spots this Deuteronomic influence in a number of texts, devoting his third chapter to Deuteronomic language in Zech. 9–14 and his fourth chapter to Deuteronomic passages that significantly parallel Zech. 9–14. Indeed, Person found so many intertexts between Deuteronomy and Second Zechariah that he concluded it turns the canonical book of Zechariah into Deuteronomic corpus (1993: 13-14, 36-37). The results of Person's work can be shown in a table (see Table 1, pp. 324-25).[4]

Person finds no fewer than ten verses/passages in Second Zechariah dependent on Deuteronomy, five of which also depend on the Former Prophets. In addition, he cites four more texts dependent on the Former Prophets alone, and finds nineteen related to Jeremiah.

By contrast, Nurmela has challenged the approach of Mason and Person, questioning whether shared themes constitute proof of influence. He thinks that a tighter criterion is needed when speaking of intertextual borrowing, namely, shared words and phrases. The presence of such

---

3. It may seem strange to speak of an appeal by 'the reuse of older prophetic documents', but I have paraphrased Mason in this way because, on the one hand, there are no explicit statements in Zech. 9–14 of the kind found in Zech. 1.4, and, on the other hand, Zech. 9–14 alludes to numerous previous texts, at times in agreement with them, at times not.

4. Person was not interested in intertexts with prophets other than Jeremiah or non-prophetic literature outside of Deuteronomy and the Former Prophets. In all the tables presented in this paper, I have attempted to report the major conclusions from each work cited. It would be impossible to list every allusion mentioned in every work.

sharing alone sometimes is insufficient to prove dependence, since different works might draw from the same source, instead of one from the other (Nurmela 1996: 21, 26-27). Sometimes not even identical words and phrases persuade Nurmela that one text was alluding to another. One such case is the well-known pair of texts where Amos' denial—'I am no prophet' (Amos 7.14)—appears again in the lips of future hypothetical prophets (Zech. 13.5).

One may grant that quotations and shared vocabulary provide the strongest evidence of dependence of one text upon another without abandoning shared themes as evidence altogether. Surely ancient writers could employ similar language (cf. the use of Exodus imagery in Isa. 43.16; 51.10) or refer to other texts without quoting them (cf. the citation of Num. 27.12-39 in Ezra 3.4, introduced by the phrase 'as it is written'). Thus, Nurmela's error seems to be in limiting intertextuality too severely. If so, one may well accept the argument of Mason and Person that Second Zechariah stands close to First Zechariah thematically and properly followed it. The next question to ask, then, is this: From what other texts does Second Zechariah borrow? A review of research into answers to that question will be the next topic in this investigation.

2. *Connections Between Zechariah 9–14 and Other Texts*

The identification of intertexts with Zech. 9–14 is well underway. These intertexts connect Second Zechariah not only with other parts of the Twelve (particularly Hosea, Amos, Micah, and Zech. 1–8) but also with Isaiah, Jeremiah, Ezekiel, Psalms, Deuteronomy, and, to a lesser extent, Genesis, Exodus, and the Former Prophets. A brief review of the scholarship establishing these connections is in order.

The first scholar to be mentioned here is Willi-Plein (1974), who subjected each pericope within Second Zechariah to a search for intertexts. Table 2 on p. 326 reproduces the results of her study.

The majority of intertexts come from the prophetic books Isaiah, Jeremiah, and Ezekiel. No more than half a dozen in Jeremiah, however, correspond to the intertexts cited by Person. Within the Twelve, Willi-Plein finds six intertexts with Hosea, two or three with Amos, and one or two with Micah. She thinks texts similar to Second Zechariah may be found in Zech. 2 and 8 and in Joel 2 and 4. She points to only three intertexts with Deuteronomy (a marked contrast with Person's study) and four with other books in the Torah and the Former Prophets.

The second scholar to be reviewed here is Larkin, who also builds upon the insights of Mason (Larkin 1994: 45) in arguing that Zech. 9–13 was an anthology of mantological wisdom comparable to Amos 7–8, Zech. 1–6, and Dan. 7–12.[5] In so doing, she identifies a number of intertextual connections between Zech. 9–14 and other texts. Her major examples are summarized in Table 3 on pp. 327-28.[6]

Larkin lists three intertexts in Deuteronomy, all also cited by Person, and two by Willi-Plein; she also lists two in Jeremiah, neither cited by Person, but one by Willi-Plein. In addition, she posits limited influence from Leviticus, an influence spotted by no other scholar reviewed here. On the other hand, she cites six intertexts with Zech. 1–8, more than with any other collection in the Twelve. Her results seem to reinforce those of Mason.

The third scholar to be reviewed is Tai (1996), whose concern is with prophecy as scriptural exegesis in Zech. 9–14. His interests stand near to those of Larkin (who traced mantological exegesis), and they are presented in Table 4 on p. 329.

Tai finds only four intertexts with Deuteronomy, two of which were cited by Willi-Plein and one by Person and Larkin. He also cites twelve intertexts with Jeremiah, of which four or five were cited by Willi-Plein, five by Person, and one by Larkin. Tai finds seven verses or passages with intertexts in Ezekiel, of which Willi-Plein seems to agree in three specific cases (Larkin in two cases) and in general with the view that Zech. 14 draws upon Ezek. 40–48. Tai finds three intertexts in Hosea; Willi-Plein agrees on one, and Larkin one. Tai also finds two each in Amos and Micah, with Willi-Plein in agreement on one in each case. Larkin finds two of his intertexts in Amos. Significantly, however, Tai finds only two intertexts with Zech. 1–8, where Larkin found six.

Early in his study Tai (1996: 7) objects to Mason's conclusion that Zech. 9–14 shares five themes with Zech. 1–8 on the grounds that the themes do not always share verbal parallels. On the other hand, Tai rejects several possible verbal parallels as evidence of intertextuality. He denies

---

5. Zechariah 14 fell outside that scheme and is best viewed as an epilogue comparable to Amos 9 and Zech. 7–8 (so Larkin 1994: 180-220, 252).

6. Larkin primarily seeks intertexts with mantological (wisdom) features, so the table reporting her work emphasizes those conclusions and does not mention all of the numerous allusions she mentions. In the comparisons of the tables that follow at the end of this paper, not all of Larkin's intertexts will be tabulated, resulting at times in under-reporting of allusions in particular that she finds.

(1996: 13 n. 15) that the root נוח ('rest') in 9.1 refers to the same root in 6.8 on the grounds that the passages differ in terms of genre and meaning. Texts do not always have to agree, however, for one to allude to another. In this case the verb appears in the first sentence of Second Zechariah: 'The word of the Lord is against the land of Hadrach and will *rest* upon Damascus' (NRSV). The phrase 'rest upon Damascus' is so startling that Moseman (2000: 493) offers a different reading of the whole sentence, taking the preposition ב, which governs both place names, to mean 'upon', not 'against' in the first place and 'upon' in the second. Zech. 6.8 also exhibits a striking use of the root נוח: 'Those who go toward the north country have set my spirit at *rest* in the north country'. Thus, while the root itself is common and would not alone prove dependence of one text on another, its use in two startling texts in close proximity dealing with 'the north' suggests that Mason was on better footing than Tai allows.

Several other such examples may be listed. Tai agrees (1996: 18 n. 47) that the phrase מעבר ומשב (two participles denoting persons 'passing through and returning') in 9.8 appears earlier in 7.14, and acknowledges that the phrase in 9.8 is either an allusion or a point of contact between the two texts. Still, he does not count it among the texts in the background of 9.1-8. He admits (1996: 49 n. 45; cf. p. 40) that 4.6 treats the theme of salvation through God's power and not the king's, as does 9.9-10, but cites Ps. 33.16-17 as the source of the latter. He also says (1996: 93) that when reading 10.6 the verb ישע causes one to remember 8.13, where the object of that verb also is the House of Judah and the House of Israel, but he does not treat 8.13 otherwise as a source text for 10.6. In light of these examples, Tai's list of intertexts between the two parts of Zechariah may be too small.

The final scholar to be reviewed here is Nurmela (1996). While his study involved intertexts between the entire book of Zechariah and the rest of the First Testament, Table 5 on pp. 330-31 reports only the results of his investigation of Zech. 9–14.

Nurmela found intertexts for five passages in Jeremiah, of which Person also identified four, Willi-Plein three, and Tai three, but only two in Deuteronomy, of which Person identified one. There is substantial agreement, however, among Willi-Plein, Tai, and Nurmela about intertexts with Ezekiel. With regard to intertexts with Hosea, Amos and Micah, Nurmela finds only one. Nurmela finds six places where Zech. 9–14 borrows from Zech. 1–8 and also thinks 8.20-23 depends on 14.16.

Do the differences in the results of these studies make it impossible to draw conclusions about intertexts between Zech. 9–14 and other texts? The answer to this question is 'no'. That is so for several reasons. It has already been noted that Person limited his study to Deuteronomy, the Former Prophets, and Jeremiah. Thus, only Willi-Plein, Tai, Nurmela, and Larkin surveyed the whole Hebrew Bible, and some of Larkin's allusions in particular are under-reported. In reaction to earlier studies (e.g. Mason), Tai argued (1996: 8) that themes alone are not sufficient for positing intertextuality. He argued for agreement of verbal parallels, theme, and theology. Nurmela, likewise, argued that only verbal parallels prove inter-textuality. Still, as mentioned in the first section of this study, such limitations on what one considers intertextuality do not seem consistent with the way writers of various eras have employed their own field of literary acquaintance. Writers use the words and phrases of other writers subconsciously, as well as consciously. They quote them for effect or to dispute them. They cite texts they assume their readers will know rather than repeat the information. Thus, it would seem unwise to restrict too severely the possible ways that one writer might have used another.

Given the present situation with regard to identifying intertexts, it is not possible to determine which of these scholars (if any) is correct, either about the method to be employed or the specific texts said to have influenced Second Zechariah. Besides, all are agreed that fairly extensive borrowing took place in the compilation of Second Zechariah and that the borrowing could involve agreement or disagreement between Second Zechariah and earlier texts. All are agreed that the borrowing took place across a variety of corpora, whether the other Latter Prophets (including other prophets among the Twelve), the Pentateuch, the Former Prophets, or the Psalter. This investigation accepts that general conclusion. Moreover, the thematic coherence between the two parts of Zechariah demonstrated by Mason and Person as well as allusions cited by several of these scholars make it appear as if Second Zechariah was composed with an eye on First Zechariah.

The difference in their tone, however, is striking. The author(s) of Zech. 1–8 anticipated a new day, which would begin with a new temple, a new high priest, and perhaps even a new king.[7] By contrast, the author(s) of Second Zechariah thought that the conduct of the leading groups in

---

7. Even Rose (2000: 208) argues that First Zechariah had in view a 'future royal figure', though he was not Zerubbabel. I remain convinced that both Haggai (ch. 2) and Zechariah (4.12-13) expected Zerubbabel to assume the role of king, whether Zerubbabel held such ambitions or not.

Jerusalem (Davidides, priests, Levites, and prophets, if any were still functioning) made such hopes impossible without a wholesale cleansing (Zech. 12.1–13.6). The rebuilding of the temple had ushered in no new day, so far as the redactor was concerned, because the 'shepherds' (the leading families) were corrupt (Zech. 11.4-17). Hence, the redactor or someone of a like mind placed these chapters at the end of Zech. 8 to answer why the good days predicted in Haggai–Zech. 1–8 had not come into fruition.

This conclusion, however, opens another line of questioning. How is Second Zechariah related not merely to First Zechariah, but to the rest of Twelve? When did it enter the Book of the Twelve? Why was it simply attached to Zechariah and not given a name of its own? How is it related to the book of Malachi, which follows it? It is possible to shed light on those questions.

3. *The Entry of Zechariah 9–14 into the Book of the Twelve*

a. *Recent Scholarship on the Twelve*
Recently, a number of scholars have been studying the Book of the Twelve as a redacted whole (Redditt 2001), a direction of study that emerged after Mason published his studies on Zechariah. Among them, Nogalski (1993a: 20-57) argues that catchwords in the seams between collections within the Twelve suggest a purposeful redaction of the whole. This redaction took place over time in a series of stages. The first stage was the uniting of the eighth-century prophets Hosea, Amos, and Micah with the seventh-century prophet Zephaniah to form an early precursor. Building on the work of earlier scholars (e.g. Wolff 1974: 3-4; Tucker 1977: 69; Weimar 1985: 97; Freedman 1987: 25-26), Nogalski calls that corpus 'Deuteronomic', because it employs a scheme for dates reminiscent of the Deuteronomistic Historian (Nogalski 1993a: 278-80). Haggai and Zech. 1–8 constituted a second precursor (Nogalski 1993a: 273). The addition of the remaining prophetic collections to the Twelve fell mainly into what Nogalski calls a 'Joel-related layer' (1993b: 275-78; cf. Nogalski 2000). Jonah and Zech. 9–14 entered subsequently about the same time (1993b: 278-79).

Though Nogalski has met with dissenters (e.g. Ben Zvi 1996), a number of scholars have agreed with him in principle. Indeed, several (e.g. Schneider 1979; Lee 1985; and House 1990), had already articulated the principle that the Twelve is a more unified book than scholars characteristically admit. Schart quickly followed Nogalski's lead, noting his relative in-difference to the rise of the 'deuteronomistic' corpus and starting there. Schart uncovers a two-volume first stage, comprised of early versions Amos and Hosea (1998: 128, 151-55; cf. Jeremias 1996); it stands behind the four-volume deuteronomistic corpus, which constitutes the second stage (Schart 1998: 156-223). Then, Schart addresses the redaction of the remainder of the Twelve, disagreeing with Nogalski about the centrality of Joel. The third stage was the expansion of the Deuteronomistic corpus with the insertion of a Nahum–Habakkuk corpus (pp. 234-51). A Haggai–Zechariah corpus (minus Zech. 14) was added in the fourth stage (pp. 252-60), a Joel–Obadiah corpus (with other redactional material including Zech. 14) in the fifth stage (pp. 261-82), and then individually Jonah (pp. 287-91) and Malachi (pp. 297-303).

Independently from Nogalski and Schart, Curtis developed his own understanding of the stages of growth of the Twelve that also does not reckon with a Joel layer. He posits two collections of three books: Hosea–Amos–Micah from the time of Hezekiah, and Nahum–Habakkuk–Zephaniah from the time of Josiah. These two corpora were joined by inserting Obadiah after Amos (with which it was programmatically and intertextually related) shortly after the destruction of Jerusalem. He thinks Haggai and Zech. 1–8 first circulated together, with Zech. 9–14 and Malachi being added, so that Haggai–Zechariah–Malachi came into the Twelve as yet another three-volume corpus (see Curtis 2000: 166-67, 171). He points, correctly, to something else that holds those three books together: the sixth-century prophets Haggai and Zech. 1–8 are at least partly responsible for the early success towards restoration signified by the rebuilding of the temple; Zech. 9–14 and Malachi are fifth-century documents bemoaning the failure of the Jerusalemite leadership in con-tinuing the restoration (p. 183). With this stroke, he shows the connection of Second Zechariah with Malachi.

Curtis accounts for the 'deuteronomistic' superscription of Zephaniah simply as a framing device that deliberately mimicked the superscriptions for Hosea, Amos, and Micah, added by the editor of the late pre-exilic corpus of six books that ended with Zephaniah. He thinks the lengthy list of kings (reaching back into the eighth century) in Zeph. 1.1 is well ex-plained by his suggestion (p. 171). Then he turns to Zeph. 3.14-20, where he argues that 3.19-20 is actually prosaic and was added when Haggai was joined to Zephaniah (p. 181). Further, this 'Zion–daughter oracle' has a literary connection with the one in Zech. 9.1-10, and the two oracles 'were editorially and thematically significant for the redactors responsible for appending Haggai–Zechariah–Malachi to the trunk of the preceding books'.[8]

Curtis acknowledges his own dependence on the earlier work of Schneider, who also argues for four stages: (1) Hosea, Amos, and Micah, assembled during the reign of Hezekiah in support of his policies; (2) Nahum, Habakkuk, and Zephaniah, prompted by the reforms of Josiah and joined with the first collection during the exilic period; (3) Joel (which was written in the pre-exilic period), Obadiah, and Jonah, with Obadiah being appended to Amos as a fitting close to it and Joel, and with Jonah being placed at the head of collections about Assyria; and (4) Haggai, Zechariah, and Malachi, included in the fifth century (Schneider 1979: 154-62).

The differences between Curtis and Schneider actually point to another issue: the original order of the Twelve. The LXX differs markedly from the MT in the order of the first six prophetic collections; the order is the same in both for the last six. Table 6 shows the differences.

Table 6. *The Order of the Book of the Twelve*

In the MT	In the LXX
Hosea	Hosea
Joel	Amos
Amos	Micah
Obadiah	Joel
Jonah	Obadiah
Micah	Jonah

The views of Nogalski, Schart and Curtis fit well with the sequence in the MT, where Joel, Obadiah, and Jonah are interspersed among the eighth-century collections, whereas Schneider's view fits better the order in the LXX.

b. *Reconstructing the Rise of the Twelve*
Solving the question of which order was primary lies outside the parameters of this study, but the differences in order point to the lack of

---

8.   Curtis 2000: 182. Whether the redactor responsible for Zech. 9–14 still held to the hopes expressed in the 'Zion Daughter' oracle (Zech. 9.9-10) may remain open. I have argued that the redactor expressed his own view of Jerusalemite leadership in the so-called 'Shepherd' passages in Zech. 10.1-3a; 11.4-17; 13.7-9, and in 12.6-7; 12.10–13.6 as well (Redditt 1989: 632-36; 1995: 102-103).

commonality among Joel, Obadiah, and Jonah. None of them contains internal information about the date of its origin, not even in their super-scription or incipit. Jonah is a narrative whose putative setting, however, is the reign of the eighth-century king of Israel, Jeroboam II (2 Kgs 14.25). As a narrative containing very little of Jonah's preaching, it is an oddity in the Twelve. Its more natural home would appear to be 2 Kings.

Joel and Obadiah are more like the other collections in the Twelve, in that they consist of sayings. Sweeney (2000: I, xxvii) argues that the reference to the Valley of Jehoshaphat in Joel 4.12 'recalls the Judean King Jehoshaphat's (r. 873–849 BCE) defeat of Ammon, Moab, and the men of Seir...in the valley of Berachah...as related in 2 Chronicles 20', whereas 'Obadiah is the name of Elijah's associate who announced the presence of the prophet to the Israelite Ahab (r. 869–850) and hid the prophets of YHWH...' While Sweeney's suggestions are plausible, they are hardly proven. Even if he is correct on both counts, however, his sug-gestions at most show that both are the products of people who adopted putative ninth-century prophets as their spokesmen, and the mystery of how the books entered the Twelve would still remain. The most plausible answers are: (1) that Joel and Obadiah constituted a corpus that came into the hands of the scribes who were assembling the Twelve (so Schart) or (2) that they were the product(s) of those scribes written for their specific places in the Twelve (as Nogalski suggests). The mystery remains unsolved.

The upshot of all of this is twofold: (1) Jonah was drawn into the Twelve despite its uniqueness. It will be necessary to ask why later. (2) Probably one can speak of three precursors to the Twelve, precursors which were themselves the results of periods of growth. Those three were a collection associated with the names of the eighth-century prophets Hosea, Amos, and Micah; a late-seventh-century collection associated with the names Nahum, Habakkuk, and Zephaniah (if Zephaniah was not already part of the eighth-century corpus as Nogalski and Schart argue); and a post-exilic collection that included at least Haggai and Zech. 1–8.

It is the growth of that post-exilic collection that is the real point of interest here. Scholars have paid much attention to that growth, the most elaborate description being that of Steck. He sees much of Joel, Obadiah, Zephaniah, and Malachi being added to the emerging corpus of Twelve in the Persian period. He lines out a series of additions to the emerging corpus of the Twelve, many of which constitute Zech. 9–14 and Malachi. Parallel to this development is the growth of the book of Isaiah (cf. Boss-hard 1987). Steck's results are summarized in Table 7 on p. 332 (which is based on Steck 1991: 196-98).

Of interest to this study is Steck's conclusion that Zech. 9–14 never existed as a separate entity, but emerged as a series of additions to Zech. 1–8 after Malachi (at least in part) had been affixed *as part of Zechariah*. The separation of Malachi from Zechariah by means of the superscriptions in Zech. 12.1 and Mal. 1.1 turned Malachi into the twelfth book in the corpus. Steck also follows Rudolph (1976: 290-93) in arguing that Mal. 3.22-24 (Eng. 4.4-6) forms the conclusion not simply to Malachi, but the Twelve as a whole.

In response to Steck, one may say that his work depends on his reconstruction of the history, not simply of Israel, but of Isaiah and the Twelve as well. In addition, Steck sees no internal integrity to Second Zechariah, reducing it instead to a series of additions to First Zechariah. That view has not as yet found much support. On the other hand, Steck does call attention to several issues that need to be addressed: the similarity of the superscriptions in Zech. 9.1; 12.1 and Mal. 1.1, and the function of Mal. 3.22-24 (4.4-6).

Other scholars as well have contributed insights to this discussion. Nogalski (1993a: 53-55) offers several pieces of evidence that Malachi was attached to Zech. 1–8 before Zech. 9–14, two of which warrant mentioning here. First, the antithesis between love and hate in Zech. 8.17 appears again in Mal. 1.2-3 in the form of God's loving Israel but hating Esau. In addition, the phrase 'entreat the face of YHWH' appears in the next to last verse of First Zechariah (8.22) and the ninth verse of Malachi. Second, he argues that Zech. 13.9 alludes to Hos. 1.9 and Mal. 3.2-3, texts at the beginning and the end of the Twelve.

That allusion is a crucial piece in this argument. Zech. 13.9 concludes the final 'Shepherd Oracle'. Zech. 13.8 says that God will strike the city, with two-thirds of its population being killed. Verse 9 expands v. 8, adding that God would refine the surviving third of Jerusalem's population. The thought is developed by means of two separate allusions, as Nogalski (1993b: 235) points out:

Zech. 13.9a Then I will send this third into the fire to *refine* them as *silver* is *refined* and to assay them as *gold* is assayed…	Mal. 3.2-3 For [God's messenger] is like a *refiner's* fire and a fuller's soap. He will sit as a *refiner* and a cleanser of *silver*, and he will purify the sons of Levi, and he will purify them like *gold* and *silver*.
Zech. 13.9b *I will say*, 'They are *my people*': and he will say, 'YHWH is *our God*.	Hos. 2.23 And *I will say* to Lo-ammi, 'You are *my people*': and he shall say, 'You are *our God*'.

In view of these intertexts, one may agree with Nogalski's conclusion that the author of Zech. 13.9 had the entire Book of the Twelve in view, including Malachi.

In addition, Zech. 14.9, which interrupts but grounds a vision of the future Jerusalem, may have alluded to several verses in Malachi.

Zech. 14.9 And YHWH will become *king* over all the earth;	Mal. 1.14 [F]or I am a great *king*, says YHWH Sebaoth, and my *name* is reverenced among the nations.
on that day YHWH will be *one* and his *name one*.	Mal. 2.10 Have we not *one* father? Has not *one* God created us?
	Mal. 2.15 Did not the *One* make her?... And what did the *One* desire?

The word 'king' appears in the remarkable title 'King YHWH' צבאות in Zech. 14.16-17, so the idea of God as the king of the whole earth is not foreign to the thought of the chapter, but the use of the title 'king' in connection with the word 'one' has more in common with Malachi than with anything else in Zech. 14 and perhaps drew upon Malachi's thought.[9]

Bosshard and Kratz (1990: 35) also add to this discussion by offering eight parallels between Malachi on the one hand and Haggai–Zech. 1–8 on the other as evidence that Malachi originally followed Zech. 8. The parallels are Mal. 1.8//Hag. 2.10-14 (קרב in the hiphil); Mal. 1.8//Hag. 1.1, 14; 2.2, 21 (governor); Mal. 1.9, 14b//Hag. 2.17; Zech. 8.9, 13 ('your

---

9.   It is not likely that the borrowing—if borrowing there was—went the other way, since much of Zech. 14 is a composite of images from earlier texts. Zech. 14.1-3 draws heavily on passage like Joel 4.1-3 (3.1-3) and Ezek. 38 and 39; Zech. 14.4, 8 draws on Ezek. 47.1; Zech. 14.5 alludes to the earthquake mentioned in Amos 1.1, if not to the verse itself; Zech. 14.10 alludes to Jer. 31.38; Zech. 14.12-15 alludes to the plagues in Egypt; and Zech. 14.17 may echo Isa. 19. Of course the oneness of YHWH and a theology of the name of YHWH are also characteristic of Deuteronomy. Indeed, Deut. 6.4 may well be the ultimate source of the emphasis on the oneness of God, but the book of Deuteronomy does not refer to YHWH as king. Other texts, of course do. Ps. 47.3 (2) praises YHWH as the king of the all the earth, Isa. 6.5 speaks of 'the king, YHWHצבאות' Jer. 10.10 calls YHWH 'the living God and the everlasting king', and Jer. 46.18; 48.15 and 51.57 contain the phrase 'says the king, whose name is YHWH צבאות'. I am unable to locate any place other than Zech. 14.9 and Mal. 1.14 which calls YHWH 'king' and employs theology about the 'name' of YHWH in such proximity. The added emphasis on the oneness of God in Zech. 14.9 and Mal. 2.10, 15 may well seal the case that Zech. 14.9 draws upon Malachi.

hands'); Mal. 1.2-5//Zech. 8.17 (love, hate); Mal. 1.4-5//Zech. 1.12-15 (people of anger); Mal. 1.6; 3.6-12 (teaching the priests and people the Torah); Mal. 2.2-3; 3.9-10//Zech. 8.9-15 (blessing and curse); Mal 3.6-7/Zech 1.1-6; 8.14 (warning and repentance of the sins of the 'fathers'); Mal. 3.7//Zech. 1.3 (identical wording).[10]

Finally, Glazier-McDonald (1987: 24-29) argues that despite the appearance of three consecutive words (משא דבר־יהוה: 'burden, word of YHWH') in the headings in Zech. 9.1; 12.1 and Mal. 1.1, the phrases are quite distinct in how they function and in their origin. She successfully challenges the view espoused by many, including Steck, that the three verses are identical superscriptions to three additions to Zech. 1–8. (See below for her argument.) Her challenge also undercuts his contention that Malachi probably was the last book admitted into the Twelve. Rather, Malachi very likely was attached to Haggai–Zech. 1–8 by means of its own superscription before the three were attached to Zephaniah.[11]

If Malachi was attached to Haggai–Zech. 1–8 before Zech. 9–14, was Zech. 9–14 the last major piece to find a place in the Twelve? Nogalski thinks not, arguing instead that Jonah was the last addition (1993b: 270-73; cf. Schart 1998: 297-303). That suggestion, however, requires that for a while, that is, until Jonah was added, there was a 'Book of the Eleven'. The significance of the number twelve in ancient Israel was so far-reaching it seems unlikely a redactor would stop one prophet shy (see Redditt 1996: 256-58). The uniqueness of Jonah within the Twelve has already been noted. It seems plausible to suggest, then, that it was added to bring the number to twelve (though not exclusively for that purpose). What is more, Jonah probably entered at the time a redactor put together the pre- and post-exilic precursors to form one volume. Regardless of whether Joel and Obadiah formed a separate precursor, as Schart argues, or formed the core of a 'Joel-related' stage, as Nogalski agues, Jonah filled the twelfth place when Haggai, Zech. 1–8, and Malachi were added to the others.

A recent suggestion concerning the role of Jonah in the Twelve leads to a similar result. Lescow (1993: 186) thinks that the deuteronomistic collections (Hosea, Amos, Micah, and Zephaniah) appear at the beginning and end of the pre-exilic corpus, framing the later collections (Joel, Obadiah, Nahum, and Habakkuk). Jonah occupied the fifth or middle

---

10. Schart (1998: 294) supplies this list, but finds it unconvincing.

11. Whether 'Malachi' is a proper name or a title ('my servant') is irrelevant to this discussion.

position in the corpus, as a didactic centerpiece.[12] This observation might suggest that Jonah entered the 'pre-exilic' collection before the 'postexilic' collection was added. Zech. 9–14 would have come last since Zech. 13.9 drew on texts from both corpora: Hos. 2.23 and Mal. 3.2.

The relative dates of Jonah and Second Zechariah impinge on this issue. A number of scholars date Jonah well into the Greek period, but such a late date is not necessary. Sasson (1990: 27), for example, expressing hesitation about dating the book at all, places the final editing of Jonah 'during the exilic, or more likely during the postexilic period' based on 'literary and linguistic features'. Trible (1996: 466) refuses to date it at all, saying only that the reference in 2 Kgs 14.23-25 makes the eighth-century reign of Jeroboam II the *terminus a quo* and the reference to the Twelve in the second-century Sir. 49.10 the *terminus ad quem*. Among those scholars who do attempt to date the narrative, some see parallels from Greek literature to the sea episodes in Jonah as evidence of a date in the Greek period, but Wolff (1977: 86) adduces parallels to Jonah from the Greek singer Arion, who flourished c. 620 BCE. Even the presence of Aramaisms no longer may be regarded as proof of a late date, because many of those words are nautical terms that are present in Ugaritic texts as well. There is, it would seem, no necessity for dating Jonah in the Greek period. Thus, several scholars choose the fifth century (Fretheim 1977: 34-37; Limburg 1988: 138), and others the fourth (Eissfeldt 1968; Fohrer 1965: 442; and Lux 1994: 210-11, who specified the late Persian period).

Scholars also frequently date Second Zechariah in the early Greek period on the basis of two passages. The first (9.1-8, 9-13) is said to follow the march of Alexander the Great to Egypt, but does not (cf. Jouguet 1985: 21-31). The second (9.13) reads: 'I will arouse your sons, O Zion, Over your sons, O Jawan' (Hebrew יון, the normal word for Greece). Even so, Ezek. 27.13 mentions 'Jawan' as one of a number of nations that sold slaves to Tyre, suggesting that Greece was involved economically with the Levant as early as the sixth century, and in trade likely to be unfavorable to Judah. Thus, a date in the first half of the Persian period for Second Zechariah is quite defensible (cf. Redditt 1994: 675-77; 1995: 94-100). The issue, however, is not which of these books was written first, an issue

---

12. Lescow's argument meshes nicely with the point made by van Leeuwen (1993: 34-48) and Cooper (1993: 160) that Jonah shares the language of Exod. 34.6-7 in Joel 2.13; Mic. 7.18; Nah. 1.2-3a; and possibly Hos. 14.3, 5. The inclusion of Jonah in the midst of the pre-exilic corpus set it among other collections examining the meanings and applications of the same text.

which cannot at this point be resolved, but which entered the emerging corpus of the Twelve first; and the point here is that Jonah need not be dated so late as to preclude its entering prior to Zech. 9–14.

c. *The Addition of Second Zechariah*

Nogalski argues that when Second Zechariah was inserted between First Zechariah and Malachi, Zech. 9.1 and 12.1 were added in imitation of Mal. 1.1, on the grounds that the exact sequence משא דבר־יהוה ('burden, word of YHWH') appears only in these three verses. A return to Glazier-McDonald (1987: 24-27) here will be helpful, since she argues differently. She thinks the three verses arose independently of each other. She translates the superscription to Malachi 'The burden of Yahweh's word, directed to Israel by Yahweh'. Zech. 12.1a also forms a superscription, but with several differences. First, the recipient is designated by the preposition על ('concerning'), not אל ('to') as in Mal. 1.1 (cf. Hag. 1.1; Zech. 4.6). Second, the role of the prophet in Zech. 12.1 is expressed by the phrase ביד ('by the hand of') as in Jer. 50.1; Hag. 1.1, 3; 2.1, etc. She concludes that the closest parallels to Mal. 1.1 are found in Jer. 50.1 and Hag. 1.1, not Zech. 12.1. In Zech. 9.1, she argues, the word משא ('burden') stands by itself, with the remaining words in v. 1a constituting the announcement of judgment in the passage: 'The word of Yahweh is against the land of Hadrach and will rest upon Damascus' (NRSV).[13]

These differences call into question an easy assumption that Zech. 9.1 and 12.1 draw upon Mal. 1.1. Even more problematic is the widely held view that they begin two separate additions to Zechariah. What holds Second Zechariah together is the work of a redactor responsible for Zech. 12.6-7, 12.10–13.6, and the so-called 'Shepherd' materials in Zech. 10.1-3a, 11.4-17 and 13.7-9 (Redditt 1989: 632-36; 1995: 103). Further, since the single word משא ('burden') formed the superscription in 9.1a, the phrase 'word of YHWH' in 9.1a is not from a late redactor at all. Finally, while the superscription in 12.1 is redactional, it stands at the head of 12.1–13.9 at most, and perhaps only ch. 12 or a portion thereof. It does not begin a separate collection added to Zech. 1–8.

---

13. Moseman (2000: 490-94) disagrees slightly with her translation, but concurs with her understanding of 9.1. He also argues that משא introduces Zech. 9–14 in its entirety, though he does not defend that claim or explain the role of Zech. 12.1.

4. *Conclusion and Implications*

The conclusion from these deliberations is that Second Zechariah very likely joined the Twelve as its last collection, later even than Malachi or Jonah. It was placed near the end of the Twelve, quite possibly by its own redactor, where it could reinterpret the Twelve from the perspective of its redactor, which appears in Zech. 10.1-3a; 11.4-17; 12.6-7, 10-12; 13.1-6, and 7-9. Those verses reshape the future expectations of much of the Twelve, which anticipated a new, purified and united kingdom, ruled by a new David, and ministered to by a cleansed priesthood. The contribution of the redactor of Second Zechariah was to temper such expectations in the light of the priests, prophets, and Davidides of his day (Zech. 12.1–13.9). Such expectations could not come about, he argued, with the leaders or 'shepherds' flourishing in Jerusalem in his day (Redditt 1989: 632-36; cf. Redditt 1993: 679-85).

In a consecutive reading of the Twelve, Malachi becomes a further indictment against priests for their contemptuous treatment of sacrifices (1.12-13) and the laity for robbing God by withholding tithes (3.8-9). Though God was like a father to them, they did not respect God (1.6; 2.10). Only the names of 'those who revered YHWH' would be found in God's 'book of remembrance' and only they would be saved (Mal. 3.16-18). Thus Second Zechariah itself articulated a reassessment of prophetic hopes, and lent to Malachi and to the Twelve that same reassessment in the process. In that sense, it not only was the last collection to enter the Twelve, but also was its capstone.

Curtis reads Second Zechariah somewhat similarly and argues (2000: 183-84) that the 'Zion–Daughter Oracles' in Zeph. 3.14-20 and Zech. 9.1-8 'mark the seams of the closure of the Twelve'. He is correct in saying that the redactor of Second Zechariah believed later generations had betrayed the restorationist ideal in Zeph. 3.14-20 and Zech. 9.1-8. One might add other texts with a similar idyllic picture of the future: Hos. 14.4-9; Amos 9.11-15, and Mic. 7.11-20, all redactional texts added to the Twelve in its process of growth. What seems to distinguish and separate the redactor of Second Zechariah (in 10.1-3a; 11.4-17; 12.6-7, 10-12; 13.1-6, and 7-9) from the hopes expressed in the Zion–Daughter Oracles, however, is his pessimism about those hopes. His inherited materials envisioned a new Davidic ruler (9.1-13), a reunited Israel (10.6-7), the return of exiles (10.8-12), with Jerusalem as its center (12.1-5, 8-9). His own view was that his contemporary leaders were worthless shepherds

(10.1-3a; 11.4-17; 13.7-9), who could not reunite the people unless they repented (12.10-14). Even prophecy itself had gone awry (13.3-6). The only hope was for Israel to turn and follow the teachings of God through God's prophets. Those prophets clearly included the 'twelve' who spoke in the Book of the Twelve.

Three implications of this study warrant mentioning here. First, since Second Zechariah seems to have entered the Twelve after the number of 'prophets' reached twelve, the redactor of Second Zechariah probably was not the redactor responsible for pulling together the Twelve.[14] He may, however, have been the one responsible for inserting Second Zechariah into the Twelve. If he made additions to the Twelve, however, it is possible other, later redactors did so too.

Second, one such addition might have been Mal. 3.22-24 (4.4-6), though the relative dates of those verses and Second Zechariah remain open, despite Steck's suggestion (1991: 198) that Malachi was separated from Second Zechariah and that parts of Malachi, including 3.22-24, were added between 220 and 190 BCE. This study suggests that the redactor of Second Zechariah likely was not the redactor that added Mal. 3.22-24. The striking feature about those verses, which close Malachi, is their appeal to Moses and their promise of Elijah. To see how striking their mention is one need only note that the name 'Moses' appears only in Mic. 6.4 elsewhere in the Twelve, and the name 'Elijah' not at all. Indeed, Moses is named only in Isa. 63.11-12 and Jer. 15.1 elsewhere in the other Latter Prophets, and Elijah not at all. Continuing, the phrase 'Moses my servant' appears nowhere else in the Latter Prophets, though Isaiah, Eliakim, David, Jacob/Israel, Zerubbabel, the 'Branch', and Nebuchadnezzar are addressed by God with the phrase 'my servant'. Likewise, Jer. 7.25; 26.5; 35.15; Ezek. 38.17, and Zech. 1.6 have God speak of 'my servants the prophets', and Amos 3.7 speaks of 'his' (i.e. God's) servants the prophets. On the other hand, Moses is called 'my servant' by God in Josh. 1.2, 7 and 2 Kgs 2.1, 'the servant of YHWH' in Josh. 1.15; 8.31, 33; 11.12; 12.6; 13.8; 14.7; 18.7; 22.2, 4, 5, and 2 Kgs 14.12, and simply 'his (i.e. God's) servant' in Josh. 9.34 and 1 Kgs 8.56.[15] It is difficult to avoid the conclusion

14. For a discussion of the social setting of the redactor of Second Zechariah, see Redditt (1989: 638-40). Whether that redactor belonged to a 'Deuteronomic' school as Person (1993) argues may be left open. For a discussion of the community of the redactor of the Twelve, see Redditt (2000: 14-25).

15. To be sure, the man Nehemiah also calls Moses 'your [i.e. God's] servant' in Neh. 1.7-8 and 9.14, and simply 'the servant of YHWH' in Neh. 10.29, suggesting that

that the author of Mal. 3.22-24 (4.4-6) did not have his eye on the Twelve, but on the Former Prophets at least when he penned those words, if not Deuteronomy or the entire Torah as well (cf. Rudolph 1976: 290-93).

Third, if this reconstruction of the rise of the Twelve is largely correct, it provides a peek into the process of canonization. Davies writes that 'A work becomes canonized; (a) by being preserved by copying until its status as a classic is ensured; and (b) by being classified as belonging to a collection of some kind' (1998: 9). In the case of the Twelve, the process involved the assembling of a variety of prophetic voices into collections bearing the names of specific 'prophets', the collecting of those 'voices' into at least three precursors. In those precursors redactors blended the 'voices' and even corrected them along the way. Eventually, one or more redactors united the precursors, the collections Joel and Obadiah, and the narrative that constitutes Jonah into a collection of Twelve Prophets. To that collection another redactor added Zech. 9–14. All this collecting was performed by scribes, who not only copied, but connected divergent voices, sewed them together in the seams between the voices, and occasionally even added their own insights. Their unity lay, not in their agreement with each other, but in their testimony to the power of YHWH's word to find fulfillment in the lives of God's people (see Steck 2000: 143).

the phrase was not simply idiosyncratic to Mal. 3.22 in the postexilic period.

Table 1. Intertextuals Listed by Raymond F. Person in his Second Zechariah and the Deuteronomic School

Second Zechariah	Deuteronomic Texts	Deuteronomic Phrases and Themes	Jeremiah
9.5-6	Deut. 23.3		25.20
9.11			38.6
10.1-2	1 Kgs 22.13-23; Deut. 18.10; 13.2, 4, 6		23.25-28
10.4			30.20-21
10.8b			23.3; 30.19-20
10.9			8.19
10.10	Deut. 1.7; 3.25; 11.24; Josh. 1.4, etc.		
10.12		'in his name they will walk'	
11.1-3			25.34-38; 49.10; 50.44
11.4-17			25.15-29
11.9			15.2
11.10		'break covenant'	15.2
11.16		'devour (human) flesh'	19.19
11.17	Deut. 34.7; 1 Sam. 3.2, 13		23.1-4
12.2			25.15-17
12.2, 6		'all the surrounding peoples'	
12.3		'all the nations of the earth'	
12.3, 9; 13.2, 4; 14.6, 8, 13		'and it will come to pass on that day'	
12.4	Deut. 28.28; 2 Kgs 9.20		
12.6	Judg. 15.4-5(?)		
12.10-11	2 Kgs 23.29-30(?)		
12.12-14			31.1, 34-35
13.2-6		false prophecy	

Second Zechariah	Deuteronomic Texts	Deuteronomic Phrases and Themes	Jeremiah
13.2	Deut. 13.6; 17.7; 19.8; 21.21; 22.21, 24; 24.7, etc.		
13.3	Deut. 13.2-4, 6; 18.20; 21.18-21		
13.6	Deut. 4.1; 25.2; 1 Kgs 18.28; 2 Kgs 9.24		
13.7	1 Kgs 22.17		10.21; 23.1-4; 25.34-38; 49.20; 50.45
13.9			33.2-3
14.1		'behold, the Day of YHWH is coming'	
14.3		'those nations'	
14.9	Deut. 6.4		
14.10	2 Kgs 14.13	'Corner Gate'	31.38
14.10		'Gate of Benjamin'	20.2; 37.13; 38.7
14.10		'Tower of Hanamel'	31.38
14.13	Deut. 28.20, 28		
14.14, 16		'year after year'	
14.14, 16, 19		'Feast of Booths'	

Table 2. *Intertextuals listed by Ina Willi-Plein in her Prophetie am Ende, p. 93*

Second Zechariah	Non-prophetic Texts	Isaiah 1–39	Isaiah 40–55	Isaiah 56–66	Jeremiah	Ezekiel	Hosea	Amos	Micah	Similar
9.1-8		29.1-8				ch. 28	2.19	1.6-8		Isa. 66.17
9.9-10		31.1-3					2.20-25			Zech. 2.14; Mic. 4.10; 5.10
10.1-2	Deut. 11.15				14.15					
10.3a, 6, 8-10, 12					23.1-3	ch. 34, esp. vv. 25-30; 6.8-10	2.23-25			
11.1-3	Judg. 9.15	2.13? 10.28[-34]			25.34-38; 49.19					
11.17					50.35-38?					
13.2-6							2.19	7.14	3.3-6?	
13.7-9			48.10			ch. 5, esp. vv. 2-3, 12; 6.8-10	2.22-25			
14.1-2, 5b (9)		[13.16b?]								
11.4-16					12.3; 23.1-4; 25.34-36	ch. 34; 37.15-28	12.9; 3.1 [-5?]			
9.9-17	Gen. 37.24; Exod. 24.3-8		42.6-7	61.7??	31.10-20					Isa. 61.1
10.3b-5, 7, 11		[14.2-4;] [22.23]			30.21					
12.1-13.1	Deut. 28.28		44.24; 51.13, 16, 17-23		2.13	(38.1–39.1;) 39.2-29; 36.25				Joel 3.1
14.1-21	Gen 8.22; Deut 6.4	[2.1-4]	40.4ff	60.19-20	2.13; 31.38-40; 25.9; 43.28	11.23; 43.1-3; ch. 47		5.20	4.1-4	Zech. 8.20-22; Joel 4.17-18; Isa. 24.23; 66.18-24

Table 3. *Intertextuals Listed by Katrina J.A. Larkin in her* The Eschatology of Second Zechariah

Second Zechariah	Type of Interext	Non-Prophetic Texts	Isaiah	Jeremiah	Ezekiel	Amos	Hosea	Zechriah 1–8
9.1	Mantological Exegesis		17.1, 7					
9.1	Formula							2.12; 3.9; 4.10; 8.6
9.1	Wisdom Influence	מׂשּׂא						
9.2a(?)	Mantological Exegesis				47.15-20			
9.5-6	Mantological Exegesis					1.6-8		
9.6	Allusion	Deut. 23.3						
9.6, 10; 13.2	Allusion	Lev. 17.10; 20.3, 5						
9.7	Echo	Deuteronomic Language						
9.7b	Mantological Exegesis					1.8b		
9.8	Formula							2.12; 3.9; 4.10; 8.6
9.8a	Mantological Exegesis		29.3					
9.8b	Quotation	Job 42.5b						
9.9-10	Mantological Exegesis	Gen. 49; Ps. 72.8						2.14
9.11-12	Typology	Genesis (Joseph)		Jeremiah				
10.1-2	Mantological Exegesis			14.22, 14				
10.6	Mantological Exegesis						9.3	
10.10a(?)	Mantological Exegesis						9.3	
10.11	Typology	Exodus						
11.1-2(?)	Mantological Exegesis		2.13-15					
11.12, 17	Formula							2.12; 3.9; 4.10; 8.6
11.4-14	Mantological Exegesis				37.15-28			
11.15-16	Mantological Exegesis				34.2-6			
11.17(?)	Mantological Exegesis			50.35-38				

Second Zechariah	Type of Intertext	Non-Prophetic Texts	Isaiah	Jeremiah	Ezekiel	Amos	Hosea	Zechriah 1–8
12.1	Wisdom Influence	מֵשָׂא						
12.4	Echo	Deut. 28.28						
12.4	Formula							2.12; 3.9; 4.10; 8.6
12.9–13.1					36.18-28			7.3-5; 8.19
13.1	Allusion	Lev. 12.2						
13.3, 7	Allusion	Levitical						
13.5	Allusion						7.14		
13.8					5.1-12			
14.9	Allusion	Deut. 6.4						
14.10-11	Allusion	Lev. 25.9						

Table 4. *Intertextuals Listed by Nicholas H.F. Tai in his* Prophetie als Schriftauslegung in Sacharja 9-14

Second Zechariah	Non-Prophetic Texts	Isaiah 1–39	Isaiah 40–55	Isaiah 56–66	Jeremiah	Ezekiel	The Twelve
9.1-8	Deut. 23.3	20.5-6			5.20-24; 3.7b-8	47.13-7; 28.3-5; 7.20-4	Mal. 1.1
9.9-10	Ps. 33.16-17; Ps. 72						Zeph. 3.14-5; Mic. 7.9; Zech. 2.14
9.11-17	Exod. 24.1-11; Deut. 15.12-18; Ps. 80.2-4			61.1-3	ch. 34; 31.10-14		
10.1-2	Deut. 11.11, 13-14				5.25; 14.13-16		
10.3-12	Exodus traditions; Josh. 4.7, 23; Ps. 89.10				23.1-4; 31.10-11, 27; 51.50		Hos. 2.25
11.1-3					22.20-23; 25.34-38; 21.14		
11.4-17						37.15-28; 34.23-24	
12.1-8	Deut. 28.28; David traditions in 1 and 2 Samuel; Ps. 18.40	10.16	42.5; 51.17-23		5.14; 51.17-23		Mal. 1.1; Zech. 3.2; Obad. 18; Joel 3.1-2
12.9-13	32.15-20		44.3-4			39.29	Joel 3.1-2
13.1	Num. 19.9, 17					36.25	
13.2-6	1 Kgs 13.18				30.14	36.25, 27	Hos. 2.18-19; Amos 7.14; Mic. 3.5-7
13.7-9	Ps. 66.10, 12				6.9	5.1-2, 11-12	Hos. 2.18, 23, 25; Amos 1.8; Joel 3.5
14.1-21	Ps. 22.28-29; Gen. 8.22; 1 Kgs 5.4-5	2.2-4; 13.10, 16		ch. 60	31.38-40	chs. 40-48	Amos 5.18; Mic. 4.1-3; 1.3-4; Zeph. 3.8-10; Hab. 3.3-6; Mal. 3.22-24

Table 5. *Intertexts Listed by Risto Nurmela in his Prophets in Dialogue*: Inner-Biblical Allusions in Zechariah 1–8 and 9–14

Second Zechariah	Non-Prophetic Texts	Isaiah	Jeremiah	Ezekiel	Hosea	First Zechariah
9.2-4				28.3-5		
9.8		29.3				7.14
9.9						2.14
9.10	Ps. 72.8					
9.13		49.2				
9.15, 17	Ps. 144.12					
9.15; 12.8		31.5				
9.16		62.3, 10				8.7, 13
10.1-2	Deut. 11.14-15		10.13-15; 51.16-18; 14.4-22			
10.3, 6-10			23.1-3; 29.14; 32.37			
10.4			30.21			
10.6						8.7, 13
10.8-10		41.17				8.7-8
10.11		11.15-16				
11.1-2		2.13				
11.2-3			25.34-38			
11.7, 10, 14, 16; 13.7-9		1.25		34.2-4, 5; 37.15-28; 5.1-12		
12.1		51.13				
12.4	Deut. 28.28					
12.7						8.7, 13
12.10-13.2				36.17, 22-32		
13.2					2.19	
13.3			14.14; 27.15			

Second Zechariah	Non-Prophetic Texts	Isaiah	Jeremiah	Ezekiel	Hosea	First Zechariah
14.4				11.23; 43.2		
14.6						8.20-23
14.8				47.1-12		
14.11				Terms from throughout book		
14.12, 16		66.23-24				
14.21				46.20, 24		
14.21				44.9		

Table 7. *Growth of Isaiah and the Twelve in the Greek Period as Proposed by O.H. Steck in his Der Abschluss der Prophetie im Alten Testament*

Isaiah	The Twelve
A. Isaiah and the Twelve in the Persian Period	
1–34, 36–39, 40–55+60–62	Much of the Twelve in place. Mal. 1.2-5; 1.6–2.9 (vv. 13-16?); 3.6-12 added to Zech. 1–8
B. Isaiah and the Twelve in the Time of Alexander the Great	
	(1) Twelve Preliminary Step I: Insertion of Zech. 9.1–10.2 (between 332 and 323 BCE)
	(2) Twelve Preliminary Step II: Insertion of Zech. 10.3–11.3 (between 320 and 350 BCE)
(3) Isaiah Expansion I: First uniting of Isa. 1–39 and 40–55+60–62 Redactional additions: 10.20-23; 11.11-16; 13.5-16; chs. 24–27; 30.18-26(?); 34.2-4; ch. 35; 51.1-3, 4-5, 6-8, 10b-11; 54.2-3, 9-10; 55.10-11(?); 62.10-12	(-) Twelve Expansion I: Addition of Joel, Obadiah, Zephaniah (slightly later)
(4) Isaiah Expansion II Redactional additions: 1.27-8; 4.2-6; 29.17-24; 33.14-16; 48.22; 51.16; 56.9–59.21; 60.17-22; 61.2; 62.8-9; 63.1-6 (between 311 and 302/1 BCE)	(5) Twelve Expansion II: Redactional addition of Zech. 11.4–13.9 (slightly later)
(6) Isaiah Expansion III: 1.29-31; 12.1-6; 14.1-3(?); 54.11-17; 56.1-8; 58.13-14; 60.12a; 61.3; 63.7–64.11 (all between 302/1 and 270 BCE); 65.1–66.24 (about 253 BCE, at same time as 19.18-25)	(7) Twelve Expansion III: Redactional addition of Zech. 14 (between 240 and 220 BCE)
C. Final Stage in the Formation of the Twelve	
	(8) Separation of Malachi from Zechariah to form twelfth book. Addition of Zech. 12.1a; Mal. 1.1; 2.10-12; 3.22-24 (Eng. 4.4-6) (between 220 and 201 or 198 and 190 BCE)

PUTTING THE ESCHATOLOGICAL VISIONS OF ZECHARIAH
IN THEIR PLACE: MALACHI AS A HERMENEUTICAL GUIDE
FOR THE LAST SECTION OF THE BOOK OF THE TWELVE

Aaron Schart

In the last decades of the twentieth century it has become increasingly clear, and may now be considered as a basis for studies in the new millennium, that the so-called Minor Prophets must be perceived as parts of the Book of the Twelve Prophets. As James Nogalski has proposed, one should therefore no longer speak of Amos, Hosea, Malachi and the other prophetic collections as *books* but rather designate them as *writings*, which were meant to form a book only in combination. Within the collection of the Twelve, the writings were combined in such a way that the meaning of the whole overruled the meaning that a certain text had in its original place. The theological position that was held by the last redactors was inferred into every part of the collection. As a result, it is imperative that commentators of single writings take into account the place and function this writing has within the book as a whole (Petersen 1995; Sweeney 2000; Weyde 2000).

If the Book of the Twelve is purposefully arranged, one should expect to find a coherent global structure that directs the reading process (Collins 1993: 65; House 1990: 67-71). Most important in this respect are the beginnings of the twelve writings, nine of which contain superscriptions.[1] Since the dated beginnings follow in a historical sequence, the reader gets the impression that the whole collection intends to unfold a certain part of the history of prophecy. The deepest break is located between Zephaniah and Haggai. At this point the Babylonian exile is obviously presupposed,

---

1. I only want to speak of a superscription if 'die Informationen, die sie enthält, auf einer Metaebene zum restlichen Textkorpus liegen und sie weder grammatisch noch semantisch eine lineare Anknüpfung an den folgenden Text aufweist' (Schart 1998: 32). This is true only for Hos. 1.1; Joel 1.1; Amos 1.1; Obad. 1a; Mic. 1.1; Nah. 1.1; Hab. 1.1; Zeph. 1.1 and Mal. 1.1.

but the redactors do not even mention it. It seems to me that the redactor deliberately highlighted and justified this silence, in so far as Hab. 2.20; Zeph. 1.7 and Zech. 2.17 stress in very similar phrases the fact that silence is the appropriate human reaction when faced with the awe-inspiring and formidable reality of the LORD. To use the words of Zech. 2.17: 'Be silent, all people, before the LORD!'

Within the last section of the Twelve, including Haggai, Zechariah, and Malachi, it is unambiguous that Haggai and Zechariah form a single unit.[2] It is much more difficult to establish, however, why and how Malachi follows Zechariah. There are reasons to argue that Malachi is not the proper name for a prophet, but rather a title ('my messenger'). If this were true, it would be even more obvious that Malachi is not just another part of the chain of prophets, but serves a different purpose.

1. *How Many Layers in Malachi?*

Evaluating the source-criticism of Malachi, it is safe to say that over the last decades there has emerged a strong consensus that Mal. 3.22-24 was added to form a conclusion not only for the Book of the Twelve, but also for the second part of the Hebrew Canon, Nebiim (Rudolph 1976: 291; Nogalski 1993b: 185; Steck 1991: 134-36; Schart 1998: 302-303; Weyde 2000: 388-93).[3] The rest of Malachi is more difficult to analyze. Among others, Bosshard and Kratz (1990), as well as Steck (1991), have proposed that one has to differentiate between two layers. Bosshard and Kratz start with the observation that Mal. 1.6-2.9 and 3.6-12 belong together because they use similar concepts. Likewise Mal. 2.17–3.5 and 3.13-21 belong together. Only the last two units mention a coming *Läuterungsgericht* ('purifying punishment'). This thematic difference is enough evidence for Bosshard and Kratz to postulate two layers in Malachi. Their oldest layer (*Grundschicht*) is comprised of Mal. 1.2-5; 1.6–2.9 (without 1.14a) and 3.6-12.[4] Since it is very common in prophetic writings to find oracles that

---

2.   Neither Haggai nor Zechariah begins with a superscription; instead, they utilize a narrative framework, which consistently uses the same dating formula—'In the second year of King Darius' (e.g. Hag. 1.1; Zech. 1.1)—and seamlessly combines the prophecies of Haggai and Zechariah.

3.   According to Steck, Mal. 1.1 also belongs to this addition. However the arguments are weak. They only gain weight when one presupposes the thesis that Malachi once followed seamlessly after Zechariah—a thesis I will consider and dismiss below.

4.   Bosshard-Nepustil (1997) repeats his earlier hypothesis (Bosshard and Kratz 1990) without mentioning any new arguments.

address present issues placed alongside those that deal with the judgment of God in the future, I see this argument of Bosshard and Kratz as very weak. Different oracles addressing different topics do not necessarily produce a source-critically relevant tension.

There are, however, some insertions. Relevant for this study is the case of Mal. 1.11-14. Elliger (1956: 198) considers the whole passage as secondary. However, I think that if one isolates Mal 1.11aβb and 1.14b as secondary elements, the rest of the passage fits into its context and should belong to the oldest layer. There are some other insertions, but they are not relevant for this investigation.[5]

2. To What Layer of Zechariah
Was the Basic Layer of Malachi Attached?

a. *Was the Malachi* Grundschicht *Attached to Zechariah 8?*
Steck (1991), Bosshard and Kratz (1990), and Nogalski (1993b) have proposed that their Malachi *Grundschicht* (not mine!) once followed Zech. 8. They compile a lengthy list of citations, allusions and thematic connections between the text passages in question. This list is at first glance quite impressive, and one has to admit that they note a lot of *Bezüge*, as they call them, which nobody has noted before. However, overwhelmed by the sheer mass of so far undiscovered *Bezüge*, they tend to overstate their case. First, it would be helpful if they would evaluate the significance of their observations. At least some of the *Bezüge* may not have been noted before simply because they are coincidental and meaningless. Second, one gets the feeling that these scholars no longer assume an oral history of the prophetic texts. Although it is true that many of the late prophetic writings belong to the literary type of *Schriftprophetie*, one should not deny up front that the writings grew out of a process of 'preaching the tradition', as Rex Mason has reconstructed it. Especially in the case of Malachi, one has the distinct impression that the written text goes back to discussions in which the prophet was involved. Shared vocabulary between different prophetic texts would be a natural consequence, if their authors took part

---

5. The one I consider most obvious is Mal. 3.1b-4, where a phrase from Joel is picked up and applied to the messenger of the covenant. This is one of the instances where it is very obvious that the redactors of the Malachi *Grundschicht* deliberately cite Joel, whereas the *Grundschicht* itself does not. The redactor wants to identify the messenger of the *Grundschicht* with the day of the LORD from Joel.

in the same debate within the community of faith.[6] In this article I do not want to evaluate all of their *Bezüge*, but only those that I think are most interesting.[7]

(1) *First Argument: Mal. 3.6-7//Zech. 8.14//Zech. 1.2-3.* These three passages share a particular concept: in the current time the LORD proclaims that the punishment of the sins of the fathers has come to an end. The LORD is prepared to start anew if this generation repents and returns to Yahweh. All three passages share the sentences: 'Return to me…and I will return to you…' It can well be argued that these striking verbal agreements stem from the oral stage. The redactional framework of the visions in Zech. 1 and 8 may stem from the same community in which the discussion presupposed by Mal. 3.6-12 was rooted.

(2) *Second Argument: Mal. 1.9, 13b//Zech. 8.9, 13.* The phrase 'your hand' (singular) in Mal. 1.9, 13b alludes to the phrase 'your hands' (plural) in Zech 8.9, 13. This allusion is not very significant. One can ask why it is not mentioned that Zech. 14.13 has the singular 'hand' three times. In Zech. 8.9, 13 we have an exhortation: 'Let your hands be strong!' The addressed audience is Israel as a whole. In Malachi it is the priesthood. The fact is stressed, that the priests are responsible for the quality of the gifts offered to Yahweh. The chance that this allusion was intentionally created is very small.

(3) *Third Argument: Mal. 1.2-3//Zech. 8.17, 19.* More significantly, in both chapters Yahweh himself states 'I hate' (*qatal* first person) something. In

---

6. 'In the second place, the suggestion that such material is the result not only of a purely literary activity but springs from and reflects the living process of "preaching the tradition" surely does bring it to life and show something of its importance in the life and faith of a living community. It is all too easy for academic biblical scholars, using the techniques of literary criticism, to present the development of the biblical material in purely literary terms. It is almost as though we discern our counterparts sitting at some oil-lit desk in an ancient prototype of the Bodleian Library engaged in a purely intellectual exercise of up-dating the text, ironing out its difficulties or re-interpreting it so as to uphold its truth when its predictions have not been seen to materialise. But preachers are engaged on a more immediate and urgent task. They are concerned from a sense of pastoral need for a community of faith. They must meet the constant threats of loss of faith or, at least, of apathy towards that faith and its observance through disappointment and disillusion' (Mason 1990: 261).

7. Compare Lescow's very critical evaluation (1993: 179-84).

Zech. 8 it is the 'oath of falsehood' (8.17), whereas in Malachi it is Esau. Only six times does Yahweh hate something in first person speech (Jer. 12.8; 44.4; Hos. 9.15; Amos 5.29). This seems statistically remarkable, but it needs to be clarified whether the allusion makes any specific sense in a larger concept of coherence or contrast between the passages involved.

(4) *Fourth Argument: Zech. 8.21-22//Mal. 1.9.* Both passages contain the phrase 'to entreat the favor'. This phrase occurs 16 times, but the imperative used in Mal. 1.9 is only employed one other time in 1 Kgs 13.6 (Weyde 2000: 134). Since the concept of entreating Yahweh is of great theological value, it may well not be by chance that this phrase occurs here and there. Nogalski rightly asks: 'Given that these two passages consistently use the same vocabulary to contrast radically different situations, and that one can sometimes detect one or the other passage appears to be shaping the contrast, the question arises: why do the passages contrast situations as they do?' (Nogalski 1993b: 199). And his answer is:

> The Haggai–Zechariah (1–8) corpus depicts a very hopeful and positive view of the times surrounding the building of the temple... Malachi, with its portrayal of the abuses of both people and priest, presents a shocking contrast to the hope in Zechariah... The situation has gone full circle, as if Jerusalem's destruction and Yahweh's subsequent deliverance have been for naught. The circular pattern of judgment, punishment, and deliverance begins again in precisely the place where one would expect a different, more hopeful, beginning. In this light, the calls of Zechariah to learn from the mistakes of the fathers (especially 1.2-6; 7.9-14, 8.9-13,14f) appear even more poignant, precisely because they went unheeded, despite the optimism with which they were delivered. (Nogalski 1993b: 200)

Although Nogalski's interpretation of the thematic progression from Zechariah to Malachi seems well taken, this does not at all exclude the possibility that Zech. 9–14 stood between Zech. 8 and Mal. 1.[8]

b. *Was the Malachi* Grundschicht *Attached to Zechariah 13?*
Steck has proposed the thesis that the basic layer of Malachi followed Zech. 13. His hypothesis is very complicated and therefore difficult to evaluate. His strongest argument seems to be that Zech. 13.8-9; Mal. 3.2

---

8. This is demonstrated by the fact that Nogalski's position resembles very much the synchronic reading of the Haggai–Zechariah–Malachi corpus by Pierce (1984). Another problem is that Nogalski does not compare Zech. 14 and Mal. 1. It would be interesting to see how many allusions he would find in this case.

and 3.13-21 have the concept of purifying punishment (*Läuterungsgericht*) in common. Again, the main question is why a thematic allusion between the passages must imply that they once followed one another immediately.

c. *Was the Malachi* Grundschicht *Attached to Zechariah (9–)14?*
As a result, one is left with the simplest thesis, namely, that the basic layer in Malachi was attached to Zechariah after ch. 14 was added to the pre-existing corpus of prophetic writings.

(1) *First Argument.* As is well known, the strongest argument for the thesis that Malachi already had Zech. 9–14 in mind is based on the super-scription in Mal. 1.1, which is of the same type as the superscriptions in Zech. 9.1 and Zech. 12.1.[9] In addition, Petersen has observed that there is a certain move behind the arrangement of the superscriptions: the first addresses a foreign nation (Zech. 9.1), the second concerns Israel (Zech. 12.1; preposition עַל), and the third refers to Israel's being directly addressed (Mal. 1.1).[10]

(2) *Second Argument.* In Zech. 14.20-21, the phrase 'house of Yahweh' occurs twice. Also mentioned is the holiness of this place. This is a fitting thematic link to Mal. 1, where prominent installations of the temple and the levitical priesthood are mentioned.

(3) *Third Argument.* The strongest verbal allusions between Zech. 14 and Malachi are in Zech. 14.9 and Mal. 1.14aβb. I quote Myers and Myers:

> Although 'Yahweh of Hosts' is surely, as indicated above, disproportionately frequent in postexilic prophecy, 'king' appears in Haggai–Zechariah–Malachi only here (vv. 16-17) and in Mal. 1.14 ('I am a great king, says Yahweh of Hosts', and 'my name is revered among the nations') in relationship to God. (Meyers and Meyers 1993: 467)

9.   Nogalski assumes that Mal. 1.1 is the oldest superscription, and that Zech. 9.1 and 12.1 were modeled after Mal. 1.1. However, this is questionable. Bosshard and Kratz, as well as Steck, argue that the superscription in Mal. 1.1 was inserted as part of the last layer in Malachi. This is questionable, too.

10.   'If I am correct in understanding Malachi as the third in a series of deutero-prophetic collections, the sequence of prepositions relating these collections to various nations or territories is especially significant: *b-* against a foreign nation (Zech. 9:1), '*al*-concerning Israel (Zech. 12:1), and '*el* to Israel (Mal. 1:1)' (Petersen 1995: 165).

It seems very obvious to me that the redactor who inserted Mal. 1.11aβb and 14b did so in order to underline and strengthen the linkage between Mal. 1 and Zech. 14, and thus stitch together these two writings within the Book of the Twelve. The redactor probably found it unsatisfying that the Joel–Obadiah corpus would conclude with Zech. 14, so Malachi was attached to Zech. 14. The redactor already had the text of Malachi in a fixed form. Some verbal allusions to the Joel–Obadiah corpus already existed within this pre-existing version of Malachi, for example the allusions to Zech. 8.20-23, the theme of worldwide reverence toward Yahweh in Zech. 14, and the allusion from Mal. 1.11aα to Zech. 14.9 (שם). The very same redactor may have inserted Zech. 14.20-21 in order to focus the reader on the place that is relevant in Mal. 1.6–2.9. The allusions were there because in the redactor's community it was common to preach and read the Book of the Ten as respected scripture and be inspired by it.

(4) *Summary*. The thesis that the basic layer in Malachi was originally attached to Zech. 14 seems to be more sound and probable than the others that have been proposed, especially since it does not exclude the possibility that the redactor who added Malachi to the pre-existing corpus also wanted to allude to Zech. 8.20-23. To be sure, I do not think that Zechariah and Malachi formed a literary stratum from the very beginning. The evidence is far too weak.[11] The redactor who attached Malachi had before him a collection of oracles, the basic layer of Malachi. This collection already shared themes and vocabulary, especially with redactional passages in Haggai–Zech. 1–14. In order to strengthen the coherence between Haggai–Zechariah, on the one hand, and the basic layer in Malachi, on the other, the redactor inserted some passages into Malachi (e.g. Mal. 1.11aβb, 14b) which presuppose Malachi's position after Zech. 14 and within the Book of the 'Twelve'. What does this mean?

3. What Meaning is Conveyed by the Redactional Arrangement?

Whatever source-critical hypotheses one considers plausible, in the end one has to explain the final, canonical order. How is Malachi's meaning to be construed when it is read after Zech. 14? In fact, Zech. 14 would form a

---

11. On the contrary, lexemes and concepts prominent in Zech. 14 are not mentioned in the basic layer of Malachi: Yahweh as king, holiness, סכות, aggression of the nations, and others. In addition, the formulas which structure the text within Zech. 14 (e.g. והיה ביום ההוא) are not used in Malachi.

glorious and satisfying end of the book. What would be more appropriate for a prophetic book, which has as one of its most central topics the coming of the Day of the Lord, than to close with a magnificent description of this event? Zech. 14 is in my view written to form the end of the Joel–Obadiah corpus. All the tensions within the Book of the Twelve are solved, and a scenario for the end time is established which is complex enough to include all aspects of the future of all the prophets within the book.[12] Why is it that something follows Zech. 14? Why does Yahweh need to send his messenger after his last prophet Zechariah has summed up the history of prophecy in such an elegant manner?[13]

a. *Arguing the Tradition*

Already the form of this last writing is important. The disputation speeches attempt to persuade the addressees.[14] At the same time they involve the reader of Malachi in typical debates. Again and again, the point is not that the opponents consciously disregard Yahweh and his laws, but that they appear surprised over the attacks of the prophet. One gets the impression that the opponents have a generally positive attitude towards the basic norms, which the prophet propagates. In addition, they are convinced that they practice these norms. It is typical that the hearers do not contradict the basic contentions of the speeches but rather ask במה ('how is that?'). However, there are obviously differences between the hearer and the

---

12. 'Ch. 14 is a summary of the eschatological teaching of almost all the preceding prophets: the assault on Jerusalem, the destruction of the City, cosmic phenomena, Yahweh's final victory, the conversion of the gentiles and their pilgrimage to the newly established City. This is certainly not intra-historical eschatology; it derives from a general picture gleaned from all the prophets and made to live in cultic circles around 331. It is the final eschatological summary, and conclusive re-interpretation of all prophecy from Amos to Zechariah' (Grech 1969: 253-54). 'Ein wesentlicher Unterschied zwischen Sach 14 und Sach 9, 1–13, 9 in Bezug auf die Anspielungen auf die älteren Texte besteht darin, daß Sach 14 einen gesamten Entwurf der eschatologischen Erwartung vorlegt und dazu die traditionsgeschichtlich vorgegebenen Vorstellungen ausbaut, während die Aussagen in Sach 9, 1–13, 9 von den Bezugstexten inspiriert, beeinflußt oder vorgeprägt sind' (Tai 1996: 229). For example, the earthquake is mentioned in Zech. 14.5, which once confirmed the message of Amos; and Zech. 14.8 alludes to Joel 4.18.

13. 'Der Übergang vom Sacharjabuch zu Maleachi ist überraschend. Nach dem endzeitlichen Kampf um Jerusalem (Sach 14) ist nun wieder von Problemen des gegenwärtigen Lebens die Rede' (Rendtorff 1983: 254).

14. In my view it is probable that the disputation speeches report real discussions in a condensed form.

prophet about the right practice in everyday life. The shift from Zech. 14 to Malachi redirects the focus from the tremendous end time vision to the small-scale problems of the proper *halachah*.

b. *The Present Situation is Important for the Future*

Malachi recognizes that the promised, glorious future of Zion is already effective in his time. This can best be demonstrated in the case of the nations. Everywhere the name of Yahweh is revered, and at the same time Edom's final destruction is already on the way. But still this future is 'impeded by the unworthy behavior of the priests in the temple, the very place where God's name should be honored most' (Collins 1993: 81). One gets the impression that if the 'religious laxity' of the hearers could be overcome, the final victory of the Kingdom of God could materialize (Pierce 1984: 410). It is not enough to wait until the day comes. Here and now one has to act as if it were already near.

c. *No Mention of Edom*

Zechariah 14 does not mention Edom, although it is one of Yahweh's preeminent enemies.

Although Zech. 14 tried to include all aspects of the Joel–Obadiah corpus, one thing was not included within the scenario: What will happen to Edom, who is—according to Obadiah—the pre-eminent enemy of Yahweh? Malachi 1 states clearly that Edom will in this present age be destroyed forever.

d. *God Judges Individuals Not Nations*

The pre-eminent achievement of Zech. 14 is the idea that after the nations conquer Jerusalem and are subsequently defeated by Yahweh, their remnant will finally take part in the cult of Israel. Within Zech. 14 the actors involved in the end time are nations. In Malachi, however, particularly in 3.13-21, it is clear that in the end God will judge every single person. The survivors of Israel and the nations, who will, according to Zech. 14, together celebrate the Feast of Booths, are not morally qualified in any sense. They are simply the ones who escaped destruction in the last days, for whatever reason. Yahweh's kingdom does justice to nations but ignores the fate of the individual person. In contrast, Mal. 3 states firmly that the final judgment will take into account every single life, even every single action (Koenen 1994: 65).

e. *Eschatological Visions Must be Counterbalanced by Torah-Practice*
Bosshard and Kratz have rightly observed that only in Mal. 2.17–3.5 and
3.13-21 can an eschatological perspective be detected. Both passages have
more features in common than a shared theme. (1) Both disputation
speeches state in the very first sentence that they are reactions to presupposed attacks from the 'you-group'. The phrase 'your words' occurs in
Mal. 2.17 and 3.13. This clearly shows that the prophet is attacked by the
'you-group' and needs to defend his case. (2) In both cases the 'you-
group' doubts that the wicked get their just punishment while the people
who cling to Yahweh get an adequate reward. (3) The rejoinder to this line
of reasoning is, in both instances, based on the expectation that the future
will bring a definite differentiation between the two groups. The wicked
will be punished and the righteous will be rewarded for being ridiculed in
the present time.

We have two lines of argumentation within Malachi. The first (Mal.
1.6–2.9; 2.10-16; 3.6-12) tries to motivate the hearers/readers to whole-
heartedly fulfill the Torah, especially in cultic matters. Specific passages
of the written Torah play an important role and are cited: Mal. 1.8 cites
Lev. 22.18-25, and Mal. 2.4 cites Deut. 18.1-8. Malachi defends the
position that the duties of a righteous Israelite are clearly stated in the
Torah. If one fulfills the Torah partially (e.g. Mal. 3.10), or gives it a low
priority (e.g. 1.7), or, in the worst case, misleads others with it (e.g. 2.8-9),
one does not do justice to Yahweh who loves his people like a father. In
the disputation speeches Malachi is aggressive and confronts people who
do not heed the Torah.

The second line of argument (Mal. 2.17–3.5; 3.13-21) treats different
problems. Malachi defends the argument that righteous behavior in the
present will be rewarded with overwhelming blessing in the future. The
righteous must not give up, but transform their expectations. The reward
will be fully experienced when the final day comes. So, what Malachi
really wants is to encourage a life according to the norms of the Torah. But
he also needs to address the claim that such a life is futile. If Malachi
cannot answer those questions, his demand to follow the Torah will go
unheard. The coming day of Yahweh is not a single event in the far future
and therefore irrelevant, but an event that in the dimension 'before
Yahweh' (3.16) already is reality and by virtue of its anticipation affects
the present. Every action is registered and archived in a book. Nothing
escapes the just sentence of Yahweh. It is wise to have this final judgment
in mind.

4. *Summary*

The glorious vision of the final day of the Lord in Zech. 14 once formed the end of the Joel–Obadiah corpus. However, the redactors of the canonical Book of the Twelve were not satisfied with this ending. They attached the writing of Malachi in order to prevent readers of the eschatological visions from misunderstanding them. The hope that Yahweh will be universally acknowledged, and that the nations and Israel will celebrate together in peaceful harmony, is needed and gives strength to the believers. However, there also needs to be a counterbalancing emphasis on not neglecting the everyday practice of Torah, which is the lifelong task of every single person.

In this respect Malachi represents an important hermeneutical guide for reading the Book of the Twelve from a canonical perspective. It is not allowed to stop reading after Zech. 14. The visions of Zechariah have to be put in their place.

A RESPONSE

Rex Mason

My reaction was two-fold when a call came from the Sheffield Academic Press telling me that Mark Boda and Michael Floyd were proposing to make my original 1973 thesis on Zech. 9–14 the basis for a series of papers and to prepare both thesis and papers for publication. The first, frankly, was surprise that after all this time a work which had been gathering dust on murky shelves in the Library of the University of London, unread by all but a handful of dedicated scholars engaged in the same area, should now be the subject of any interest whatever. The readership of such work even as I have published sometimes falls short of the astronomical, and it therefore surprised me that anyone should be interested in an unpublished work. Indeed, I had to read it myself to see what I had said all those years ago.

That initial reaction of surprise was swiftly followed by one of gratitude for their interest and concern, a gratitude which has grown as I have seen the enormous amount of work they as editors have done to put the carbon copy of an old typed work into modern digital form and make my erratic and antiquated reference systems such as modern publishers could deal with. And my gratitude to them includes also all those who took the time to prepare the papers which now accompany it and which I have found so exciting and informative, revealing as they do so many new lines of scholarly research and development which go far beyond my amateurish and puny efforts at the start of my academic and teaching career. That is why this short article is a 'response'. In no way is it intended as an 'answer' to those who have raised fully justifiable questions about my work, its assumptions, its methods and its claimed 'conclusions'. It is I who have everything to learn from them.

I should, perhaps, explain why the work was never published, although as I do so I am uncomfortably mindful of the French saying, *Qui s'excuse, s'accuse*. I had always meant to prepare the thesis for publication at some time, but that time never seemed to come. Its examiners, George W. Anderson and Robert Murray, suggested that it needed some 'popularizing' before I presented it to a wider public. But at that time I was just beginning teaching the Old Testament with all the preparation that requires, and, as some of you will know, the demands of denominational theological colleges (and the denominations they serve) on the time and energies of their staff are multifarious and ceaseless! And then there always seemed to be some new publishing task to absorb such spare time and energy as I had. Even when retirement came, the odd jobs still presented themselves and, eventually, I felt that the immense amount of work needed to bring it up to date outweighed any possible value it now might have. In the event, it is the work of the editors and all the contributors to this volume who have filled the gap between the state of Deutero-Zechariah studies as I saw them in 1973 and those studies as they have developed so enormously and profitably between then and now.

The publication of the thesis gives me an opportunity to acknowledge my immense debt to Professor Peter Ackroyd who was my supervisor and who became friend and endless source of inspiration to me over the years. Several contributors to this volume rightly point out that I was by no means the first to examine the influence of 'earlier' biblical literature apparent in Zech. 9–14. (See, e.g., Stade 1881; 1882; Delcor 1952.) It was Ackroyd, however, who was one of the pioneers in the use of the term 'inner biblical exegesis' and its practice. One has only to think of his article on the interpretation of the Babylonian exile (Ackroyd 1974) and many others conveniently now gathered in his 1987 volume of essays. Indeed, it was he who suggested the title for the thesis! The names of others who developed the method are mentioned by contributors to this volume and by me in my 1990 article on inner biblical exegesis. I would especially like to single out one not otherwise mentioned here, namely, J. Weingreen, for his seminal work on 'rabbinic-type glosses' (Weingreen 1976).

Re-reading the thesis has been an interesting (and often chastening) experience. I can only hope that readers will make some allowance for my tender youth and inexperience in 1973! But one section of it with which I remain content is the Introduction. For there I did try honestly to face some of the difficulties about the method of detecting 'earlier biblical influences' on a particular text. Thus I was quite open early in the thesis in acknowledging the fact that the study of the resonance of one text with another is an imprecise and, often, to a marked degree, subjective process, and I anticipated many of the objections which have since been levelled at the method. I acknowledged that, even where there may be identity of vocabulary, even, perhaps, vocabulary or syntax peculiar to the two passages, we cannot be certain which is quoting which, or even if quotation is taking place at all. Two passages may be citing a common source or reflecting a common vocabulary or set of ideas. Then there is always the danger that once a scholar has found a so-called 'dependence' in one place, he or she can go on finding it everywhere in a circularity of argument. Further, there is always the difficulty of establishing the date of the final form of any text as we now have it and so of knowing just exactly what it was the author had in front of him (Mason 1973: iii-v).

Of course, to say that one has anticipated or recognized problems and difficulties is certainly not to assert that one has met or dealt adequately with them. It is worth pointing out, however, that an element of subjectivity is not peculiar to this method of biblical study. It characterizes all methods, as I can call my friend John Barton to witness (Barton 1996: *passim*). The answer is, surely, not to abandon them, but to use them with care and humility, acknowledging that each is but one tool among many available to the biblical scholar and by no means the one master key that unlocks every secret. My own method was a cumulative one, trying to test results step by step and waiting until there was, or was not, a sufficient body of evidence to infer that any one kind of practice was at work.

Following on from this, then, I have found it most interesting and instructive to see the way various contributors to this volume have written about these problems. David Petersen, a scholar to whose work I owe an immense debt, has put me still more deeply in that debt by his perfectly justified and constructive call for some kind of system and order in one's use of terminology. How right he is to say that imprecision in vocabulary at once masks and encourages imprecision in *method*. I freely confess that my normally pallid features reddened just a little with embarrassment as I saw how I had bandied, even in the Introduction (let alone the main body of the work), words like 'exegesis', 'allusion', 'quotation', 'echo' and many others as indiscriminately as one sprinkles pepper on a goulash. I welcome his call for some attempt, at least, for order and system in one's use of terminology, an attempt amply and ably demonstrated by the various scholars to whose work he so fruitfully calls attention.

But the problem is not only how one finds the proper words to describe the interaction of texts, but how one recognizes and establishes that there is any such interaction in the first place. All the contributors to this volume have exercised meticulous scholarship and painstaking care in examining the various criteria that must be met in order to establish 'dependency' of one text on another. They differ from one another, and that is not surprising where the method cannot be termed in any way a precise science. Risto Nurmela and Eibert Tigchelaar both insist on close, and often exclusive correspondence of vocabulary and phrasing between passages and demonstrate great care and skill in the way they seek to establish this. Paul Redditt, on the other hand, thinks that this is to limit evidence of intertextuality 'too severely'.

Nevertheless, when struggling with the difficulty of establishing where intertextual relationships exist, and just what to call them when one does claim to have found them, there are one or two grains of comfort to be found, I think. The first is that it is not only biblical scholars who experience the difficulty. This has been well illustrated in Richard Schultz's excellent book *The Search for Quotation: Verbal Parallels in the Prophets* (1999). Examining the phenomenon not only in biblical literature, but in that of the ancient Near East more widely, and then in that of more modern Western literature, he shows that the same vexed issues constantly arise in all comparative literary studies. There is some comfort to be derived from that!

There is further comfort, for me at least, in finding that, if one has sinned, one has done so in good company. Schultz cites the example of Otto Kaiser who, in his *Introduction to the Old Testament*, uses five different terms for the process on one page, 'alteration of saying', 'phrases taken over', 'quotations', 'distinctive recasting' and 'echoes' (Schultz 1999: 217 n. 15). Perhaps it is a case of 'Let him that is without exegetical sin cast the first footnote' (and it would be an interesting exercise to discover whether that should be called an example of 'allusion' or 'echo', or given some other name!).

The third grain of comfort, perhaps even a little act of self-defense on my part, is to point out that the influence exerted by one text on another can be an extremely complex and varied process. In my initial response to the early papers read at Denver I cited an example from my Sunday School days as a boy in a very theologically conservative, Bible-based, Baptist church. In those days there was only one English version in common use (in such circles) and that was the King James Version. We learned verses and, indeed, whole passages from it and were required to recite them each Sunday. Consequently we were steeped in its language and its imagery. When, therefore, one week our teacher said to us some-

thing about his earlier life, describing it as 'when I was in Egypt', no one
needed to explain to us what he meant. We knew he was not referring to
some tour of the Upper Nile undertaken under the auspices of Thomas
Cook. He meant 'before I became a converted Christian'. Yet think of the
complex exegetical process that we as biblical scholars would have to
trace in order to explain that 'echo'. Such an analysis would need to say
something of the deuteronomistic setting of the account of the Exodus
which has presented it and interpreted it as a redemption of the Israelites
from slavery by God in order to call them into a covenant relationship with
God as the people of this God. It would need to trace the way the theme
became celebrated in the liturgy of the temple as reflected in many Psalms.
It would need to consider the reinterpretation of that event by Second
Isaiah and its application to the return from exile in Babylon. It would
need to move on into the New Testament and think, among many other
elements, of the Matthaean account of the infancy of Jesus re-enacting the
story of Israel as he goes down to Egypt, returns, is tempted in the wilderness and passes through the waters of the Jordan. It would need to recall
incidents like the Lucan account of the Transfiguration in which Moses
and Elijah appeared and spoke to Jesus of the 'Exodus' he was about to
accomplish in Jerusalem (Lk. 9.31), apart from other appearances of the
tradition in the New Testament. Then we should have to trace the history
of the tradition among the Church Fathers, and throughout the history of
the Church since, not forgetting its power to evoke the imagery of the
Negro Spiritual and still to prove a force in the work of Liberation
Theology. My point is simply that, while analysis and correct nomencla-
ture are an important and extremely helpful part of our scholarly study of
the whole process, we have, in the end, to acknowledge that the processes
by which written texts exert influence on those who use them are
extremely complex and fluid. And in this connection I found Michael
Floyd's use of different examples of the very varied ways in which more
recent literary works have 'depended on' earlier works extremely valuable
and enlightening.

There is one other complicating factor in determining 'dependence'
from the use of parallel vocabulary and ideas. It seems too elementary
even to mention that ancient prophets and writers, while they must have
had written sources whose growing recognition and worth generated the
whole process of 'allusion', would not have had our modern ease of facili-
ties for looking up references. The codex form, not to mention the invention of indexes and concordances, make the present-day scholar's task of

'checking her or his references' much easier. To some extent the words of mine cited by Aaron Schart from *Preaching the Tradition*, though originally making a different point, also have their bearing on this issue. Because verbal similarity between texts 'is the result not only of a purely literary activity but springs from and reflects the living process of "preaching the tradition"' (Mason 1990: 261), variations between one text and another may not be as significant as we often try to make them appear.

But beyond the vexed questions of how we detect and label inter-textuality there is the further issue of who, or which group, might have employed it in this way. I said, again in the Introduction, that one hoped-for result from the method I was using was 'to see if it affords any clue to the place of this author, or authors, in the developing traditio-history of the community of post-exilic Judaism' (1973: ii). I was just a little, well, 'abashed' is perhaps the right word, to read how Mark Boda, in quoting this, goes on to say that my 'focus was unabashedly historical'. Of course I fully understand what he is saying in context, and he is justified in saying it. But I have always thought of myself as one who has never found much interest or concern in the alleged 'historical' context in which a work was written. This is partly because, as I say often throughout the thesis, the text does not usually provide unambiguous evidence about this, and that anyway the period in which Zech. 9–14 is supposedly set is so little known to us. Further, I agree strongly with his point that one must ask both 'diachronic' as well as 'synchronic' questions of a text. This is because every text comes to us with a long history of growth and as a result of a complex transmission process in the course of which it has been edited and re-edited as it has been applied to a succession of situations. Strangely, I consider myself even a little less 'historical' than he is, in this respect. I read with the greatest interest his masterly examination of the extremely difficult 'Shepherd Allegory' in 11.4-16 (how eagerly we await his forth-coming commentary). I am indebted to him for his suggestion that the speaker may not be the prophet, an idea which had frankly never occurred to me, which shows the value of reading the work of one's colleagues (although I think I still incline to the view that the most natural 'first-person' speaker would be the prophet). His study of the passage in comparison with the relevant Ezekiel passages makes a fascinating case for the idea that the whole passage represents a rejection of the resumed Davidic linc instituted by the Persians with Zerubbabel. He may well be right, but I would myself wish to be a little less precise. Even if it began in that exact historical context it would not be difficult to see how it could be developed and reapplied in later situations of discontent. One has only to think of the use made of these chapters in the New Testament to see that. Michael Floyd also, although more broadly, gives an 'historical' context for these chapters as constituting a re-evaluation of the Persian period in favour of the Greek/Hellenistic era. I find his argument that such a reading depends not merely, or indeed not primarily on verbal parallels to be important and interesting as further illustration of the truth that no one method of approach to the text offers the single secret to unlock all its 'treasure'. Many keys are needed in order to 'bring out the treasure'. Raymond Person's valuable and interesting assertion that the chapters are the product of a continuing post-exilic deuteronomistic 'school' draws attention to many undeniable parallels that exist between these chapters and the work of that 'school'. My only caveat would be that the 'Deuter-onomists', whether pre-exilic, exilic or post-exilic, remain a somewhat shadowy and elusive group. That in no way lessens, however, the force of his argument that these chapters come from those who might well be termed their 'spiritual successors'.

My point in citing these invaluable studies, however, is not primarily to argue about their precise conclusions. I wish to draw attention to, and applaud, the fact that they concentrate not only on establishing whether literary dependence may be traced and how, and with what terminology we describe it, but on who produced this literature and for what purpose. For these too are important, even essential, matters of investigation. In a way the same may be said of those contributors who, rightly, insist that we should not read these chapters in isolation, but see them in their place within the scriptural canon. This is an area of study that was not far advanced in 1973, but it is a fascinating and important one, and I found the studies that deal with it most valuable. This is particularly so of the articles by James Nogalski, Paul Redditt and Aaron Schart. These, too, raise ques-tions about the circles from which this material emanated, even if their concern is with the process a little further down the road in its 'reception history'. As with all our methods of approach, this does not entirely escape the possibility of subjectivity, since we can only discern the mind of the compilers from the finished work, but it is another valuable tool in the scholar's workshop.

If, in conclusion, I try to stand back from my re-reading of my thesis, and the stimulus of these accompanying papers, not to mention the vast amount of work that has been done by others on these chapters between 1973 and now, I ask myself what my overriding impressions are all this time later. First, I suppose I am glad, and relieved, that for all the difficulties about method and terminology, there does seem to be widespread agreement that there actually *is* a good deal of use of other Scripture in these chapters. It would have been something of a 'let-down' to find that the entire basis of the thesis was generally considered to have been misplaced! I am also interested to see that there is considerable agreement that they emanate from circles critical of the official leadership of their day, while there is natural disagreement about what their day was and against whom they were reacting. Readers might be interested to know that for me this idea proved a turning point in my whole work. I was almost in despair of finding any coherent and unifying theme in Zech. 9–14 at all. The material seemed at times to be no more than a chance, almost random collection of prophetic and eschatological sayings as, now, John Barton finds Joel 2.28–3.31 to be (2001: 22). There are those who still believe this of Zech. 9–14. A forceful and impressive paper by Johannes Tromp of Leiden entitled 'Bad Divination in Zechariah 10.1-2' will be appearing in the Tromp (2003) published transactions of a joint Oxford/Leiden colloquium held in January 2002 which argues just this. For me, however, the 'echo'(?) of the phrase 'the sheep doomed to slaughter' in Zech. 11.4 from Jer. 12.3, opened up the possibility that these chapters (for all that the individual items in them are of disparate provenance and age) might be the work of a group, whether sectarian or 'mainstream', who rejected the official leadership of their day and found valuable source material in Jeremiah's criticism of the 'shepherds' of his time for justifying their stance. I am interested to find that there are those who share some form of that view today.

For the future, I think the issue of just why people use earlier material is one which, while it has been dealt with marginally in the thesis and the accompanying papers, deserves to move to centre stage. But I do not propose to attempt that here. I gave it a preliminary airing in a paper read at the joint Oxford/Leiden colloquium mentioned above and that paper will be appearing in due course.

In a cemetery I once read the cheering tomb inscription 'Remember thine end'. At my age I don't need many gratuitous hints of mortality, but I always get them whenever I go down to investigate the stacks of a college or university library. There, mouldering untouched, may be found the works of the academic 'giants' of one's youth, seldom read now any more, and referred to only in glancing footnotes of ever diminishing frequency. But their works were the stepping-stones on which we all trod to get farther along the way. I am very happy that my thesis has finally seen the light of day. If it proves even to have offered one stepping-stone by which others have been able to stride much further forward, I shall be glad. Or, to change the metaphor, if it proved to be a 'No Through Way' notice which led others to turn to much more promising ways ahead, then that too would have been a real gain. I am most excited by all the new work which is going on in biblical studies in general, and in Zechariah studies in particular, so well demonstrated in all these accompanying papers, and I am encouraged that it is going much farther than I ever achieved and in such promising new directions. And, again, my very sincere thanks to all those who have made this volume possible.

BIBLIOGRAPHY

Aalen, S.

1952   *Das Begriff 'Licht' und 'Finsternis' im Alten Testament im Spätjudentum und in Rabbinismus* (Skrifter utgilt av Det Norske Videnskaps-Akademi; Oslo: Jacob Dybbad).

Abrams, M.H.

1993   *A Glossary of Literary Terms* (New York: Harcourt Brace Jovanovich, 6th edn).

Ackroyd, P.R.

1950–51   'The Teraphim', *Expository Times* 62: 378-80.

1958   'Two Old Testament Historical Problems of the Early Persian Period', *JNES* 17: 13-27.

1962a   'Zechariah', in Black and Rowley 1962: 646-55.

1962b   'The Vitality of the Word of God in the Old Testament', *ASTI* 1: 7-23.

1967   'History and Theology in the Chronicler', *Concordia Theological Monthly* 38: 501-15.

1968a   *Exile and Restoration* (London: SCM Press).

1968b   'Meaning and Exegesis', in P.R. Ackroyd and J. Lindbars (eds.), *Words and Meaning: Festschrift for D. Winton Thomas* (3 vols.; Cambridge: Cambridge University Press): 1-14.

1970   'The Old Testament in the Making', in P.R. Ackroyd and C.F. Evans (eds.), *The Cambridge History of the Bible* (3 vols.; Cambridge: Cambridge University Press), I: 67-112.

1971   'Aspects of the Jeremiah Tradition', *Indian Journal of Theology* 20: 1-12.

1973   *I & II Chronicles, Ezra, Nehemiah* (TBC; London: SCM Press).

1974   'An Interpretation of the Babylonian Exile: A Study of II Kings 20, Isaiah 38–39', *SJT* 27: 329-52.

1982   'Archaeology, Politics and Religion: The Persian Period', *Iliff Review* 39: 5-24.

1987   *Studies in the Religious Tradition of the Old Testament* (London: SCM Press).

Albrecht, K.

1896   'Das Geschlecht der hebräischen Hauptwörter', *ZAW* 16: 41-121.

Anderson, G.W.

1959   *A Critical Introduction to the Old Testament* (London: Gerald Duckworth).

Ap-Thomas, D.R.

1957   'Some Aspects of the Root HNN in the Old Testament', *JSS* 2: 128-48.

Avi-Yonah, M.

1954   'The Walls of Nehemiah', *IEJ* 4: 239-48.

Bartel, A.
1979   'Once Again—Who Was Sheshbazzar?' [Hebrew], *Beth Mikra* 79: 357-69.
Barton, J.
1996   *Reading the Old Testament: Method in Biblical Study* (London: Darton, Longman & Todd; Louisville, KY: Westminster/John Knox Press).
2001   *Joel and Obadiah: A Commentary* (OTL; Louisville, KY: Westminster/John Knox Press, rev. edn).
Beal, T.K.
1992   'Glossary', in Fewell 1992: 21-24.
Beale, G.K.
1999   'Questions of Authorial Intent, Epistemology, and Presuppositions and their Bearing on the Study of the Old Testament in the New: A Rejoinder to Steve Moyise', *IBS* 21: 152-80.
2001   'A Response to Jon Paulien on the Use of the Old Testament in Revelation', *AUSS* 39: 23-34.
Beek, M.A.
1972   'The Meaning of the Expression "the Chariots and the Horsemen of Israel" (II Kings ii 12)', *OTS* 17: 1-10.
Ben Zvi, E.
1996   'Twelve Prophetic Books or "The Twelve": A Few Preliminary Considerations', in Watts and House 1996: 125-56.
Ben-Porat, Z.
1976   'The Poetics of Literary Allusion', *PTL: A Journal of Descriptive Poetics and Theory of Literature*, 1: 105-28.
1985   'Intertextuality' [Hebrew], *Ha-Sifrut* 34: 170-78.
Ben-Yashar, M.
1981   'On the Problem of Sheshbazzar and Zerubbabel' [Hebrew], *Beth Mikra* 88: 46-56.
Berger, P.R.
1971   'Zu den Namen ששבצר und שנאצר', *ZAW* 83: 98-100.
Beuken, W.A.M.
1967   *Haggai-Sacharja 1–8* (Assen: Van Gorcum).
Bewer, J.A.
1911   *A Critical and Exegetical Commentary on Obadiah and Joel* (ICC; Edinburgh: T. & T. Clark).
Beyse, K.-M.
1971   *Serubbabel und die Königserwartungen der Propheten Haggai und Sacharja* (Aufsätze und Vorträge zur Theologie und Religionswissenschaft, 52; Berlin: Evangelische Verlagsanstalt).
Bianchi, F.
1994   'Le rôle de Zorobabel et de la dynastie davidique en Judée du VIe siècle av. J.-C.', *Transeu* 7: 153-66.
Bič, M.
1962   *Das Buch Sacharja* (Berlin: Evangelische Verlagsanstalt).
Black, M., and H.H. Rowley (eds.)
1962   *Peake's Commentary on the Bible* (London: Thomas Nelson).

Blenkinsopp, J.
2000   *Isaiah 1–39: A New Translation with Introduction and Commentary* (AB, 19; New York: Doubleday).

Boda, M.J.
2001   'Oil, Crowns and Thrones: Prophet, Priest and King in Zechariah 1:7–6:15', *Journal of Hebrew Scriptures* 3: Art. 10 (reprinted as 'Oil, Crowns and Thrones: Prophet, Priest and King in Zechariah 1:7–6:15', in J. Stafford [ed.], *Proceedings of the Currents in Biblical and Theological Studies Conference 2001* [Winnipeg: University Of Manitoba Press, 2002]: 89-106).

2003a   'Majoring on the Minors: Recent Research on Haggai and Zechariah', *CRBS* 11.

2003b   *A Century of Haggai-Zechariah Research* (Tools for Biblical Studies; Leiden: Deo).

2004   'From Fasts to Feasts: The Literary Function of Zechariah 7–8', *CBQ* 66 (forthcoming).

forthcoming *Haggai–Zechariah* (Grand Rapids: Zondervan).

Bosshard, E.
1987   'Beobachtungen zum Zwölfprophetenbuch', *BN* 40: 30-62.

Bosshard-Nepustil, E.
1997   *Rezeptionen von Jesaia 1–39 im Zwölfprophetenbuch: Untersuchungen zurliterarischen Verbindung von Prophetenbüchern in babylonischer und persischer Zeit* (OBO, 154; Freiburg: Universitätsverlag; Göttingen: Vandenhoeck & Ruprecht).

Bosshard, E., and R.G. Kratz
1990   'Maleachi im Zwölfprophetenbuch', *BN* 52: 27-46.

Bright, J.
1962   'Isaiah—1', in Black and Rowley 1962: 489-515.
1965   *Jeremiah* (AB, 21; New York: Doubleday).
1970   'Jeremiah's Complaints—Liturgy or Expressions of Personal Distress?', in J.I. Durham and J.R. Porter (eds.), *Proclamation and Presence: Old Testament Essays in Honour of G. Henton Davies* (Richmond, VA: John Knox Press): 189-214.

Brockington, L.H.
1962   'I and II Samuel', in Black and Rowley 1962: 318-37.
1969   *Ezra, Nehemiah and Esther* (NCB; London: Marshall, Morgan & Scott).

Brouwer, C.
1949   *Wachter en Herder* (Wageningen: H. Weenman en Zonen).

Burney, C.F.
1918   *The Book of Judges* (London: Rivingtons).

Carroll, R.P.
1986   *The Book of Jeremiah: A Commentary* (OTL; London: SCM Press).

Carter, C.E.
1999   *The Emergence of Yehud in the Persian Period* (JSOTSup, 294; Sheffield: Sheffield Academic Press).

Charles, R.H.
1914   *Between the Old and New Testaments* (London: Williams & Norgate).

Chary, T.
1955   *Les prophètes et le culte à partir de l'exil* (Bibliotheque de Theologie, Series
            III.3; Tournai: J. Gabalda).

Childs, B.S.
1962   *Memory and Tradition in Israel* (SBT, 37; London: SCM Press).
1972   'Midrash and the Old Testament', in J.H.P. Reumann (ed.), *Understanding
            the Sacred Text: Essays in Honor of Morton S. Enslin on the Hebrew Bible
            and Christian beginnings* (Valley Forge, PA: Judson Press): 45-60.
1979   *Introduction to the Old Testament as Scripture* (Philadelphia: Fortress
            Press).

Clayton, J., and E. Rothstein (eds.)
1991   *Influence and Intertextuality in Literary History* (Madison: University of
            Wisconsin Press).

Clements, R.E.
1965   *God and Temple* (Oxford: Basil Blackwell).

Coggins, R.J.
1968   'The Old Testament and Samaritan Origins', *ASTI* 6: 38-48.

Cohn, E.W.
1986   'The History of Jerusalem's Benjamin Gate: A Case of Interrupted
            Continuity?', *PEQ* 118: 138-43.

Collins, T.
1993   *The Mantle of Elijah: The Redaction Criticism of the Prophetical Books*
            (The Biblical Seminar, 20; Sheffield: JSOT Press).

Condamin, C.
1910   'Le sens messianique de Zach.12,10', *RSR* 1: 52-56.

Conrad, E.
1999   *Zechariah* (Readings: A New Biblical Commentary; Sheffield: Sheffield
            Academic Press).

Cook, S.L.
1993   'The Metamorphosis of a Shepherd: The Tradition History of Zechariah
            11.17+13.7-9', *CBQ* 55: 453-66.
1995   *Prophecy and Apocalypticism: The Postexilic Social Setting* (Minneapolis:
            Augsburg–Fortress).

Cooke, G.A.
1936   *A Critical and Exegetical Commentary on the Book of Ezekiel* (ICC;
            Edinburgh: T. & T. Clark).

Cooper, A.
1993   'In Praise of Divine Caprice: The Significance of the Book of Jonah', in P.R.
            Davies and D.J.A. Clines (eds.), *Among the Prophets* (JSOTSup, 144;
            Sheffield: JSOT Press): 144-63.

Cresson, B.C.
1972   'The Condemnation of Edom in Post-exilic Judaism', in J.M. Efrid (ed.), *The
            Use of the Old Testament in the New and Other Essays: Studies in Honour of
            W.F. Stinespring* (Durham, NC: Duke University Press): 125-48.

Cross, F.M.
1958   *The Ancient Library of Qumran and Modern Biblical Studies* (New York:
            Doubleday).

1966   'The Divine Warrior in Israel's Early Cult', in A. Altmann (ed.), *Biblical Motifs* (Philip Lown Institute of Advanced Judaic Studies, Studies and Texts, 3; Cambridge, MA: Harvard University Press; London, Oxford University Press): 11-30.

Culley, R.C.
1967   *Oral Formulaic Language in the Biblical Psalms* (Toronto: University of Toronto Press).

Cunliffe-Jones, H.
1966   *Jeremiah* (Torch Bible Commentaries; London: SCM Press, 2nd edn).

Curtis, B.G.
2000   'Zion–Daughter Oracles: Evidence on the Identity and Ideology of the Late Redactors of the Book of the Twelve', in Nogalski and Sweeney 2000: 166-84.

Curtiss, J.B.
1957   'The Mount of Olives in the Judaeo-Christian Tradition', *HUCA* 28: 137-80.

Dahood, M.
1972   'Ugaritic-Hebrew Parallel Pairs', in L. Fisher (ed.), *Ras Shamra Parallels* (3 vols.; AnOr, 49; Rome: Pontifical Biblical Institute), I: 71-382.

Davidson, A.B.
1916   *The Book of the Prophet Ezekiel* (rev. A.W. Streane; Cambridge: Cambridge University Press).

Davies, P.R.
1998   *Scribes and Schools: The Canonization of the Hebrew Scriptures* (Library of Ancient Israel; Louisville, KY: Westminster John Knox).

Delcor, M.
1951a   'Les allusions à Alexandre le Grand dans Zacharie 9.1-8', *VT* 1: 110-24.
1951b   'Un Probleme de Critique Textuelle et Exegese', *RB* 58: 189-99.
1952   'Les sources du Deutéro-Zacharie et ses procédés d'emprunt', *RB* 59: 385-411.
1953   'Deux passages difficiles: Zach. 12.11 et 11.13', *VT* 3: 67-77.
1962   'Le Tresor de la Maison de Yahweh des Origines l'Exile', *VT* 12: 352-77.

Dentan, R.C.
1956   'Zechariah 9–14', *IB*, VI: 1089-17.

Dodd, Charles H.
1952   *According to the Scriptures: The Sub-Structure of New Testament Theology* (London: Nisbet).

Donne, J.
1967   *Sermons on the Psalms and Gospels with a Selection of Prayers and Meditations* (ed. E.M. Simpson; Berkeley: University of California Press).

Draisma, S. (ed.)
1989   *Intertextuality in Biblical Writings* (Kampen: Kok).

Driver, S.R.
1892   *A Treatise on the Use of the Tenses in Hebrew and Some Other Syntactical Questions* (Oxford: Clarendon Press, 3rd edn).
1906   *Minor Prophets: Nahum, Habakkuk, Zephaniah, Haggai, Zechariah, Malachi* (The Century Bible; Edinburgh: T.C. & E.C. Jack).
1913   *Notes on the Hebrew Text and Topography of the Books of Samuel* (Oxford: Clarendon Press, 2nd edn).

Eaton, J.H.
1964   'The Origin and Meaning of Habakkuk 3', *ZAW* 76: 144-71.
Eichrodt, W.
1970   *Ezekiel* (trans. C. Quin; OTL; London: SCM Press).
Eisenbeis, W.
1969   *Die Wurzel שלם im Alten Testament* (BZAW, 13; Berlin: W. de Gruyter).
Eissfeldt, O.
1937   'Eine Einschmeltzstelle am Tempel zu Jerusalem', *Forschungen und Fortschritte* 13: 163-64.
1965   *The Old Testament: An Introduction* (trans. P.R. Ackroyd; New York: Harper & Row).
1968   'Amos und Jona in Volkstümerlicher Uberlieferung', in R. Sellheim and F. Maass (eds.), *Kleine Schriften* (4 vols.; Tübingen: J.C.B. Mohr), IV: 137-42.
Elliger, K.
1951   *Buch der zwölf Kleinen Propheten. II. Nahum, Habakuk, Zephanja, Haggai, Sacharja, Maleachi* (ATD, 25.2; Göttingen: Vandenhoeck & Ruprecht).
1956   *Buch der zwölf Kleinen Propheten. II. Nahum, Habakuk, Zephanja, Haggai, Sacharja, Maleachi* (ATD, 25.2; Göttingen: Vandenhoeck & Ruprecht, 3rd edn).
1964   *Buch der zwölf Kleinen Propheten. II. Nahum, Habakuk, Zephanja, Haggai, Sacharja, Maleachi* (ATD, 25.2; Göttingen: Vandenhoeck & Ruprecht, 6th edn).
Eslinger, L.
1992   'Inner-Biblical Exegesis and Inner-Biblical Allusion: The Question of Category', *VT* 42: 47-58.
Fewell, D.N. (ed.)
1992   *Reading Between Texts: Intertextuality and the Hebrew Bible* (Literary Currents in Biblical Interpretation; Louisville, KY: Westminster/John Knox).
Finkelstein, L.
1969   *New Light From the Prophets* (London: Vallentine/Mitchell).
Fishbane, M.
1985   *Biblical Interpretation in Ancient Israel* (Oxford: Clarendon).
1988   *Biblical Interpretation in Ancient Israel* (Oxford: Clarendon Paperbacks).
Floyd, M.H.
2000   *Minor Prophets, Part 2* (FOTL, 22; Grand Rapids, MI: Eerdmans).
2002   'The *Maśśā'* as a Type of Prophetic Book', *JBL* 121: 401-22.
Flügge, B.G.
1784   *Die Weissagungen welche den Schriften des Propheten Zacharias beygebogen sind, übersetzt und critisch, erläutert, nebst einigen Abhandlungen* (Hamburg).
Fohrer, G.
1952   'Die Gattung der Berichte über symbolische Handlungen der Propheten', *ZAW* 64: 101-20.
1955   *Ezechiel, mit einem Beitrag v. K. Galling* (HAT; Tübingen: J.C.B. Mohr).
1965   *Introduction to the Old Testament* (trans. D.E. Green; Nashville: Abingdon Press).
1968   *Die symbolische Handlungen der Propheten* (ATANT, 54; Zurich: Zwingli Verlag, 2nd edn).

1970   *Introduction to the Old Testament* (trans. D. Green; London: SPCK).
Freedman, D.N.
1987   'Headings in the Books of the Eighth-Century Prophets', *AUSS* 25 (Spring): 9-26.
Fretheim, T.E.
1977   *The Message of Jonah* (Minneapolis: Augsburg–Fortress).
Friebel, K.G.
1999   *Jeremiah's and Ezekiel's Sign-Acts: Rhetorical Nonverbal Communication* (JSOTSup, 283; Sheffield: Sheffield Academic Press).
2001   'A Hermeneutical Paradigm for Interpreting Prophetic Sign-Actions', *Didaskalia* (Spring): 25-45.
Gaide, G.
1968   *Jerusalem, voici ton roi: Commentaire de Zacharie 9–14* (LD, 49; Paris: Cerf).
Gelin, A.
1951   *Agée, Zacharie, Malachie* (La Sainte Bible de Jérusalem; Paris: Editions du Cerf, 2nd edn).
Genette, G.
1982   *Palimpsestes: la littérature au second degré* (Paris: Seuil).
1997   *Palimpsests: Literature in the Second Degree* (trans. C. Newman and C. Doubinsky; Lincoln: University of Nebraska Press).
Glazier-McDonald, B.
1987   *Malachi: The Divine Messenger* (SBLDS, 98; Atlanta: Scholars Press).
Gowan, D.E.
2000   *Eschatology in the Old Testament* (Edinburgh: T. & T. Clark, 2nd edn).
Gray, G.B.
1912   *Isaiah I–XXVII* (ICC; Edinburgh: T. & T. Clark).
Gray, J.
1961   'The Kingship of God in the Prophets and the Psalms', *VT* 11: 1-29.
1964   *I & II Kings* (London: SCM Press).
1970   *I & II Kings* (London: SCM Press, 2nd edn).
Grech, P.
1969   'Interprophetic Re-Interpretation and Old Testament Eschatology', *Aug* 9: 235-65.
Gressmann, H.
1905   *Der Ursprung der israelitisch-jüdischen Eschatologie* (FRLANT, 6; Göttingen: Vandenhoeck & Ruprecht).
1929   *Der Messias* (FRLANT, 43; Göttingen: Vandenhoeck & Ruprecht).
Grether, O.
1934   *Name und Wort Gottes im Alten Testament* (BZAW, 64; Berlin: W. de Gruyter).
Grützmacher, G.
1892   *Untersuchungen über den Ursprung der in Zach. 9–14 vorliegenden Prophetien.*
Hanson, P.D.
1979   *The Dawn of Apocalyptic: The Historical and Sociological Roots of Jewish Apocalyptic Eschatology* (Philadelphia: Fortress Press, rev. edn).

Hatch, E., and H.A.A. Redpath
1897   *Concordance to the Septuagint and the Other Greek Versions of the Old Testament* (Oxford: Clarendon Press).

Hatina, T.R.
1999   'Intertextuality and Historical Criticism in New Testament Studies: Is There a Relationship?', *BibInt* 7: 28-43.

Hays, R.B., and J.B. Green
1995   'The Use of the Old Testament by New Testament Writers', in Joel B. Green (ed.), *Hearing the New Testament: Strategies for Interpretation* (Grand Rapids: Eerdmans): 224-38.

Herrmann, J.
1924   *Ezechiel übersetzt und eklärt* (KAT, 11; Leipzig, A. Deichert).

Hertzberg, H.W.
1964   *I & II Samuel* (trans. J.S. Bowden; London: SCM Press).

Hill, A.E.
1982   'Dating Second Zechariah: A Linguistic Reexamination', *HAR* 6: 105-34.

Hoftijzer, J.
1953   'A propos d'une interprétation récente de deux passages difficiles: Zach. xii.11 et Zach. xi.13', *VT* 3: 407-409.

Holladay, W.L.
1988   *A Concise Hebrew and Aramaic Lexicon of the Old Testament* (Leiden: E.J. Brill).

Hollander, J.
1981   *The Figure of an Echo: A Mode of Allusion in Milton and After* (Berkeley: University of California Press).

Hölscher, G.
1924   *Hezekiel* (BZAW, 39; Berlin: W. de Gruyter).

Hooke, S.H.
1947   *In the Beginning* (The Clarendon Bible, 6; Oxford: Clarendon Press).

Hooke, S.H. (ed.)
1958   *Myth, Ritual and Kingship* (Oxford: Clarendon Press).

Hoonacker, A. van
1902   'Les chapitres ix–xiv du livre Zacharie', *RB* 11: 161-83, 345-78.
1908   *Les douzes petits prophètes* (Paris: Librairie Victor Lecoffre).

Hopkins, G.M.
1918   *Poems of Gerard Manley Hopkins* (ed. R. Bridges; London: Humphrey Milford).

Horst, F.
1964   *Die zwölf kleinen Propheten: Nahum bis Maleachi* (HAT, 14; Tübingen: J.C.B. Mohr).

House, P.R.
1990   *The Unity of the Twelve* (JSOTSup, 97; Sheffield: Almond Press).

Hyatt, J.P.
1941   'Torah in the Book of Jeremiah', *JBL* 60: 385-87.
1942   'Jeremiah and Deuteronomy', *JNES* 1: 156-73.
1951   'The Deuteronomic Edition of Jeremiah', in R.C. Beatty, J.P. Hyatt and M.K. Spears (eds.), *Vanderbilt Studies in the Humanities* (3 vols.; Nashville: Vanderbilt University Press, 1951), I: 71-95.

1956   'The Book of Jeremiah', *IB*, V: 775-1142.

Irwin, W.A.
1943   *The Problem of Ezekiel* (Chicago: University of Chicago Press).

Jansma, T.
1949   *Inquiry into the Hebrew Text and the Ancient Versions of Zechariah 9–14* (Leiden: E.J. Brill).

Japhet, S.
1982   'Sheshbazzar and Zerubbabel—Against the Background of the Historical and Religious Tendencies of Ezra–Nehemiah', *ZAW* 94: 66-98.

Jensen, J.
1984   *Isaiah 1–39* (Old Testament Message, 8; Wilmington, DE: Michael Glazier).

Jeremias, J.
1985   *Der Prophet Amos* (ATD, 24/2; Göttingen: Vandenhoeck & Ruprecht).
1996   'The Interrelationship between Amos and Hosea', in J.W. Watts and P.R. House (eds.), *Forming Prophetic Literature: Essays on Isaiah and the Twelve in honor of John D.W. Watts* (JSOTSup, 235; Sheffield: Sheffield Academic Press): 125-56.

Johnson, A.R.
1958   'Hebrew Conceptions of Kingship', in Hooke 1958: 204-235.
1961   *The One and the Many in the Israelite Conception of God* (Cardiff: University of Wales Press, 2nd edn).
1964   *The Vitality of the Individual in the Thought of Ancient Israel* (Cardiff: University of Wales Press, 2nd edn).
1967   *Sacral Kingship in Ancient Israel* (Cardiff: University of Wales Press, 2nd edn).

Jones, D.R.
1955   'The Traditio of the Oracles of Isaiah of Jerusalem', *ZAW* 67: 226-46.
1962a   *Haggai, Zechariah and Malachi* (Torch Bible Commentaries; London: SCM Press).
1962b   'A Fresh Interpretation of Zechariah IX–XI', *VT* 12: 241-59.

Jouguet, P.
            Alexander the Great and the Hellenistic World (Chicago: Ares).

Kaiser, O.
1972   *Isaiah 1–12* (trans. R.A.Wilson; London: SCM Press).
1981   *Das Buch des Propheten Jesaja: Kapitel 1–12* (ATD, 17; Göttingen: Vandenhoeck & Ruprecht).

Kapelrud, A.S.
1965   *The Ras Shamra Discoveries and the Old Testament* (Oxford: Basil Blackwell).
1966   'New Ideas in Amos', in P.A.H. de Boer (ed.), *Geneva Congress Volume* (VTSup, 15; Leiden: E.J. Brill): 193-206.

Kessler, J.
1992   'The Second Year of Darius and the Prophet Haggai', *Transeu* 5: 63-84.

Kilian, R.
1986   *Jesaja 1–12* (NEchtB; Würzburg: Echter).
1994   *Jesaja 13–39* (NEchtB; Würzburg: Echter).

Knabenbauer, J.
1886   *Commentarius in prophetas minores* (Cursus scripturae sacrae; Commentarii in vetus testamentum, 3.5; Paris: Lethielleux).

Koch, K.
1970   *Ratlos vor der Apokalyptik* (Gütersloh: Güterloher Verlagshaus/Gerd Mohn).
1972   *The Rediscovery of Apocalyptic* (trans. M. Kohl; SBT, 2nd Series, 22; London: SCM Press).

Koenen, K.
1994   *Heil den Gerechten—Unheil den Sündern! Ein Beitrag zur Theologie der Prophetenbücher* (BZAW, 229; Berlin: W. de Gruyter).

König, E.
1893   *Einleitung in das Alte Testament: mit Einschluss der Apokryphen und der Pseudepigraphen Alten Testaments* (Bonn: E. Weber).

Kosmala, H.
1969   'The Term *geber* in the Old Testament and in the Scrolls', in *Congress Volume: Rome, 1968—International Organization for the Study of the Old Testament* (VTSup, 17; Leiden: E.J. Brill): 159-69.

Kraeling, B.
1924   'The Historical Situation in Zech. 9.1-10', *AJSL* 41: 24-33.

Kraus, H.J.
1966   *Worship in Israel: A Cultic History of the Old Testament* (trans. G. Buswell; Oxford: Basil Blackwell).

Kremer, J.
1930   *Die Hirtenallegorie im Buch Zacharias* (Alttestamentliche Abhandlungen, 11.2; Münster: Verlag der Aschendorffschen/Verlagsbuchhandlung).

Kuhl, C.
1961   *The Old Testament: Its Origins and Composition* (trans. C. Herriott; Edinburgh: Oliver & Boyd).

Lagrange, M.-J.
1906   'Notes sur les prophéties messianiques des derniers prophètes', *RB* 13: 67-83.

Lamarche, P.
1961   *Zacharie IX–XIV: Structure littéraire et messianisme* (EBib; Paris: J. Gabalda).

Langhe, R. de
1958   'Myth, Ritual and Kingship in the Ras Shamra Tablets', in Hooke 1958: 122-48.

Larkin, K.
1994   *The Eschatology of Second Zechariah: A Study of the Formation of a Mantological Wisdom Anthology* (CBET, 6; Kampen: Kok Pharos).

Lee, A.Y.
1985   'The Canonical Unity of the Scroll of the Minor Prophets' (unpublished dissertation; Waco, TX: Baylor University Press).

Lescow, T.
1993   *Das Buch Maleachi: Texttheorie-Aulegung-Kanontheorie* (AzTh, 75; Stuttgart: Calwer Verlag).

Leske, A.M.
2000   'Context and Meaning of Zechariah 9.9', *CBQ* 62: 663-78.

Liddell, H.G., and R.A. Scott
1883   *Greek–English Lexicon* (Oxford: Clarendon Press, 7th edn).
Limburg, J.
1988   *Hosea–Micah* (Interpretation; Atlanta: John Knox Press).
Lindblom, J.
1938   *Die Jesaja-apokalypse, Jes. 24-27* (Lunds Universitet: Acta Universitatis Ludensis, n.s. Lund Universitets Årsskrift, n.f., avd. 1, v. 34, no. 3; Lund: C.W.K. Gleerup).
1962   *Prophecy in Ancient Israel* (Oxford: Basil Blackwell).
Lisowsky, G.
1958   *Konkordanz zum Hebräischen Alten Testament* (Stuttgart: Württembergische Bibelanstalt).
Litwak, K.D.
1998   'Echoes of Scripture? A Critical Survey of Recent Works on Paul's Use of the Old Testament', *CRBS* 6: 260-88.
Lods, A.
1932   *Israel, From Its Beginnings to the Middle of the 8th Century* (trans. S.H. Hooke; London: Routledge & Kegan Paul).
Lust, J.
1987   'The Identification of Zerubbabel with Sheshbassar', *ETL* 63: 90-95.
Luther, M.
1953   *A Commentary on St Paul's Epistle to the Galatians* (ed. P.W. Watson; Cambridge: James Clarke).
Lutz, H.M.
1968   *Jahwe, Jerusalem und die Völker: Zur Vorgeschichte von Sach 12.1-8 und 14.1-5* (WMANT, 27; Neukirchen–Vluyn: Neukirchener Verlag).
Lux, R.
1994   *Jona: Prophet zwischen 'Verweigerung' und 'Gehorsam'* (FRLANT, 162; Göttingen: Vandenhoeck & Ruprecht).
Mandelkern, S.
1964   *Veteris Testamenti Concordantiae Hebraicae atque Chaldaicae* (Tel Aviv: Schocken Hierosolymis, 6th edn).
Marguerat, D., and A. Curtis (eds.)
2000   *Intertextualités: La Bible en échos* (Geneva: Labor et Fides).
Masing, U.
1938   'Die Proklamation des Tab'al sohnes', dargebracht von einem Kreise von Freunden und Kollegen, *Piam Memoriam Alexander von Bulmerincg* (Riga: Pilates): 117-26.
Mason, R.A.
1973   'The Use of Earlier Biblical Material in Zechariah 9–14: A Study in Inner Biblical Exegesis' (dissertation, University of London).
1976   'The Relation of Zechariah 9–14 to Proto-Zechariah', *ZAW* 88: 227-39.
1977   *The Books of Haggai, Zechariah and Malachi* (CBC; Cambridge: Cambridge University Press).
1982   'The Books of Haggai, Zechariah and Malachi: Some Examples of Inner Biblical Exegesis in Zechariah 9–14', *SE* VII (TU, 126; Berlin: Akademie Verlag): 343-54.

1984   'Some Echoes of the Preaching in the Second Temple? Tradition Elements in Zechariah 1–8', *ZAW* 96: 221-35.

1990   *Preaching the Tradition: Homily and Hermeneutics after the Exile Based on the 'Addresses' in Chronicles, the 'Speeches' in the Books of Ezra and Nehemiah and the Post-Exilic Prophetic Books* (Cambridge: Cambridge University Press).

1997   Review of 'Prophets in Dialogue: Inner Biblical Allusions in Zechariah 1–8 and 9–14' by Risto Nurmela, *Society for Old Testament Study Book List 1997*: 73-74.

2003   'Why is Second Zechariah so Full of Questions', in C. Tuckett (ed.), *Zechariah and Its Influence* (Aldershot: Ashgate, forthcoming).

Mauchline, J.
1962   *Isaiah 1–39* (TBC; London: SCM Press).
1970   'Implicit Signs of a Persistent Belief in Davidic Empire', *VT* 20: 287-303.

May, H.G.
1956   'Ezekiel: Introduction and Exegesis', in *IDB*, VI: 39-338.

Mays, J.L.
1969a   *Amos* (London: SCM Press).
1969b   *Hosea* (London: SCM Press).

Melamed, E.Z.
1961   'Break-Up of Stereotype Phrases as an Artistic Device in Biblical Poetry', in C. Rabin (ed.), *Scripta Hieroslymnitana: Studies in the Bible* 8 (Jerusalem: Magnes Press): 115-53.

Meyer, L.V.
1977   'An Allegory concerning the Monarchy: Zech 11.4-17; 13.7-9', in A.L. Merrill and T.W. Overholt (eds.), *Scripture in History and Theology* (PTMS, 17; Pittsburgh: Pickwick Press): 225-40.

Meyers, C.L., and E.M. Meyers
1987   *Haggai, Zechariah 1–8: A New Translation with Introduction and Commentary* (AB, 25B; New York: Doubleday).
1993   *Zechariah 9–14: A New Translation with Introduction and Commentary* (AB, 25C; New York: Doubleday).

Meyers, E.M.
1985   'The Shelomith Seal and Aspects of the Judean Restoration: Some Additional Reconsiderations', *ErIsr* 18: 33*-38*.
1987   'The Persian Period and the Judean Restoration: From Zerubbabel to Nehemiah', in P.D. Miller, P.D. Hanson and S.D. McBride (eds.), *Ancient Israelite Religion: Essays in Honor of Frank Moore Cross* (Philadelphia: Fortress Press): 509-21.

Miller, J.W.
1955   *Das Verhältnis Jeremias und Hesekiels sprachlich und theologisch untersucht* (Assen: Van Gorcum).

Mitchell, H.G.
1912   *A Critical and Exegetical Commentary on Haggai and Zechariah* (ICC; Edinburgh: T. & T. Clark).

Moore, G.P.
1895   *A Critical and Exegetical Commentary on Judges* (ICC; Edinburgh: T. & T. Clark).

Bibliography 365

Morgenstern, J.
1960 'The King-God Among the Western Semites and the Meaning of Epiphanes', *VT* 10: 138-97.
Moseman, R.D.
2000 'Reading the Two Zechariahs as One', *RevExp* 97: 487-98.
Mowinckel, S.
1959 *He That Cometh* (trans. G.W. Anderson; Oxford: Oxford University Press).
1962 *The Psalms in Israel's Worship* (2 vols.; trans. D.R. Ap-Thomas; Oxford: Basil Blackwell).
Moyise, S.
1999 'The Language of the Old Testament in the Apocalypse', *JSNT* 76: 97-113.
Moyise, S. (ed.)
2000 *The Old Testament in the New Testament: Essays in Honour of J. L. North* (JSNTSup, 189; Sheffield: Sheffield Academic Press).
Muilenburg, J.
1956 'The Book of Isaiah: Chapters 40–66', in *IDB*, V: 381-773.
1962 'Ezekiel', in Black and Rowley 1962: 568-90.
Myers, J.M.
1965 *Ezra, Nehemiah* (AB, 14; New York: Doubleday).
Nicholson, E.W.
1967 *Deuteronomy and Tradition* (Oxford: Basil Blackwell).
1970 *Preaching to the Exiles: A Study of the Prose Tradition in the Book of Jeremiah* (New York: Schocken Books).
1973 *The Book of the Prophet Jeremiah: Chapters 1–25* (CBC; Cambridge: Cambridge University Press).
Nielsen, K.
2000 'Intertextuality and Hebrew Bible', in A. Lemaire and M. Saebø (eds.), *Congress Volume: Oslo 1998* (VTSup, 80; Leiden: E.J. Brill): 17-31.
Nogalski, J.D.
1993a *Literary Precursors to the Book of the Twelve* (BZAW, 217; Berlin: W. de Gruyter).
1993b *Redactional Processes in the Book of the Twelve* (BZAW, 218; Berlin: W. de Gruyter).
1996 'Intertextuality and the Twelve', in Watts and House 1996: 102-24.
2000 'Joel as "Literary Anchor" for the Book of the Twelve', in Nogalski and Sweeney 2000: 91-109.
Nogalski, J.D., and M.A. Sweeney (eds.)
2000 *Reading and Hearing the Book of the Twelve* (Symposium, 15; Atlanta: Society of Biblical Literature).
North, C.R.
1964 *The Second Isaiah* (Oxford: Clarendon Press).
Nurmela, R.
1996 *Prophets in Dialogue: Inner-Biblical Allusions in Zechariah 9–14* (Åbo: Åbo Akademi University Press).
O'Day, G.R.
1999 'Intertextuality', in J.H. Hayes (ed.), *Dictionary of Biblical Interpretation* (2 vols.; Nashville: Abingdon), II: 546-48.

Oesterley, L.A., and T.H. Robinson
1958   *Introduction to the Books of the Old Testament* (London: Macmillan, 3rd edn).

Oort, H.
1889   'Ezechiel xix, xxi, 18, 19b, 24.', *Theologisch Tijdschrift* 23: 504-514.

Otzen, B.
1964   *Studien über Deuterosacharja* (Copenhagen: Munksgaard).

Overholt, T.W.
1970   *The Threat of Falsehood* (SBT, 2nd Series, 16; London: SCM Press).

Paterson, J.
1962   'Jeremiah', in Black and Rowley 1962: 537-62.

Paulien, J.
2001   'Dreading the Whirlwind: Intertextuality and the Use of the Old Testament in Revelation', *AUSS* 39: 5-22.

Perdue, L.G., and B.W. Kovacs (eds.)
1984   *A Prophet to the Nations: Essays in Jeremiah Studies* (Winona Lake, IN: Eisenbrauns).

Person, R.F., Jr
1993   *Second Zechariah and the Deuteronomic School* (JSOTSup, 167; Sheffield: JSOT Press).
2002   *The Deuteronomic School: History, Social Setting, and Literature* (Studies in Biblical Literature, 2; Atlanta/Leiden: Society of Biblical Literature/E.J. Brill).

Petersen, D.L.
1984   *Haggai and Zechariah 1–8: A Commentary* (OTL; London: SCM Press).
1995   *Zechariah 9–14 and Malachi: A Commentary* (OTL; Louisville, KY: Westminster, John Knox Press; London: SCM Press).

Pfeiffer, R.
1952   *Introduction to the Old Testament* (London: A. & C. Black, 1st edn).

Pierce, R.W.
1984   'A Thematic Development of the Haggai/Zechariah/Malachi Corpus', *JETS* 27: 401-11.

Plöger, O.
1968   *Theocracy and Eschatology* (trans. S. Rudman; Oxford: Basil Blackwell).

Pomykala, K.E.
1995   *The Davidic Dynasty Tradition in Early Judaism: Its History and Significance for Messianism* (Early Judaism and Its Literature, 7; Atlanta: Scholars Press).

Porteous, N.
1961   'Jerusalem-Zion, the Growth of a Symbol', in A. Kuschke (ed.), *Verbannung und Heimkehr: Festschrift für W. Rudolph* (Tübingen: J.C.B. Mohr [Paul Siebeck]): 235-52.

Powis Smith, J.M.
1911   *A Critical and Exegetical Commentary on Micah, Zephaniah and Nahum* (ICC; Edinburgh: T. & T. Clark).
1912   *A Critical and Exegetical Commentary on the Book of Malachi* (ICC; Edinburgh: T. & T. Clark).

Price, J.L.

1972   'Light from Qumran Upon Some Aspects of Johannine Theology', in R.E. Brown and J.H. Charlesworth (eds.), *John and Qumran* (London: Geoffrey Chapman).

Rad, G. von

1958   *Der Heilige Krieg im alten Israel* (Göttingen: Vandenhoeck & Ruprecht).

1962   *Theology of The Old Testament I* (trans. D.M.G. Stalker; 2 vols.; Edinburgh/ London: Oliver & Boyd).

1963   *Genesis* (trans. J.H. Marks; OTL; London: SCM Press, 2nd edn).

1965   *Theology of the Old Testament II* (trans. D.M.G. Stalker; 2 vols.; Edinburgh/ London: Oliver & Boyd).

1966   *Deuteronomy* (trans. D. Barton; London: SCM Press).

Radday, Y.T., and D. Wickmann

1975   'The Unity of Zechariah Examined in the Light of Statistical Linguistics', *ZAW* 87: 30-55.

Rahlfs, A. (ed.)

1950   *Septuaginta: id est, Vetus Testamentum graece iuxta LXX* (Stuttgart: Württembergische Bibelanstalt).

Redditt, P.L.

1989   'Israel's Shepherds: Hope and Pessimism in Zechariah 9–14', *CBQ* 51: 631-42.

1993   'The Two Shepherds in Zechariah 11.4-17', *CBQ* 55: 676-86.

1994   'Nehemiah's First Mission and the Date of Zechariah 9–14', *CBQ* 56: 664-78.

1995   *Haggai, Zechariah, Malachi* (NCB; Grand Rapids, MI: Eerdmans; London: Marshall Pickering/HarperCollins).

1996   'Zechariah 9–14, Malachi, and the Redaction of the Book of the Twelve', in Watts and House 1996: 245-68.

2000   'The Production and Reading of the Book of the Twelve', in Nogalski and Sweeney 2000: 11-33.

2001   'Recent Research on the Book of the Twelve as One Book', *CRBS* 9: 47-80.

Rendtorff, Rolf

1983   *Das Alte Testament: Eine Einführung* (Neukirchen–Vluyn: Neukirchener Verlag, 3rd edn).

Reventlow, H.G.

1963   *Liturgie und prophetische Ich bei Jeremia* (Gütersloh: Gütersloher Verlagshaus).

1993   *Die Propheten Haggai, Sacharja und Maleachi* (ATD, 25.2; Göttingen: Vandenhoeck & Ruprecht).

Riesenfeld, H.

1948   *The Resurrection in Ezekiel XXXVII and in the Dura-Europos Paintings* (Uppsala Universitets Årsskrift 1948, 11; Uppsala: Lundequist; Leipzig: Harrassowitz).

Rignell, L.G.

1950   *Die Nachtgesichte des Sacharja* (Lund: C.W.K. Gleerup).

Robert, A.

1935   'Les attaches littéraires bibliques de Prov. 1–9', *RB* 44: 512-17.

Robinson, G.L.
1896   'The Prophecies of Zechariah with Special Reference to the Origin and Date of Chapters 9–14', *AJSL* 12: 1-92.

Robinson, H.W.
1927   'Prophetic Symbolism', in T.H. Robinson (ed.), *Old Testament Essays* (London: C.H. Griffin).

Rose, W.H.
2000   *Zemah and Zerubbabel: Messianic Expectations in the Early Postexilic Period* (JSOTSup, 304; Sheffield: Sheffield Academic Press).

Rowley, H.H.
1925–26 'The Text and Interpretation of Jeremiah 11.18–12.6', *AJSL* 42: 217-27.
1939   'Zadok and Nehushtan', *JBL* 58: 113-41.
1945   *The Rediscovery of the Old Testament* (London: James Clarke).
1947   'Was Amos a Nabi?', in J. Fück (ed.), *Festschrift Otto Eissfeldt* (Halle: Max Niemeyer): 191-98.
1956–57 'The Marriage of Hosea', *BJRL* 39: 200-233 (reprinted in *idem, Men of God* [London: Thomas Nelson, 1963]: 66-97).
1963   *The Relevance of Apocalyptic: A Study of Jewish and Christian Apocalypses from Daniel to the Revelation* (London: Lutterworth, rev. edn).
1965   'The Nature of Old Testament Prophecy', in *idem, The Servant of the Lord* (Oxford: Basil Blackwell, 2nd edn): 95-134.

Rudolph, W.
1949   *Esra und Nehemia samt 3 Esra* (HAT; Tübingen: J.C.B. Mohr).
1976   *Haggai—Sacharja 1-8—Sacharja 9-14—Maleachi* (KAT, 13.4; Gütersloh: Gerd Mohn).

Russell, D.S.
1964   *The Method and Message of Jewish Apocalyptic* (London: SCM Press).

Rylaarsdam, J.C.
1952   'Exodus', in *IB*, I: 831-1099.

Saebø, M.
1969   *Sacharja 9–14: Untersuchungen von Text und Form* (WMANT, 34; Neukirchen–Vluyn: Neukirchener Verlag).

Sasson, J.M.
1990   *Jonah* (AB, 24B; New York: Doubleday).

Sawyer, J.P.A.
1965   'What Was a Mošia'?', *VT* 15: 475-86.
1967/8   'Spaciousness', *ASTI* 6: 20-34.
1972   *Semantics in Biblical Research* (SBT, 24; 2nd Series; London: SCM Press).

Schaberg, J.
1990   *The Illegitimacy of Jesus* (New York: Crossroad).

Schaefer, K.
1992   'Zechariah 14 and the Formation of the Book of Zechariah' (dissertation: Ecole biblique et archéologique française, Jerusalem).
1993a   'The Ending of the Book of Zechariah: A Commentary', *RB* 100: 165-238.
1993b   'Zechariah 14 and the Composition of the Book of Zechariah', *RB* 100: 368-98.
1995   'Zechariah 14: A Study in Allusion', *CBQ* 57: 66-91.

Schart, A.
1998   *Die Entstehung des Zwölfprophetenbuchs: Neubearbeitungen von Amos im Rahmen schriftenübergreifender Redaktionsprozesse* (BZAW, 260; Berlin: W. de Gruyter).

Schmid, K.
2000   'Innerbiblische Schriftauslegung: Aspekte der Forschungsgeschichte', in R.G. Kratz, T. Krüger and K. Schmid (eds.), *Schriftauslegung in der Schrift: Festschrift für Odil Hannes Steck zu seinem 65. Geburtstag* (BZAW, 300; Berlin: W. de Gruyter): 1-22.

Schneider, D.A.
1979   'The Unity of the Book of the Twelve' (dissertation, Yale University).

Schultz, R.L.
1999   *The Search for Quotation: Verbal Parallels in the Prophets* (JSOTSup, 180; Sheffield: Sheffield Academic Press).

Scott, R.B.Y.
1956   'The Book of Isaiah: Introduction and Exegesis', in *IB*, V: 151-381.

Simpson, C.A.
1952   'The Book of Genesis: Introduction and Exegesis', *IB*, I: 437-829.

Skinner, J.
1936   *Prophecy and Religion* (Cambridge: Cambridge University Press).

Smith, G.A.
1972   *Jerusalem: The Topography, Economics and History from the Earliest Time to A.D. 70* (New York: Ktav).

Smith, H.P.
1899   *A Critical and Exegetical Commentary on the Books of Samuel* (ICC; Edinburgh: T. & T. Clark).

Snaith, N.H.
1946   *The Book of Amos* (2 vols.; Study Notes on Biblical Books; London: Epworth Press).
1947   *The Jewish New Year Festival* (London: SPCK).

Snyman, G.F.
1996   'Who is Speaking? Intertextuality and Textual Influence', *Neot* 30: 427-49.

Sommer, B.D.
1996   'Exegesis, Allusion and Intertextuality in the Hebrew Bible: A Response to Lyle Eslinger', *VT* 46: 479-89.
1998   *A Prophet Reads Scripture: Allusion in Isaiah 40–66* (Stanford: Stanford University Press).

Stacey, D.
1990   *Prophetic Drama in the Old Testament* (London: Epworth Press).

Stade, B.
1881   'Deuterosacharja. Eine kritische Studie', *ZAW* 1: 1-96
1882   'Deuterosacharja. Eine kritische Studie', *ZAW* 2: 151-72, 275-309.

Stalker, D.G.M.
1968   *Ezekiel* (Torch Bible Commentaries; London: SCM Press).

Steck, O.H.
1991   *Der Abschluss der Prophetie im Alten Testament; Ein Versuch zur Frage der Vorgeschichte des Kanons* (Biblisch-Theologische Studien, 17; Neukirchen–Vluyn: Neukirchener Verlag).

2000   *Prophetic Books and their Theological Witness* (trans. J.D. Nogalski; St Louis: Chalice).

Stern, E.
1984   'The Persian Empire and the Political and Social History of Palestine in the Persian Period', in W.D. Davies and L. Finkelstein (eds.), *The Cambridge History of Judaism. I. Introduction: The Persian Period* (3 vols.; Cambridge: Cambridge University Press): 70-87.

Stoppard, T.
1968   *Rosencrantz and Guildenstern Are Dead* (New York: Grove).

Strack, H.L., and P. Billerbeck
1922–28   *Kommentar zum Neuen Testament* (Munich: Beck).

Sweeney, M.
1996   *Isaiah 1–39 with an Introduction to Prophetic Literature* (FOTL, 16; Grand Rapids, MI: Eerdmans).
2000   *The Twelve Prophets* (2 vols.; Berit Olam; Collegeville, MN: Liturgical Press).

Tai, N.H.F.
1996   *Prophetie als Schriftauslegung in Sacharja 9–14: Traditions- und kompositionsgeschichtliche Studien* (Calwer Theologische Monographien, A17; Stuttgart: Calwer Verlag).

Taylor, C.L.
1956   'The Book of Zephaniah: Introduction and Exegesis', in *IB*, VI: 1007-34.

Taylor, V.
1953   *The Gospel According to St Mark* (London: Macmillan).

Thompson, J.A.
1956   'The Book of Joel', in *IB*, VI: 727-60.

Thomson, J.G.S.S.
1955   'The Shepherd-Ruler Concept in the Old Testament', *SJT* 8: 406-18.

Tigchelaar, E.J.C.
1996   *Prophets of Old and the Day of the End: Zechariah, the Book of Watchers and Apocalyptic* (OTS, 35; Leiden: E.J. Brill).

Tollington, J.
1993   *Tradition and Innovation in Haggai and Zechariah 1–8* (JSOTSup, 150; Sheffield: JSOT Press).

Torczyner, H. (Tur Sinai)
1936   'Presidential Address', *Journal of the Palestine Oriental Society* 16: 1-8.

Torrey, C.C.
1936   'The Foundry of the Second Temple of Jerusalem', *JBL* 55: 247-60.
1943   'The Evolution of a Financier in the Ancient Near East', *JNES* 2: 295-301.
1947   'The Messiah ben Ephraim', *JBL* 66: 253-77.

Touzard, J.
1917   'L'âme juive au temps des Perses', *RB* 36: 126-33.

Trible, P.
1996   'The Book of Jonah' *NIB*, VII: 463-529.

Tromp, J.
2003   'Bad Divination in Zechariah 10.1-2', in C. Tuckett (ed.), *Zechariah and Its Influence* (Aldershot: Ashgate, forthcoming).

Tucker, G.M.
1977   'Prophetic Superscriptions and the Growth of a Canon', in G.W. Coats and
            B.O. Long (eds.), *Canon and Authority: Essays in Old Testament Religion
            and Theology* (Philadelphia: Fortress Press): 56-70.
Unterman, J.
1987   *From Repentance to Redemption: Jeremiah's Thought in Transition*
            (JSOTSup, 54; Sheffield: Sheffield Academic Press).
van Leeuwen, R.C.
            'Scribal Wisdom and Theodicy in the Book of the Twelve', in L.G. Perdue,
            B.B. Scott and W.J. Wiseman (eds.), *In Search of Wisdom: Essays in
            Memory of John G. Gammie* (Louisville, KY: Westminster/John Knox
            Press): 31-49.
van Seters, J.
1972   'The Terms "Amorite" and "Hittite"', *VT* 22: 64-81.
van Wolde, E.
1989   'Trendy Intertextuality?', in Draisma 1989: 43-49.
Vaux, R. de
1961   *Ancient Israel: Its Life and Institutions* (trans. J. McHugh; London: Darton,
            Longman & Todd).
Vermes, G.
1961   *Scripture and Tradition in Judaism* (Leiden: E.J. Brill).
Vries, S.J. de
1975   *Yesterday, Today and Tomorrow: Time and History in the Old Testament*
            (Grand Rapids: Eerdmans).
Waterman, L.
1954   'The Camouflaged Purge of Three Messianic Conspirators', *JNES* 13: 73-78.
Watts, J.W., and P.R. House (eds.)
1996   *Forming Prophetic Literature: Essays on Isaiah and the Twelve in Honor of
            John D.W. Watts* (JSOTSup, 235; Sheffield: Sheffield Academic Press).
Weimar, P.
1985   'Obadja. Eine redaktionskritische Analyse', *BN* 27: 35-99.
Weingreen, J.
1957   'Rabbinic-Type Glosses in the Old Testament', *JSS* 3: 149-62.
1963   'Exposition in the Old Testament and in Rabbinic Literature', in F.F. Bruce
            (ed.), *Promise and Fulfillment, Essays Presented to S.H. Hooke* (Edinburgh:
            T. &. T. Clark): 187-201.
1968   'הוצאתיך in Gen. 15.7', in P.R. Ackroyd and B. Lindars (eds.), *Words and
            Meaning: Essays Presented to David Winton Thomas* (Cambridge:
            Cambridge University Press): 209-215.
1976   *From Bible to Mishna* (Manchester: Manchester University Press).
Weis, R.
            'A Definition of the Genre *Maśśā'* in the Hebrew Bible' (dissertation,
            Claremont Graduate School).
1992   'Oracle', *ABD*, V: 28-29.
Weiser, A.
1961   *Introduction to the Old Testament* (trans. D. Barton; London: Darton,
            Longman & Todd).
1962   *The Psalms* (trans. H. Hartwell; London: SCM Press).

1969   *Das Buch Jeremia* (ATD; Göttingen: Vandenhoeck & Ruprecht).

Wellhausen, J.
1892   *Die kleinen Propheten mit Noten* (Berlin: Georg Reimer).

Westermann, C.
1969   *Isaiah 40–66* (trans. D.M.G. Stalker; London: SCM Press).
1970   *Das Buch Jesaja: Kapitel 40–66* (ATD, 19; Göttingen: Vandenhoeck & Ruprecht, 2nd edn).

Weyde, K.W.
2000   *Prophecy and Teaching : Prophetic Authority, Form Problems, and the Use of Traditions in the Book of Malachi* (BZAW, 288; Berlin: W. de Gruyter).

Whitehouse, O.C.
1905   *Isaiah. I. Isaiah I–XXXIX* (2 vols.; The Century Bible; Edinburgh: T.C. & E.C. Jack).

Wildberger, H.
1972   *Jesaja. I. Teilband: Jesaja 1–12* (BKAT, 10.1; Neukirchen–Vluyn: Neukirchener Verlag).
1978   *Jesaja. II. Teilband: Jesaja 12–27* (BKAT, 10.2; Neukirchen–Vluyn: Neukirchener Verlag).
1982   *Jesaja. III. Teilband: Jesaja 28–39; Das Buch, der Prophet und seine Botschaft* (BKAT, 10.3; Neukirchen–Vluyn: Neukirchener Verlag).

Willi-Plein, I.
1971   *Vorformen der Schrift-exegese Innerhalb des Alten Testament* (BZAW, 123; Berlin: W. de Gruyter).
1974   *Prophetie am Ende: Untersuchungen zu Sacharja 9–14* (BBB, 42; Cologne: Peter Hanstein).

Williamson, H.G.M.
1985   *Ezra, Nehemiah* (WBC, 16; Waco, TX: Word Books).
1988   'The Governors of Judah under the Persians', *TynBul* 39: 59-82.

Witt, D.A.
1991   'Zechariah 12–14: Its Origins, Growth and Theological Significance' (dissertation, Vanderbilt University).

Wolff, H.W.
1974   *Hosea* (trans. G. Stansell; Hermeneia; Philadelphia: Fortress Press).
1977   *Dodekapropheten 3: Obadja und Jona* (BKAT, 14, 3; Neukirchen–Vluyn: Neukirchener Verlag).

Woude, A.S. van der
1984   *Zacharia* (De Prediking van het Oude Testament; Nijkerk: Callenbach).

Wright, N.T.
1996   *Jesus and the Victory of God* (Philadelphia: Fortress Press).

Ziegler, J.
1950   'Die Hilfe Gottes "am Morgen"', in H. Junker and J. Botterweck (eds.), *Alttestamentliche Studien: Friedrich Nötscher Festschrift* (Bonn: Peter Hanstein): 281-88.

Zimmerli, W.
1969   *Ezechiel* (BKAT, 13; Neukirchen–Vluyn: Neukirchener Verlag).
1972   'Deutero-Ezechiel?', *ZAW* 84: 501-16.

INDEXES

INDEX OF REFERENCES

BIBLE